MEMOIRS OF A RADICAL LAWYER

MICHAEL MANSFIELD

with Yvette Vanson

BLOOMSBURY

LONDON · BERLIN · NEW YORK

First published in Great Britain 2009

Copyright © by Michael Mansfield 2009

All court transcripts reproduced in this book are Crown copyright

Material from *Strangeways 1990: A Serious Disturbance* by Nicki
Jameson and Eric Allison as quoted in the *Guardian* © Larkin
Publications and reproduced by kind permission of the authors

Extract from transcript of Martin Bashir's *Panorama* interview with
Princess Diana © BBC 1995 and reproduced by kind permission

All photographs reproduced are from the author's own
collection, except where credited otherwise

The right of Michael Mansfield to be identified as the author of this Work has been
asserted by him in accordance with the Copyright, Designs and Patents Act, 1988

Bloomsbury Publishing Plc
36 Soho Square
London W1D 3QY

www.bloomsbury.com

Bloomsbury Publishing, London, New York and Berlin

A CIP catalogue record for this book is available from the British Library

ISBN 978 0 7475 7654 9

10 9 8 7 6 5

Typeset by Hewer Text UK Ltd, Edinburgh
Printed in Great Britain by Clays Ltd, St Ives plc

To Yvette – without whom this book
would never have been written

and

To all my lay and legal clients – without whom
there would have been no story to tell

CONTENTS

PREFACE

This is a memoir. Not an autobiography – cradle to grave – let alone some tedious detailed diary, but a collage of recollections and reminiscences, which are gathered together around issues that I feel are important, and which arise from some of the cases I have undertaken. Personal stories punctuate the themes, but only where there is a natural connection. No confidential information about anyone I've ever represented is used or divulged; not every trial, not every person gets a mention – which does not imply that the omissions are less important. Where a case is described in some detail, I do so to highlight what went right or wrong, or what needs to be changed in our legal system.

Roll up the shutters in a riverside storage warehouse and there it all stands. Forty-two years' worth of my working life contained in rows of battered cardboard boxes, neatly stacked. I am possibly the only barrister to have kept pretty well every brief I've undertaken. Originally just in case the notes and statements might be useful at some unknown future time for the purposes of another trial or appeal. And some have been.

But now it's time to move on to a different future. Maybe some benevolent agency will adopt my archive. Meanwhile, I felt I should try to make some sense of the years I've spent in the law. This book is an attempt to do just that. It may be on the large side, but then so am I! But always, my aim has been to keep an eye on the main point: justice being done, and being seen to be done.

Nothing stays still for long in the law. In the time that I have spent writing this memoir a number of the cases and issues I refer to have come back to life. Some have reached new conclusions, others remain unresolved, but the reader should know that the book he or she is about to read was up to date at the time of going to press!

Michael Mansfield, QC, 7 June 2009

PROLOGUE

Veins and Vanity

Camp Zeist in Holland. I am attending as an observer at the first Lockerbie appeal. My flight's delayed; my taxi driver gets me lost; I rush to get in; security's tight – so tight that a burly police officer doing the body search, when rubbing up and down my legs, asks, 'Have you got something concealed in your trousers?' I protest that there is nothing besides my legs, but the waiting queue is getting agitated – so the police officer threatens a full strip-search in another room. The hearing has started. I can't stand queues or officialdom at the best of times. So I drop my trousers on the spot to reveal hard, bulbous, knotted varicose veins. This is a passport to a speedy entrance to the appeal.

Flashback to the late 1940s: I'm one of three 'musketeers' – Jeremy, Robin and I are all about eight. I am thin and look a bit like William Brown from *Just William* – grey flannel shorts, socks round my ankles and always a cap askew. We spend our free time roaming the wilds of north London and setting impossible challenges for each other. Normally these revolved around the rapids of what we thought was a vast river, but was in fact a rather turgid brook called Dollis, which runs from Barnet all the way through to the Thames somewhere near Chiswick. Little did I know that these challenges were to become a formative part of my psyche, because we each chose for another a task that tested our ability to face up to our weaknesses and fears. For example: wading through deep water, handling 'poisonous' snakes, climbing gigantic trees and crawling through damp, dark tunnels. My particular fear was jumping from high branches, so when commanded to climb the tallest tree on the river bank, I reluctantly clambered up, but prevaricated for too long about taking the final leap. The two others decided I needed some encouragement. Suddenly I felt a sharp pain in the back of my right leg, and left the branch immediately. I had been shot by a German air pistol that my brother had brought back at the end of the Second World War, and which we regularly sneaked out from the garage where my mother had hidden it. The pellet penetrated my trousers and left a wound that caused a massive bruise.

Needless to say, I couldn't tell Mother how this was caused. She was forty-one when I was born in 1941, having had my two brothers Gerald and Ken in her early twenties. There was still the legacy of an earlier beauty discernible in her face and stature, although by this time she was distinctly portly. I inherited her large, pale-blue eyes. Mother was patient, kind and tolerant – but, like so many women of her generation, paid due deference to my father. She kept a bamboo cane above the kitchen door in case of misdemeanours. She never used it, but threatened to 'tell your father' if things went wrong. We both knew he'd never catch me to cane me, as he'd lost the whole of his left leg in the First World War, but I wasn't taking any chances over the air-pistol wound and eventually I suffered for my secrecy with varicose veins the size of drainpipes . . .

What happened to the other musketeers? Robin became an aerial photographer who worked on the Oscar-winning film *Gandhi*; Jeremy pursued his love of all animals exotic and became a game warden in Tanzania.

As for me, my vanity got the better of me, after years of horrified glances at swimming pools and on beaches. Soliciting the advice of Mary, a friend who is a specialist in lumpy legs, I went for venal analysis at Charing Cross Hospital. This consisted of me standing stark naked, as Mary – with roller in hand – endeavoured to detect the extent of the damage to my arteries and the likelihood of deep-vein thrombosis. As she knelt in front of me, a passing colleague called out, 'Oh, Mary, same position, different man!'

The consultation that followed with The Prof. began with a roving anecdotal discussion about the Old Bailey bombing in 1973 and other terrible events we had both experienced over the last twenty-five years in London, I as a lawyer, he as a doctor. I thought he was trying to prepare me for the worst – amputation! Instead he was refreshingly candid about the shortcomings, imprecision and unpredictability of medical science. Having presented me with the pros and cons of the treatment then available, and because I wasn't in pain, he left the final choice to me. So I still have hideous legs.

'MICHAEL, YOU SEE WHAT YOU WANT TO SEE!'

From Finchley to Philosophy

It was a strange-looking bottle – tall, narrow, square-shaped – and according to the label, it contained Camp Coffee. I had discovered it in my favourite childhood retreat, the larder set into the wall beneath the stairs at 73 Naylor Road, and there could be no mistaking that it was number 73, as my father Frank had painstakingly carved the two numerals, in large relief, in the top of the privet hedge a few feet from our front door.

Our kitchen was what an estate agent would call 'conveniently compact', and my mother Marjorie always referred to it as the scullery. Yet somehow this tiny space managed to contain a large white enamel sink, a gas cooker that gave off more gas than rice puddings, and a bulbous silver American-style fridge, taller than me and adorned with an enormous metallic bronze handle. Stick four wheels on it and it might have passed for a Cadillac or a Buick.

Alongside that fridge was my haven, the recessed larder, shelved from floor to ceiling. Most of the shelves were empty, but there was always a small store of carefully preserved items, preciously obtained during that late-1940s era of ration books: a jar of home-made gooseberry jam from the allotments on the other side of the Northern Line at the bottom of our garden; packets of digestive biscuits; tins of corned beef, spam, sardines and condensed milk; sugar, tea – and coffee.

Not instant coffee or beans, let alone ground coffee. This coffee, in its strange bottle, had 'chicory' written on the label, which left me little the wiser, and what really intrigued me was that no one – not my parents, or my older brothers – ever seemed to drink it.

I speculated that maybe it had turned solid over the years, or maybe the fact that nobody went near it had something to do with its odd name. Whatever the reason, for ages it had apparently remained untouched by human hand, until I found it. From time to time I would take down the bottle from the shelf and scrutinise its label, which depicted a tented, exotic Far Eastern location with a resplendent gentleman in a turban holding an embossed gilt tray, perfectly placed in the middle of which was a bottle of Camp Coffee.

That bottle on the tray bore exactly the same label, showing the same man, complete with turban, tray and bottle. And the bottle on the label of the bottle on the tray also showed the man in the turban, and *his* bottle had the same label – and so on, and so on, and so on . . .

One day, my mother found her inquisitive eight-year-old in the larder, holding my father's magnifying glass close up against the label. 'What on earth are you up to?' she exclaimed.

'Well,' I replied, 'does it ever end? Or is it down to the skill of the artist?' And I asked her, if you reversed the process, with ever larger bottles and larger and larger labels – some the size of the larder itself – how large could the bottle get?

Amused by these random perceptions, my mother observed, 'Michael, you see what you want to see!'

Now this was not exactly my Stephen Hawking moment of parallel universes, let alone the calculus of the infinitesimal, but unwittingly I had stumbled into a world unknown – and it wasn't so much my own ruminations as my mother's reaction to them which struck a chord.

What she said bothered me then, and still does – and it lies at the heart of forensic science, the area of the judicial process with which I was to become so deeply involved in later years. For a sizeable proportion of what passes as science depends upon the eye of the beholder and is highly subjective, and the perception of physical phenomena is hugely susceptible, both consciously and unconsciously, to all sorts of personal beliefs and predilections. Without rigorous awareness and precautions, such a situation can

have disastrous consequences, including, particularly in my area of
the law, wrongful conviction and imprisonment.

Born on 12 October 1941, when Gerald was sixteen and Ken
fifteen, I was the Last Chance Saloon. A Blitz baby, I still retain
clear memories of wartime London in the blackout: all our windows
blocked in with hardboard and blackout blinds; the corrugated-iron
Anderson shelter covered in sandbags in next door's garden, into
which we were herded during raids; my Mickey Mouse gas mask in
its brown cardboard box, the red string handle looped around my
neck; and, perhaps most ineradicably of all, the shrill terror of the
air-raid sirens.

Even now, sixty-odd years later, whenever a siren goes off I find
the sound very unsettling. For in my mind it still heralds a wave
of German bombers passing over London – bombers, moreover,
that following their raids on the railways around King's Cross were
quite likely to dump any remaining bombs on the streets around our
house. I clearly remember the drone of these planes as they passed
the anti-aircraft battery at the top of our road, the sky brightening
as the searchlights hunted for them and the ground rippling with
shockwaves from the pursuing guns. I have a constant reminder on
my desk, a chunk of bomb which hit King's Cross station, retrieved
by Gerald and now used as a paperweight.

In spite of the mayhem going on all around, mine was a very secure
and modest upbringing, by parents who were far from wealthy, in
Whetstone, then (as now) an unpretentious north London suburb,
but an area with its own place in history as the village where, during
the Wars of the Roses, soldiers sharpened their swords before the
Battle of Barnet in 1471.

My father had lost his left leg in October 1917 while serving
on horseback in Palestine with the City of London Yeomanry,
gunned down in a hail of Turkish machine-gun bullets; he was then
twenty-one years old. I remember him as a tall, imposing man of
silent disposition, both conservative and Conservative at the same
time. There were odd flashes of humour, such as when he would
use a pencil to tap out a rhythm on his false leg while sitting on
the London Underground, much to the consternation of fellow
passengers. Sometimes, for a joke, he would dislodge the false leg

from his stump – and, as his leg seemed to grow longer and longer, so did my embarrassment.

His civilian career was with British Railways, and during the Second World War he had a critically responsible job controlling the nocturnal movement of emergency rail traffic at a secret headquarters in Gerrards Cross in Buckinghamshire. This entailed my mother driving him there – a distance of some fifteen miles – in complete darkness, save for the cat's eyes in the road. Because of the wartime dangers, I was left asleep and alone at home, in the firm expectation that I wouldn't even know she had gone. I can still vividly remember one night when I was about three, and as usual was tucked up in bed at number 73, with Mrs Kimber the next-door neighbour listening out for me, should I wake up.

On this occasion Mrs Kimber didn't hear my crying when I was awakened by the noise from the anti-aircraft guns. Frightened by their persistent pounding, I called out for my mother. Nothing. I called again. Still nothing. I was rapidly beginning to find the lack of any response more distressing than the hammering from the guns, so I got out of bed and walked around the house in total darkness in search of my mother. No one could be found, and in complete panic I made for the front door. Being just too small to reach the handle, I dragged a telephone directory across the hall and, clambering up onto it, managed to open the door – and walked into a terrifying outside world where there was no light and no people, just unspeakably awful noise. It was plain to me that I was the only person left alive on Earth, and I began screaming – at which point Mrs Kimber finally heard me, scooped me up from the pavement and took me into her house to await my mother's return. After that, I always went with my parents in the car for those blacked-out drives to Gerrards Cross – journeys which in the dead of night, I found rather exciting.

On account of my father's work he was entitled to special rations, including bananas, and obviously felt that, with no bombs actually dropping on our house and enjoying a more comfortable existence than most others, we were in a privileged position. Therefore my mother stockpiled our banana ration so that they could be distributed among the less well-off families she came across as she carried out her duties in the London Ambulance Service.

Bundled into the back of what she called her 'sit-up-and-beg' Ford Popular – polished royal blue – I was taken to various addresses, where, since she clearly considered it quite inappropriate for me to come in with her, she ordered me to 'sit tight' while she deposited brown paper bags containing a banana or two to each of the families.

I could never quite understand what it was about these bananas which meant that those families could eat them, but I could not. Did they contain some mystical property that transformed the inhabitants into super-humans? In this and other simple ways, without having to preach the gospel, my parents led by example and gave me small but telling lessons in how to care for others without making a meal of it.

Theirs was a very stiff-upper-lip world, but one imbued with a strong sense of fair play and propriety: my brothers both away fighting for their country in the services; church every Sunday; the *Daily Telegraph* as preferred reading (in addition to sympathising with its politics, my father liked to practise his calligraphy by copying the font); no television (at least until the mid-1950s), only the wireless and *Workers' Playtime*; roses and irises in the garden. It was all thoroughly middle-class and conventional, and thoroughly English.

This upbringing encouraged unquestioning loyalty to Queen and Country. Ours was a household of servicemen and women. Gerald was an artist by temperament and a talented draughtsman, but to satisfy the patriotism of my father, and almost out of spite to 'prove himself a man', he joined up in 1943, and eventually became the bass drummer in the regimental band of the Scots Guards: the bass drummer was the lynchpin of the band, as it was he who had to keep the marching rhythm going. I remember, years later, Gerald teaching me to drum on a stool between my knees, with a cork mat on top to soften the noise. I still dabble on the drums.

Ken, the happy-go-lucky brother, but still fifteen years my senior, volunteered for the Fleet Air Arm and served on HMS *Ocean*, an aircraft carrier in the Mediterranean. He survived too and returned to work on the railways, which pleased my father. Ken was a good sportsman and played football for Loughton. Then he met a blonde bombshell and fell hopelessly in love. Even Mother and Father were captivated by her *joie de vivre*. One morning my mother woke to find a note from Ken: he had left to catch the P&O liner to South

Africa, because the bombshell had dropped him. He planned to work on the railways in Africa, and in fact did so for the rest of his life. I remember being pushed into the car as we rushed down to Southampton to try and stop him. As we arrived on the dockside we were in time to see the ship pulling away. Mother cried; Father was mutely distraught. I was ten and, not knowing how else to console them, bought a big plant from the shop at the end of the road the next day. It was small solace, compared with the joy he brought into our lives on regular visits back home with his wife Sylvia and their five effervescent children. I loved the startled look of disbelief whenever I was introduced as uncle while still wearing short trousers.

The service mentality pervaded our home right into the late 1950s. By this time I was at Highgate and my behaviour at school was generally so good that I was nicknamed 'Goodchild' by my school mates. I volunteered for the Combined Cadet Force (CCF) – to avoid music appreciation on a Tuesday afternoon. I was proud of my uniform. Gerald taught me to Blanco my belt and gaiters and to melt boot polish to get a mirror shine on my boots. Mother sewed creases in my trousers so that they were always razor sharp. I chose to specialise in developing one of the elite squads of twelve boys – the CCF Drill Squad. I was quite tyrannical. But as a result we were really good and gave exhibitions at school Open Days. We were *so* good I was invited to Sandhurst on a special course. At seventeen I became one of the Army's first ever Junior Under Officers (a special rank had been created between non-commissioned officers (NCOs) at school level and commissioned officers who went to Sandhurst). Interestingly one of the course tests at Sandhurst involved standing up and speaking off the cuff for two minutes on an unknown subject. This was the first time I realised that I could speak in public – mind you, for two minutes! Perhaps if things had turned out differently I might have ended up a Colonel in Iraq . . .

Aside from her largesse towards the local poor, my mother mostly kept herself to herself, which made it all the more astounding when she took on the local Finchley constabulary over the issuing of a parking ticket.

This was a mother who loved Ivor Novello; who considered it her public duty to become a blood donor; who embroidered kneelers for the church; who was shocked to the core when I was sent home for a week from Holmewood Primary School for gripping the hand of my girl partner with too much enthusiasm in the snaking line on the platform of Totteridge station; who later cajoled me into joining the Young Conservatives, principally so that I should learn the quickstep and 'meet the right type of girl' at their dances. For years she did her bit for the local Conservative Party, addressing and sticking down envelopes containing election messages and manifestos, inveigling her youngest son to help her deliver them, and canvassing for the local MP, one Margaret Thatcher – who, after each election, would invariably send a glowing note of thanks for my mother's efforts. (I've often wondered whether I could have changed the course of history by dumping my entire supply of election leaflets into the nearby Dollis Brook.)

My mother was pro-Establishment to the core, but falling foul of the law while out shopping one afternoon in Whetstone changed her for ever. A local police officer accused her of parking within the marking studs near a pedestrian crossing, and issued her with a ticket. She insisted that she had done no such thing and, incensed, first refused to pay the fine, and then mounted her own spirited defence in court – when her courtroom *coup de grâce* was calling my father as a surprise witness. Unseen by the police, he had been sitting in the car at the time of the alleged offence, and was now called upon to back up my mother's story. He had developed a distinctive gait by hopping on his good leg and sweeping his false leg alongside, aided by a walking stick, and I can imagine that making his way through the court to the witness box was a true show-stopper – the stuff of *Perry Mason*.

Mother was acquitted, triumphant, but the ramifications of the case went far beyond that simple verdict. The fact that the police – 'Bluebottles', she called them – had been prepared to lie in such a small case appalled her, and ever afterwards she would repeat to me: 'Never trust a man in uniform.'

It was a formative experience for me, as the case clearly lies at the root of my long-standing suspicion of the police, and my mother's words still come back to me when I am engaged on cases where police corruption, malpractice or simple incompetence has led to a serious miscarriage of justice. It is not fanciful to consider that it was my mother's sense of having been wronged – even over such a comparatively trivial matter – that produced in me the anger which has been the driving force of my legal career.

One ever-present motif of my childhood was the railway. By the early 1950s my father had worked his way to the position of Deputy Chief Controller for the Great North-Eastern Region of British Railways. As well as having a railway line at the bottom of our garden, all holiday travel was by rail, and occasionally my father allowed me to accompany him out of King's Cross as far as Potters Bar on the footplate of a steam locomotive heading north.

In the circumstances it will come as no surprise that I spent hours building my own railway with a clockwork Hornby train set. This construction became so complex that, rather than take it down every night, my father made a table the size of my bedroom with a hole in the middle and with my bed beneath, so that I could stand on it in order to operate the trains which occupied the whole of the tabletop. I used cigarette butts to get the effect of steam and torch bulbs for the station lights, which were wired up to a huge square Eveready battery.

I loved that model railway, but even more I loved to cycle over to Oakleigh Park station, where a sturdy iron pedestrian bridge crossed over the main lines, to watch the real thing. Amazingly elegant engines, like the *Mallard* and the *Flying Scotsman*, emerged into daylight from the long tunnels under the hills of north London, as I stood on the iron bridge, positioned exactly above the path of the oncoming train, in order to be enveloped by noise, smuts and smoke. I could hear the locomotives inside the distant darkness, building up a head of stressed steam, which exploded once released outside the tunnel, invariably accompanied by a warning sound akin to a hollow tubular siren. The pitch of this sound seemed quite distinct from the engine itself, changing magically from high as it approached to low as the engine passed beneath my feet. I didn't know then that Christian Doppler had noted this effect more than a hundred years before![1] These trains were land-speed record-breakers, and by the time the cloud of smoke had evaporated, the train had vanished towards Potters Bar, Hatfield and beyond.

My father worked long hours on the railway to pay for my education at Highgate public school, where I started in 1954. He had had to fight hard to get where he did, but he never moaned about his lack of leg. I have no idea if he was in pain, since he always maintained a stoical front.

Because his own sporting ambitions were cut short, he took enormous vicarious pleasure in watching my somewhat chequered progress. First-eleven soccer was a treat because my mother could drive him virtually onto the pitch. However, I hardly dared tell him about my other pathetic attempts. Being on the heavy side, athletics was a nightmare, so I focused on fringe activities, such as the shot put and the 'hippy' mile walk. As for boxing, my father was thrilled when he discovered I was heavyweight champion one year. Why hadn't I told him? For one thing, my style was embarrassingly camp; for another, there were only ever two of us competing for the title; and for a third, because Father had a somewhat disarming habit, when his supportive enthusiasm got the better of him, of letting slip his nickname for me: 'Winxie'.

As Father worked harder and harder to pay my school fees, so I saw less and less of him. It was never mentioned to me that he was dying of cancer of the throat – a particularly painful type, as he couldn't swallow easily. I learned later how he had dutifully taken to work the food that my mother had prepared for him, but had been unable to eat it. He wouldn't have dreamed of explaining or complaining, and I never really knew how ill he was.

Such things were hidden, and my mother refused to let me see him either just before or after his death in 1960. She was trying to be kind, but I felt sad that I couldn't be with her, or him, at such a difficult time. I was eighteen when he died and had just passed my driving test, so was able to make a small contribution by driving my mother to the funeral home. She went in. I sat and waited outside.

Shortly after his death I received a letter from a close friend, Bill McGregor. He saw me every day, but had decided he wanted to put his condolences on paper, and wrote movingly of the ways I would miss my father: the times I'd walk into the room and he'd not be in his high-backed mahogany armchair; the times he'd no longer pop into my room at night after work; the umbrella stand full of his walking sticks to remind me of his strange limping gait. It wasn't my father's words I would miss, but his unspoken presence, the lack of him. Bill was so right.

My father never saw me succeed at university or witnessed my later career – and maybe that's just as well, as he wouldn't have approved of some of the causes in which I believe. But I wish I'd had long discussions with him, in the way I do with my own children.

Within days of his death I learned that I had failed to gain admission to Peterhouse, Cambridge, where my brother Ken had gone on a Fleet Air Arm scholarship after the war. A few days after that disappointment I learned that I had also failed to get a place at Keele, which was particularly galling because Bill, who had achieved the same O and A Level results as I had, did get in.

I decided not to take this rejection lying down – and now I think that it was a combination of anger, at not knowing my father well before he died, and the seeming injustice of university rejection that propelled me onto a train to Stoke, the town nearest to Keele University.

My father's boss, a magnanimous railway manager named G. F. Fiennes, had discovered the identity of the Keele admissions tutor and, crucially, had also found out his address. So at lunchtime on the first Sunday after I had learned that I had been turned down, I arrived at Keele, situated on a windswept hill in North Staffordshire, near the towns comprising 'the Potteries'. The main building was Sneyd Hall, beyond which were wartime Nissen huts converted to student accommodation and teaching rooms, while staff accommodation was in typical 1950s semi-detached suburban houses nearby. I soon found the object of my journey.

Hugh Leech and his wife were enjoying their Sunday lunch when I knocked on their door unannounced, but although he could hardly believe (any more than I could) the audacity of my trip, he had both the good grace and the humour to invite me in to partake of an Angel Delight gooseberry fool, a culinary speciality of the 1960s, and then dug out my file and conducted an interview with me on the spot.

The only question he asked was, 'What would you do with a million pounds?', to which I responded, 'I'd give half to my mother so that she can enjoy things she's never had, especially as my father has just died. And the rest I'd spend going round the world, instead of coming to university.'

He pronounced, 'You're in. When do you want to start?' – and to his amazement I replied, 'Tomorrow.' I'd brought a bag containing all the necessaries with me. There's a fine line between confidence and arrogance . . .

Keele University was the brainchild of A. D. Lindsay, the political philosopher and author of *The Modern Democratic State*, who wished to re-create a collegiate ethos akin to that of his alma mater, Balliol College, Oxford; and the unusual – and critical – aspect of the course was a compulsory foundation year, which provided all students with a shop window on the world, from astronomy to zoology (sensibly omitting the law). So within weeks of arriving I was looking at the heavens and learning about how recent our existence is, all recorded history being the equivalent of the last few seconds before midnight in the history of the universe on a twenty-four-hour model. That stunning realisation certainly puts everything into sharp perspective and cuts you down to size – and from then on I listened to every new subject with added intensity.

It was only after the first year that you were allowed to select your degree subjects, and most people changed from their original choice – in my case English and history. Instead of English, I was tantalised by philosophy, of which I had no knowledge and little experience, though from childhood I remembered Professor C. E. M. Joad on *The Brains Trust* on the BBC always beginning his answers with 'It depends what you mean by . . .'

If you chose a major arts or humanities subject, as I had, you were compelled to study as a subsidiary a completely different discipline, usually science. This ultimately enabled me to fuse the two, by studying the philosophy of science and its methodology – which was to prove an essential intellectual tool for what was to follow in my legal career. Had I been merely confronted with pure science or mathematics, I would have seized up – the thought of grappling with hieroglyphics and formulae was far too daunting – but the philosophy and methodology of science neatly cut through these symbolic barriers to reach the core rationale of this branch of learning. I remain for ever indebted to this enlightened form of liberal education, which has since been destroyed by the ravages of political short-sightedness and subservience to market forces.

I studied philosophy under the exacting eye of Professor A. G. N. (Antony) Flew, who belonged to the British empirical school

(Hume, Locke and so on) and had a formidable reputation –
understandably, as he demanded commitment of the highest order.
All argument was subjected to intimate dissection, requiring precise
and incisive formulation: the dialectic of thesis versus antithesis
producing synthesis.

Flew was initially highly sceptical about my potential, and
told me so. And whether he said this in order to provoke me or
whether he really thought I was a no-hoper, I was galvanised by
his scepticism and redoubled my efforts to prove him wrong.
Throughout the course he encouraged me to apply the rigorous
discipline of logic, which in the case of science means ensuring that
in any investigation there is an adherence to first principles, and in
particular that assumptions are identified and challenged. In my
legal career this has involved the questioning and exposure of so-
called scientific expertise and objectivity, and I take pride in the fact
that some aspects of forensic science have become recognised over
time as being in fact a subjective interpretation of what appears to be
concrete and indisputable – as is art.

At Keele I wasn't exactly the heart and soul of any political party.
Having scraped in at the last minute, I did not intend to jeopardise
my opportunity by doing anything other than working hard for a
degree, while immersion in study was also a way of coming to terms
with the death of my father barely one month before I had started
there, and the fact that my mother was at home alone trying to do
the same. I had to succeed for them.

So for a good while I was completely unaware that Keele had a
thriving Students' Union, mostly controlled by a clique at the left-
wing end of the Labour Party. This seemed to have little to do with
me, until one rainy afternoon towards the end of my first year I
was waiting to catch the campus bus going into the Potteries when
I was approached by two fellow students, who announced that they
wanted me to stand as a presidential candidate in the forthcoming
Union election.

As far as I was concerned, I was a nobody, barely more recognisable
to my fellow students than the bus stop itself, but that, they insisted,
was irrelevant. By standing and getting myself known, although I
wouldn't make it to President, I could sweep to power as Secretary
against someone on whom they were not too keen. The rain was

getting heavier and my bus was approaching, so in order to cut the conversation short I agreed – and, to my astonishment, duly became Secretary of the Union.

I loved every minute of my time in that role, doing things I never imagined I could undertake: chairing meetings, speaking in public, attending conferences, and even enjoying the quickstep with Princess Margaret, the University Chancellor. (There you go, Mother: that time in the Young Conservatives was not wasted.)

My first stab at public speaking was a debacle. I was so nervous that I wrote it all out, punctuated with studious philosophical allusions, and read it word for word to a stunned Union audience. I fondly imagined that the silence with which it was greeted was a sign of reverence, until I sat down and realised that it was a sign of bemusement and boredom. A lesson never forgotten, and from that day on I have only once written down or read out a public speech.

However, none of this occasioned any kind of political awakening in me, so that when a student whistleblower kindly informed everyone, on special breakfast placemats, of the whereabouts of all the top-secret regional seats of government (which were a central plank of contingency plans in the event of nuclear warfare), I could genuinely tell the Special Branch investigators who came to interview me about whether I knew who had done it that – in the words of the Spanish waiter – 'I know nothing.'

At the end of my final year Professor Flew told me, with a twinkle in his eye, that I had achieved a first-class grade in philosophy. Well, blow me down! Now it was time to concentrate on my ambition to begin a career in law.

2

GETTING INN

A Brief Life

Once a television set had eventually been installed in 73 Naylor Road in the mid-1950s, I found the small silver screen in the corner of the living room completely seductive, and later one of the programmes I watched most avidly was an American drama series called *The Defenders*. Every week a father-and-son team took on seemingly hopeless legal cases, all of which contained a strong social or moral theme. Winning was rare, and the real point of it all was ensuring that people got the best representation possible and were able to air and explore their grievances in the face of institutional indifference.

Even at a very young age – and doubtless influenced by my mother's victory concerning the parking summons – this idea was immediately attractive to me, and provided a constructive channel for my feelings of anger over various forms of social injustice, being a tangible, concrete service with a clear goal.

Once I had begun to consider the law seriously, even before I went to Keele, the odds appeared to be stacked against me. Before he died my father had told me that, in his view, no progress could be made in that profession unless I became a Freemason – and since he thoroughly disapproved of everything that Freemasons stood for, he felt I should stick to trains. Others thought that to succeed in law you needed to be a member of the landed gentry, or at least know someone who was. Above all, you could not survive without some kind of family stipend to get you through the lean years, which in my case was a mountain altogether too steep and too far to climb.

So when I went up to university I had put all these thoughts on the back burner. Fortunately for me, they did not stay there long because I met (at a dance class: Mother was right once again) and fell in love with Melian Bordes, a tall, handsome and striking young woman. We both had a strong interest in sport, and her father, Commander Breon Bordes (like my own father) had Huguenot roots. She was reading French and maths, subjects in which she has maintained an interest throughout her life.

The first summer after we met I went, on my own, to Florence on a British Council arts course. I missed Melian deeply, and when I returned to England we discussed our future together. I mentioned my ambition to go to the Bar, and it so happened that one of her uncles, Andrew Monroe-Kerr, was a barrister practising on the Western Circuit. He gave me invaluable advice, mainly to the effect that I should not be put off by all the paraphernalia, if it was something I really wanted to do.

I started to read up on what was involved. First, join one of the four Inns of Court – Middle Temple, Inner Temple, Lincoln's Inn and Gray's Inn – which back then contained all the sets of chambers in London. I chose Gray's Inn because it seemed more off the beaten track (by about 200 yards) and because it had a strong Irish student intake, and I really liked the Irish.

All the Inns were much the same, ancient foundations shrouded in mystery and mystical ceremony – I could see why my father thought membership of a Masonic Lodge might help – and they have survived by means of their insular and inscrutable cloistered confines. Their traditions are jealously guarded and preserved, and if you walk into one of them off the street you are confronted with another age. Scratch the surface and you discover a thoroughly British substratum that is reflected in all the major public schools, Oxbridge colleges, Sandhurst, the Foreign Office, the Church and the monarchy. For someone like me, well outside the magic circle, it required a markedly deep breath as well as a blind eye for me to join this pillar of the Establishment.

My saving grace, I thought at the time, was that Melian (who had become my wife in 1965) and I intended to emigrate to Australia, where I could practise law and see a bit of the world. There was an interesting scheme, euphemistically called 'Assisted Passage', whereby successful candidates would have their journey subsidised for a down-payment of just £10. Since the Australian Government was very fussy about who it took, this could be regarded as a form of middle-class deportation, and our idea was therefore for me to pass the Bar exams after my degree and then we'd set off.

Besides the weighty task of trying to get through all these exams in time, I had not allowed for the fact that you are also required to *eat* your way to professional status: thirty-six dinners had to be consumed prior to qualification. Fond though I am of food, this was quite a challenge, so I started the 'eatathon' while I was still at university. A student friend, Maureen Ritchie, who had a mossy Morris Traveller and returned to London regularly to see her parents, kindly took me to Gray's Inn every term for the purpose of attending these dinners. Without her help I would never have made it, because my grant did not even cover the barest expenses and my vacation jobs working 'on the dust', and then delivering new cars, merely provided money which I gave to my mother.

My fellow workers 'on the dust' in Finchley could not fathom why on earth I was refuse collecting. They thought I was an undercover toff gaining experience for some kind of magazine exposé, so they presented me with a cup and saucer for my tea instead of a mug. They simply couldn't believe I really did need the money.

One of the most revealing experiences of the job was the weekly collection at the Friern Barnet Mental Hospital, a vast asylum built like a Victorian prison. Up until then I had never encountered anyone suffering from serious mental illness and, like many people, I was afraid because of my ignorance. Some patients were allowed into the grounds where the bins were and often sat on them awaiting our arrival, at which point we engaged in extraordinary and entertaining conversations about what was going to happen to the rubbish we removed. My fear was soon displaced by a realisation that they were probably saner than I was.

The Gray's Inn dining experience was both breathtaking and nerve-racking. One moment I was living and studying close to the Pottery towns – immortalised by Arnold Bennett in such novels as *Anna of the Five Towns* (1902), *The Old Wives' Tale* (1908) and *Clayhanger* (1910) and an area seared by economic deprivation – and the next minute I was thrust into a highly privileged and exclusive club.

The walls of the Inn were bedecked with portraits of illustrious and famous legal luminaries, such as Bacon, Cecil, Holt, F. E. Smith and Atkin. An ornate carved screen had been presented by Elizabeth I, and fine examples of heraldic stained glass filtered daylight into this historical domain. The dining hall contained long mahogany tables with wooden benches; raised slightly above these was another table for the elders of the Inn, otherwise known as Masters of the Bench, or Benchers. Against this backcloth it's easy to see why I never expected to be joining their number – which I did, however, when I was elected in 2007.

Each student was robed, and we dined in a group of four (a mess); one took the role of senior and another that of junior within the mess; the plates had to be passed round one way and the wine another. You were obliged to toast, by name, each member of your mess, followed by those in the mess above you and below you on the table. What I found to be complete anathema were the penalties incurred for minor infringements of dining etiquette. Somewhat like a forfeit, the culprit was required to stand up and perform a recitation or song. No doubt it was thought to be all jolly good fun and not to be taken seriously, but for most of us it was nothing short of public humiliation, particularly for the women students, whose numbers were small and who had to suffer the usual round of sexist comments.

There was, however, a far more important activity promoted by the Inn, which I found invaluable: the Moot. This was a mock trial prosecuted and defended by students in front of real, experienced judges, and it provided precisely what the law courses did not, namely a practical exercise of advocacy skills. A brief was prepared outlining a set of facts, which then required analysis to establish what legal liability arose. You were judged not only on the content of your submissions, but on other qualities, notably presentation. The tips handed down by eminent High Court judges such as the Lords Edmund Davies and Donaldson were all sound and necessary, although I can't say that I've always managed to stick to them: be clear, concise and non-repetitive. One of the judges, the Honourable Sir William McNair, kindly took the trouble to write to me after each Moot suggesting improvements: watch your posture; look the court in the eye; don't doggedly read out texts of legal authorities; speak with conviction; observe the general reaction; adjust your tone and tenor; listen intently to questions and queries and address them directly; be wary of the judicial seduction that begins, 'Well, Mr Mansfield, isn't *this* what you really mean?' Receiving encouragement of that kind was worth its weight in gold.

The Inn also provided other much-needed practical help, in my case money. I was awarded an Exhibition (a bursary) for three years following a written examination in jurisprudence, which was just up my street because I saw this as a natural extension to the philosophy degree.

Meanwhile, as far as the Bar exams themselves were concerned, I was not doing so well. Melian had taken a year out to teach in France as part of her French degree, which meant that I had finished mine before her, so I decided to remain in the Potteries while she completed her final year and take a correspondence course for the Bar. This was somewhat unconventional and more than a little mind-numbing: so far as I could see, the endless notes which I was sent in grubby brown envelopes were no more than sophisticated shopping lists. When I eventually managed to attend some lectures in London, which weren't much better, I wondered what the point was.

No lawyer worth his salt wanders round with all this information – Roman law, Equity law, company law, all very Byzantine – in his head. Surely, I reasoned, they should be teaching me about where to find the law you need to know and how to apply it; but the answer from the examiners was a resounding 'no', and so I had to keep doing retakes until I felt like a crammed parrot.

By the summer of 1967 that parrot was hanging on to his perch by one leg, having scraped through all the exams except one: land law. I think it was a case of three strikes and you're out, and I had failed twice, so I had to make it this time or it was curtains.

The result of my final shot would be published at the end of August, and at the beginning of that month, on the 7th, Melian gave birth to our first child, Jonathan – a wonderful, but unplanned arrival. At the same time we had got through the screening process at Australia House, and our passage to Adelaide was booked for

November. If I managed to pass the exam, I could be called to the Bar just before departure. Everything was becoming rather tight, and I felt very edgy. Maybe I'd taken on too much; maybe I wasn't cut out for the law anyway; maybe emigrating for four years (the minimum we had agreed on) was mad. Wasn't that what had happened to the Tolpuddle Martyrs?

Instead of trying to ease the pressure by cutting something out, I seem to have a natural response that does quite the opposite. Prepare for the worst, but hope for the best – and now preparing for the worst entailed thinking about alternative careers.

Most people thought I'd lost it when they heard that I had taken up devising weird inventions. There was the knife-cutting fork, handy for those parties where you have to eat standing up, trying to juggle a glass, cutlery and a plate. I managed to persuade Viners, a well-known cutlery firm in Sheffield, to consider a prototype, and even took out a provisional patent. At the same time I thought it might be useful for the plate to be designed with a notch cut into its circumference to accommodate the stem of a wine glass. Then there was the electronically operated self-opening umbrella, which popped out of a small pack strapped to your back like a parachute. Finally there was a bed which gently raised itself into the vertical position in the morning, so that you could step out of it and then hide it away in a cupboard. (Wallace and Gromit went a step further in the film *The Wrong Trousers* by contriving a chute down which Wallace was propelled from the bed through the floor into a pair of waiting trousers.) The world was saved from these mechanical machinations because the examiners finally took pity. I passed.

Hoping for such an outcome, I had made some other preparations. Once you've secured your exams and eaten your dinners, there is a further stage of training called pupillage, which took twelve months and which had to be paid for. I thought I might complete at least six months before going to Adelaide, not having realised that you weren't supposed to start your pupillage before you were called to the Bar, let alone before you had passed all the exams. On top of this I did not know quite how you obtained a Pupil Master. Nowadays it's all highly regulated and centralised, but back then I set off using my well-tried method of walking around till I found the right door.

Opposite the Royal Courts of Justice there is a large black door on the Strand, which leads into the Temple. So I went through there, believing this to be the heart and hive of legal activity. I asked the porter where I could find pupillage, and he directed me to the Treasurer's office, where the person I saw had an obvious military demeanour: perfectly polite, but plainly astonished that anyone should come in and ask for a pupillage as if it were a loaf of bread. He probably thought that the easiest way to deal with someone so naive was to palm me off on a nearby friendly barrister, who would put me straight.

Within minutes I was sitting in a tiny room in Crown Office Row in front of a bespectacled P. G. Wodehouse-style figure called Quentin Edwards, and I soon came to respect the enduring humanity with which he had embraced my unannounced arrival. There could not have been many who were prepared to take in someone like me without further thought. He had a remarkable legal practice, which embraced everything from ecclesiastical tree-root damage to licensing applications for pubs and clubs, while in his spare time he acted as a Nonconformist lay preacher. Like Professor Flew, Quentin was a strict disciplinarian and expected me to be in the office from eight in the morning until six in the evening, and was rigorous about the briefs I was allowed to read, ensuring that I knew them inside out. Once I had mastered the instructions, he would then set me a series of questions that would require further research (which is what I thought the Bar schools should have been doing). All this made me realise that presentation depends on preparation, and that I had a very long way to go before reaching even the foothills of the television scenarios I'd so eagerly consumed.

Weeks before I was due to embark on the voyage to Australia, Quentin suddenly suggested that I might like to reconsider going at all, as he had a friend and colleague in a top criminal set who might be prepared to give me a second six months' pupillage straight away. I am a firm believer in not only looking for opportunities, but taking them whenever they come along: they hardly ever occur when you want them to, so you have to be flexible and receptive when they do.

Melian and I spent a weekend pushing Jonathan around Hampstead Heath, weighing up what we should do. We'd already said our goodbyes to numerous friends (many of whom had never thought we'd go anyway), but the chance I had been offered seemed too good to miss. After a great deal of heart-searching we decided to forfeit our £10 and stay in England.

Five Paper Buildings was a very different set-up from Quentin Edwards's practice. It was a high-profile prosecution set, where the lawyers were housed in large rooms with leather-backed chairs and beautiful views across Temple Gardens to the River Thames, and where a pupillage was like gold dust. The engine room of the set was an old-school senior clerk called Tom, who divvied up the work and kept a beady eye on everyone.

My Pupil Master was Brian Leary, a slick, super-confident prosecutor with a generous spirit. In your second six months you are allowed to take on small cases on your own – and as he thought the best way of learning was to jump in at the deep end, within days of my arrival I was sent to Hampstead Magistrates' Court to prosecute a shoplifter. I hadn't been to any criminal court by this time and was completely terrified, but Brian told me not to worry and just get on with it, a lesson that has remained with me throughout my professional career.

He wrote out exactly where to go, where to stand in court, when to get up, what to say – and, crucially, not to forget to ask for costs – and it all worked like a dream. The shoplifter was convicted, and to Brian's amazement the case even found its way into the local newspaper, the *Ham & High*.

Mind you, the defendant had pleaded guilty . . .

3

DRUGS, ROCK AND LAW

'Operation Julie', The Cambridge Two

Although I had that first courtroom success as prosecutor, my real interest – in line with the inspiration I had received from watching so many episodes of *The Defenders* – was in defending.

I was called to the Bar in 1967, and throughout my early years as a barrister one of the hottest issues – both political and social – was the increase in drug use, in particular cannabis.

As for my own experience of cannabis, I'm not going to fall back on that overused cop-out that I smoked but didn't inhale, because I didn't smoke at all. Many of my contemporaries did, however, and I soon got drawn into the campaign to legalise – or, more precisely, decriminalise – the drug.

In my spare time I was a volunteer at two centres in London providing advice to addicts: one run by the Association for the Prevention of Addiction (APA) in King Street, Covent Garden, and the other a walk-in centre under Hungerford Bridge. Many of the people who used these centres were addicted to heroin and in a state of such extreme distress that, while I was in my twenties, as were some of them, it was as if they were living on a different planet.

Through the volunteering I met Bernard (Bernie) Simons, a hugely generous, witty and cultured person who spread his life across many interests, particularly the National Theatre: he became a close friend, but sadly died prematurely in the late 1980s. Another volunteer was the acclaimed writer Anthony Masters. His work was amazingly eclectic, from children's books to political biographies.

His breadth of interest also encompassed running soup kitchens for addicts and the homeless, and championing the cause of Travellers. Both he and his wife Robina became close friends. His early death in 2003 was yet another real loss. I also came to know Jon Snow (now presenter of Channel 4 News), who shared our concern about drugs as well as many other issues over the intervening years.

The centres brought me into contact with individuals who'd intentionally broken the law, but who felt they had no alternative; and before being able to offer advice, I wanted to understand who they were, their motivation and the roots of their addiction – essential if you have to represent someone, but an approach not generally approved of by the majority of the Bar at the time.

There was a large amount of public ignorance and misinformation, especially in relation to LSD and cannabis – pronounced 'canaaarbis' by the higher echelons of the legal fraternity at the time. Fine distinctions between physical addiction and psychological dependence were not appreciated then. I started attending government committees along with others like Bill Deedes, the well-respected journalist, and all the while Bernie was instructing me on a series of drug cases, which took up a great deal of court time in the early 1970s.

Bernie knew that I was outraged by the consummate hypocrisy of those who were vehemently hostile to drug-takers while imbibing excessive quantities of claret – in any case, he really didn't know too many other barristers whom he could brief. We began to write a book together, and helped launch a new magazine called *Drugs and Society* by co-writing a regular legal column.

Looking back on the articles I wrote, they seem somewhat tame now, but at the time they were regarded as quite radical. For example, in July 1973 I penned an article entitled 'Private Drug Use – No Crime?',[1] a critique of the first Misuse of Drugs Act of 1971. Like so much social legislation, the Act had been passed with very little informed debate, and I sought to question two aspects: the jurisprudential basis on which the criminal law was invoked to sanction certain types of behaviour, and a lack of provision for the education and treatment of addicts.

The central thrust of my argument was based on the work of John Stuart Mill contained in his essay *On Liberty*, which distinguished between self-regarding and other-regarding acts. In essence, self-regarding acts which do not encroach on the life and liberty of someone else should not attract state sanction, whereas with other-regarding acts, which do, the state may intervene to protect good order. This was a strictly libertarian viewpoint reflected in part by Professor H. L. A. Hart in *Law, Liberty and Morality*, and opposed by Lord Devlin in *The Enforcement of Morals*. I tried to suggest that people who pursue dangerous activities purely for themselves, and who are not endangering anyone else, should not be criminalised. I have shifted position since then, because it is almost impossible to postulate any activity that can be isolated in such a way that it can have no effect on anyone else. The real question is what kind of regulation society wishes to have in place to deal with the social repercussions: this has assumed considerable importance recently with the civil procedures that have been introduced to deal with anti-social behaviour.

In 1973 articles along these lines were adding to the image I seemed to be engendering with the cases I took, as someone who needed to be watched, and I have no doubt that some form of MI5 file on me was opened. At the time I certainly felt that what I was doing was risky and frowned upon, an apprehension heightened once I began representing Irish defendants.

I'm sure that this image cannot have been helped by the fact that I joined a rock band of fellow lawyers called The Mindless Pleasures. We played at lawyers' parties, street festivals and in a pub in Stoke Newington on Saturday nights, and because I was the drummer we were definitely off-beat. My kit was fourth-hand and tatty, but its well-worn appearance lent a certain depth and implied that I had a track record, whereas there were no tracks and no records . . .

Meantime I continued taking drugs cases. My first appeal in the Court of Appeal was in front of the Lord Chief Justice, Lord Widgery, in 1971, the year before he presided over the first Bloody Sunday inquiry. The appeal concerned a nice point of law, which has remained as an authority right up to the present day and can be found in every criminal practitioner's handbook (known as *Archbold*), under the title *Searle and Others*, and it came down to this: before you could be convicted of joint possession of drugs found in a place you occupied with others – such as a room, a minibus or a car – it would not be enough for the prosecution to show mere knowledge of the presence of drugs; they would also have to prove that you had an element of control, which might arise if you were able to take what you wanted from a common pool of drugs.

There were many other drug cases which gave rise to extraordinary and bizarre issues. When two men called Ameer and Lucas were arrested for trading in cannabis in a hotel in west London, they claimed it was a police sting set up by an agent provocateur.

Geoffrey Robertson (now a leading authority on international human-rights law) was my co-counsel and Alan Green (an incisive advocate, later Director of Public Prosecutions) was prosecuting. The judge was Bernard Gillis, meticulous and punctilious. At trial in 1977 the agent provocateur suggested that the police had licensed him to deal, and had rewarded him with slabs of cannabis from the deals. When challenged by the prosecution to prove such outlandish claims, the informer said he kept some of the cannabis seals under his mother's bed at home – and the next day he produced in court the seals themselves, which exactly matched the ones in our case.

After the acquittal of the defendants, the journalist David May of the *Sunday Times* constantly pressed the police authorities for an explanation, but, so far as I'm aware, to this day none has ever been forthcoming.

In 1978 the *Daily Express* trumpeted a police investigation called 'Operation Julie', which had broken the world's biggest drug ring, responsible for the manufacture of six million doses of LSD. I considered that part of my task in defending one of the people charged (who pleaded guilty) was to attempt to take the heat out of the gross exaggerations being made about the effects of LSD. The conventional wisdom at the time about how to present a plea in mitigation concentrated on the personal circumstances and the role of an individual defendant. No one would have dreamed of challenging the legislation itself and its rationale – completely unacceptable and far too political. This did not deter me, but on reflection maybe I was wrong to underestimate the detrimental effects of LSD.

It was only a few years earlier that cannabis had been viewed as the greatest evil on Earth, with both the police and the courts displaying considerable ignorance even about the various forms that it took.

I had a friend (I'll call him Eric, to protect the guilty) who was growing a few plants in the window box of his basement flat somewhere in Tufnell Park in north London. The local bobby on his rounds commented on the verdant growth, only to be informed by Eric that it was a form of nettle he was cultivating for soup.

When Eric moved with a few friends to a large Victorian house, so the story goes, the plants went with him, and come harvest time he took them inside. The house had one of those clothes-drying racks that can be raised to the ceiling via a pulley, and Eric said he used to hang the cannabis leaves over this to dry. Somebody must have tipped off the police, for late one evening they arrived on his doorstep, accompanied by sniffer dogs. Fleet of foot and with great presence of mind, Eric rapidly stuffed the leaves into the laundry basket and rushed out into the back garden wondering where to hide the stash – then in a moment of panic emptied the basket over the fence into the neighbour's garden. The dogs sniffed around for a while, but the prey had flown . . .

Eric's neighbour was a member of the aristocracy, and the next morning Lady Whoever-She-Was awoke and looked out into the garden, where she was amazed to see a pile of leaves, from a tree she didn't possess, at a season that was not autumnal. Without further ado, she went outside and swept the leaves neatly into a pile, then set fire to them. The aroma penetrated the slumbers of he who had so carefully harvested them – and soon, his nose pressed to the window, Eric was watching the soaring flames of the bonfire and the remains of his precious cannabis floating gently up in the breeze . . . her Ladyship swaying delicately in the wind.

There is of course a serious side to all this. I have always recognised the substantial risks to health of all forms of drugs, including prescription drugs and alcohol. But imprisonment is not the answer to the drugs problem, and should be reserved for the rarest of extreme cases. The original idea for the registration and management of heroin addicts was a British initiative and was along the right lines, but the current emphasis on penalties distracts from the crucial task of examining the causes and providing essential education.

It was for these reasons that much later in my career I was glad to be able to help Ruth Wyner and John Brock, who became known as the Cambridge Two.

They both worked at Wintercomfort, a drop-in centre in Cambridge for homeless young people, most of whom were dependent on drugs – Ruth was Director and John the Day Centre Manager – and both were dedicated charity workers. Established in 1989, Wintercomfort provided a facility not offered by anyone else in the area and had the backing of reputable academics at Cambridge University, and yet the local police regarded it as a centre for drug dealing.

The police action began in February 1998 when two undercover policemen calling themselves Ed and Swampy began calling at the Wintercomfort Day Centre and involving themselves in secret drug deals taking place between some of the homeless. An extensive surveillance operation was mounted, backed up by a camera hidden under the roof of a building on the opposite side of the street.

In May the operation was concluded with the arrest of eight drug dealers and of Ruth and John, and the couple were charged with 'permitting premises to be used for the purpose of supplying a class-A drug'. The trial began eighteen months later at King's Lynn Crown Court and lasted seven weeks, involving evidence from 300 hours of videotape.

No one suggested that either Ruth or John had been personally involved in any of the drug deals, or that they had been present at the time these took place. The case against them was simply that they had 'turned a blind eye' to what was going on and had not done enough to stop it. Ruth and John argued forcefully that they had done as much as was humanly possible without compromising the whole object of the Day Centre, based as it was on client confidentiality and trust. Wintercomfort was an essential first step in getting homeless people off the streets in order to address their problems – what's more, they argued, involving the police could put their staff at risk of reprisals.

On 17 December 1999 Ruth and John were convicted and sentenced to five and four years respectively – particularly harsh sentences, which had serious repercussions for other social workers in this field.

The astonishing campaign launched on their behalf by the homeless people who had used the Day Centre has been graphically chronicled by Alex Masters in his book *Stuart: A Life Backwards*.

Stuart and others organised a march of the homeless and a 'sleep-out' over three days outside the Home Office, and also won the support of Alan Bennett, Joan Baez, Victoria Wood, several MPs, a large number of Cambridge academics and the trade union Unison.

By the time I came on board for their appeal in December 2000, a good head of steam had been raised in favour of Ruth and John. Each of them had two children and their families had suffered greatly, while John himself was close to breakdown – and all because of their honest endeavours to help people come off drugs and rebuild their lives without constantly begging on the streets and harassing members of the public. For my part, I felt a palpable sense of anger about the iniquity of their situation.

We got leave to appeal both conviction and sentence – and lost on conviction, but won on sentence. The law as interpreted by the Appeal Court judges was in my view quite unrealistic, determining as 'irrelevant' a defendant's belief that the steps he had taken to prevent dealing were reasonable. My contention was that a jury should not reach its conclusion solely on an objective basis, by overriding the genuine, bona-fide subjective belief of what was reasonably possible in the circumstances, held by a professional worker in the field. I lost on this point, and I still feel that this was an erroneous decision, which will have to be revisited at some point if there is ever to be a constructive and sensible approach to this ever-increasing problem. Fortunately, the judges substantially reduced Ruth and John's sentences to allow their immediate release.

We have to try and think laterally about how we get people off hard drugs, and mentoring seems to be an idea that works on a very practical level. I remember a BBC television programme in which a lawyer became a mentor to a woman coming off heroin: it was a good demonstration of how, if you don't lock someone up, but have someone willing to be a 'best friend' (and, in a sense, usher the person gently back into life) things can change. Just being there – setting up contacts, listening, nothing too heavy, but providing reliable support – can work. The woman wrote a wonderful letter to her mentor thanking him for backing her, acknowledging how much she owed him and saying that he had given her back her life: she'd finally made it and come off heroin. This was true innovation, with the courts providing the opportunity and somebody on the outside being prepared to give up time just to be alongside that person in need.

And yet I can't believe I'm still having to argue this case, almost thirty-five years after Bernie and I blazed a trail on these very same points in the articles we wrote.

4

PRINTS AND IMPRESSIONS

The Angry Brigade and the Fallibility of Forensic Science

The drugs cases of my early years as a practising barrister made me ever more aware that for most legal practitioners science was a blind spot – as it had been for me – principally on account of there being a lamentable dearth of scientific training and education. I started to put the principles of scientific method to the test.

In so many of the drugs cases on which I cut my legal teeth there was an issue about the nature and amount of the drug, as well as where it had been found, and my clients regularly made allegations that the drugs had been 'planted'. Sometimes a drug had in fact been planted in a pocket, but sometimes not. On other occasions there was merely a claim that it had been found there. In those circumstances I began to ask what appear now to be rather simple and obvious questions. For example:

Has anyone examined the pocket for traces of the drug concerned?
Unheard of; never done; too time-consuming.
Has any wrapping been examined for fingerprints?
Not considered.
Has the substance been matched with any other drug recovered from the same source?
Not contemplated.

In one particular case, drugs had been stolen from a chemist's shop, and in the process a window had been broken and particles of glass ended up on the intruder's clothing – particularly in the turn-ups of his trousers. A match was said to have been achieved between the shop glass and the glass found on my client. This was based on what is called the 'refractive index' of the glass itself – refraction is like the bent image you get when you stick your finger in water – and as usual everyone expected that this evidence would go unchallenged as being incontrovertible. To the chagrin of the judge, I did not allow the expert's report to be read, but asked him to attend for cross-examination. I wanted to discover what methods, protocols and procedures were in place at the laboratory; furthermore, I wanted to know how the refractive index had been calculated.

The expert wasn't used to having to testify. He arrived with a well-worn, brown Home Office briefcase in which he carried his papers and the exhibits. When my turn came to put my questions, I asked him to produce the test tube containing the particles of glass. He fumbled in the case and drew it out. In a moment of seeming satisfaction he held it aloft and shook it – and to his amazement the test tube was silent. From then on I nicknamed him 'Tinkerbelle'. But that was not all. It turned out that he had signed a statement for work he had not carried out himself, and that there were no adequate records from the lab about the examination, let alone the methods used. It goes without saying that it is absolutely vital to preserve the sample whenever possible and record precisely the methods and results of the tests, so that another scientist can come along and replicate everything in order to verify it. (These are the principles of 'interverifiability' and 'reproducibility'.)

The chance to explore these avenues in a more significant way came in 1972 with my first major case. Gordon Carr, in his book about this case,[1] dubbed the accused 'Britain's first urban guerrillas'. Like most other European countries in the early 1970s, the UK had its own brand: there was the Baader-Meinhof Group in Germany and the Red Brigade in Italy; ours had the rather Monty Pythonesque name of the Angry Brigade. I had read about them in the papers, but only with passing interest. Their main targets were banks, embassies and the homes of senior Conservative politicians, like the Attorney General Sir Peter Rawlinson, all attacked between 1970 and 1971. But in all the twenty-five bombings attributed to the Brigade – including one audacious attack on the Post Office Tower in central London – no one was killed. So they were seen as more of an embarrassment to the government than a serious threat, a 'leftist cult of hippies and weirdos', as the papers put it, though in fact they were campaigning against Lord Donaldson's Industrial Relations Bill, which at the time proposed serious restrictions on trade-union rights.

I scarcely noticed the reports of eight young people being arrested after a police swoop on a north London house in August 1971, and when Bernie turned up at my home in Priory Gardens, off the Archway Road, late one Sunday evening to talk about a client, I assumed it would be another drugs case. But this case turned out to be different – so different that he hadn't felt able to discuss it over the phone – and it was the first time I had been offered something with serious social and political overtones. For his part, Bernie was in a state of excitement, because it was a high-profile event, and as soon as I had heard him out, I agreed to act as barrister for his client. I had no idea what I was letting myself in for.

Bernie had been instructed by a young telephonist called Angela Weir, who along with seven other defendants had been charged with planting small explosive devices outside London businesses and the home of Employment Secretary Robert Carr, in 'an attempt to awaken democracy'. Also known as the Stoke Newington Eight, the group held a mish-mash of libertarian and militant beliefs strongly influenced by anarchism and the Situationists, the radical international political and artistic movement.

The defendants included John Barker; Jim Greenfield; Hilary Creek and Anna Mendleson, the daughters of a leading landowner and the Mayor of Manchester respectively; and Stuart Christie, a peripatetic anarchist who had previously been imprisoned in Spain for carrying explosives with the intent to assassinate the dictator General Franco. The trial of the Angry Brigade was the culmination of 1960s radicalism.

I hadn't met any so-called 'terrorists' before, but Angela struck me as a very unlikely one. She was small, articulate and polite, and we talked a great deal about her life, her views, her politics: she was clearly very bright and not a bomber. As we talked, I wanted to be able to identify with her as much as I could, to be standing in her place; I wanted to be able to feel as she did, so that I could genuinely communicate those feelings in court. It may sound like acting, but it isn't. You have to be able to activate those emotions in yourself in order to be convincing. A dispassionate delivery just doesn't work.

As the case entered court on 30 May 1972, public sentiments were riding high on a tide of media prejudice. As it happened, the prosecutor was a well-known, senior Treasury Counsel John Mathew, who was a leading member of my own set of chambers, highly skilled and thorough and with a reputation second to none. The chambers at Five Paper Buildings was regarded as a top prosecuting set, and for me to develop high-profile defence work there was slightly quirky – especially when the opposition was in the room next door. John was meticulously professional and I learned a massive amount from his ordered and focused techniques. There were no tensions within the set, but it was not easy from a public point of view to explain the apparent contradiction in this working relationship.

The prosecution's case against Angela rested mainly on a scientific assessment of a false passport the police had found in the name of 'Rosemary Pink', which they claimed had been forged by Angela. Usually such cases depended on a prosecution expert witness claiming that the 'questioned' handwriting contained characteristics that were the same, or similar, to those in the 'control' sample belonging to the accused. The defence customarily produced a different expert to say that it wasn't the same, or that he or she couldn't be sure that it was. Then it was up to the jury to decide. In those days juries tended to trust the prosecution, but to me this approach lacked an important element of scientific rigour. So I tried something that had never been done before.

I asked not one but a number of handwriting experts to conduct blind tests independently of, and unknown to, each other. Some felt so threatened that they refused, but finally three agreed to look at a series of different, unidentified samples of handwriting. Some were Angela's (the control sample), some were her relatives', others were by unrelated persons and still others were from the ('questioned') passport. This meant that the experts did not know where any of the samples had come from or whether more than one had been written by the same person. The key question I posed was whether they could determine if any of the samples were written by the same person. This entirely novel approach was intended to counteract the inevitable influences of preconception, preconditioning and prejudice – for science, unlike beauty in art, should not reside principally in the eye of the beholder.

It was an unprecedented challenge. In those days no one questioned experts, especially not your own. No one put their proficiency to the test. But I did, and I had to explain to the Legal Aid Board why there was a need for so many witnesses and their costs. There was judicial consternation when I clearly showed that handwriting 'expertise' was not a science but an art, and a highly subjective one at that. In Angela's case all the experts disagreed, and the resulting confusion and conflict between the 'scientific' views ensured her acquittal.

I remember Mother sitting at the back of the Old Bailey, slightly bemused.

I incurred judicial disapproval in two ways during this case. First, I was prepared to help Anna Mendleson, a co-defendant who was granted bail on very strict conditions, by driving her to court every day from the home of her solicitor, Michael Seifert, an old school friend who lived round the corner from me. This was unheard-of conduct – before the Angry Brigade trial and even possibly since.

Second, I encountered the judicial phrase 'Mr Mansfield, I cannot see you', which was directed at you if you appeared before a judge in clothing that was sartorially unacceptable. I disliked the uniform worn by most barristers in that early period – black jacket, waistcoat and pinstriped trousers – and instead invested in what I thought was a rather smart double-breasted, dark-blue blazer with gun-metal buttons. The height of chic! I was invited 'round the back' to the judge's chamber for some elliptical words of advice.

In those days there were other arcane customs at the Bar. Barristers never shook hands with one another – I mean, you had to have a hand forever ready to draw your sword. They never addressed each other by their first names: whatever next, for familiarity breeds . . . I could never get used to all this and often faced retreating, wincing fellow members of the Bar.

During the trial there was a wonderful moment. One afternoon a co-defending counsel stood up with a seemingly serious application about the appalling cell conditions at the Old Bailey, and when taxed by the judge about the exact nature of the complaint, produced from underneath his seat a huge pink birthday cake with candles – which he had asked me to light while he was speaking. It was his client's birthday and the jailers had refused to let the cake into the cell, so he produced it in court. His client was very touched and so was the judge, but in a different way.

The Angry Brigade trial was one of the longest criminal trials in English history, lasting over six months from May to December 1972. Four of the defendants were convicted, but – with a jury rider for mercy on the grounds that their motivation was understood, which the judge graciously implemented – they only got ten years in prison each. Stuart Christie went on to become a prolific writer, best known for *My Granny Made Me an Anarchist.*

In the end it was a triumph for Angela, for Bernie and for me, as Angela was acquitted and went on to make a reputable and successful career in gay-rights advocacy as Director of Stonewall, the gay/lesbian pressure group, and Director of the UK Government's Women and Equality Unit. She was awarded an OBE in 1999.

A triumph, but this was just the beginning of a long battle against the unquestioning use of scientific evidence in British courts, culminating in the very basis of forensics being challenged in the notorious 'fingerprint on the bomb' case in 2001. But more of that later . . .

For me, another repercussion of the Angry Brigade case lay in its political context, and it was not long before whispers about my being a dangerous subversive started to reach my ears. Me a subversive? Nothing could have been further from the truth. My upbringing and political experience had been thoroughly middle-class and conventional, and it was hardly surprising that the emergent radical consciences of the mid-1960s had not featured on my radar before my involvement in the Angry Brigade case. I was not much older than the eight in the dock. They were intelligent and articulate; I was politically naive. The ideas and issues raised during the trial concerning the injustice wrought by the exigencies of capitalism, and the operation of state agencies in perpetuating this, gave me considerable food for thought. I was familiar from university with the concept of anarchism, but Situationism was a new one on me.

From the late 1950s this had been a movement describing, with considerable foresight, the way in which rapidly developing new technologies were creating an unreal society, one indirectly experienced by all of us. Over the years I have characterised this as a screen culture that has vastly increased with the advent of the Internet, cable and satellite television, mobile phones and laptops. We have become an audience in Marshall McLuhan's 'global village',[2] susceptible to being manipulated and controlled, and this may explain my long-standing hostility to the corruptible information highway of websites and emails.

My first brush with radicalism had aroused only a spirit of enquiry rather than a conversion, so the whispers about my subversiveness didn't bother me that much. It all struck me as typically British: you show interest or regard for other people and you run the risk of being branded a revolutionary, when in fact revolution (let alone armed revolution) could not have been further from my thoughts. Of course it was a risk being associated with what was then called 'alternative thinking', but it was a risk I was prepared to take, and the special benefit was that I was soon being asked to take on other controversial and high-profile cases.

Henceforward I was the Red under every legal bed – and funnily enough, Keele had been known as 'the Kremlin on the Hill', while the 'Kremlin' label had also been applied to Cloisters, the chambers to which I moved in 1973.

The Head of Cloisters was John Platts Mills (JPM), an eccentric, erudite, maverick ex-Labour MP, and I was part of a team led by him in another groundbreaking forensic exercise.

In 1975 Cornelius McFadden and seven others were accused of a conspiracy to cause explosions in clothing shops in Uxbridge, Welwyn Garden City and London's West End by means of firebombs contained in cigarette packets. Many of these did not detonate and were therefore recovered, and one of McFadden's fingerprints was alleged to have been on the face of an alarm clock used as a timing device. The defendant vehemently denied touching the clock, but there was no innocent explanation for the fingerprint's presence, so we had to examine whether it was possible for it to have been planted.

Despite some reluctance and resistance by those experts we approached to the very idea that a print could be moved, we were able to work out in principle how this could happen. When it came to cross-examining the prosecution fingerprint expert, JPM, a tall, quizzical figure peering over his pince-nez, began by feigning ignorance and asking seemingly unambiguous and straightforward questions. In essence, if a mark made by grease from sweat on the skin can be lifted from a crime scene and then deposited onto a laboratory slide, is there any reason why it cannot also be placed on any other surface?

The expert was of course adamant this was not possible. The cross-examination went something like this:

But if it was, asks JPM, *what kind of surface provides the best receptor?*

Glass.

As if by magic, JPM produces from below his bench a small sheet of plate glass. *Like this? How do you detect the mark?*

By dusting it with powder.

What kind of powder do you use?

Ninhydrin.

JPM produces some fine aluminium powder in a tin, like talcum powder. *How do you put the powder onto the mark?*

With a brush.

Out comes a fine-art paintbrush. *Like this?*

JPM then proceeds to brush the powder delicately onto the thumbprint he has left on the glass. This reveals the contours and ridge characteristics of his mark.

So now, how do you get the dusted mark onto a laboratory's glass slide?

With sticky tape.

JPM picks up a roll of Sellotape and cuts off a section. We are nearing the climax, as JPM places the tape on the dusted mark and then transfers it deftly onto another glass surface I swiftly hand him. Hey presto!*

It was a masterclass in logic and finesse so gripping that in court you couldn't even hear the proverbial pin drop. Mr Justice Melford 'Truncheons' Stevenson had an apoplectic fit and docked

---

* Staggeringly over thirty years later I am watching an episode of *Wallander* (BBC1, December 2008) starring the excellent Kenneth Branagh when a technical 'nerd' character does exactly the same thing – lifts a print with tape – for the purpose of accessing a locked computer.

all our fees. We were accused of being mere 'mouthpieces' for wicked allegations being contrived by enemies of the state, and in those circumstances we could not expect the hand that fed us (legal aid) to underwrite such calumny with any money for all the time 'wasted' on this part of the case. The Court of Appeal disagreed and reinstated our fees.

There were, however, some complications from a forensic point of view with JPM's exposition. How do you remove the Sellotape from the transposed mark without leaving an outline of the sticky tape? How do you prevent some of the fingerprint powder remaining on the transferred mark? Most of all, the whole operation would necessitate corruption on a massive scale by SOCOs (Scene of Crime Officers), laboratory assistants, liaison officers, exhibits officers and fingerprint experts themselves.

McFadden was convicted, but JPM had shaken the self-satisfaction of experts and caused a reappraisal of the apparently irrefutable.

Thereafter, he travelled the world on diplomatic missions to Iron Curtain countries and left-wing regimes as an unofficial troubleshooter, and was my predecessor as President of the Haldane Society of Socialist Lawyers. A favourite image is from the notorious and long-running Grunwick dispute in the late 1970s. A group of Asian women had been denied the right to join a trade union, and Grunwick had swiftly become a symbol for the assertion of workers' rights, drawing hundreds of protesters from all over the UK to the processing laboratories in north London. On more than one occasion the pickets were famously led by JPM, resplendent in bowler hat and pinstripes.

JPM was an outstanding and courageous barrister, and I was thrilled when in the final years of his life he joined my chambers at Tooks Court, where he was still practising at the age of ninety.

Fingerprinting was once again put under the microscope in 1998 when I took the appeal of Gilbert 'Danny' McNamee.

He had been born into a strife-ridden Crossmaglen, Northern Ireland, in September 1960, and after graduating from Queen's University, Belfast, became an electronic engineer employed by Kimball's in Dundalk, making circuits for gaming machines.

McNamee led a seemingly ordinary life until he was arrested on

16 August 1986 at his home by the British Army and Royal Ulster Constabulary and flown to London, where he was charged with conspiracy to cause explosions in the Hyde Park bombing in July 1982, which had killed four soldiers and seven horses. At his trial at the Old Bailey he denied even having sympathy for the IRA, and no evidence was presented that he had any paramilitary links.

The Crown's case rested on three fingerprints: one each on short lengths of insulating tape in two caches of explosives-making equipment discovered near Pangbourne in Berkshire and in Salcey Forest in Northamptonshire, and a left thumbprint on a Duracell battery recovered from the debris after a controlled explosion in Kensington.

The Crown argued that the 'artwork' used in the manufacture of circuit boards found in these locations was so similar that all the boards were made by 'the same original master' – who, they asserted, was McNamee. This evidence, together with all the emotive links to the Hyde Park bombing, added up to what seemed an impressive case.

At his trial, McNamee's defence was that, although he was unable to explain the thumbprint, there was an innocent explanation for the two fingerprints, in that he may have touched parts of the reels of tape in his everyday work as an electronic engineer. If bomb-making had been going on, he was unaware of it. The judge, however, claimed that 'two prints . . . could have an innocent explanation; but three prints are beyond coincidence'.

After five hours of deliberation by the jury, McNamee was found guilty on all charges and sentenced to twenty-five years in prison. He then lost his appeal and, facing a lifetime behind bars, in September 1994 joined six other prisoners in trying to escape from Whitemoor Prison, shooting and wounding a prison warder as they went, before being captured two hours later. I represented a co-defendant in that trial, which collapsed when the *Evening Standard* published prejudicial material and was held to be in contempt of court.

McNamee's case was eventually referred to the Court of Appeal by the Criminal Cases Review Commission in 1998, when I was briefed by Gareth Peirce along with my junior Henry Blaxland.

I had known Gareth for a number of years and had worked with her on all manner of criminal matters. She has a strong civil-rights background in the USA and a deep sense of injustice, and we gelled from the beginning, each knowing exactly what the other needed for a case. Her preparation is immaculate and immense – each brief or set of instructions reads like a book – and she has a facility for entering the lives of others completely. Every dimension of a case is explored, something I'd always tried to do from my early days in the drug-advice centres. Gareth Peirce was and remains unique, with a quiet and deliberate persistence that is unnerving and capable of unravelling the most complex situations.

The McNamee case really set me thinking, and I decided to practise analysis of the swirls and whorls of my own thumbprint at home while preparing for court. But what should I use to transfer my print to paper for the purpose? My second wife Yvette came up to my study one evening to find sheets of apparently blood-stained thumbprints scattered around the room.

What on earth had I been doing? Well, I'd sneaked down to the kitchen and taken my favourite vegetable out of the fridge, then conducted my own tests with beetroot juice. It was fascinating.

The point is that individual prints are unique, but analysis depends on the clarity of reproduction. In an ideal world of controlled conditions, it is straightforward to obtain two prints from the same finger, which can be compared – but not so when the same finger is placed, often inadvertently, on a contaminated surface during the commission of a crime. The ability to discern a match of characteristics may then become highly subjective. In order to minimise this risk, it is once again crucial to ensure an element of blind testing. A number of different independent experts need first to examine the crime-scene mark to establish a consensus on which characteristics are capable of comparison. When it comes to the control print, the examiner should not know whether it belongs to a suspect, an arrestee or A. N. Other. Strictly speaking, there should be several controls submitted, blind; and with the help of computer imaging this exercise should be possible against a databank of retained prints.

As it happens I witnessed a demonstration of computer imaging whilst addressing the annual conference of the Finger Print Society in Manchester in March 2009. A Scene of Crime Officer (SOCO) using compact portable equipment can now electronically image a finger mark at the scene of a crime, and then transmit it electronically from the scene direct to the laboratory. This process provides speed, accessibility and, most importantly, high resolution imagery.

Over the course of seven days at the McNamee appeal, I took on the scientists, this time challenging the basic tenets of fingerprinting. Fourteen different experts from at least five different fingerprint bureaux throughout the UK were called, and the spectrum of disagreement over McNamee's mark was enormous, from 'unreadable' to 'more convinced than ever'. It even became apparent that different experts had assigned the same characteristic to different parts of the same thumb. In the court's judgment this was both 'remarkable and worrying'. For there to be no unanimity between them and very substantial areas of disagreement came as a shock, considering that all the experts save one were currently employed in various police forces across the land.

It was also revealed during the hearing that although the police had found a solitary print of McNamee's in the Pangbourne cache, they had found on the same circuits twenty-four much more prominent prints belonging to known IRA bomb-maker Desmond Ellis. But this evidence had not been disclosed at McNamee's original trial.

The Court of Appeal upheld McNamee's appeal on 17 December 1998,[3] and in the wake of this verdict the evidential standard of sixteen ridge characteristics for court purposes has been revisited, as have the protocols for quality control and independent verification. Danny McNamee is now a practising solicitor in Belfast.

Nevertheless, the risks remain amply demonstrated by a recent miscarriage of justice in Scotland involving a police officer, Shirley McKee, accused of touching a surface near the scene of a murder. And in another case in the USA in 2004, Brandon Mayfield was wrongly linked to the Madrid train bombings by FBI fingerprint experts.

These anomalies prompted a senior lecturer in cognitive neuroscience affiliated to University College London and Cognitive Consultants International to examine how objective the science really was. Dr Itiel Dror[4] carried out his investigation by seeing if the same expert would make the same decision on the same fingerprint if presented with it in a different context: another form of blind testing.

Dror approached six international experts, including one in the

UK, with eight crime-scene marks and eight control prints from suspects. The experts had in fact previously compared them in earlier cases and had deemed four matches and four exclusions. None of the experts knew they were re-examining marks they had seen before or that they were participating in a research project, and only two of the six experts came up with the same decision they'd made previously. The majority had changed their opinions. QED.

Meanwhile, back at the lab, the show goes on. The latest hot forensic tool is the analysis of earprints, which is going through all the perennial problems I've described so far. It seems the lessons have to be learned all over again.

The earprint (like the fingerprint) is unique to each of us and has features that are genetic and formed in the womb: its overall dimensions, the outer rim or helix, the lobe, the semicircular protrusion next to the jawbone called the *tragus* – these are the gross anatomical features. But in addition there are minutiae such as creases, notches and nodules. Unlike the finger, however, the ear has a very different interaction with the surface it presses against. Questions arise about whether the same ear can produce the same mark on more than one occasion under similar conditions or, more importantly, whether different ears might produce similar marks. Much will depend on pressure and malleability.

Mark Kempster was arrested in connection with a number of burglaries carried out in 2000. The case against him on the main burglary rested on an earprint found on a downstairs window pane. Either burglars are getting more careless or no one spotted the possible use of earprints before, despite everyone knowing about finger-, foot- and shoeprints. It seems the would-be intruder susses out his target by listening hard by a window for sounds of movement inside. Glass, as we've seen, is a perfect surface for retaining marks – unless, that is, it's raining or the windows are cleaned regularly . . .

Kempster was apprehended before any earprint comparison had been made. When interviewed by police he strenuously denied any involvement in the burglary, although it transpired that he did know the occupier and had done work at the address. Once the police received the firm and positive opinion of the expert, Cheryl

McGowan, that his ear had made the mark on the window, they naturally accepted its cogency. Thereafter they forcefully confronted Kempster with this result. He too, quite naturally, thought the evidence must be incontrovertible and, while maintaining his innocence, felt obliged to try and explain how his earprint could have got onto the window; his approach set the framework for his defence at the trial that followed. As a result, the earprint comparison was not seriously challenged, or examined in detail, beyond the production of a transparent earprint overlay by McGowan. This was a black-and-white outline of Kempster's control print placed on top of the crime-scene mark, suggesting an exact match. Another expert approached by the defence agreed with Cheryl McGowan, but as the defence were mounting no challenge, he was not called to give evidence before the jury.

Kempster was convicted in March 2001 at Southampton Crown Court, and subsequently appealed on the basis that earprint evidence was not yet a fully fledged science, but his appeal failed despite some impressive international testimony. I became involved in 2007 when a second appeal was opened up by the diligence of my solicitor Steve Bird, who tracked down one of the few experts in this uncharted territory, Dr Michael Ingleby, whose experience with a European Union-funded research project in 2006 meant that he was able to highlight the need for minutiae to be identified before a firm opinion should be attempted.

This derived from yet more blind testing, where a known print was scanned with a databank of 7,580 samples from 1,229 donors in the UK, Holland and Italy. In 95 per cent of cases it came out in the top five of near-matches. This means that there are still at least four others with which the known print could be confused.

While preparing the second appeal it became clear to me that neither the prosecution nor the defence experts had satisfactorily explained how they had reached their conclusions. For example, Cheryl McGowan's original trial statement merely said that she had made the comparison and had formed the view that the mark on the window was Kempster's.

I asked Dr Ingleby to find out what original working notes or papers had been retained by the prosecution. It was dismaying in the extreme to find that in fact there was very little. It was at this point that Dr Ingleby discovered that the overlay used at trial was misleading. In 2008 he demonstrated to the Court of Appeal by the use of different colours on the overlay that the two sheets had not been properly aligned and therefore did not provide a match. There was, in his view, a mismatch of gross anatomical features as well as no comparable minutiae.

The Court of Appeal allowed the appeal on this point, but Kempster remained convicted on other counts.

What needs to happen in these cases is: first, the establishment of a consensus amongst the scientific community about what gross features and what minutiae are capable of providing a reliable comparison. Second, when a mark is lifted from the scene and sent to the laboratory, before any comparison is made a detailed analysis of the mark must be recorded, indicating what particular features are present. This record should include graphic, narrative and digitalised computer formats. Where possible these features should then be run through the databank to see if there are any comparators. When a suspect's control print arrives at the laboratory, it should be examined quite separately, in the same way as the crime-scene mark. The final stage, I suggest, should be conducted by a senior expert who has not been previously involved. Then, and only then, should the critical comparison be made between the crime-scene mark, the control and any databank product.

This one simple, little-known case highlights the potential for fallibility and weakness in the science of identification. It also demonstrates how the course of justice can be diverted.

None of this is to say that the shortcomings of forensic science render it useless, or to undermine the enormous contribution it has made to the detection of crime. It is more a case of ensuring that a better recognition and accommodation of the risks attached to subjectivity do not irretrievably convert science into art.

PARENTS AT RISK

Angela Cannings and the
Frontiers of Forensic Science

When Angela Cannings walked free from the Appeal Court in London in December 2003, it was the end of a four-year nightmare. The forty-year-old had served twenty months of a life sentence after being found guilty of smothering two of her babies – but now her protestations of innocence had been heard.

What made the Cannings case especially notorious is that there could scarcely have been a better illustration of how, harking back to my mother's comment when she found me with the Camp Coffee bottle at number 73, people see what they want to see.

For me, children are altogether more stimulating and fun than adults. When I attend large social gatherings, if there are children present I tend to gravitate in their direction, and I love devising games and imaginary stories, which repeatedly land us all in trouble. I have six children of my own, and they're all grown-up now, despite enduring my mad moments and tomfoolery: monsters in the dark, chasing and capturing fantasy animals, putting on silly unrecognisable voices on the telephone and the inevitable dressing-up.

With each of the six there came a moment in their early lives, when they were between twelve and eighteen months old, when, seated in my big armchair, I would place them on my right foot with my legs crossed and raise and lower them rhythmically to simulate 'Ride a Cock Horse to Banbury Cross'. They also liked – or at least

I thought they liked – being thrown up in the air to free-fall back into my arms. Later the new-age baby technology replaced my right leg with a bouncer, an elastic contraption suspended from the door lintel. Strapped into a sort of harness, babies were propelled up and down, back and forth, by their tiny legs. Innocent fun? Yes – or maybe no. Given what I now know from cases regarding infant death, I wouldn't dream of doing the same things with my grandchildren.

At an even younger age, when children are newborn, parents are faced with the dilemmas of accepted medical wisdom: do you place the baby face down to sleep, with the risk of smothering, or face up, with the risk of choking? What about the mattress? Thick or thin? Foam or not? Is an alarm of any use during the night or while you're downstairs? You try to make informed decisions, but the one thing you know is that whatever you do it's nearly always wrong. We all tread an extremely fine line – an inch on the wrong side and you could end up in the dock.

I felt this most acutely when I first met Angela Cannings, for whom I had been engaged as defence barrister for her trial in 2002. She had been a caring young mother with an honest and straightforward family, all of them trying to make their way without too much fuss and certainly any bother. Then, like a bolt from the blue, disaster struck. No warning. No ready explanation. Just the absolute nightmare of nightmares, from which we wake to find our lives crushed by death around us – like the brutal ten seconds of the China earthquake in 2008.

In 1989, at the age of thirteen weeks, Angela's firstborn, Gemma, died suddenly at home. Two years later so did her second child, Jason, at seven weeks. Jade was born in January 1996 and is now a teenager. Finally Matthew was born on 5 July 1999, and Angela and her husband Terry thought the worst was behind them and they could look forward to a trouble-free future. Four months later, at the age of eighteen weeks, Matthew too was dead.

Such a sequence of events is something everyone finds difficult to comprehend. As I was to remind the jury, in the words of Oscar Wilde's Lady Bracknell: 'To lose one parent, Mr Worthing, may be regarded as a misfortune; to lose both looks like carelessness.'[1] So where does that leave you if it's three? For Angela it meant arrest, charges of murder, and conviction. Nature abhors a vacuum, and so does human nature. In such circumstances we crave an explanation, and if there is no known medical cause for so many deaths, then it has to be murder.

The cause written on the first two death certificates was SIDS (Sudden Infant Death Syndrome): cot death. This acronym, however, denotes a category rather than a cause, and according to the CESDI survey,* it's a category embracing the single largest proportion of infant deaths in the UK (at ages between one and twelve months), and means that after careful and thorough investigation, no natural or unnatural cause of death can be ascertained. This is to be distinguished from the unascertained category, which merely suggests there is insufficient evidence to reveal a known cause.[2]

In the Angela Cannings case, what science – and no doubt the trial jury – could not countenance were three instances in the same family. At the start Angela had been charged with the murder of the three children who had died. Prior to trial, when the case was before the Examining Magistrate whose job it is to consider whether to commit or send a defendant to trial, she ruled there was no case in relation to Gemma. The immediate cause of death for all three was apnoea – cessation of breathing – but why? If there is no discernible natural cause, then unnatural smothering appears to be all that is left.

Enter, stage left, Professor Roy Meadow, a leading light in paediatrics. He undoubtedly pioneered a better understanding of the risks encountered with that incredibly small group of parents who do cause harm to their babies – for example, those who batter their babies – but these are by no means the same group as those who commit terrible assaults on older children like Victoria Climbié, who was abused and murdered in 2000 by her guardians.

The problem for Professor Meadow was the steady transformation of warning lights into the fixed theme of guilt, for a specialism may carry within it the seeds of its own demise by creating a dogma out of signs and symptoms which should be no more than signposts or indicators. Professor Meadow crossed the Rubicon from uncertainty to certainty with his notoriously erroneous statistical assertion in

---

* Confidential Enquiry into Still Births and Deaths in Infancy, 7th Annual Report 2000, www.cemach.org.uk

the case of Sally Clark – who earlier in 2003 had been released after being wrongfully imprisoned for more than three years following the death of her two sons – that the chances of more than one death in the same family (or, put more precisely, the chances of two SIDS deaths in one affluent, non-smoking family) were one in 73 million. What Professor Meadow had done was to treat the two deaths as independent of each other and then, using the base probability of one death (which had been calculated at one in 8,500), he went on to merely square this figure to produce one in 73 million. The problem is that while this is arithmetically correct, it is statistically erroneous, because the deaths cannot be treated as independent (for example, there may be a genetic cause). Statistical research has demonstrated that while it is rare for a cot death to occur, where such a death has occurred in a family, there is a much greater risk of it happening again.

In Angela's case all sorts of other circumstances were employed by the prosecution. The deaths all occurred while she was at home alone; she did not immediately call the ambulance on all occasions; two deaths were preceded by episodes characterised as an ALTE (acute life-threatening event), and it was also suggested that Jade had suffered such an episode, although of course she did not die. These sorts of factors are resorted to because smothering may not leave any signs of injury: no facial bruising, no haemosiderin in the lungs (the iron left behind from a prior bleed), no petechial haemorrhages (small dots) in the eyes. In the absence of these features, therefore, the question arises as to whether there is a discernible pattern of events which in itself gives rise to suspicion.

Professor Golding, an epidemiologist originally approached by the prosecution but called by me at the trial, did not believe there was one. Beside the absence of a pattern, there were no other corroborative elements: no violent predisposition in Angela, no explosions of temper, no psychological or psychiatric disturbance, not even a hint of Professor Meadow's favoured hypothesis of Munchhausen's Disease by Proxy, wherein a parent may self-harm or harm a child in order to gain attention for a personal, social or economic privation.

By 2002, over thirty years since my tangle with the expert witness I nicknamed 'Tinkerbelle', you might have thought experts expecting to give evidence would have their notes available for inspection. Well, *you* might, but not if you're Professor Meadow. He had told his secretary to shred most of his research material even though there were trials pending, for reasons of confidentiality and storage. Once again we had to accept the word and memory of an expert. It also goes without saying that Meadow was unwavering in his own belief that Angela had smothered her children.

To comprehend the magnitude of this suggestion, you only have to step back a moment and imagine a loving mother, recognising that she is capable of committing the ultimate crime against her own children, going on to give birth to more children, whom she proceeds to kill. It's nothing short of a re-enactment of the Greek tragedy *Medea*.

I was well aware that the task we all faced in defending Angela was monumental. In practical terms, we had to prove her innocence – which, remember, is not something that the law requires, because the onus or burden of proof is on the prosecution rather than the defence.[3]

I was fortunate to have a closely knit team of committed and well-informed lawyers: my junior Jo Briggs had medical science coming out of her ears and at her fingertips, while my instructing solicitor Bill Baiche, a big man exuding a quiet and calm confidence, was assisted by Jackie Cameron, who gave Angela and her family unstinting support.

Every medical avenue was explored to see if there was any conceivable, viable explanation. Altogether approximately eighteen different experts were assembled, from a large number of diverse disciplines. Could there, for example, have been a cardiac problem, which gave rise to an irregular heartbeat, or arrhythmia (the prolonged QT syndrome)?[4] To test for this, electrodes are attached to different parts of the body and produce different wavelengths on a graph, and I spent hours studying the output from an electrocardiogram machine.

We also looked at whether there was an immunodeficiency, which might have provided a gateway through which other potential dangers such as infection might pass. Then there was the coincidence of other infant deaths over the same period of time in the same Wiltshire village where the Cannings family lived. Could there have been clandestine environmental factors bearing on all of these children, including those in Angela's family? Was it because they all lived near a railway line, or beneath pylons carrying power cables, or close to a disused ammunition dump? Nothing seemed to provide the answer. Maybe we were all trying too hard. Maybe there wasn't a single explanation and we should have been engaging in a multifactorial approach.

In a sense the whole exercise was not just proving that Angela had not committed murder, but proving that murder had not been committed at all.

We did not succeed. Angela was convicted and sentenced to life imprisonment. We all have dark days, but for me this was one of the very worst, similar to the second Birmingham Six appeal and to the trial of Barry George. I spent hours trawling back over every inch of the case. Where had I gone wrong? What had I missed? You're not supposed to take defeat personally, but in a way I do, because without that strength of feeling you can't begin the reappraisal necessary to prevent it happening again. In retrospect, I now think we over-egged the pudding, with the result that the jury may have thought we were trying to be too clever by half.

The repercussions for Angela were unbearable. If you're convicted of this kind of offence you get hell from other prisoners, and she faced constant abuse and assault, on one occasion having a pot of boiling tea poured all over her. Jade had already been subject to care orders and supervised visits throughout the time Angela had been waiting for her trial. Her husband Terry, who had been stalwart throughout, also faced a bleak and uncertain future. Yet as far as I was concerned, here was another client whose persistence shone through, and there could be no giving up.

We were already aware, through tracing the genealogy of Angela's extended family, that there had been other instances of premature infant death, five altogether. We were also aware of the possibility that there may be a gene responsible for cot deaths.

Alongside our efforts, journalist John Sweeney and his BBC team undertook intrepid research – undeterred by the admonitions delivered by Lord Taylor to an earlier generation of journalists. John discovered three other infant deaths on the Irish side of Angela's family. When the documentary *Angela's Hope* was broadcast just before the appeal hearing in December 2003, one viewer was prompted to act immediately.

Angela, it turned out, had a half-sister, of whose existence she had been wholly unaware, the result of a liaison which her father had kept secret, and one of this sister's children had had breathing problems from birth. Professor Michael Patton from the South West Thames Regional Centre at St George's Hospital in south London regarded this as significant.

It was not, however, this development alone that won the appeal, but rather a comprehensive understanding of the science by the court itself. The appeal was upheld on 10 December 2003, and the judgment delivered by the appropriately named Lord Justice Judge on 19 January 2004 is without equal:

> We recognise that the occurrence of three sudden and unexpected infant deaths in the same family is very rare and therefore demands an investigation into their causes. Nevertheless the fact that such deaths have occurred does not identify let alone prescribe the deliberate infliction of harm as the cause of death. Throughout the process great care must be taken not to allow the rarity of these sad events, standing on their own, to be subsumed into an assumption or virtual assumption that the dead infants were deliberately killed, or consciously or unconsciously to regard the inability of the defendant to produce some convincing explanation for these deaths as providing a measure of support for the prosecution's case. If on examination of all the evidence every possible known cause has been excluded, the cause remains unknown.[5]

The court went on to caution against future prosecutions without additional cogent evidence extraneous to the expert evidence, which tends to support the conclusion that the infant was deliberately harmed. In other words, another form of corroboration known as confirmatory material is desirable.

I had also asked the court to consider whether in cases like this it was time to require juries to return a verdict with reasons. When a court sits without a jury, a judge has to do this, and all concerned then have a better idea of where the decision-maker has gone wrong – or, for that matter, where they have got it right. With the incorporation of the European Convention on Human Rights into English law (effectively in 2000), this is precisely what a jury in an inquest may be asked to do, by describing their reasons in the form of a narrative.

At the Angela Cannings appeal, the court felt it was not necessary for the purposes of the appeal to decide this question, and left it for another occasion.

Outside the High Court, Bill Baiche told waiting journalists what we all felt about the case:

> These are extraordinarily difficult matters. Still nobody knows what causes cot death, and until a good deal more information is known about that, it would seem to me that prosecutions of the kind that have been brought against her and, for that matter others, should not continue.

He added that the scientific evidence given against Angela was 'wholly inconclusive, and that is the nub of the issue . . .'[6]

The anguish suffered by Angela was brought home to me even more forcibly when my daughter, Anna, telephoned me in February 2009, a few days after she had given birth to my grandson, Luca. One evening both she and her husband, Carlo, had noticed that Luca's breathing was extremely shallow, there was a general lack of response and 'floppiness'. These were all signs with which I had become familiar and were consistent with an ALTE. I could barely contain my anxiety and rushed to the hospital straight away. Anna and Carlo had had the presence of mind to summon an ambulance immediately, which arrived within four minutes and undoubtedly saved the day. We are all so vulnerable. Luca is doing fine now, but Anna and Carlo are ever alert.

Since Angela's case other similar ones have gone back to the Court of Appeal, which is a start. That is just in the criminal arena, but there are thousands of cases in the civil arena, and this is a much worse position, where the authorities have powers without going to court. Children are taken away in the night on the back of the opinion of an expert who says there has been abuse, or smothering, or whatever they believe it is, and often the mother finds the second child is taken away too, without redress. Parents are told: if you make a fuss, it goes to court. Following the Cannings judgment, many of these parents are coming out and demanding that their cases be reassessed, in order to see if the nature of that evidence was reliable in the first place.

There is, however, a long road to travel, as Nicky and Mark Webster discovered to their cost on 11 February 2009. They were seeking the return of their three eldest children, who had been removed from them and adopted in December 2005. The local authority believed that one child had suffered non-accidental injuries inflicted by one or both parents. In 2007 fresh evidence suggested that the fractures may have related to iron deficiency caused by a feeding disorder and not to deliberate assaults. The court was unable to undo the formality of the adoption orders and observed that if there is a lesson to be learned from the case, it is the need to obtain second opinions on injuries to children at the earliest opportunity, particularly in cases where, as here, the fault was unusual.[7]

Angela was finally reunited with her family and, as others before her have done, she has lent her support to those facing a similar predicament. Her own ordeal has taken its toll, however: she and Terry are no longer together.

On the positive side, the Attorney General instigated a full review of 200 other cases to ensure there had been no other miscarriages of this kind, and they were referred back to the Court of Appeal. I handled four of these cases, which were heard at the same time in June 2005. It was a daunting and mammoth undertaking, accomplished with a great legal team. It was the research connected with them which gave me cause for concern and made me think about how we all handle our own children.

Medical opinion had considered that one of the main features of baby shaking was the presence of a subdural haemorrhage, combined with brain swelling brought about by the direct impact between the brain and the skull. This was usually illustrated to a jury by comparing the impact involved in a child being hit by a car travelling at forty miles per hour: in other words, hardly something that would arise by accident, or in the rough and tumble of everyday play, or from the occasional fall from a bed, highchair or climbing frame.

However, following groundbreaking work carried out by three

distinguished experts – English neuropathologist Dr Jennian Geddes, anatomical forensic pathologist Dr John Plunkett and American biomechanical engineer Dr Kirk Thibault – it became clear that catastrophic injuries could be occasioned by a small degree of force. In one tragic US case a grandmother happened to video her granddaughter at play on an indoor climbing frame when the little girl fell awkwardly only a few feet from the ground, with fatal consequences.

No one is suggesting that this sort of sad occurrence is inevitable, or anything other than rare. What is being tested is whether the working hypothesis used to trigger child-abuse investigations can be satisfactorily transformed into a conviction. In other words, great care has to be taken before jumping to conclusions based on criteria customarily associated with Shaken Baby Syndrome, which had almost reached the status of a dogma. If three types ('a triad') of intracranial injury were found – encephalopathy, subdural haemorrhage (SDH) and retinal haemorrhage – then there was a strong presumption of deliberate injury inflicted by the child's carer.

In the light of the fresh medical evidence, the Court of Appeal judges said:

> On our view of the evidence in these appeals, the mere presence of the triad on its own cannot automatically, or necessarily, lead to a diagnosis of non-accidental head injury.[8]

Twenty-one experts in different fields had brought their experience to bear on a complex series of interrelated cases, and in the crucible of a courtroom it is often easy to forget the emotional impact and tragedy that have been inflicted on families who have not only lost a loved one, but have also been subjected to the microscope of public scrutiny.

This was particularly so for a young couple whom I met in 2005: Angela and Ian Gay, who had been convicted of poisoning three-year-old Christian Blewitt by force-feeding him with salt. I had read about their conviction in a newspaper and felt that there was something inherently wrong with it. I was in contact with Bill Baiche, the solicitor who had taken over their case and with whom I had worked on the Cannings appeal. It seemed that similar mistakes and similar assumptions were being made.

Angela and Ian had been through the difficult business of adopting Christian, and not long after the adoption had been concluded, the little boy was rushed to hospital, where it was discovered that he had a very high concentration of sodium (salt) in his body plasma. The amount was calculated to be equivalent to 30g or approximately six teaspoons full of dry salt – roughly the same as drinking 1 litre (1¾ pt) of triple-strength saline or sea water. At trial the jury were left with only one viable explanation: forcible ingestion.

Despite no sensible or plausible method being postulated as to how a three-year-old infant could possibly have been made to consume such quantities without being violently sick, both Angela and Ian were convicted of manslaughter. Once you begin to think about it, contesting this requires going back to the drawing board and approaching the whole matter from first principles, and fortunately there was somebody able to do this in time for their appeal.

Dr Glyn Walters, a committed and passionate scientist then nearing retirement, got down to brass tacks. You may get a high concentration of sodium because in one way or another you have taken too much on board; alternatively, you may have too much sodium concentrate, because you have lost a great deal of water and haven't replaced it; finally, there could be a problem with the regulatory mechanisms which govern the delicate balance between total body water – 60 per cent of body weight is water – and sodium. Total body water is normally maintained within narrow limits, and is kept inside those limits through the action of the anti-diuretic hormone (ADH), which is made in the part of the brain called the hypothalamus. There are sensors or receptors that tell the brain when it is necessary for the body to get rid of fluids like water, as well as when not to, and of course when to drink, and all of this is known collectively as the osmostat – a bit like a thermostat.

What had not been appreciated during the trial were the problems that might arise with the osmostat. Most obviously, its function could be disrupted by brain disease, but what Dr Walters discerned was the possibility that while the sensors may *not* have been affected by a brain disease, they may have been reset at too high a level by an unknown natural cause. This means that instead of the normal 140 threshold, a much higher level of 170 may have been set, for some unknown reason, in this particular case. Dr Walters noticed that while Christian was (counter-intuitively) being treated in the hospital with a saline solution, this regime never took Christian below 157. He was therefore effectively operating at a higher level, excreting the amounts being administered. Dr Walters could not be sure that this was the explanation, but equally he could be sure that this was not a case of hypernatraemia (salt poisoning), if for no other reason than the 30g of salt were not being excreted. The obvious answer to this was that Christian had never taken that amount in the first place.

The Court of Appeal ordered a retrial, which took place in 2007, conducted successfully by a good friend and colleague in Tooks Chambers,[9] Michael Topolski. Angela and Ian Gay were acquitted, but they had had their lives blighted by an allegation that they had punished Christian for his misbehaviour by forcing salt into his body in some way or another. Worse, they had lost their lovely adopted child.

These are complex and unusual cases where a jury can hardly be expected to make informed judgments on the basis of a science which is barely proven and whose frontiers are uncertain.

The problem is often discerning where these frontiers are. What are you dealing with? Where does it fit in? Where do you look to find out more? Who are the right experts? It's taken all my professional life for lawyers to realise that the all-purpose, ubiquitous jack-of-all-trades defence expert is long gone.

This was never more pertinent than for Kevin Callan.

Kevin was a Manchester-born, United football fan who left school at fourteen when the family moved to Gorton in Derbyshire. Bored, he was allowed by the authorities to spend his last compulsory years of schooling painting and decorating old people's homes. He enjoyed it. He learned to drive early and eventually became a lorry driver, going back and forth to the Continent.

He had two failed marriages and two kids, with whom he always stayed in contact. But there was one woman, Les, who kept coming in and out of his life, until in 1985 he tracked her down and moved in with her. Les Allman had two young daughters, Mandy and Natalie; Mandy had cerebral palsy (a neurological condition from birth, which makes speech and movement difficult, although many sufferers are very bright indeed). The combined new family got on really well and Kevin became very involved in Mandy's care: he helped her 'walk' with the aid of splints and learn the alphabet. This was a long, slow process that required hours of patience, but Les and Kevin enjoyed the challenge, as did Mandy. The family moved to Wales to be near a special school for Mandy, close to Kevin's parents and not far from Les's. They planned to get married in 1990.

Kevin kept up a rigorous exercise regime with Mandy, supervised by her Child Development Unit and physiotherapist. They used a sponge roll to strengthen her arm and leg muscles, and Mandy had fun in the process. But things began to go wrong for her when she had a couple of accidents at the school, involving bruising and, more seriously, a '2cm-deep laceration to the crown of her head'[10] caused by falling onto the corner of a table. Les took her away from the school.

Mandy was very upset by the incident and started vomiting and becoming listless. Kevin told me later on how he saved her life at night more than once, by preventing her from choking on her own vomit. He and Les were very worried for her. She was in pain from the stitches in her head and on 14 December 1990 they took her to a paediatrician, who told them not to worry. Kevin was certain the deterioration in Mandy was a result of the fall at school.

Les and Kevin felt ignored by the health professionals and couldn't seem to get any help, despite asking repeatedly. Finally in March 1991 both Les (who had had a minor gynaecological operation) and Mandy went into Tameside Hospital for tests. But for some unexplained reason Mandy didn't have her tests; and a week later Les learned that she herself might have been pregnant at the time of her operation. She would now need another operation to remove their unborn child. The couple were devastated.

Things seemed to be going from bad to worse for this once-happy family. At the beginning of April, Mandy fell off a worktop in the kitchen when Kevin rushed into the other room to attend to a crying Natalie for a few seconds. Mandy had bruises all down the side of her body and the cut on her head reopened, but she wasn't seriously hurt and seemed fine.

But a few days later she came back from school unwell, and two social workers turned up and took Mandy to see a Dr Marie Lawrence, who said that she wasn't concerned as the injuries were consistent with the fall that Kevin had described. Les and Kevin realised they were under scrutiny, although what they actually wanted was scrutiny for Mandy by committed health professionals.

Mandy went back to school for two days, but Kevin and Les were so worried that they called out their GP, Dr Susan McClure, who – despite hearing Mandy's symptoms – simply looked in her ears and said she was all right. But she wasn't. On the Friday she stayed off school, but bumped herself again when her frame toppled over. (This falling is common in children with cerebral palsy: they are very uncoordinated and unsteady, but have to be encouraged to try and become independent and mobile.)

Mandy had a fun fourth birthday with her grandparents on 14 April, playing with a cardboard baby pram that Kevin had made her, but the next day Les had to go into hospital for her remedial operation. Mandy had another fall – this time down the stairs, but she seemed not to be concerned at all. She and Natalie stayed with Kevin all day, helping to make a path in the garden. A health visitor called unexpectedly, but Mandy was asleep upstairs. In the afternoon a couple of visitors came and saw Mandy playing happily on the slide in the garden.

When Les came back from day surgery she sat and watched the kids on the swing, but suddenly Mandy went very white. Kevin brought her in, but her eyes glazed over and she cried and pointed to her head and belly – as she had done whenever these incidents had occurred. They put her down for a rest, and some time later Les insisted on going to the local shops for some things. Kevin cleared up and decided to get Mandy ready for bed proper. Coming out of her bedroom to say goodnight to her mummy, Mandy started to vomit ferociously and began struggling for air. Kevin rushed her to the bathroom to try and unblock her airway. He was in a panic and started mouth-to-mouth resuscitation; when Les heard his shouts, she rushed up the stairs and then down again next door to phone for an ambulance. Her neighbour Margaret came back with her and saw Kevin pushing on the little girl's stomach and chest: he got something out of her mouth and she started gurgling. A medic appeared and told Kevin, 'Carry on, mate, you're doing a good job.' The medic soon took over and, using a suction unit, unblocked Mandy's airway and she was rushed to Tameside Hospital.

After the couple had waited for what seemed like hours, a doctor finally came to tell them that Mandy had died from a 'brain haemorrhage'. Les's father Neville asked if they could see her medical records, but was refused.

The family were obviously deeply distressed, but within a short time they were to become even more so. Kevin was arrested on 16 April 1991 for the murder of his young stepdaughter.

At the trial Les was pressured into being a witness for the prosecution. In fact she was a wholly positive witness for Kevin, maintaining that he was not guilty, was an excellent father and had achieved 'minor miracles' with Mandy. But her evidence was overshadowed by the two prosecution experts: Dr Geoffrey Garrett, a Home Office pathologist with thirty years' experience, and Dr Jeffrey Freeman, the Consultant Paediatrician at Tameside Hospital. They both asserted that Mandy had been forcibly shaken to death, so the jury found against Kevin and he was convicted. He spent the next four years trying to clear his name.

Over the preceding months his relationship with Les had become more and more strained, not helped by the fact that social services had threatened to take Natalie away: in fact, after he was found guilty, they came to Kevin and said they were considering wardship proceedings. Kevin refused to say that Les was an unfit mother, but the corrosive effect of the situation was too much for both of them and their relationship ended. Although Les met someone else and became pregnant again, she retained a deep affection for Kevin.

Kevin was determined to prove his innocence and went to the Wakefield Prison library, asking for medical books on head injuries. Several were suggested, but he liked the sound of *Head Injury: The Facts* by Philip Wrightson, Dorothy Gronwall and Peter Waddell.[11] He read and reread the book, which seemed to verify everything that had happened. From his prison cell he wrote to the authors, who specialised in neuropathology. Unfortunately they lived in New Zealand.

He also wrote to Campbell Malone – a jovial, open-hearted northerner who has proved himself a tireless campaigner for sufferers of miscarriages of justice. He's down to earth and really knows what he's doing, but as with most good legal aid lawyers is badly under-resourced. Kevin asked us both to represent him. We agreed. Then Philip Wrightson replied and said he'd like more information on the case as it raised serious concerns. Things were beginning to move.

Kevin conducted his own research, reading everything he could get his hands on about cerebral palsy, brain surgery and neuropathy. Philip Wrightson agreed to work on the case for nothing, and by this time Kevin had written to specialists all over the world to gain knowledge and help for his case. He started to get support from campaign groups and the local paper, but the prison authorities seemed to put everything in the way to stop him – even down to refusing him typewriter ribbons and Tipp-Ex. In 1992 Kevin had a surprise visit from Les. He was pleased she was still supporting him, but couldn't work out why she wasn't campaigning to clear his name, as he was.

Kevin had always said that the initial head injury at the school in November 1990 was crucial, as were the subsequent falls from the slide and down the stairs, which could have caused the fatal haemorrhage, particularly in a child with cerebral palsy. But no scans or relevant tests were ever done. And the blocked airway after her vomiting had contributed to cerebral oedema and irreversible brain damage. In March 1993 Philip Wrightson wrote summarising his findings, and they showed exactly that: Mandy had not been killed by shaking. Kevin was overcome with relief.

Campbell contacted another eminent consultant forensic pathologist, Helen Whitwell, whose report concurred with Wrightson's and maintained that Dr Garrett's evidence and post-mortem report had been seriously flawed. The papers went in to the Appeal Court.

On 15 April 1994, the third anniversary of Mandy's death, the court turned down Kevin's application in an unduly summary fashion. Lord Justice Tucker wrote:

> I see no reason to grant such a long extension of time.* I would not have granted leave in any event. It was open to your advisors to obtain this [new] evidence at the time of trial. The fact that two new experts have now been discovered does not enable you to reopen the matter in my opinion.[12]

---

* An application for leave to appeal has to be lodged within twenty-eight days of the date of conviction and sentence. Thereafter you have to obtain leave from the Appeal Court to lodge an application out of time.

This is the informal, unspoken doctrine that you can't have 'two bites at the cherry'. It's short-sighted and based on the hidden premise underlying the beliefs of some of the traditional higher judiciary that most people who have been convicted by the courts are ne'er-do-wells who are just playing the system.

This was a major blow, but we plodded on until finally in October leave to appeal was granted. And then a prosecution scientist agreed with our two experts, and the game was up. The case against Kevin was formally dropped on 6 April 1995 and we won his appeal without opposition, barely one year on from Lord Justice Tucker's summary refusal.

Afterwards Kevin had support from Paddy Hill, one of the Birmingham Six (see Chapter 17), who warned him of the emotions that might overcome him now that he was released and of the intense media attention – and he was right about both. Kevin developed severe pains in his stomach, no doubt due to the stress he was experiencing. He and Les agreed to visit Mandy's grave, and not long afterwards got back together. Life was tough in a caravan with Natalie and Jade, her new sister. They had had no compensation and little help from the authorities. Kevin was also twice visited by the police about other crimes. Campbell complained on his behalf, but it certainly unnerved Kevin.

At last some friends on the caravan site offered the family a new home to rent. Then life looked up and Kevin had his other two kids to stay, too. The compensation came through; Les and Kevin finally got married. They were very happy, but suddenly in 1996 Kevin had to have emergency surgery for a burst duodenal ulcer. He was lucky to survive – but, unfortunately, not for long. His experiences had scarred him irreparably, and Kevin Callan died prematurely in 2003 at the age of forty-five.

Although his case attracted little attention and went largely unnoticed, his legacy is immense. The main point is simple. Certain infant head injuries (such as a double haematoma or bruising) clearly suggest the possibility of maltreatment, and such a natural assumption must be investigated. But an open mind is imperative, because the injuries may not necessarily have been caused deliberately by blunt impact or shaking at the hands of a carer. Judgments about this cannot be left to paediatricians or ordinary pathologists alone. In Kevin's case no one – no lawyer, no police officer, no social worker, no doctor, no judge – had spotted that there was no input from the specialist field that mattered most, neuropathology.

It took Kevin himself, from his prison cell, to find this out. We are all indebted.

The time is long overdue to take action over the shortcomings of forensic science as well as the failings of forensic scientists.

There are several deficiencies common to many of these cases, although not all of them. Frequently, a prosecution is embarked upon when it is clear from the start that there is a serious division of opinion between reputable experts about the cause of particular injuries. Sometimes the dispute is over basic issues from the original findings – in other words, what can actually be discerned from scans, X-rays, the histology and so forth.

The process nearly always involves at least two stages: the findings and then the interpretation, often with the added complication that the original samples have been used up or lost, and occasionally that the appropriate examinations were not all done in the first place.

What remains, therefore, tends to be the opinion of one expert against another. This provides a nearly impossible situation for any fact-finding tribunal, whether jury and judge or judge alone. On what basis can a non-scientist arrive at a conclusion of guilt or innocence when the choice may merely come down to a preference in presentation? Rarely will there be exhibits that can be pored over, and even if there are, they are often unintelligible.

In the Cannings case, the Court of Appeal provided some extremely sensible guidance. Lord Justice Judge suggested that where an investigation into two or more sudden unexplained infant deaths was followed by a serious disagreement between reputable experts, then the prosecution should not be started or continued without additional cogent evidence.

Unfortunately, this advice has not been heeded, and cases go forward in the absence of corroborative evidence. Even when experts have been discredited, cases proceed by substituting other experts who will come up with the same theory or a new one, or who stray beyond their own area of expertise. In short, the same old assumptions are dragged out, propped up and maintained.

None of this should be happening, but one of the reasons why it is continuing to take place is because in the UK we have not had a proper forensic-science facility independent of government facilities. We don't have a tradition of challenging scientists, and forensic science has been considered the monopoly of the government state service. The defence has to go to a small number of private practitioners or occasionally to universities to obtain expertise, and this is increasingly difficult because there are cutbacks in legal aid or it's hard to get authorisation for the expert that you really need. Sometimes you may have to go abroad, particularly in DNA cases, because there may be no one in the UK outside government service with this specialism.

It is time that the criminal-justice system took a firm grip of the situation by establishing a clear regulatory structure with obligatory protocols and guidelines. This has been raised endlessly in professional debate, parliamentary reports, reviews and Royal Commissions, but there persists an extraordinary reluctance to act.

In my view, what is needed is a National Institute of Forensic Science to lay down standards and guidelines for experts who give evidence in court, and such an institute needs to be properly resourced in order to provide for education, training, inspection and registration. The recently established Council for the Registration of Forensic Practitioners was not comprehensive, and membership was purely voluntary.[13] However, in March 2009, the government announced that the Council was to be wound up. I hope that the forensic science regulator will establish a national and obligatory register of accreditation.

In all cases where forensic science is involved there needs to be, as there is in the USA, a preliminary hearing – which they call Frye – where the trial judge assesses the admissibility of expert evidence. Frye is named after a 1923 District of Columbia court decision refusing to allow a jury to learn the results of a crude predecessor of the modern lie-detector test. The court insisted on a precondition of 'general acceptance'. The judges in Frye ruled:

Just when a scientific principle or discovery crosses the line between experimental and demonstrable stages is difficult to define. Somewhere in this twilight zone the evidential force of the principle must be recognised, and while courts will go a long way in admitting expert testimony deduced from a well-recognised scientific principle or discovery, the thing from which the deduction is made must be sufficiently established to have gained general acceptance in the particular field in which it belongs.[14]

Essentially, the courts in the USA now exercise a form of quality control. Using the Daubert Test,[15] the judge decides which experts are capable of giving evidence and the areas in which they are qualified to comment. This ensures that certain basic thresholds are achieved: that the theory or technique employed can be or has been tested, subjected to peer-review or publication and scrutinised for any known rate of error; and that it has been identified whether there is a consensus within the scientific community.

In the UK the present deficiencies have been given a recent and stark illustration by the conviction in February 2007 of a so-called expert forensic psychologist. Gene Morrison was convicted of twenty offences, involving a deception that he had practised for twenty-seven years. His qualifications had been bought from a website, and he had no genuine academic credentials or forensic-psychology skills. Up to 700 cases may now have to be reviewed because of the bogus opinions he proffered.

Besides wondering why forensic scientists, police officers, solicitors, barristers and judges never asked a single fundamental question that would have exposed this individual, what that case really illustrates is systemic failure on a grand scale. Obligatory accreditation, and hearings before the admission of such evidence, would have weeded out Morrison twenty-seven years ago.

An improvement in standards and training would also help to prevent future cases from going to trial where the expert evidence is disputed. In addition there should be fully funded, adequate resources for the independent sector used by the defence.

I am aware that in this chapter I have concentrated on parents, rather than children who are at risk. I have long been conscious from my first contact with a child-abuse case – Maria Caldwell, who died in 1975 – that children need and have a right to be protected.

Every year there seems to be one more horrifying case after another: Victoria Climbie, who was killed by her guardians, and whose parents were represented by two members of my chambers in 2000; in 2007 a small girl with cerebral palsy thankfully survived malnutrition and terrible injuries inflicted on her by her parents: it was only when the child's grandmother phoned for help that she was rescued by social services; and in 2008 we learned of the sickening case of 'Baby P'.

So often I have been appalled by these stories, and two features stand out. First and foremost is the repeated failure by the authorities to implement the many recommendations that are carefully constructed in the wake of each case, the main ones being inter-agency cooperation and multidisciplinary working. Lord Laming conducted a review after the 'Baby P' case, which was published on 12 March 2009. He characterised child protection as a 'Cinderella service'. More than 350 children had died at the hands of abusive or violent parents/carers between Victoria Climbie and 'Baby P', both of whose deaths occurred in the London Borough of Haringey. Two of his main observations were the need for a more efficient IT system to log essential information about children at risk, and the need for a national agency to oversee swift and effective implementation of the report's recommendations.

The second feature to stand out is the fact that in so many of these cases there must have been *someone* who knew what was going on and who could have saved a life. The 'I can't get involved' syndrome is almost as pernicious as the abuse itself.

One of the most vociferous and committed campaigners for children's rights is Esther Rantzen,[16] famous as the presenter of BBC Television's *That's Life!* for twenty-one years. The show changed the traditional role of the consumer programme, from simply exposing faulty domestic appliances and dodgy salesmen to investigating life-and-death issues, such as the need for more organ donors. In 1986 Esther produced and presented *Childwatch*, which alerted the British public to the prevalence of child abuse and successfully campaigned for a number of legal reforms, such as the introduction of the videolink for child witnesses in court. Even more importantly, perhaps, it helped launch the first national helpline in October 1986 for children in danger or distress, ChildLine – the first line of its kind anywhere in the world and now open twenty-four hours a day throughout the year. On the very first night 50,000 calls were made to ChildLine, which now has twelve bases around the UK; and hundreds of thousands of children with serious problems – including physical, sexual and emotional abuse – have been counselled by trained volunteers (one of whom was my second PA, Susie Haig). ChildLine has now merged with the NSPCC, providing it with extra resources, and the helpline has been emulated in 150 countries around the world. Countless children have been protected, and countless lives have been saved.

In 1989 Esther courageously exposed abuse at Crookham Court, a school near Newbury operated by a paedophile, who employed two paedophile teachers. Arrests took place, followed by a trial at Reading Crown Court. Esther was due to be a prosecution witness and sought my advice about what was going to be involved.

This was very unusual, but in my view entirely proper: witnesses do not receive sufficient support and explanation before engaging in what can prove a harrowing process. There are now various witness-support schemes, and some senior investigating police officers go out of their way to provide reassurance, but the problem is that the lawyers for the prosecution do not represent the witnesses being called, and in any event there is a professional rule precluding barristers from talking about the facts of the case to their own witnesses who are giving evidence.

What happens on television is familiar to all of us, and particularly to Esther; what happens in reality is quite another thing. In order to build confidence you have to start with the bare essentials, such as: where does the judge sit? How do you address him or her? Where is the jury box? Does the jury ask questions? Who are the barristers? In what order do they examine a witness? What happens if you have a memory lapse? And so on.

I made it clear to Esther that I could not 'coach' her, but I was able to give her a flavour of what to expect, and I accompanied her to the court throughout the two long days she gave evidence. She was quite naturally on edge, despite the fact that she had faced millions of viewers on a weekly basis, but she felt that she owed it to the abused children to give of her best. I remember her attention to detail – in particular, what kind of outfit she should wear – but the overriding memory was what she taught me about the children she counselled, and the categorical imperative that they are to be listened to *and believed.*

Until then I think I had fallen into the conventional trap often portrayed in the courts, that children tend to live in some fairytale land when it comes to talking about their personal experiences. She showed me how wrong that approach could be.

In the Crookham Court case, one defendant pleaded guilty, and the other two were convicted by the jury. The case also led to changes in the Children's Act, which enabled social workers to intervene in private boarding schools.

There is an obvious tension between the rights of the wrongly abused child, on the one hand, and the wrongly accused parent, on the other. How do you ensure the sanctity of the former without infringing the integrity of the latter? As usual there is an extraordinarily sensitive balance to be struck between doing absolutely nothing (turning a blind eye) and raising regular false alarms and interventions.

There are two major factors bearing on this exercise. First, one thing is for sure: it cannot, and should not, be left to the professionals – the social workers, doctors, teachers – alone. Each one of us bears a responsibility (whether we are a relative, neighbour or friend) to be alert and unafraid to confront or report untoward or disturbing behaviour towards children. This is not to advocate 'grassing on your granny', but straightforward civic awareness.

Second, our awareness (professional and lay) has to be sensitised by well-grounded information and not prejudiced by the prism of presumption. The 'well-to-do' are no less predisposed to violence than the less well-off, and the appearance of injury may belie a medical propensity. Discerning which is which requires careful, time-consuming and considerate enquiry. This should be expected and welcomed as a matter of course. It's not the 'nanny state', but the caring community.

6

1984

Miners and Milestones

1984 was a momentous year: politically, professionally and
personally. The miners embarked on their longest and most
acrimonious strike, which changed the course of history, and I made
decisions that changed the course of *my* history.

On 1 May – a propitious date – I established a new set of
chambers at Tooks Court, part of the rationale behind which was to
provide a collective base for young entrants to the Bar who wished
to pursue cases of a political/civil-rights nature, rather than merely
take anything that was around. Originally the idea was for Stephen
Sedley (now Lord Justice Sedley) and I to head this project jointly
– he would lead on the civil side and I would do the crime – but the
potential birth was so painful for the set that we were both in at the
time (Cloisters under John Platts Mills) that our project, as originally
planned, was stillborn. In order to smooth ruffled feathers, Stephen
stayed and I left.

At this period I was involved in a complex 'spy' trial, representing
Michael Bettany, an MI5 officer convicted of passing sensitive
information to the Soviet Embassy in London. This was a stressful
case for a number of reasons: much of it was held in camera; most
of the paperwork was secret and had to be held in safes; and I was
so concerned that our every word was being bugged that I ended up
having conferences in lifts. It was a doubly stressful time, not only
because of the gravity of the case but also because my family life
was imploding. Melian and I both accept equal responsibility for the

breakdown of our marriage, but there's no doubt that the innocent victims were our five lovely, long-suffering children.

Stephen Sedley's place at Tooks Court was taken by Paddy O'Connor, a passionate, intellectual high-flyer. We began with a small, diverse band of young and enthusiastic colleagues, 40 per cent black and 50 per cent women, and wanted to be outside the confines of the Inns of Court, without the usual hierarchy of clerks and the internal arrangement of most chambers: in other words, we were a form of collective. We employed clerks on PAYE (resisting the percentage fee structure commonly used); we sought the ultimate democracy with weekly meetings to discuss policy and politics; and our fees were to be pooled so that all tenants received equal remuneration, a utopia which we never actually achieved.

Not long after our inception, the senior clerk, overwhelmed by the amount of work and the arrogance and demands of the barristers, as he saw it, literally jumped on his bike and left us for France. In his absence three young barristers – Sandra Graham, Christiana Hyde and Janet Plange – stepped into the breach and sorted the administration until I persuaded him to return to a suitably admonished band of brothers- and sisters-in-law. Looking back, I can't really blame him. Barristers can be a difficult lot: something to do with their self-employed status and with the uncertainty of where the next case (and therefore the next fee) is coming from; but there's no excuse for tantrums, and I've seen my fair share of those. Yet we are still going strong.

It was not only the establishing of Tooks Court which made 1984 a momentous year for me, for it was then that I met Yvette, an independent television producer and director. She was (and remains) dynamic, political, intelligent and sexy – a combination I just couldn't resist. Yvette was researching and producing, for the BBC's Community Programme Unit, a film about the miners' strike called *Taking Liberties*, and came to interview me with the director Steve Connelly, as I had been recommended as a useful lawyer who might explain the laws on picketing and so on. She was not au fait with the law, but she was very bright and asked all the right questions – and we hit it off immediately. It was, quite simply, love at first sight.

In my recorded interview with Yvette I was able to point out the freedoms that, from the earliest days of the strike, were being threatened – freedom of association, movement and speech – and she expressed herself delighted that I had given her 'the structure of the film'. Less of a boost to my ego was the fact that I was so verbose that I was left on the cutting-room floor (though Yvette never thought that my ego needed much boosting!).

While making the film, Yvette and her crew spent time in Yorkshire and stayed in mining communities, exposing the scale of the police intervention and the violence inflicted on so many families in these small pit villages. The footage was a revelation.

She met Terry ('My friends call me Tex') Dunn, who opened doors to a community that was sceptical or even hostile towards the media, and with good reason. Tex became not just a source of great inside information, but also a close personal friend.

At one point the film crew decided to challenge the freedom-of-movement restrictions imposed by the police by taking Tex and another miner in a van to Nottinghamshire. Inevitably they were stopped at a roadblock, and the sequence in the film would be almost comical, were it not so chilling, as the police were both abusive and dismissive at the same time. The crew kept filming, but were told to turn round and go back to Yorkshire or they would be arrested. I had half-hoped they would keep going so that we could challenge the policy in court, but Yvette had to think of the miners, whose future livelihoods and freedoms were at stake, so back they went, with Tex commenting, 'Is this Poland, or what?'

The background to the 1984–5 miners' strike is long and complicated, but at its centre was the hatchet man Ian MacGregor, who a few years earlier had been brought in to decimate the steel industry and in 1983 was appointed Chair of the National Coal Board, with the full approval of 'Iron Lady' Margaret Thatcher, to do the same to the coal industry. The rousing miners' leader Arthur Scargill (whom I came to represent on more than one occasion), President of the National Union of Mineworkers, was determined to protect the conditions – and ultimately the jobs – of hundreds of thousands of miners who worked in the industry at that time, while Women Against Pit Closures was an amazingly resilient and successful movement led by a committee of ferocious campaigners, including Arthur's wife, the irrepressible Anne Scargill, who shares my birthday and is exactly the same age. She and I are like twins, and remain great friends. Stir into the mix the police, media and judiciary – whose role it became to label and condemn miners as criminals – and it made for one of the most bitter industrial disputes of modern times.

Following a vote for an overtime ban against pit closures and a paltry pay rise of 5.2 per cent at a time of double-figure inflation, many miners were laid off, and several local disputes erupted. Face-workers' basic wage for a shift was £29 – with added bonuses from productive pits (mostly in Nottinghamshire) – and many surface workers relied on income supplement and housing benefit. The work was hard, dirty and dangerous, but miners needed their jobs, and they knew that if they lost this strike, the NCB would close seventy pits. (And it did.) After the closure of Cortonwood pit in Yorkshire was announced on 1 March 1984, with nine years of coal remaining, 55,000 Yorkshire miners came out on strike, and the national strike (including coalfields in Yorkshire, Scotland, South Wales and Kent) was solid within a fortnight. Nottingham proved to be less staunch, although the local leadership did call their men out following the death of twenty-four-year-old David Jones, who collapsed while picketing at Ollerton colliery.

There then commenced one of the biggest and most brutal police operations against citizens that Britain has ever seen. One and a half million police from forty-three forces were deployed, at an estimated cost of £2 million a week.[1] Roadblocks sealed off the county of Nottinghamshire from any outside picketing; lorries carrying coal to steelworks and driven by non-unionised men willing to cross picket lines were heavily protected; miners were beaten and arrested and their leaders attacked.

But this didn't stop the miners. They found paths through woods and across farmers' fields. Clapped-out cars fuelled by supporters' donations transported miners disguised as market traders down country roads to appeal to their dithering Nottinghamshire colleagues to show unity. But by then the propaganda war was on to convince the Notts miners to scab – that is, to betray their comrades by crossing the picket line – and, spurred on by their right-wing leaders, scab most of them did, with a few notable exceptions, such as Ernie Barber and the gentle giant Stefan Wysocki (from Derbyshire, where the strike was also less solid), two miners whom I came to know and respect thoroughly for sticking to their principles. By mid-March most Nottinghamshire miners were working again, which cut a deep rift in the solidarity of the strike.

Mining was an industry labelled 'uneconomic', despite the fact that many pits had years of coal remaining, but it wasn't the money that made the miners fight: it was the fact that there was no alternative. Between 1972 (the year of the previous strike) and 1984 more than 100,000 miners' jobs had been lost and 115 pits shut down – and when the mines closed, with them went their communities. So in 1984 the miners knew that the stakes were high.

The state intervened to try and immobilise the strike. Despite sustained support from UK and European dockers, huge consignments of coal were secretly transported from Poland and South Africa via non-union ports on the east coast. NUM funds were sequestrated; deductions were made to already meagre state benefits given to striking miners' families; and pressure was applied to get miners to return to work. Miners and their families suffered tremendous hardship and were isolated by the betrayal of the TUC leadership under Len Murray and Ted Willis, whose major role was to negotiate a 'surrender deal' with the government and the NCB. Politicians of all hues had been baying for the miners' blood and the Labour Party leadership under Neil Kinnock did little to counteract the tumult.

But what can never be underestimated, and should not be forgotten, was the huge support and solidarity shown by other trade unionists, both in the UK and internationally, and the generous support of the public, both in their fundraising and in their physical participation in the strike. My own in-laws, Paul and Sally Vanson, both staunch Labour supporters, were among those who collected money and clothing, and together Yvette and I drove with them to Yorkshire to distribute the goods. The miners and their families were courageous in their commitment to saving their pits and their livelihoods during the longest industrial dispute ever in the UK, and earned huge respect for doing so.

But they suffered. A total of 766 miners were sacked by the NCB and never returned to work in the depleted coalfields, while almost 10,000 were arrested and, according to Home Office figures, 7,874 were charged with everything from breach of the peace through unlawful assembly to riot. Our great friend Tex was thrown through a plate-glass window at his pit by police and then charged with 'criminal damage'. He was also sacked for that alleged offence, and this loyal, committed miner was hounded out of his industry and his community. He went on to gain a degree at the LSE and to help many other trade unionists fight for their jobs and rights via a charity in London, but the loss of his pit and his family left Tex an ill man. He has rebuilt his life with a new wife and son, but I suspect he will never really get over the strike and its aftermath.

Despite the hardships, there were funny moments. One of the apocryphal stories involves a much-hated, haughty Chief Superintendent. Arriving on a picket line one cold winter's morning, he was confronted by a huge replica of himself made out of snow, complete with pips, buttons, cap and smirking mouth. Less than amused by the snowman blocking his way, he ordered the miners to demolish it, and of course they refused. Furious, he jumped into his Range Rover and drove it at speed at the offending snowman. What he didn't know, until a mighty crunch ensued, was that the grinning snowman had been built around a large concrete bollard – and so ended the life of the Chief Superintendent's rather fine police vehicle.

Fortunately, many of the hundreds of actions taken against individual miners arrested on public-order charges, both minor and serious, in the magistrates' and Crown courts proved unsuccessful, thanks to a great team of defence lawyers who took on the system and won: the Tooks contingent virtually removed themselves to Yorkshire to defend them. Having put ourselves on the line in this way, we were reliant on an equally small band of committed solicitors to brief us.

One of the most important trials of my life involved defending Bernard Jackson, President of the Wath Main branch of the NUM in South Yorkshire, along with another local lad, David Moore, and Craig Waddington from Scotland, three of the fifteen defendants in the crucial Orgreave trial of 1985.

Orgreave was owned by British Steel, supplying coke to its steelworks in Scunthorpe, and miners began picketing the plant from early in the strike, asking for and receiving support from the steel workers, who refused to cross their lines. By late May 1984 there had been mass pickets as pressure was put on the steel workers to resume work, and scab lorry drivers were brought in to transport the coke, with 200 lorries a day roaring past the pickets because the coke was so vital to continuing steel production. Arthur Scargill had already been arrested once, along with many others.

Bernard was a white-haired, pipe-smoking miner with a solid commitment to his industry, who was hugely politicised by the strike. David was a quiet, mild-mannered, religious man, genuinely astonished by the state savagery he experienced. And Craig was a young, feisty lad who would take no nonsense from anybody, and who maintained this spirit despite many attempts to curb it.

For what was called 'the most important trial of public order this century', we faced the daunting task of ensuring these innocent men were found not guilty, though by the time of the trial they had been pilloried and maligned in the national press as rioters and men of violence. Eighty-odd others were charged with similar offences, and the outcome of our trial would almost certainly determine their futures as well.

Yvette and I rented a 'granny flat' attached to a farm overlooking Orgreave itself, a large industrial site, a huge black, smoking, fiery blot on the surrounding countryside – much of which was given over to rapeseed production, so beautiful in the spring with its bright-yellow hue and such a contrast to the coking plant.

On 18 June 1984, a beautiful early summer's day, the largest picket of Orgreave assembled. Thousands of miners from all over the country were escorted onto a field next to the plant and then surrounded by police – the miners in T-shirts or bare-chested, the police in full riot gear with batons, shields, helmets and dogs, and mounted contingents waiting in the wings. (This tactic of corralling or 'kettling' of protesters has been used regularly ever since – right up to the G20 demonstrations in April 2009.)

What followed – at least, what the prosecution said had followed – was described at length in the opening speech of Brian Walsh, QC, in the imposing Victorian courtroom in the centre of Sheffield, not two miles from Orgreave itself. Standing by an axe, ball bearings, a mallet and a metal bar, which he termed 'but a tiny sample of an arsenal of weaponry with which these men . . . equipped themselves', Walsh described how 'the pickets put their plan into action. They charged forward against the police lines, hurling missiles in a quite terrifying display of violence which lasted several hours ... They were sick minds who organised this.'

Later, in 1986, Bernard Jackson, who had kept his own record of the trial, wrote a book with Tony Wardle to support the powerful film which Yvette produced and directed for Channel 4, *The Battle for Orgreave*. In it Bernard describes in detail, and very movingly, the whole build-up to the strike; his own experiences of being smashed in the face with a shield and held in a painful and dangerous armlock, 'damn near strangling me'; his time in prison on remand; the trial; and his feelings about the struggle to keep their jobs and communities intact:

> The anger I felt was the anger of injustice. I felt anger towards the media who had consistently chosen selectivity, right from the start of the strike, in what they pictured and what they reported. How many pictures had been shown of a poor bleeding policeman when for every policeman there were a hundred injured pickets – fractured arms and legs, split skulls and livid truncheon weals? I felt anger at the state which had not only allowed this to happen but was obviously pulling the strings, planning it and providing the resources to make it possible. I felt anger at the men who should have been supporting us, the Kinnocks and Willises, when openly and arrogantly the state was intent on smashing working-class organisations. How dare they pretend to represent, to speak for the working class? History will judge them and it will not forgive easily.[2]

For me the summer of 1985 was a stimulating and tense time. It was a year since the events at Orgreave, the strike was over and many pits had closed, but until I moved up to Yorkshire and visited the homes of miners and working men's clubs I had no real idea of the extent of the sacrifices and daily struggles faced by mining families: burning their own furniture to keep warm; surviving on food parcels and soup kitchens; and running the gauntlet of cocky Metropolitan police officers from down south, flaunting their pay packets stuffed with overtime.

My clients had been anticipating the trial with trepidation and the stakes were high, for the miners charged with riot faced life imprisonment, and there was no doubt that the state was more than willing to hand down such a punishment. Fortunately, the fate of my clients was to be decided by their peers, twelve men from Sheffield and its environs, who sat on the jury for forty-eight days as the evidence unfolded – in front of His Honour Judge Coles, no less . . .

I shared Bernard's anger at the response to the strike, but in my line of business I have to direct that anger forensically at those in front of me in court. That I did in my week-long cross-examination of the man in charge of the police at Orgreave on the day: Assistant Chief Constable Anthony Clements, a man with greying hair and a small moustache. He came into the witness box and answered Brian Walsh with a firm, steady, well-spoken voice. He appeared to have a complete grasp of the 'facts' surrounding 18 June, and his demeanour was one of a reasonable man horrified by the violence he had seen: his last words to the prosecution were: 'In thirty-three years of policing I have never seen anything quite like it.'

Listening to his description of his deployment of Police Support Units (PSUs), officers with long shields, short shields, horses and dogs because the stone-throwing at 8 a.m. was of such intensity, I realised that I had to undermine this voice of authority with evidence. In my experience, policemen cannot always be believed, but I had to demonstrate this to the jury.

As I challenged Clements about the details of his evidence and suggested that his men had gone berserk, his protestations about their bravery and the violence of the pickets became more vociferous. He admitted that he had sent in the horses without warning, and when I asked him if he was worried that some of the 6,000 demonstrators might be trampled underfoot by the galloping horses, he replied, 'Not in the slightest.'

Clements alluded to a restricted-circulation manual of instructions written by members of the Association of Chief Police Officers (ACPO) for use by the police in public-order situations. I was thus able to call for the manual to be disclosed: only a few pages were shown to us, but this move enabled me to expose the premeditated nature of their strategy. Clements said that their orders were to 'disperse the crowd and make arrests of the criminal offenders', and when I pressed him, he conceded that this didn't mean just stone-throwers.

'So *no one* had the right to be there?' I asked.

'That is right,' he replied.

In one short answer Clements had summed up the situation in our so-called liberal democracy: simply by deciding that a protest is not in the public interest, the police can criminalise ordinary people for demonstrating in support of their basic rights.

Then I asked him about the case of Russell Broomhead, who had been beaten about the head with a truncheon by an officer said to be PC Martin. The assault was shown on national television, and yet despite the fact that Russell had sustained severe injuries, he was later charged with riot, *just for being at Orgreave*. According to Clements, 'If he was in that situation, he probably was rioting.'

Over many days I cross-examined Clements about several issues, such as the wall of reverberating noise caused by the police banging on shields to intimidate the miners; the fact that the police spat at, punched and kicked those arrested; the use of illegal head-locks to restrain prisoners, which leads to the blood circulation being stopped. There was a particularly shocking stretch of film shot by an amateur cameraman/miner who had hidden himself up a tree close to the action. Unbeknown to the riot squads below, he captured a sequence depicting a snatch-squad of two or three officers who targeted a perfectly innocent picket, pinned him to the ground and throttled him with a tight lock around his neck with an arm and truncheon. As they maintained this hold, he was dragged protesting along the ground towards the police lines while being audibly abused by the police. Other issues included the deployment of officers without identification (once again a feature of G20, 2009); the arsenal of weapons produced in court, which Clements insisted were 'an important element in the day's happenings', but not one of which was mentioned in his statement, nor was any evidence of their use ever produced; the case of photographer Lesley Boulton, who was famously protecting her head as a mounted policeman swung at her with his yardstick – she was calling for help for a seriously injured miner – and nearly had her skull smashed in the process. And much, much more.

I had got Clements to build up a picture of *his* version of events for the jury: that Scargill had provoked his men at 8 a.m.; that the use of horses (which advanced at a walk) was justified; that deploying riot police in 'snatch-squads' was necessary because, following a 'push' of ten minutes against the police cordon, there was a hail of missiles; that by 8.20 a.m. 'the sky was black with missiles'; and so on.

In his book Bernard Jackson describes how Clements spoke as if this was reality, and not merely opinion: 'But I knew something which Mr Clements didn't know. I knew that a trap was being set for him, and with each answer he was getting himself deeper and deeper into a morass from which he would find it impossible to escape. I could not wait for the trap to be sprung.'[3]

And that afternoon I sprang it.

I asked that the jury be shown the police's own video of the day. This came as bit of a bombshell to Clements and the court. They knew of the film's existence, but thought the defence didn't.

The first videotape, timed and recorded from the roof of a building behind the police lines, was as clear as daylight, and contradicted all of Clements's assertions. There were hardly any pickets at 7.30 a.m.; there was no action by miners, no stones, nothing. In fact it was really boring.

Tape 2 showed a build-up of pickets, but the scene was still peaceful. The occasional plastic bottle was seen floating through the air, but mostly miners were standing around, shirtless, talking, and the sky was definitely not black with missiles. At 8 a.m. Arthur Scargill was nowhere to be seen; the 'appalling crush' against police lines was timed at fifty-eight seconds, and was no more than the sort of ritual push that happened on all picket lines, more symbolic than effective. But then suddenly the cordon parted and the horses cantered out, straight at the gathered protesters.

There it was on the police video: no barrage of stones, just horses charging into a crowd of unarmed men; there followed the assault of the short-shield officers; then the sound of clapping from the police cordon, as miners tried to carry away their bleeding and injured comrades. It was shocking.

In court, it was some consolation for the defendants to see the disintegration of Clements under fire – and then he dug another hole for himself by insisting that Arthur Scargill had slipped down a bank and was 'not hit by anything carried by an officer'. When I was dramatically able to reveal a photograph showing the attack by two policemen with short shields on Arthur and those around him, I felt my job had been done for the moment and I sat down.

The trial continued as the prosecution began to put the individual cases against the fifteen in the dock, and as the weeks went by a pattern began to emerge of at least two officers to each defendant being arrested, and statements being dictated by members of the Serious Crime Squad to ensure that a case was foolproof. But there were some more surprises to come . . .

Bryan Moreland was a thin, worried man from Durham who had been terrified by mounted police chasing fleeing pickets and had been struck by a long-shield-carrying officer. He had lost three stone waiting for the trial and his marriage had collapsed under the pressure.

Bryan's lawyer, Vera Baird (later to join Tooks and then become Solicitor General in Gordon Brown's government), suggested that there was strong evidence that the officer concerned may have forged a signature on a fellow officer's statement. When the incriminating statement was found to be missing over lunch, the judge was furious and the game was up: a few days later the case against Bryan was suddenly dropped. There was huge relief all round at this decision, and it gave hope to defendants and barristers alike that maybe we were beginning to expose the frailty and falsity of the prosecution case.

On 18 June 1985, as the trial crawled forward, we celebrated the anniversary of the Battle for Orgreave with a party that Arthur and Anne Scargill attended. There was a cake, and an excellent wig-and-gown impersonation of Ed Rees, one of the barristers. Bernard made a moving speech on behalf of the defendants, insisting that their faith in their leadership had not diminished: the fight had been right, and now they were confident that their great legal team would make sure that justice was done. I looked across at Gareth Peirce, solicitor and friend, and caught her eye – then held my breath and, although not a believing man, prayed that he was right.

The remaining individual cases were put by the prosecution, who accused the miners generally of erecting barricades and wires across the lane up to the village, of hurling bricks, and so on. Miners are not angels, and by the time the protesters had been driven up the field by short-shield units, been charged at by horses and witnessed their comrades being beaten and battered, they instinctively retaliated. By 1.30 p.m. on that day, stones were being hurled at the police, and although I don't condone it, who could blame them? As for tripwires and mallets and a catalogue of other weapons, there was no proof whatsoever of them.

'Geordie' Foster was an amiable, easy-going guy accused of throwing half a brick. In fact the photos show in his hand a pork pie, which he'd just bought in the village – and very annoyed he was not to be able to eat it. Nevertheless he was accused of riot.

Gradually the claims of the police grew more and more hollow, and the recurring themes of falsehood and cover-up began to pall, but fortunately there was another moment of light relief.

Greg Taylor was an exuberant Welsh barrister representing gentle Bill Greenaway, fifty-one years old, who had had his wrist fractured in two places, and James O'Brien, who had a terrible gash over his eye from a truncheon blow: a photograph showed the blood streaming down his face and torso as if from a war wound. Both incidents occurred over the bridge near the village of Orgreave, where miners had finally fled to escape the marauding police.

A number of officers claimed that they had been injured by bricks thrown by miners which had bounced off the ground. PC Kearns from Merseyside, ex-army service in Northern Ireland, claimed that he found Orgreave 'frightening' and reported a bouncing half brick hitting his wrist. Another officer, Sergeant Smith, provided a graphic description of the propensities of a bouncing brick which was nothing short of Olympian. Akin to a knight in shining armour he advanced carrying a long shield, wearing padded gloves, a body protector, shin-pads, a cricket box and a riot helmet. Lo and behold a full house brick ricocheted off a nearby long shield onto the ground and bounced up underneath his own long shield hitting him in the groin with such force that he fell to the ground.

Greg put this convoluted sequence to the test. He entered court bearing a bright orange carrier bag containing his experimental equipment. From the bag he withdrew an ordinary house brick and in his lilting Welsh accent put the following questions to the officer: 'I thought you might be interested, we've been doing a little practising in the car park. We've been throwing bricks, full house bricks and do you know what? No matter how hard we throw them or at what angle we can't get them to bounce. Now there's interesting, isn't it? But just in case, we threw some half bricks . . .' He produced one from the bag. 'And would you believe it, they won't bounce either. We're not having much luck with bouncing bricks.' Laughter in court! An offer to bowl one down the aisle in court towards the witness box to finally prove the point was smartly declined.

Then Paddy O'Connor, representing George Foulds, accused of stone throwing, asked another officer, Sergeant Hill, under cross-examination whether he had noticed anything distinctive about his client. He hadn't. When asked what George had said, the officer maintained that he had stated 'I ain't been throwing or owt'. Paddy then asked George to stand and say something, but the prosecution and judge quickly intervened to stop him. We all knew that George was a Scot with such a broad accent that none of us could understand a word he said. A Yorkshire 'owt' would never have passed his lips. Eventually the jury would have heard George in the witness box and the game would have been up.

Another day Vera Baird, a strikingly tall figure in court, wished to demonstrate the incredibility of some police evidence, and when she came to cross-examine one of the officers who had been dressed in riot gear on the day, she carefully took him through what he had to wear and carry, putting on the equipment herself. First she placed on her head a large blue riot helmet, with a visor covering her face; then she produced a full-length riot shield strapped to her left arm, behind which she stood; and in her right hand she wielded a truncheon. Under these conditions she could barely see the witness box, let alone identify anyone, run after them and arrest them, with both her hands already full. It appeared to the jury from this simple exposé that officers who claimed to identify and pursue rioters in this gear were talking out of the back of their helmets.

Still the trial continued, and Yvette filmed the defendants for the documentary for Channel 4, taking them back to Orgreave for the first time since that day to re-create what had happened to all of them, which was simultaneously a traumatic and cathartic experience. Young David Bell had had his leg broken by the police; Dave Coston from County Durham was watching, horrified, as many miners were forced down the steep railway sidings onto the live railway tracks below, when he was 'stabbed' in the kidneys with a truncheon; Eric Newbiggin had been beaten so badly with a truncheon that his skull had been fractured; sixteen-year-old Kevin Marshall was pushed onto a car bonnet and struck by an officer, then dragged by one leg, hopping on the other, as he was arrested by the men in blue. There was so much independent photographic evidence, from photographers who had taken risks to record the events, that it was possible to verify these attacks, and it became impossible for the police not to be revealed as fabricators.

Over the weeks and months Yvette developed a friendship with some of the miners, which has lasted to this day, but it was a nerve-racking experience – filming, hearing evidence day after day, living and breathing the events over and over again. In particular, the interview that Yvette undertook with Arthur Critchlow on the steps of the 'police holding centre' is distressing, compelling television. Arthur had been in hospital for two weeks and had to have fluid drained from his brain, following a cosh on the back of his head by a policeman. He is such an honest, brave man, and it is painful to watch him sobbing as he relives the humiliation that he and his family suffered at the hands of the authorities – whenever I see it, the footage still leaves me crying along with him. But Arthur is proud too, and he was determined that his story should be told and his actions vindicated: 'When my children know I've been to prison, they won't be ashamed. They'll hold their heads up high and say: "Our dad's Arthur Critchlow, and he fought for what he knew was right." '

On 17 July 1985, when this epic trial was just two days short of a half-century, the prosecution caved in. Undoubtedly the jury had come to see that the defendants in the dock were ordinary men fighting for their livelihoods, and that the police evidence about organised violence was simply not true. The final straw came when a policeman who was about to give evidence passed the Orgreave plant on the road into Sheffield as he drove to court – and had to turn back. Word went round that he was 'sick at the sight of Orgreave'.

Eventually Bernard Jackson and his colleagues received damages for wrongful arrest and malicious prosecution, but their lives had been traumatised and their pits were duly closed.

Bryan Moreland lost his health; some – such as David Bell – lost their lives prematurely. Who knows what ordeals these men really experienced? They were not perfect, but they were honest, decent men. And what of the police who perpetuated these acts? Not a single one was disciplined or charged with assault arising out of the events on 18 June 1984.

What was deeply shocking was the role of the media in the strike. On 20 June 1991, Tony Benn, MP, asked a question in the House of Commons:

> Is the Leader of the House aware that the award of £500,000 or more in damages and costs to thirty-nine miners who were injured, maliciously prosecuted and in other ways damaged by the South Yorkshire police is unprecedented in the history of British law? Does he recall that on 19 June 1984 the then Prime Minister and the then Home Secretary, who is now a Commissioner in Brussels, described what happened as 'mob rule', that the then Home Secretary said that those charged with riot might face life imprisonment, that the case was tested in the courts and that the courts threw out the charge of riot, and that the men were proved innocent?
>
> Is the Leader of the House aware that the other day when the settlement was made it was clear that in so far as there was violence, it was on the part of the police, and it was admitted during the riot trial that the BBC transposed the film to show stones being thrown before the cavalry charge although the police video confirmed otherwise? Indeed, the ministerial responsibility for what happened was established on 22 July 1985 when I made public the text of the 'public order tactical operations manual' which the Home Secretary had approved. This is a matter of ministerial responsibility on which the Home Secretary should make a full statement.[4]

But I don't think he ever did.

This trial was only part of a much bigger picture. Similar charges were brought in relation to other days at Orgreave, involving a total of nearly 150 miners. Between January and September 1985 not one defendant was convicted of such allegations and not one police officer was disciplined, let alone charged.

These outcomes received nothing like the banner headlines that blazoned the original events. An honest and dignified community had been vindicated. But the much-acclaimed victory of capital, and the demise of union power, has been a hollow and short-lived affair. It heralded unmitigated privatisation, untrammelled deregulation, and the growth of a society built on asset-stripping, self-interest and a culture of unashamed bonanza bonuses. Regularly described now – twenty-five years on – as a shadow economy of sub-prime mortgages, unsecured credit and derivatives, it apparently went undetected by those who took up where Margaret Thatcher left off. The damage is immense and is wreaking havoc among the working population with ever-rising levels of unemployment.

None of this is the result of unseen and unpredictable international forces, but rather it is the consequence of deliberate policies aimed at bolstering the institutions of capital, and readily explains why striking miners were demonised as the 'enemy within'. Lest anyone should doubt this analysis, just take a look at the Ridley Report, which had been commissioned by the Tories in opposition, and which had drawn up contingency plans over ten years before the strike for a premeditated confrontation and defeat of the miners.

It was in the midst of a spiralling economic downturn on 11 March 2009 at the House of Commons that some of us who had been closely involved with the miners' strike launched a new People's Charter for Change.[5] It set out six policy priorities concerning a new model for the finance industry and an end to expenditure on war and weapons; new jobs with an emphasis on green technology; an end to half-baked privatisation programmes; renationalisation; affordable social housing; free education for all students; and equality in the workplace. It is an attempt to reset the agenda and the objectives for a future marked by social justice, rather than the excesses of market indulgence.

As for me, I was privileged to be made an honorary lifetime member of the National Union of Mineworkers. I had got to know Arthur and Anne Scargill very well, and admired their tenacity and courage. Both had been subjected to the full panoply of state surveillance and pressure, coupled with outrageous and scandalous claims in the tabloid press, yet they stood firm – and Arthur was totally right in his predictions about what would happen to the mining industry. I represented him on various occasions and was impressed by his leadership qualities and his outstanding oratory, and as far as I am concerned he has definitely earned his place in history.

Unsurprisingly, my association with Arthur resulted in a few snide comments in the legal profession – in some quarters I was regarded as some kind of armed revolutionary – and it was at about this time that I ran into trouble with the Bar on account of someone's animosity getting the better of them. A serious but false accusation was made that I had in effect been fabricating defences for miners and coercing other barristers to fall into line, and in addition it was suggested that I was 'touting' for work.

The allegations surfaced at the very time I commenced the defence of miners charged with riot at Orgreave, and I felt that this was no coincidence: the stress of knowing that a major investigation into my behaviour was taking place would, it was doubtless hoped by some, destabilise my work. This matter took more than two years to resolve, by which time the strike and the trial were over, and no charges were preferred – and I subsequently learned from one of the investigators, a former police officer, that they had found no truth in any of the allegations, just as I had proclaimed from the start.

One of the most important lessons I learned from the experiences of the miners in the face of aggressive public-order policing tactics and policies was the need for vigilant independent observers, such as Policewatch in Sheffield. Without the benefits of their accounts (written and taped) and the prolific photographic material from professional and amateur bystanders, it would have been far more difficult to challenge and controvert police testimony during the trials. As a result, it occurred to me that the protection of the right to collective protest required a proactive approach pioneered originally by Liberty, under its former name of the National Council for Civil Liberties (NCCL), when it was monitoring the activities of the black shirts and the fascists in East London in the 1930s. With others I helped to establish a voluntary ad hoc group which we called LOG: Legal Observers Group. It was intended to provide a service to those organising protests, demonstrations, marches and picket lines. We recruited qualified and trainee lawyers working in pairs, in fluorescent marked bibs, to monitor police action in a systematic way. On-the-spot legal advice was available, together with cards setting out the participants' legal rights and telephone numbers of on-call solicitors. In this way, one observer kept an eye on proceedings, maintained contact with headquarters and compiled an end-of-day report, whilst the other recorded events of interest either in writing or photographically.

One of the first occasions this idea was put into practice was for the dispute between Fleet Street printers and Rupert Murdoch's News International in 1986. It was the second protracted and bitter struggle to challenge Thatcher's industrial legislation. The scenes outside the new Wapping plant were exceptionally violent, with 1,262 arrests and 410 police injuries over the course of a year.[6] The police were accused of being heavy-handed and aggressive in dealing with strikers and residents alike. I witnessed this at first hand on more than one occasion when I attended as a legal observer.

Yvette was pregnant when we went the first time; we had no idea it was going to turn into a dangerous scrum, otherwise she would obviously have stayed away. It was extremely scary being suddenly thrust into a maelstrom of hundreds of protesters and unrestrained riot police, some on horseback, who rode straight at us. Had I not unceremoniously shoved Yvette into the gateway of a block of flats, we would undoubtedly have been trampled under the advancing hooves. I rushed Yvette to the house of an acquaintance who I remembered lived in Cable Street – ironically where there were confrontations in the 1930s between the Jewish and East End working-class communities and Oswald Mosley's Fascist 'blackshirts'. This friend kindly took in a shaken Yvette, while I went back out to try and observe and record the frightening events taking place. Our endeavours worked well and there developed quite a large and active network of members of LOG. There seems to be an equivalent today – advice on setting up such a group can, of course, be found on the Web.[7]

It's strange, and worrying, how history seems to repeat itself. In 2006 I was approached by a young group of independent documentary-makers to participate in a film uncannily entitled *Taking Liberties*, the same name as Yvette's film in 1984. This later film catalogues the destruction of civil liberties by the Blair/Brown government, and the opening sequence so mirrors the one in the first documentary that it makes my heart sink.

Two decades on from the miners' strike, the sequence is of a police roadblock set up to deter protesters against the use of American bases in the Iraq war from reaching the US Air Force base at Fairford in Gloucestershire. Like the miners, the protesters are turned back, this time imprisoned in their buses and escorted by police outriders all the way to London – a journey of several hours, allowing no stops even for basic necessities.

The similarities are chilling. Have we come so far from the roots of our democracy that now state interference allows such humiliation to be routinely inflicted on our own citizens? In the case of both the miners and the Fairford protesters, the police action was unlawful and the House of Lords gave an important ruling supporting the right to peaceful demonstration. That, of course, received far less publicity than the original roadblock.

Most recently in April 2009 these issues surfaced again during the Metropolitan Police handling of the G20 protests. Perhaps the most significant aspect of this concerns the Met's public statements about what had happened before they realised that there were photographers capturing numerous incidents on the streets. It appears that most of the images which then appeared on our television screens were from people who happened to be nearby at the time. In the case of Ian Tomlinson, a news vendor who died, the initial response was that there had been no contact with police. The second response was that there had been *some* contact but it had been carried out in order to move Mr Tomlinson out of danger. Once photographic material became available neither of these versions could be sustained and subsequently an officer was interviewed in relation to possible charges of manslaughter. Again this demonstrates the absolute necessity for independent monitoring and observation.

It is utterly reprehensible, therefore, that in 2008 the government should have pushed through Parliament provisions within the Counter-Terrorism Act which potentially outlaw taking photographs of officers on duty. The new offence contained within Section 76 is worded as follows: 'eliciting, publishing or communicating information on members of the armed forces, intelligence services and police officers which is likely to be useful to someone committing or preparing an act of terrorism'.

This provision went largely unnoticed and received scant public debate. It is a thoroughly oppressive measure because of its unlimited scope and because it does not require any intention to assist 'someone committing or preparing an act of terrorism'. For example, were I to photograph a member of the Household Cavalry standing guard outside a Royal palace, and then put it on YouTube, this could undoubtedly be 'useful' according to the section. Clearly it is arguable that under this provision the police are empowered to prevent the photos being taken in the first place, by confiscating the camera. This is not a matter of concern only to members of the media, but to all of us.

Tooks Court was an important resource during the miners' and printworkers' disputes, providing high-quality defence for many hundreds of strikers. But the set was not designed just to give human-rights advice; it was to have another function as well: to bring together like-minded, caring people to form a community, ending the splendid isolation of old-style sets.

Getting this mix off the ground on a day-to-day basis cannot be achieved by barristers, who are usually not sitting behind their desks every day of the week. They are often away from chambers for long periods, doing cases in far-flung places, and we rely heavily upon a team of people – clerks – who are there all the time: to pick up the phone, field emails, slot cases into the diary, negotiate fees, right through to finding lost items of clothing or (in my case) a collapsible bike: I swore blind that I'd left it in chambers for safety. One clerk, Lennox, checked every frame of the CCTV, while Kieran and Natasha scoured the locality. I still maintained that it must be there somewhere, until weeks later while walking to Farringdon Tube station I found myself admiring an identical red Brompton – same pannier, same bell, same lights. As I dreamed of past pleasures, I slowly realised that it was mine, chained by me to a lamp post in a rush to catch a train. Explaining to the clerks how the bike had suddenly reappeared was like watching judicial expressions of disbelief in the Court of Appeal on a bad day.

Fortunately, the clerks have been at Tooks a long time, most of them for the best part of fifteen years, and they are used to my moments of madness. Martin Parker, the senior clerk, is a tall, slim,

stoical Scot – and he has to be stoical when you consider the range
of demands placed upon him 24/7. He and I have been Arsenal fans
for years, but I think we'll get over it soon . . . He also plays a mean
guitar. His quiet authority is matched by his attire, and as he arrives
each day – in a black wide-brimmed trilby hat, a neat overcoat
concealing a crisp shirt underneath, with a pair of imposing braces
– he could be mistaken for Clint Eastwood. He has kept the helm
steady through thick and thin with a cool nerve. He would make a
brilliant poker player.

The team alongside him is loyal and fun. You need a sense of
humour, otherwise the job would drive you nutty. Lee Wakeling
has a taxing task, literally: he deals with the fees and finances.
Without him keeping an eye on everything, we would all dry up
with worry. The vast majority of our work is publicly funded and,
quite rightly, every minute expended on a case has to be accounted
for and explained. Lee ensures we forget nothing. But, like all the
other clerks, he often works well beyond the call of duty. Anxious
about the welfare of that wandering red bike, he personally drove a
hired van to ensure that, along with other personal effects, it got to
The Hague for me to use during a case I was undertaking for over
a year.

Lee sits opposite Carol Thomas in the ultra-modern premises
we recently leased, instead of the cramped, Dickensian conditions
we endured off Chancery Lane. Finding somewhere upon which
everyone could agree was like cooking by committee: it takes for ever
and you're never sure that you'll be able to recognise the finished
product. After six years of tortuous searching there was unanimity
for a striking conversion in a small street off the Farringdon Road
in Clerkenwell – a little to the left of the *Guardian*, as we liked to
describe it. Originally the building housed stables for the workhorses
used in Smithfield. Now it's just unbridled lawyers, cheek by jowl
with graphic designers and motorcycle couriers. The building has
been cleverly redesigned around an atrium, so that every working
room has natural daylight from above, as well as large windows.
This futuristic architecture provoked one newspaper cartoon that
depicted me as Captain Kirk astride the *Starship Enterprise*.

Carol is hugely experienced as a clerk and she has been a friend for
many years. After a spell abroad in the West Indies, she returned in

1993 at exactly our moment of greatest need, after a series of rapidly changing senior clerks. Knowing everything there is to know about the mysteries of clerking and who to contact to get things done, she took on the task. Since then Tooks has been on a settled path, with her successor Martin and twelve other clerks, while Carol has taken over the coordination of the many extramural activities the set undertakes and has helped us create a unique and vibrant ambience. Throughout the years, I have kept in mind the example set by Anthony Masters, the writer I met right back at the start of my career. At the heart of his endeavours was a belief that literature and the arts are gateways to a better quality of life for everyone. This was the stimulus for his initiatives, aimed particularly at motivating children and harnessing their natural creative abilities. 'Book Explosion' workshops and 'Event Operas' were spontaneous enactments of real-life events, which he staged using merely found objects.

By 2009 I like to think we have definitely achieved a unique kind of community. But not only in the way you might imagine.

Look up, not down. That is what I try to do when I am walking around the streets of London (though sometimes it's a bit tricky, given the potholes, and is certainly to be avoided while riding a bicycle). There is a fascination and an intrigue in the world above our heads – always some fresh perspective or insight to behold. The blackbird riding a moving CCTV camera; the bicycle tyre looped over the top of a thirty-foot-high lamp post; a small tree struggling to grow between the roof-tiles; two window cleaners sitting in their cradle between floors, ten storeys up, drinking tea and reading newspapers.

This exercise in inquisitive observation and enquiry has been part of my daily life since an art teacher at Highgate insisted on making his pupils aware of the environment we moved in, and especially aware of the extraordinary visual pollution with which we put up, and to which we become anaesthetised. A Royal Academician whose Welsh mountain paintings and seascapes are without equal, Kyffin Williams was an inspiration. His work communicates a feeling for the atmosphere of a moment, but he also keeps an acute eye on the smallest detail, which at once lends both depth and life to his pictures. He would get us slovenly lot of schoolboys to describe what we had seen on the way to school: no, not what we had 'seen', or what we had looked at – which might be rather obvious – but what needed to be 'looked for', and then questioned. He started with things beneath our feet, then moved on to things above our heads. This soon became a competition in the obscure, the outrageous and, sometimes, the fantastical, but it set us thinking, and responding, and for me it led to an entertaining and educative search for differences, for shades, for reflections, and for the unnoticed but enigmatic detail.

This last aspect was at the core of Kyffin's art. Sadly, he died not long ago, but a perfect example of his talent hangs beside my front door: a simple, almost single continuous-line ink drawing of an elderly Welsh countryman, gently walking off into the distance. Everything one needs to know about the man is in the contours of his cloth cap. This sort of observation is important for all of us, but particularly for lawyers, for while standing back to get the bigger picture may be desirable, the real clue may lie in the tiniest detail.

My early cultural influences opened my eyes and ears to a creative world that was as far from Whetstone as was Mars: Winifred Atwell; *Quo Vadis*; Glenn Miller and Benny Goodman; *The Goons*; the British Council 1961 summer arts course in Florence; Stoke Theatre in the Round every Saturday night for £1; the Halle Orchestra . . . and later, with my kids, the Unicorn Theatre and the Little Angel Marionettes in Islington; then, later still, Magritte and Picasso's *Guernica*; virtuoso guitarist Antonio Forcione; Northern Broadside's *Cleopatra Off Broadway*, with a stunning Ishia Bennison in the title role and a charismatic Barrie Rutter as her Antony; wonderful jazz at the 606 Club in Chelsea.

I am a firm believer that culture, or art in its broadest sense, has the capability to challenge fixed notions and to open people up to fresh possibilities and ideas. The Bar, so often represented as traditional, reserved and conservative in all things, is not often linked in the public mind with the avant-garde, and certainly not with those who produce overtly polemical works or who espouse openly political causes.

It has been a great joy to me, therefore, to have had the opportunity for Tooks Chambers to be a platform for a variety of artists and art projects. Varying widely in media and in approach, the artists involved have included Rasta performance poet Benjamin

Zephaniah, who was Poet in Residence sponsored by the Poetry Society at the time of the Stephen Lawrence inquiry and as a result wrote many incredible poems based around our cases in his brilliant anthology *Too Black, Too Strong*; talented painters Tim Dolby, Gavin Maughfling and Val Clay; a steel band and gospel choir that included our administrator, Sandra; French designer Cyril Bresset's fabulous fashion show; a celebrity auction for Show Racism the Red Card in sport; a celebration of International Women's Day with excerpts from *The Vagina Monologues*; installation art curated by Sarah Strang on the impact of the killing of Jean Charles de Menezes; and a women's photography collective from Madagascar, whose cameras were bought by Tooks and whose work was displayed during Black History Month. The results of these and other collaborations have been witnessed in chambers by many who have visited us, either as part of their job or as guests at special events.

Apart from inviting members of chambers to see Tooks as a resource for a wider community, these artistic projects have elicited extraordinary responses from all involved. Many barristers have spoken to me of how they have found themselves reappraising their work after seeing others interpret what they do through the prism of art. Visual translations of universal suffering, such as were displayed in Ricky Romain's exhibition *In the Absence of Justice* (co-sponsored by Tooks, Bail for Immigration Detainees and Amnesty International), reminded me that we do not work in a vacuum. It can be easy to become lost in the minutiae, to refine a matter down to a tally of bald facts or statistics. This, though, is to lose sight of the very real, human cost of each and every case that is tackled and the necessity of remaining cognisant of the needs, feelings, problems and views of others.

In 2006 I was invited to speak at a fundraiser for the Marine Theatre in Lyme Regis, an event that had surprising and unforeseen consequences, for at the end of the evening I was presented with a file that revealed that my ancestors had actually hailed from Lyme.

It transpires that not only are many Mansfields to be found in the cemetery – including my great-great-great-grandparents Mary and Joseph – but in the Lyme Museum hangs a picture of one of the last ships to be built in the town on the Cobb, by one William Mansfield, a wealthy shipwright. The author John Fowles, in his capacity as Curator of Lyme Museum, wrote a short biography of William.

Uncomfortably for me, however (and not a little ironically, in the light of my stance on human rights), it appears that at the time of writing this book a branch of my family called Manfield (without the 's') occupies Court Hall Farm in Uplyme, which after the Monmouth Rebellion had been put down in 1685 was apparently used as a courtroom during the Bloody Assizes – by none other than the 'Hanging Judge' himself, Judge Jeffreys.

THE SLENDEREST THREAD

A Case of Who Dunnit?

By the afternoon of Monday 2 July 2001 the jury had been deliberating for the best part of six days. This was not the longest wait for a verdict that I've had – in the Fertiliser Conspiracy trial a few years later (see Chapter 20) it was nearly seven weeks – but whatever the length of time, I find this is the most difficult part of the trial to handle. Juries have an onerous task and take their responsibilities very seriously; therefore you can rarely expect a verdict within hours, after sitting for many days and weeks listening to detailed and complex evidence and arguments. This trial had been going since Wednesday 2 May, two months earlier.

It had taken place in Court Number One at the Old Bailey, the scene of many famous trials in the past, including those of John Christie (10 Rillington Place) and Ruth Ellis. Given this history, and the somewhat sombre grandeur of the setting, there was no doubt in anyone's mind about the gravity of the occasion. No one connected with the trial can leave the building, in case the jury suddenly returns with a question – or, of course, with the verdict – and this could happen at any moment. Even though I've been there many times before, I am always on tenterhooks at this juncture of a trial, and it's very difficult to devise ways of occupying the time; it's even worse for the family involved, in this case the defendant's sister, let alone for the person downstairs in the cells. And this was a murder case, so just imagine what it must have been like waiting for the verdict.

The Central Criminal Court stands in what was the bailey[1] of the City of London wall and occupies the site of Newgate Prison, within which executions took place up until 1902. The defendant I was representing had been in custody for more than twelve months, since his arrest the year before.

Much of my time is spent with my client discussing the trial, the body language of the jurors when they come into court, the meaning of any questions they ask and the possibilities of an appeal should it all go wrong. On this occasion there was a dedicated team of people who were all able to ease the burden: my instructing solicitor Marilyn Etienne, my junior Myriam Syed and the psychologist Dr Susan Young.

Unusually, the jury had been sent each night to a hotel. When I first started, this was standard practice in order to ensure no interference from outside sources and, in particular, no risk of prejudice from untimely or irresponsible press reporting, but in the end the cost of this exercise was thought to outweigh the possibility of prejudice.

Once we got to the weekend with this trial, it was decided that the court would sit on the Saturday, to enable the jury to continue with its deliberations, which it is not supposed to do other than when they are all together and assembled in the jury room, with the jury bailiff outside. When this happens it is always a little odd, since Saturday is not a normal court day and the building is eerily empty.

The Old Bailey has been my professional home for over forty years and I am familiar with every step and every brick, and I appreciate that it's the people who work there who make the place tick: the police officers on the front door, the stewards on the Lord Mayor's entrance at the back, the prison officers, canteen staff, court ushers, Matron, court clerks, shorthand writers/stenographers, journalists, telephonists, cleaners and, last but by no means least, my fellow colleagues at the Bar. With many of the staff I am on first-name terms, and I can be assured of a helping hand when I've lost something or I'm not feeling well (rare in my case). The grapevine of information from this network is crucial in gauging the temperature of the day – prison vans stuck in traffic, a juror late, the judge a bit on edge, a bomb scare – and out of hours you can be treated to some lovely vignettes. Late one evening after the courts had risen I went back to court to retrieve some papers, and noticed that the small court next door appeared to be sitting. It has oak panelling throughout, and a large, high-sided wooden dock beneath which is the well of the court, flanked by a witness box similar to a pulpit and the jury box; the judicial bench spans the width of the court at a level slightly above all this. Through the small glass panels of the court door I could see that there was someone sitting in the witness box and another person sitting in the high-backed leather judge's chair. It was two women cleaners taking a breather: they had entered into the spirit of the place and were re-enacting the events of the day as they imagined them, punctuated by some mighty fine one-liners – until, that is, my clapping broke up the party. The backstage crew in the Theatre of Law is just as vital as it is at the Victoria Palace.

At the top of the Old Bailey are the barristers' robing rooms – one for women, another for men – and a further small room for Silks. The conditions are cramped; my locker, no bigger than a tallboy, is shared with four others. Tatty wigs, soiled wing collars, discarded papers are scattered about. Everyone is friendly, but normally in a rush. Studs go missing, and in my case my spare trousers; riding in by bike, I need a complete set of court clothes as well as the gown, wig and waistcoat.

There is a canteen for barristers called the Bar Mess. Forty years ago this was an austere dining room, with deep-green leather-backed chairs and a corner for a tipple of pre-prandial sherry. There was also an unspoken pecking order, whereby the top established Silks and Treasury Counsel (specialist prosecutors), usually from half a dozen sets, all sat proprietorially at the top table. All that has changed and now the 'mess' is a bustling melee of barristers.

Normally at lunchtime I cannot be bothered to eat a meal, so I grab a sandwich and sit in the adjacent tiny Bar Library. There is always more preparation to be done, but most importantly it provides an opportunity, when I spy someone relevant through the little glass window, to pop out and discuss the case with co-defending or prosecuting counsel. In my view, this is crucial to the effective management of a trial.

There are very different stances adopted over this exercise. Some lawyers, reflecting the adversarial nature of the process, feel that contact should be kept to a bare minimum; others, especially in cases with a political hue, are deeply suspicious and believe that nothing should be given away; but a large proportion feel that regular interchanges are perfectly acceptable. I have endeavoured to steer a middle course – not too close and not too far. The fundamental requirement is trust. All concerned must know you mean what you say: don't bluff, and don't pull any fast ones.

A great deal can be achieved by sensible dialogue and negotiation, whether it's a contested trial or a guilty plea. The most obvious example is agreeing what evidence can be read without challenge, or can be reduced to admissions to save court time and money. Another is giving notice of legal submissions and attempting to distil the core issues out of court. If you don't, it merely leads to unnecessary argument and hostility – and an adjournment in any event. Neither judges nor juries appreciate trials that are consumed with personal duels fought out in public, so I have studiously tried to avoid these.

The prosecutor in the trial was Treasury Counsel Orlando Pownall: tall and imposing, with an affable, persuasive manner, he is regarded by his many admirers as 'the matinee idol'. Many years before, I had led him on a different murder case where our defence had involved unravelling the mental effects of insulin deprivation. There had been a plethora of points of law to be sorted before the trial got going, and our working relationship enabled this to be accomplished without fuss or bother.

But back to the long wait.

By the close of play on the Saturday there was still no verdict, and I was becoming increasingly nervous, because in this case the longer the jury was out, the more likely I felt the chances of a conviction. Normally it's the other way round, because you believe that the doubt you must have engendered by the defence case is causing the jury to hesitate and think hard. This time I made the mistake I had guarded against over many years, of allowing myself to believe that we had achieved an acquittal. I was not alone in this: the vast majority of observers right through to the press benches believed the same, as was clear from the publicity that followed the verdict. But as the wait went on, my confidence in this result was slowly ebbing away.

That weekend I was supposed to have been with Yvette and some close friends in Sussex. It was a beautiful summer afternoon, and as I stood on the pavement outside the Old Bailey contemplating the quickest way of joining them, my worries must have been written all over my face, because a passing member of the public took a photograph of me standing there looking somewhat bemused – and kindly sent it to me later. The rest of the weekend I could not take my mind off the case, and kept trying to work out what was causing difficulties for the jury.

On the Monday, when we returned to the Old Bailey, we discovered that one juror had been discharged because a family member had died. That meant we were down to eleven, and the majority-verdict direction was given by the judge: if you have twelve jurors you can return a verdict of eleven to one or ten to two (this was brought in by the Juries Act 1974 to circumvent what was perceived to be the problem presented by perverse jurors); where the number drops to eleven or ten, you can only have one disagreement; below that you have a hung jury, with the possibility of a retrial, which most participants wish to avoid. I am an inveterate optimist, and it ran against the grain to give up hope when so much effort had been expended. It is extremely hard to maintain a positive demeanour, but this I strive to do, without being unrealistic or raising false hopes, both for myself and for those around me.

When the jury returned just after 4 p.m. on the Monday and, by a majority of ten to one, convicted Barry George of the murder of the television presenter Jill Dando, I could hardly contain my feelings of pain, distress and anger. How could this be? I barely had time to compose myself before the next stage of the trial: sentencing. Although the sentence for murder is mandatory life imprisonment, mitigating factors may be brought to the attention of the trial judge. In fact there was nothing more to add, and in any event I've always found it incongruous at the end of a hotly contested trial to have to switch gear and mitigate for someone who has contended throughout that he didn't commit the crime.

I felt that I might explode and, after seeing Barry George in the cells, I decided to get home as quickly as possible. I rang Yvette on her mobile, but it was switched off, and it was only then that I remembered that for the first time in thirty-five years I had managed to procure some tickets for Wimbledon, and she was there with her close friend Ishia. This was even more frustrating, because at times like this I need to be able to share the emotional turmoil with

Yvette, and if I couldn't get to talk it all over with her, then the only way to release the pent-up angst was to walk it off. The distance from the Old Bailey to home at that time was roughly seven miles, so off I went, pounding the pavements, going over and over what might have gone wrong and what I had misjudged, effectively rerunning every minute of every day of the trial. I could not achieve reconciliation, and it seems that this was the same for one juror, who a few days later made contact with my instructing solicitor and the court, expressing concerns about the verdict.

This is a rare occurrence and, although not unknown, usually reflects substantial disquiet. A juror is not allowed to reveal the content of any jury deliberations, which means that where a juror has felt compelled to report a concern, it has to be handled confidentially by the court administrator and then the judge. There have been revelations in which the court has permitted the juror's reservations to be aired on appeal, if the jury has acted improperly in some way: for example, if it has visited the crime scene without permission or had recourse to a Ouija board. In the Jill Dando case, the Court of Appeal refused my application to have the matter investigated, and therefore it is not clear what was troubling this juror.

My own state of unease remained until Barry George was finally acquitted by a second jury seven years later, in the summer of 2008. He had spent eight years in prison for a crime he did not commit.

There are some striking reasons why the assertion that he did not commit the crime has rung true from the moment this terrible killing occurred. In any investigation it's important to keep one's eye on the ball and not wander too far from the original crime scene, which usually yields the most relevant pointers and indicators.

As a defence barrister, I am often brought in quite late in the day, after a large number of other people have trawled over the scene and the evidence, formed their views and left their mark on the case, which makes it quite difficult to be independent and uninfluenced by what has gone before.

There used to be a quaint habit whereby the defence brief would arrive in chambers tied up in a pretty pink ribbon, and over the years I've seen all sorts of improvised uses for that ribbon – substitute trouser belt, shoelace, makeshift fan belt and gift wrap among them. From the days of a single 'back sheet' enclosing a couple of statements, the brief now comprises a truckload of ring-backed files, and even more recently computer-generated disks, as we head towards the prospect of a paperless, fully electronic court hearing. No matter how the material is produced, the task of distilling its essence remains the same. To achieve this and overcome the risk of being predisposed to the previous analyses, I have tried to develop a system that puts them to one side for as long as possible, while I look at the crime scene as it is described in the statements and at the exhibits which have been sent to me. As I go through them line by line, I mark them up in glorious Technicolor: blue for police, yellow for experts, green for eyewitnesses and red for the defendant. I find all this helps to impress the detail on my memory, but more importantly I have a checklist of questions I ask myself, as if I were in the shoes of the statement-maker. I have no doubt that many of these questions will have been asked already by others, but there are always a few that have been missed. The chronology of events is vital, so I construct timelines and flowcharts that I stick up on the wall, because although one thing coming before another does not necessarily mean that the former caused the latter, I can nevertheless discern patterns, which may disclose an underlying connection which is not coincidence. Alan Bennett in *The History Boys* has a wonderful line for defining history: 'One fucking thing after another.'

A few years ago, the Legal Action Group (LAG) organised an exercise for lawyers to encourage lateral thinking and careful dissection of the scene of a crime, which may have been committed in a matter of seconds. An actual crime was reconstructed and each lawyer chose to put himself or herself in the shoes of a police officer, a witness and an alleged culprit, and no one was told in advance how the whole thing had panned out in reality. Part of the most telling evidence against the perpetrator derived from what an office worker claimed to have observed from his third-floor window, looking down onto a street scene below, where it was said the culprit was tampering with the handles of car doors. We all stood at the window trying to assess angles of sight; the presence or absence of trees, foliage and buildings; the height of the witness; whether he wore glasses – but no one thought of the knockout blow. The crime itself had been committed several months before, during the winter months, whereas this exercise was being conducted in the summer. The weather in the winter had been quite different. It was raining, the central heating was on full blast in the office and the windows were closed. The result was substantial condensation and misting of the glass, with seriously impaired visibility.

In the case of Barry George, the murder had occurred outside Jill Dando's house in Fulham, west London, on Monday 26 April 1999, but he was not arrested until more than a year later, on Thursday 25 May 2000, and during the time between the crime and the arrest there had naturally been a huge amount of publicity and a mass of speculation in the media. All kinds of theories were floated, because there had been a plethora of different sightings of the possible perpetrator: a man running in Fulham Palace Road, another man sweating at a bus stop, yet another behaving oddly in Bishop's Park, and a Range Rover that could not be traced. The murder, went one theory, had been carried out by someone embittered by Jill Dando's work as a presenter of BBC's *Crimewatch*; or was it a copycat murder after another doorstep killing in Surrey; or the work of a known stalker; or a revenge attack by a Serbian hit-squad; or did it have something to do with her personal life? With so much out there before I became involved in the early summer of 2000, there was quite a bit of ground clearance to do in order to get back to the doorway of 29 Gowan Avenue, where the murder had taken place.

Once I had covered that ground, there were two outstanding features of the case that rose above everything else and excluded Barry George. The first concerned the window of opportunity within which this crime must have been committed, and the second the scientifically examined crime scene.

By April 1999, Jill Dando was not living at number 29. She had put the house on the market in February, and it was in the process of being bought by a relative of her next-door neighbour at number 31, Richard Hughes. Jill was spending most of her time with her fiancé Alan Farthing in Chiswick, though she returned occasionally to Gowan Avenue as quite a few of her belongings remained there, including business papers and clothes. There was no pattern to her movements: they were sporadic because she was heavily involved with recording two television series, one a holiday programme that took her abroad, the other an antiques programme that took her outside London. Thus it would have been extremely difficult for someone to predict when she would visit number 29: which day of the week, what part of the day and for how long. In fact she had been there on Saturday 24 April, just two days before her murder.

On that fateful Monday, Jill left Alan Farthing's address at about 10.10 in the morning, but she did not go straight to number 29. First she stopped at a petrol station, where she did some shopping which was captured on CCTV, and then shortly before 11.30 (at 11.23 a.m., to be precise) she went to Copes fish shop near Gowan Avenue. Time was running a bit tight because she was due to attend a charity lunch with a friend in central London.

Gowan Avenue was not far from where I lived at the time, so before the trial I went there on a number of occasions to size up how Jill Dando's last moments could have occurred. The road is a narrow Victorian street of terraced houses with parking on both sides, and as I normally went on a bicycle there was no parking problem. But for a car it was usually difficult to find a space in which to park, and quite remarkably, after Jill had left the fish shop in her BMW, she arrived in Gowan Avenue to find a parking space immediately outside her house: the distance between her parked car and her front door was only a matter of feet. Each house has a tiny strip of front garden barely big enough to contain a dustbin. Richard Hughes next door heard the click of her car alarm, and very shortly after that a scream. Such a time lapse is incredibly difficult to quantify, but all the estimates placed it somewhere between ten and forty seconds. In that short time someone had appeared out of nowhere, walked up behind her, forced her down towards the front doorstep and, with the gun pressed against her head in 'hard contact' to muffle the sound, had shot her once, clinically and mercilessly, through the left side of her head.

You have to pause at this point to consider a number of significant questions. Whoever did this had to have been right there, out of sight, on the spot with a loaded gun, to have been able to reach Jill in the seconds it took her to lock her car and walk to her front door. Barry George did not drive and did not have a car, and there has never been any suggestion that he was driven to the scene by someone else. As everybody knows, he is very much a loner and suffers from severe epileptic seizures. He could not have known that

Jill was going to arrive that Monday morning at about 11.30 a.m., so had he been intent on shooting her that day he would have had to wait right outside number 29 for hours, and there was no evidence of anyone hanging about in a position to effect a precision killing within seconds. There had been controversial and hotly contested sightings of a man said to be George in a different part of Gowan Avenue much earlier in the morning (between an hour and a half and two hours before the killing). It's amazing who is at home on a weekday morning in a suburban street, alert to activity outside, and no one standing that close to number 29 for more than thirty minutes would have escaped the beady eyes of others.

There were two important witnesses to the crime scene itself: the next-door neighbour Richard Hughes and Geoffrey Upfill-Brown, who lived opposite. Both of them saw a man leaving the scene in a hurry, wearing what appeared to one of them to be a dark waxed jacket like a Barbour. Upfill-Brown was spotted by Hughes as he emerged from his house over the road. Both of these witnesses attended identification parades, but did not identify Barry George as the man they had seen.

The murderer managed to evade detection before and after the shooting. If you factor in the random nature of Jill Dando's arrival and the precise way in which the shooting was done, it begins to look like an operation far beyond that of an eccentric loner. What follows is speculation, but it is based on the parameters of circumstance I have already described.

It would have been possible for anyone planning this crime (as opposed to anyone happening along by chance) to have discovered that Jill Dando was in London, but not living at number 29. Her car could have been identified and followed on previous occasions without her realising it. Once this had been done, surveillance could have been mounted, with the anticipation that she would go to one of two base addresses. On the day in question it appears from all the enquiries and the CCTV footage that she was not followed, but this cannot be excluded altogether. Nevertheless the important information was the time at which she left Alan Farthing's address, and this could have been communicated by mobile phone to others and/or the gunman. This scenario entails more than one person being involved in the murder.

A strong possibility has to be that the perpetrator with the loaded weapon arrived earlier in the street in a vehicle, and remained in the vehicle unnoticed. Someone in a car merely sitting and waiting, even if noticed, could be mistaken for a minicab driver and pass from the memory. Afterwards he could either leave the scene in the same car or in another one that picked him up round the corner, since there was no further trace of the man seen leaving the scene by the two eyewitnesses.

The second feature which tends to support this thesis, and exclude Barry George, is what was found on the doorstep of number 29.

The first trial in 2001 was very high-profile. Jill Dando was a popular presenter and my client was a complicated loner; their worlds were oceans apart. Security was high. Occasionally at such murder trials the jury accompanies the judge and lawyers to the scene of the crime, so that they have it firmly in their mind's eye during the ensuing proceedings – this is called a 'view' – and when the jury in the Barry George trial was taken to Fulham to see the crime scene, I decided to cycle there while the rest travelled in an escorted coach. I arrived shortly after the others, to be met by a police cordon at one end of the road. Sporting my tracksuit and trainers, I suppose I didn't look much like a QC, and the police refused to let me through. There was no budging them, so knowing the stubborn mindset of some cops, I decided to cycle round to the other end of the road and join the view that way. Same problem: the police didn't recognise me (why should they?) or believe me, and again refused access. I was stuck – and then luckily I spotted the judge outside number 29 and waved frantically at him, with the result that the police reluctantly let me through.

A few days later, my opening speech to the jury was unusual in that I had written it down and I read it out. Normally I would not dream of doing this because you lose spontaneity and impact, and I had never done so before or since. But this case was finely and delicately balanced, and I wanted to be clear and concise. I began by pointing out that the case against Barry George hung by the slenderest of threads: a particle of firearms discharge residue (FDR) found in the inside pocket of an overcoat recovered a year later at his home address. This particle was measured in micron units, approximately one-hundredth of a millimetre in diameter, but had been at the heart of the Crown's case and provided the only direct link between Barry George and the crime scene. When a round is discharged or fired, the chemical ingredients in the primer fuse into metallic particles, and in this case some were recovered from Jill Dando's hair and analysed in order to determine the ingredients used for this particular bullet. There are three standard components – lead, barium and antimony – and these may be combined with other chemicals such as silicon and aluminium. Needless to say, you may only recover enough to determine one or two of these, but in this instance the prosecution scientist determined that the primer must have had the three basics plus aluminium.

During the trial we called as a defence witness Dr John Lloyd, who had helped me with the Birmingham Six and other cases, and I asked him this question: 'From a forensic-science point of view, what significance do you attach to the finding of one particle in this case?'

Lloyd answered:

There could scarcely be less residue at all. The presence of a single particle does raise serious doubts as to where it may have come from. It might have been something which is just a casual contamination. Some laboratories have in fact not reported findings as significant when so little residue is found. It should be said that in this case, this is the first occasion when it has been suggested that the single particle could be a relic of an event which has occurred a year ago, it is quite a unique suggestion ... The claims that it is so related are based on scientifically unsupported assumptions. The evidence is dependent on flawed police procedures. It is my view that this evidence is not reliable as evidence of the defendant's involvement in the shooting.[2]

Much of the trial had been taken up with the issue of contamination. This need not be explored any more, because after the second appeal (conducted by Bill Clegg, QC) this slender thread was broken and formed no part of the second trial. Barry George was free again.

This may close the chapter on Barry George being the gunman, but it does not close the book on the crime. Other material was found on the doorstep of number 29 besides FDR: there was a cartridge case and the bullet itself. The bullet would normally have rifling marks from its passage down the barrel of the gun – the interior of the barrel is scored spirally in order to increase accuracy – and if these marks are absent, it means that the gun the murderer used had a smooth bore. Yet so far as is known, no commercial manufacturer in the world makes a 9mm semi-automatic pistol with a smooth bore. A number of possibilities ensue, all of which entail specialist equipment, knowledge and expertise, none of which could be attributed to Barry George. The murder weapon could have been a blank-firing pistol that had been altered to fire real bullets; or a gun with a smooth barrel over twenty-four inches in length which had been shortened; or a handgun that had been deactivated to remove it from use after the ban on handguns, but then reactivated for illegal use. Modifications of the first and third kind require the barrel to be drilled and replaced with a piece of smooth metal tubing.

The cartridge case had the maker's mark stamped upon it: *R-P .380 auto*. R-P denotes an American manufacturer, Remington Peters. The experts could also infer that the use of a .380 round meant that the weapon used was a 'short' as opposed to a 'parabellum',[3] and that it was a 9mm-calibre handgun.

Usually it would be possible to derive further clues about the gun from markings that it would leave when the firing pin hit the end of the cartridge and when it was extracted from the gun by the ejector mechanism, but there were no sufficient markings left from which to make any sensible extrapolations. What there were, at the other end of the cartridge which held the bullet before it was discharged, were some very unusual markings, regarded by some as unique. It is not unusual for a cartridge case to be reused, housing another bullet: this is accomplished by employing a machine that leaves three identical pinch marks or indentations around the rim of the cartridge where it holds the bullet, and the term used to describe this process is 'crimping'. Here there were six crimp indentations, but not identical ones, as though they had been tapped in by hand. Because there were only faint markings of ejection on the casing, it was possible that this round had not been fired before – in which case it was difficult to understand why anybody would want to open it up and alter its composition in the first place. Alternatively, perhaps it had not been fired by an automatic at all, but by a custom-built device manufactured with specialist machines or tools.

Among the unused materials disclosed by the prosecution before the trial was a letter from a member of the public with military experience who was living in the south of England. He pointed out that manually crimped rounds were commonplace in his experience amongst the armies of the former Soviet bloc, which included the Balkans, Yugoslavia and Serbia in particular. We adduced this evidence through a defence witness, Major Mead.

The significance of all these points was that first, although Barry George had an interest in firearms, no murder weapon was found in his possession; no FDR was found on any surface or tools at his premises; there were no tools with markings that could be matched with the indentations; it was not shown that he had any knowledge of or expertise for carrying out this adaptation; and there were no documents among the many thousands of bits of paper found at his address that would have shown him how to do it.

Second, there was other material which gave support to the Serbian link. Three days before Jill Dando's murder, on 23 April, during the war with Serbia, NATO forces had attacked the headquarters of Serbian television, owned by Slobodan Milosevic, with a cruise missile that killed seventeen people. The day after Jill's murder the Chief Executive of BBC News, Tony Hall, received a telephoned death threat which declared: 'Because your government, and in particular your Prime Minister Blair, murdered, butchered seventeen innocent young people – he butchered, we butchered back. The first you had yesterday, the next one will be Tony Hall.'[4] Quite rightly, this was taken very seriously by the BBC, and personal security was stepped up for a number of senior executives.

With her image on the front cover of the *Radio Times* and the BBC's intention of making her one of the main presenters for their coverage of the millennium celebrations, Jill Dando had become a key part of the public face of the BBC. In addition she had already made a successful appeal on television for Kosovan refugees who had become part of the genocide or 'ethnic cleansing' carried out by the Milosevic regime (see Chapter 22). Hit-squads operated in Serbia – a couple of weeks before 26 April the owner of a newspaper that had criticised Milosevic was shot dead outside his home in Belgrade – and the police had intelligence from an anonymous source that a Serbian hit-squad had been dispatched to the United Kingdom. Originally this line of enquiry was dismissed by the police as far-fetched, partly because the intelligence they had from within the exiled Serbian community in London did not support it.

At the moment this material does not prove that it was a Serbian hit, but it does suggest a potential line of reinvestigation, especially in the light of the work being carried out by the court in The Hague, the International Criminal Tribunal for the former Yugoslavia (ICTY). It was this tribunal that tried Milosevic and other alleged war criminals, and which arrested Radovan Karadzic in the summer of 2008. A good starting place for tracking down the killer of Jill Dando might be to seek assistance from the seventy-five-year-old Serbian company manufacturing ammunition, Prvi Partizan.

Some months after I had completed the draft for this chapter, the London *Evening Standard* revealed that Scotland Yard is to interview three witnesses about a confession by a West Midlands petty criminal of Serbian descent. It is claimed that he told people in the Portobello Bar in Belgrade in September 2001 that he had killed Jill Dando in retaliation for the death of a Serbian TV personality during NATO bombing raids on Belgrade.[5]

THE NEED TO KNOW

The Marchioness *Disaster, the*
Murder of Stephen Lawrence

When, as a small boy, I stood on the footbridge spanning Oakleigh Park station and thrilled to the sensation of the *Mallard* or *Flying Scotsman* thundering past directly beneath me, I often found myself wondering what would happen to such titans of the track if their brakes didn't work, or the old-fashioned mechanical signals failed, or a wooden sleeper was loose or out of place.

As we all know, the last twenty years have seen several major tragedies on the rail network. Two of these, at Potters Bar and Hatfield, were on the very line that ran through Oakleigh Park, while the other places whose names will for ever be synonymous with railway catastrophe include Clapham, Southall and Paddington. But tragedy is plainly not limited to one form of transport, or to man-made causes. Natural disasters – such as flash floods, tsunamis, earthquakes, fires, droughts, tornadoes, some of which are no doubt provoked by global warming – affect every corner of the world.

And when these disasters take place, there is a desperate need to know. What happened? How did it happen? Why did it happen? Who bears responsibility? These are not academic questions: they are vital in helping grieving relatives and friends to achieve some form of inner reconciliation, and ultimately closure, and they are vital in bringing reassurance to the wider public and in minimising the chances of recurrence.

It is one thing to agree about the need to know. It is quite another to get answers from institutions, corporations and government departments – and usually a mammoth task. Given the centrist cabinet-run democracy we currently endure, it is a vain hope that leaving matters to politicians will get you far, and what I have learned, more than almost anything else over the last forty years, is that progress is brought about by the extraordinary efforts of ordinary groups of families, friends and individuals – who care the most, who fight for what is right and who initiate change. They occupy the moral high ground, and their courageous stand benefits us all. None of us should ever sit back and think there is nothing we can do.

There have been two effective forums in which crucial questions can be asked of the very people who often remain invisible, or at least in the shadows: one is the inquest, the other the judicial public inquiry, and the latter often results from issues raised in the former, which is what happened with both the *Marchioness* disaster on the River Thames in 1989 and with the racist murder of Stephen Lawrence in 1993. The product of these processes is enormous, and has far-reaching repercussions for the safety of the public at large.

I recognise that there are times when lawyers are surplus to requirements or even get in the way – although I wouldn't go as far as Shakespeare in *Henry VI, Part 2*: 'The first thing we do, let's kill all the lawyers.' But inquests and inquiries are not such occasions, for there is such a painful emotional charge that it can be difficult for those most affected to compose their thoughts coherently and formulate all the questions they would like asked. And if there is more than one person involved, there is likely to be a difference of opinion about what the questions should be, and about the general strategy. This is only to be expected when people from varied and disparate backgrounds are thrown together by the chance of the disaster itself, and it is then important to ensure that everyone pulls in the same direction. This can be facilitated by focusing on a common purpose and in particular a common target, and it is usually not difficult to create an enduring bond, though in rare cases where the differences between affected people are insurmountable, separate representation is necessary.

A brief word about the nature of an inquest. There is a real lack of understanding of the English system of holding inquests, manifested most starkly during those held in 2007–9 into the deaths of Princess Diana and Dodi Fayed (see Chapter 18). The inquest is unique in English law, because it is inquisitorial rather than adversarial, which means that a judicial figure runs the whole show from beginning to end, from the moment that the body or bodies of the deceased arrive within his jurisdiction to the moment when a verdict is returned.

An inquest is not a trial: no one is in the dock; no civil or criminal liability can be determined; there are no parties to the proceedings, only interested persons. The coroner decides what evidence to adduce, either by live witnesses or by documentation, while the representatives of interested persons have no right to call anybody and only have a right to ask questions. This is the kernel of the exercise: it is a genuine search for the truth, exploring all the possibilities – those raised by the family as well as those canvassed by commentators in the public arena – and all kinds of perfectly legitimate and honestly held beliefs should be examined by the coroner. Unlike in criminal and civil litigation, the lawyers representing the various interested persons do not have an obligation to put a particular case, but on the basis of the available material they do have an obligation to ensure that every reasonable avenue is pursued. Beyond asking questions and making representations about the law, the lawyers are not allowed to make opening or closing speeches, which are entirely within the remit of the coroner alone.

What is often forgotten is that the coroner has an obligation to hold an inquest when he has reasonable cause to suspect that the deceased died a violent or unnatural death; died a sudden death of which the cause is unknown; or died in prison or in such a place or in such circumstances as to require an inquest. The coroner also has to summon a jury if at any stage he has reason to suspect the death was in prison or police custody; was caused by an accident at work; or occurred in circumstances the continuance or possible recurrence of which is prejudicial to the health and safety of the public (even if this has happened abroad).[1]

When the tabloid press thinks it knows the answer to a suspicious death and that therefore there is no need to have an inquest, it is wrong. In the circumstances outlined above an inquest is a legal requirement, and if anyone from those newspapers had suffered like the families I have met, they too would be shouting from the rafters for a proper inquiry.

The inquest is steeped in history, its roots going back to at least 1194 with the Articles of Eyre or Assize, which empowered the coroner to look after the interests of the Crown on a peripatetic basis. Originally all inquests had to have a jury, and it is not difficult to see that were the jury-based system to be used expeditiously and courageously, it would have the potential for satisfying the paramount need for justice. (In recent years this has been demonstrated most clearly by the Oxford coroner Andrew Walker, in his enquiries concerning military deaths in Iraq.)

While all this theory is fine, in practice there have been substantial impediments to getting legal representation, especially for families, the main one of which has been a lack of public funding, because for some completely unfathomable reason, until fairly recently it was not thought important enough for families to receive this kind of help. Nearly every other organisation is funded – the police, the military, medical, local-authority and public corporations and, for that matter, private companies – but families have to be supported on a voluntary basis, and for most of my forty years as a lawyer the majority of inquests I have undertaken have been pro bono – that is, *pro bono publico*, 'for the public good' – which means that I do it for free, as I have always been prepared to do when there is no funding. Since 1981 a voluntary organisation called INQUEST has provided invaluable and incalculable practical advice and support to bereaved families, despite having to walk an economic tightrope, with the threat of closure at every step.[2]

On 20 August 1989 fifty-one people were killed when the pleasure-boat *Marchioness*, which had been hired as a disco boat for a private party, sank on the River Thames near Southwark Bridge, run over – literally – by a nautical juggernaut in the form of a dredger named the *Bowbelle*, which plied its trade between the North Sea and Battersea and which, in my view, should not have been on the river in the first place. In order to maximise its economic viability and profit, it was essential for the dredger to catch all the right tides, which might entail a tight turnaround time and a departure downriver at night. At 262 feet (not far short of the length of a football pitch), the *Bowbelle* was hugely long to be plying that stretch of the Thames, and had no proper visibility over the bow or adequate communication system. The Master was situated on a bridge at the stern, while a lookout was positioned at the bow, and if something in the way was spotted, the lookout had to wave or shout. Given the *Bowbelle*'s size, tonnage (gross 1,472 tons) and speed (average 8.5 knots through the water on the basis of a 3-knot tide),[3] stopping within a few feet could not be accomplished, and so the consequences of it coming across another craft in its way were potentially horrendous.

The *Marchioness* disaster raised a large number of questions about the management of the River Thames. There had been previous collisions on the river between Battersea and London Bridge, and there had been earlier reports about deficiencies in visibility, so in one sense this was an accident waiting to happen, and it was also clear that much greater provision for rescue and assistance was urgently required, because many people were left stranded in the water.

An internal inquiry was set up under the Marine Accident Investigation Bureau, but this did not allow the families proper representation or means of eliciting the facts of what had happened, and its conclusions were unsatisfactory. Fobbed off with bland platitudes, the families were being stymied at every twist and turn, and perhaps most upsetting was the refusal to let many of the families see the victims' bodies, because the hands of twenty-five of the deceased had been cut off 'for identification purposes' – a macabre and unjustified act that characterised years of official prevarication.[4]

On two occasions the Captain of the *Bowbelle*, Douglas Henderson, faced charges. Both times the jury was deadlocked, and eventually he was formally acquitted. Neither Henderson nor the company that owned and operated the *Bowbelle* incurred any penalty.

Once a criminal charge is laid, the inquest is adjourned pending the outcome. It is possible for a coroner subsequently not to resume the inquest, if he decides the relevant issues have been given due consideration during the criminal process. The first coroner, Dr Paul Knapman, did refuse to reopen the inquests, but was overturned on appeal and a different coroner, Dr John Burton, took over.

My initial involvement arose at this stage when, on behalf of Ivor Glogg, whose wife Ruth had perished on the *Marchioness*, I attempted to mount a private prosecution against the company that owned the *Bowbelle*. Despite a very sympathetic hearing at Bow Street Magistrates' Court this action also failed, due to the shortcomings in the law relating to corporate manslaughter: you had to be able to pin responsibility onto the 'brains' of the company by showing that such a person had actual knowledge of what was going on, and since there was no obligation on the company to disclose its records, it was virtually impossible to show who knew what, when.

It was not until the inquest was resumed in 1994 that the families could begin to see results. Although Dr Burton was known for his mercurial and quirky habits, he allowed the relatives full rein to express their anguish and their proposals for change. He also had the good sense to transfer the hearings from a tiny coroner's court to the copious council chamber in Hammersmith Town Hall, and each morning we would all foregather in a consultation room to thrash out that day's questions and tactics. Some relatives were always early, others always late, some combatant, others passive; but all were devoted to seeing justice done. The solicitor, who carried their burden from the early days and long before I came on the scene, was Louise Christian, whom I have known for many years as a fearlessly outspoken comrade and friend. Tireless and conscious of the political dimensions inherent in such cases, she also represented many families who had been involved in the Paddington, Southall and Potters Bar rail disasters, and gave everyone with whom she dealt momentum and inspiration. And my junior Terry Munyard was unstinting in his support and ability to empathise with the stresses and strains felt by the families.

Preparing them to give evidence in the witness box, to relive their experiences, to voice their misgivings and where necessary to vent their anger had to be carried out with meticulous care. Whether at an inquest or a trial, lawyers are not allowed to suggest what clients may say, but they can give straightforward guidance about what questions to expect; about the need to listen and reply carefully; about the importance of speaking more slowly and clearly than in everyday conversation. Not everyone wanted to say their piece at the *Marchioness* inquest, but those who did were utterly moving and compelling.

At an inquest, even the verdict is unusual. Strictly, it has to be expressed in answer to four questions: who was the deceased? Where, when and finally, how did he or she die? And it is the fourth 'how' question that gives rise to controversy and more extensive enquiry, as it is not restricted to the immediate cause of death, but encompasses 'by what means and in what circumstances'. So, for example, in the case of the *Marchioness* the immediate cause was drowning, but the more important issue was what had caused the drowning and the collision. For ease of reference, there is a 'short-form verdict' which summarises the broad conclusions: accident, unlawful killing, lawful killing, suicide or open – with various 'forms' or versions, such as unlawful killing/murder, manslaughter, gross negligence, etc. After 2000 and the introduction of the Human Rights Act, the jury at an inquest can in addition be invited by the coroner to answer various questions on the facts of the case. This is known as a 'narrative' verdict.

At the *Marchioness* inquest the jury found that it was an unlawful killing, not murder but manslaughter, and went on to recommend a large number of improvements for river safety. This was a real victory for the collective spirit among the families, and the papers were sent to the Director of Public Prosecutions for reappraisal. No further prosecution was authorised – no surprises there – but our battle seemed far from over.

The families relentlessly pressed their case for a judicial public inquiry, to cover the ground from which inquests are precluded – in this case systemic failure well beyond the actions of the *Bowbelle* itself – and in response there was all the obfuscation and delay of the kind with which everybody is so familiar: 'There has been an internal inquiry, two attempted prosecutions and an inquest, so what more do you want? . . . The cost is too great . . . We have to move on; let's not reopen old wounds . . .', and so on.

But none of this put the families off their objective, and there was no let-up in their regular meetings with government ministers and with anyone who could be persuaded of the rectitude of their arguments. Ultimately they did convince the government, which in February 2000 announced two inquiries: one into river safety, the other into the *Bowbelle* collision, which was held at the Methodist Central Hall, Westminster, under Lord Justice Clarke, who oversaw a model of efficiency, clarity and alacrity.

This was a weird experience for me, since the venue had singularly strong childhood memories. It's an imposing building with a striking baroque dome, tucked away behind Parliament Square. Every year between the ages of eight and fourteen I was bused in to attend an

annual rally of Crusader Bible classes from all over the country. It was
a brilliant opportunity to rush about exploring the maze of corridors,
stairs and basements – one of which was the largest air-raid shelter
in the Second World War. My class was in Woodside Park in North
Finchley and I attended religiously every Sunday afternoon: my
parents were anxious to keep me off the streets and out of Dollis Brook,
which was in general terms the object of its founder, a missionary
who spotted the need for his services in around 1900 while tramping
the streets of Crouch End, where I ended up living in the 1970s. He
called his mission 'Crusaders' – a term that many of my recent clients
would find disturbing, given the 200 years of brutality perpetrated
under this banner during the eleventh and twelfth centuries.

A few years before my evangelical escapades in the Hall, the
inaugural meeting of the United Nations General Assembly was
held there in 1946. Fifty-odd years later it was time for the Captain
of the *Bowbelle*, Master Henderson, to explain his behaviour in
far more detail than previously, but at last we also had a chance to
confront the company managers. Robert Samuel was the General
Manager of South Coast Shipping, and from 1985 was the designated
officer ashore, with responsibility for monitoring the technical and
safety aspects of the company's trade. Given that aspect of his role,
I wanted to discover how much he knew about the history of the
Bow fleet, particularly on the stretch of river between Nine Elms in
Battersea at least as far as Tower Bridge. If he didn't know about this
history, why not? And if he did, the really important question was:
what had he done to investigate the causes and prevent a repetition?
My chance soon arrived:

Question, MICHAEL MANSFIELD: Did you know by 1988 at least
this, that there had been a collision between two Bow vessels on
the river in November 1987, one of which was in fact the *Bowbelle*?
Did you know that?
Answer, ROBERT SAMUEL: Yes.
Q: Yes. Was it a navigational problem or not?
A: It was a navigational or lookout problem.

This of course was one of the principal issues of concern. In
February 1988, a few months after the 1987 incident and on the

same stretch of river as the *Marchioness* disaster, the *Bowbelle* had struck Southwark Bridge, the very bridge with which the inquest was concerned. And Mr Samuel said that he did know about that. Later in 1988 another vessel in the same fleet, *Bowsprite*, although not on the River Thames, went down with the loss of life off the Belgian coast. Mr Samuel claimed that it was not his responsibility. I pressed the matter further:

Q: Once you are aware of these three separate incidents, and by the end of 1988, as we know, you're responsible for safety, were not bells beginning to ring in your mind about the integrity of the Bow fleet?
A: In what respect are you referring to?
Q: Well, is it a safe fleet? Collision on the river between two vessels, a collision between one of the same vessels and a bridge, and now another one sinks with the loss of life off the Belgian coast. That's quite a lot within one year, is it not?
A: As I explained earlier, with regard to the tragic loss of the *Bowsprite*, to this day we do not know why the vessel sank. We do not know why the hull split in two. This is after considerable exploratory work carried out by the Department.
Q: Did you after December 1988 say, 'I'm going to take the initiative as the *Merchant Notice 1188* suggests, initiatives should come from the top'? Do you agree?
A: I agree.
Q: Did you take an initiative at the top and say, 'Right, I want a full and thorough review of navigation and safety on these vessels on my desk within four weeks'? Did you do anything like that?
A: Not specifically. No.

There were in fact a large number of other incidents that cumulatively provided a catalogue of disaster – between 1981 and 1989 nine incidents involving the Bow fleet and collisions with either passenger vessels or bridges, or both – and as I went through each one, it became clear that Mr Samuel knew little or nothing about any of them save the ones mentioned above. It followed that not a great deal had been done to make proper assessments about the safety of the fleet as a whole.

There were some fairly remarkable exchanges relating to specific areas of concern, including the matter of the Master of the *Bowbelle*:

Q: Had you known that on the night Mr Henderson had consumed at least six pints of beer before going back on duty, what would have been your reaction to that at the time if you'd known?
A: He would have been disciplined.
Q: He would have been disciplined? He would have known that at the time, would he, that if in fact he was found to have been onshore drinking that he would have been disciplined? He would have known that?
A: Yes.
Q: Yes. So it demonstrates, at least, he was quite prepared to run the risk of a disciplinary proceeding for drinking, does it not?
A: That can be assumed, yes.
Q: It is a shocking indictment that the captain of the vessel on the night was prepared to run that risk, is it not?
A: Yes.
Q: Put generally, is it right that you expected crews at that time not to leave the vessel while it was docked at Nine Elms, or what was the position?
A: That would be the case. Yes. The standing orders refer specifically to that.
Q: So it's not just a case of drinking. It's also the case that they were in breach of the general policy that they should not leave the vessel at Nine Elms?
A: Yes.

One of the most important questions was of course the extent to which the Master could see beyond the fo'c'sle and bow, onto the surface of the distant water, in order to avoid a collision.

Q: Were you aware before the collision how substantially impaired visibility was from the wheelhouse of the *Bowbelle*?
A: The vision from the bridge was not perfect, agreed.
Q: Well, would that not be regarded as the understatement of the century? It was not only not very good; it was substantially impaired, was it not?

A: It was impaired.

Q: Yes. Substantially – on a river – impaired, was it not?

A: It was impaired. You have to define substantially, I am afraid.

Q: Oh yes, I will. How badly impaired was it? Did you know, for example, that it was three times over what it should have been in terms of blind distances ahead? [That is, the distance of surface water beyond the bow obscured from the view of the wheelhouse.] Did you know that?

A: That, I believe, relates to the trim of the vessel.

Q: That is right. Did you know that at the time?

A: Not at that time. No.

Q: No. In addition to the trim, of course, is the dredging gear on the deck itself. You knew that impaired vision, did you?

A: Yes.

Q: How far ahead did you think, therefore, leaving aside the trim at the moment, in normal conditions could the Master see something on the water surface? A ship's length, two ships' lengths?

A: It is something I did not address.

Q: So how do you know, when you say you're not prepared to accept it was substantially impaired, if you have not addressed it? You do not know then, do you, what the kind of impairment was?

A: Put that way, that is correct.

Q: Why did you not know?

A: I did not know.

A little further on I finally reached the key point about the lookouts:

Q: Did you know there was no lookout system on the *Bowbelle*?

A: The evidence suggests there was a system of lookout on the *Bowbelle*.

Q: Does it? May I just summarise it to you? Captain Henderson did not know who the lookout was that night. Mr Blayney [a member of the crew] said he wasn't the lookout that night, he was the 'look about'. The next person on the fo'c'sle said that he certainly wasn't the lookout, but he thought Blayney was. Is that a system, Mr Samuel?

In answer to this and a number of other specifics, Samuel's response was mainly to the effect that as he wasn't on the ship that night, he really didn't know.

The findings of the inquiry were telling:

> The striking feature of the various reports, minutes and letters that followed the 1983 collisions is that almost without exception they anticipated the navigational and operational factors which played a part in the collision that eventually occurred in 1989.[5]

Another conclusion was that the panel did not think that Mr Samuel 'can have been designated as (or in fact regarded himself at the time as) the designated person with responsibility for safety . . . because he had no relevant expertise'.[6]

Most importantly, the main conclusion was that the collision was the result of a failure by both vessels, the *Bowbelle* and *Marchioness*, to keep a satisfactory lookout procedure.

> That failure to keep a proper lookout was the responsibility of the Master of the *Bowbelle*, Captain Henderson, the skipper of the *Marchioness*, Mr [Stephen] Faldo, the owners and managers of the *Bowbelle* (East Coast Aggregates and South Coast Shipping) and the owners and managers of the *Marchioness*.[7]

At the end of the public inquiry in 2002, Lord Justice Clarke magnanimously – as this is not a course usually permitted during the final stages of submissions – allowed one of the families to address him personally.

Eileen Dallaglio, the mother of Lawrence (of England rugby fame), but also of the youngest victim, Lawrence's sister Francesca, a nineteen-year-old with a bubbly personality and a bright future in ballet, was struggling to cope with the cruel loss of her child. Eileen summarised the feelings of everyone who had been touched by the tragedy in an eloquent, powerful, personal plea:

> 'As we approach the twelfth Christmas without our children, our brothers and sisters, our family and friends, we ask this investigation to begin the process of fundamental change in

legislation, which still allows the sector of corporate greed to overshadow responsibility and accountability. Never again must companies such as Ready Mixed Concrete, East Coast Aggregates, South Coast Shipping and Tidal Cruisers be allowed to operate their vessels along English waters and the high seas with complete and utter disregard for the safety of the general public at large. Never again must companies be allowed to fail us, the general public, by allowing inexperienced personnel with substandard intelligence, inherent drink problems, forged certificates; thereby perverting the course of justice over eleven years and [with] total disregard for the safe operation of their vessels. Never again must managing directors appoint themselves designated safety officers without any experience of such matters. They have to know that they will be held accountable both in criminal and civil law.'

Tirelessly pursuing justice, she addressed the Home Affairs and Work and Pensions Committees at the House of Commons in 2005:

'I am Eileen Dallaglio. I am a founder-member of Disaster Action, a founder-member of the Marchioness Action Group, and currently with the Marchioness Contact Group. The aims have always been very clear . . . We want some peace from this disaster and we want to make sure that this Bill for corporate accountability and corporate responsibility is pushed through Parliament . . .'[8]

In practical terms a great deal has been achieved by this historic struggle. It contributed to the momentum for a Corporate Manslaughter and Corporate Homicide Act following sixteen years in which successive governments dragged their feet. On the river there is now a Royal National Lifeboat Station, with dedicated rescue craft able to lift survivors easily and directly out of the water. These craft can travel at great speed and reach most parts of the tidal Thames within ten to fifteen minutes. New grab-chains have been placed on the banks; more life jackets, life rafts and belts are on shore and on river boats. Furniture on boats is supposed to be secured to the deck; the stern of each boat should have a large, yellow, luminous reflective square; all bridges should have illumination from beneath. I now use the Thames regularly to commute by river bus from

Putney to Blackfriars, and I am acutely aware of, and thankful for, the improvements that have been brought about by people who should not have had to fight for so many years for these simple remedies. Eileen died in 2008, and I just hope she knew how much she had contributed and achieved.

Having the chance to represent people at inquests and inquiries has been one of the most rewarding and purposeful experiences I have had, and none more so than the years I spent with Neville and Doreen Lawrence after the death of their son Stephen. As with the *Marchioness*, the Stephen Lawrence case was to bring about far-reaching changes to institutional mindsets that had atrophied over many decades.

Born on 13 September 1974, Stephen was the eldest son, and from an early age he apparently slept little, but was full of creativity, energy and life: he was a good athlete and an enthusiastic supporter of Arsenal. Soon the Lawrence family had grown, and Stephen had a brother, Stuart, and a sister, Georgina.

An extrovert who liked to look stylish, Stephen was not perfect (according to his mother), but he was caring and political, and insisted on going on the protest march against the violent racism that had killed Rolan Adams in Thamesmead in 1991 – the same racism which killed Rohit Duggal in Well Hall Road in 1992 and injured Gurdeep Bhangal in Eltham High Street in 1993.

By then Stephen was eighteen, exerting his independence and railing at the normal constraints of family life. He was studying A Levels at Woolwich College and his lifelong ambition to be an architect seemed not such a distant dream. Doreen herself was studying for a Humanities degree, and Neville, unable to get work as a plasterer due to a downturn in the building trade, was helping in the house and looking after the kids.

On 22 April 1993, Doreen returned home at about 9 p.m. from a short field trip to Birmingham. It was natural for Stephen to be out until about 10.30 p.m. on weekdays, but this evening, instead of the sound of a key in the door, came a knock. It was the Lawrences' neighbours, the Shepherds: their son Joey had been at the same bus stop as Stephen and had seen him and his friend Duwayne Brooks being attacked by four or five white boys.

Within a few hours Doreen and Neville were being shown the body of their eldest son, who had been knifed to death: it gradually emerged that, in an unprovoked attack, Stephen had been brutally murdered by a gang of five white racist thugs.

Within minutes of the assault, names were being circulated in Eltham – the same names of local youths known in the community for their notorious racist attitudes and aggression. Within the first twenty-four hours a man whose real identity was known to the police walked into Plumstead police station; it was Friday 23 April at 7.45 p.m. He was given the pseudonym 'James Grant'. The information he provided was regarded by the Macpherson Inquiry as the most important of all. What he told the police was recorded in Message 40:

A male attended 'RM' [Plumstead] and stated that the persons responsible for the murder of the black youth, are Jamie and Neil Acourt of 102 Bournbrook Road SE3 together with David Norris and 2 other males identity unknown. That the Acourt Brothers call themselves 'The Krays'. In fact you can only join their gang if you stab someone. They carry knives and weapons most days. Also, David Norris stabbed a Stacey Benefield a month ago in order to prove himself. Benefield was taken to the Brook Hospital and told police he didn't know who assaulted him. He then went on to say that a young Pakistani boy was murdered last year in Well Hall, that Peter Thompson who is serving life was part of the Acourts gang. That in fact one of the Acourts killed this lad. They also stabbed a young lad at Woolwich town centre called 'Lee'. He had a bag placed over his head and was stabbed in his legs and arms in order to torture him. Jamie is described as white, 17 years, about 5' 9", black hair, medium build. Neil is described as white, also 17 years, about 5' 5", black hair, stocky build. Both are 'twins', apparently the house they live in was occupied by their mum, who has since left. Believed identity of informant established.[9]

Similar information was also provided in a detailed letter left in a phone box in Eltham on the same day:

The people involved in last night's stabbing are:
1. Neil Acourt, 2. David Norris, 3. Jamie Acourt, 4. Gary Dobson.

Names 1 and 2 are also rumoured with Wimpy bar stabbing (Eltham).

Name 1 was definitely seen in the area prior to stabbing.

Names 2 and 1 are ringleaders and are positive knife users.

Names 1, 2, 3 share house in Bourne Brook Rd, Kidbrooke.

Name 4 lives in Phineas Pett Rd.

One of these names stabbed that poor lad.

The names 1 and 2 are very dangerous knife users who always carry knives and quite like using them.

Names 1 and 2 have stabbed before. Stacey Benefield was their victim about 6 weeks ago. He lives in Purneys Road off Rochester Way.

These bastards were definitely involved and must be stopped because they keep getting away with it.

This is not a BNP related incident. (You must stress this.)

Approach these shits with care. Do us all a favour and pursue it. Good Luck.[10]

Anonymous callers also gave the Lawrences the names of Gary Dobson and the Acourts, one of whose mates, David Norris, was also named time after time, and a short while later Luke Knight's name was added to the list of suspects. But the Brook Estate where some of them lived was not sealed off: there were no police roadblocks that night, no house-to-house questioning or searches.

Jamie and Neil Acourt were not visited by the police until four days later, by which time clothes had been washed and vital forensic evidence destroyed. Their house was being watched intermittently by a civilian photographer on his own (with no mobile phone or means of communication with the police station), and one photo showed Neil leaving with a black sack, containing who-knows-what evidence being taken away and disposed of. The next day another photograph showed Jamie doing the same, but still the police did not intervene – not, that is, until it was too late.

It is recognised throughout the police force that there is a precious period of time after a murder known as the 'golden hour', which does not mean literally one hour, but usually connotes a period of about twenty-four hours within which it is crucial to follow up leads, particularly forensic ones, before the trail goes cold and vital clues evaporate.

The police signally failed to follow up speedily, or develop, the intelligence provided by 'James Grant'. One of his handlers was DS John Davidson, who was described in the Macpherson Report as 'a self-willed and abrasive officer who more than once became excited and angry in the witness box'.[11] This occurred during my cross-examination. Davidson's nickname among the police was 'OJ', which stood for 'Objectionable Jock'. He claimed to have registered Grant as an informant, but no documents proving this exist. Yet Grant's source was a crucial one: a young man told him he had seen the Acourts and the others in their house that night, all with wet hair, claiming they had taken a bath together, and yet there was no attempt to find the young man for over a week.

Certain officers stalled and prevaricated. Notes were lost, witnesses mismanaged. There was a calculated indifference which at the public inquiry led me to accuse the police of 'gross negligence, or worse'.

Why? We were never able to 'prove' it, but the relationship between certain police officers and these known criminal families – particularly the Norris clan – was not a healthy one. A woman caller had described them as the 'Krays' and told of the stabbing of Stacey Benefield, who had been too frightened of the gang to complain to the police, but bravely came forward after Stephen's murder and identified Norris and one of the Acourts as the two who had stabbed him.

On 7 May 1993 – more than two weeks after the murder of Stephen Lawrence – the five were finally arrested. The inquest, as is routine, was adjourned once this happened.

The Lawrences' dedicated solicitor was Imran Khan, whom I now consider a close friend and colleague. He's *almost* as handsome as the ex-cricketer turned political campaigner of the same name, and is certainly as committed and stalwart in his opposition to injustice, while approaching everything and everyone with good grace and humour – and he takes on so much that I'm not sure when he sleeps.

Imran briefed me early on in the Lawrence case, and I agreed to be involved, because for many years I had represented black families and he felt that my experience might be useful. But as always in the early stages of a case, I had no real idea where this was going. Was it just another murder – all too common in London – or was it going to reveal some lingering long-term malaise?

While the Lawrences were still in Jamaica, where they had gone to bury Stephen, they were dealt a huge blow with the news from the Crown Prosecution Service (CPS) on 29 July that they were dropping the charges against the five suspects for 'lack of sufficient evidence'. This was an enormous setback for the family, and for the campaign that had grown up around them, and there were immediate calls for a public inquiry. The police were hugely resistant to this, and decided on an internal inquiry instead under Detective Chief Superintendent John Barker. They clearly resented a black family 'interfering' by harnessing the media and drawing supporters like Nelson Mandela to their cause.

The police also seemed over-diligent in discrediting the key witness to the murder, Duwayne Brooks. In the autumn of 1993 he had attended a protest meeting outside the British National Party (BNP) headquarters in Welling and – by then deeply frustrated by the inability of the police to move against the five suspects – had hurled a missile as well as abuse. Out of the hundreds involved that day, only six people were charged, and Duwayne was one of them. The police pursued him with vigour and resolve right up to trial (had they showed a similar vigour in pursuit of Stephen's murderers, things might have been very different) and the CPS, showing no compassion for the trauma that Duwayne had been through when witnessing his friend's murder, had refused to drop the case against him on public-interest grounds. Meanwhile he was rapidly being designated 'an unreliable witness'.

The police reappraisal of the handling of the case – the Barker Review – continued. The Lawrences complied fully and voiced their concerns at the way in which the case had been handled: the focus on Stephen and his friends, instead of on the named suspects; the stalling over the searches and arrests; and the indifference shown by the police liaison officers. Doreen and Neville felt that perhaps at last they were being heard, but in November the press reported that the review had found that 'the investigation had been progressed satisfactorily and all lines of inquiry correctly pursued'. In fact the Metropolitan Police implied that the team had been under 'undue pressure from outside influences'. This is correct: they *had* been called to account by two parents and their supporters, who were trying to get at the truth. But the phrase 'undue pressure' was an insult to the Lawrences and their campaign, and made us all the more determined to get a public hearing and scrutiny of the real evidence.

Legally there had to be an inquest, as in any suspicious or unusual death, but there is no legal aid for the victim's family, so Imran and I took on the case pro bono, and the inquest opened at Southwark Coroner's Court on 21 December 1993. I had advised the Lawrences that it would be best if it were adjourned, so that any potential future prosecution would not be prejudiced by the information canvassed, and fortunately the coroner agreed.

Meanwhile the police were supposed to be continuing the investigation, with various officers involved: Detective Chief Superintendent Bill Ilsley, Chief Superintendent John Philpott and Detective Superintendent Brian Weeden, who was the senior investigating officer. Doreen felt the racism coming from many of the officers, and their irritation at her determination. They hid behind the 'wall of silence' they claimed had surrounded the case, but there was no such wall. The community had come forward from day one, and it was the brick wall of police obduracy that was the main problem.

Around the same time, David Norris was charged with the attempted murder of Stacey Benefield. Clifford Norris (David's father), known to be a big-time criminal involved in drugs and wanted by Customs and Excise, had supposedly been on the run for many years – whereas in fact he'd been living comfortably, untroubled by the law, in a Sussex oast-house cottage. According to the Macpherson Report, there was undoubtedly evidence of corruption, or attempted corruption, of a vital witness in the Stacey Benefield stabbing case. The strong inference is that Clifford Norris was behind that corruption and that he was closely involved in trying to pervert the course of justice by bribing Stacey Benefield and another witness involved in the case, named Matthew Farman.[12]

The trial of David Norris started at the Central Criminal Court on 15 November 1993. Towards the end of the case one of the jurors – the foreman, as it turned out – approached the chauffeur or escort for Norris, no doubt arranged by his father, and assured him the verdict would be one of not guilty. Although the matter was reported, no application was made to discharge the juror in question or to ask for a fresh trial. The juror was in fact awaiting trial himself on charges of fraud and handling a stolen cheque worth £23,000. David Norris was acquitted, and the Norris family continued their cosseted lives, leaving Stacey Benefield without justice.

By now Yvette had approached the Lawrences about making a documentary about the case, but they were very reticent as they didn't want to be seen to be exploiting Stephen's death in any way (even though there was no financial gain to be had from participating in such a venture). Good publicity is often the vehicle for change, and soon they realised that the documentary might be a way of getting their version of events across.

However, it was not to prove that simple, as no TV channel would commission a film. Yvette's company was well known by this time for its hard-hitting, award-winning films, but this case was considered too hot to handle. It seems incredible now, given the amount of media attention the case eventually generated, but at the beginning no one wanted to know. BBC's *Panorama* finally decided to fund an initial couple of days' research and filming, to see if the idea 'had legs', and Martin Bashir was assigned to the story, but suddenly the BBC withdrew, with an explanation that the 'suspects' might not get a fair trial. Later it appeared that Bashir had a more pressing story to follow, an exclusive interview with Diana, Princess of Wales – and later still he was the only British journalist to interview some of the five suspects for ITV and give them airtime. I considered this behaviour shameful.

It was not until 1996 that Robin Gutch of Channel 4 agreed to commission an hour-long documentary, and I remember the first long interview on camera that Doreen and Neville Lawrence ever gave, conducted by Yvette. It was painful for Stephen's parents to have to relive the awful events of the night he died, but they were as honest and dignified as they have always shown themselves to be. When I came into the room at the end of the filming, I found Yvette in floods of tears. For some reason, she had asked Doreen off-camera when Stephen's birthday was, and was told that it was 13 September, the same date as our son Freddy's. This has always made me feel a deeper connection to Stephen – not very logical, I appreciate, but somehow a link that made my involvement all the more poignant. The finished film, named *The Stephen Lawrence Story*, managed to be both incredibly moving and properly analytical.

Two days before the first anniversary of the murder, Paul Condon, then Commissioner of the Metropolitan Police, finally agreed to meet the Lawrences, after which he reluctantly instigated a reinvestigation under a new team headed by Commander Perry

Nove, who kept us informed of events and reinvigorated the process. Detective Chief Inspector John Carnt took over day-to-day operations, while Detective Superintendent William Mellish became senior investigating officer when Brian Weeden retired. Quite rapidly, given that he'd reputedly been 'on the run' for over four years, Clifford Norris was arrested after being found at his home in possession of a couple of pistols and a sub-machine gun. (Nice people, the Norrises.) He got eight years.

Suddenly a great deal of information came to light. Jamie had kicked a black kid down some stairs at his school, then kept kicking him until he was unconscious; Neil had threatened another black boy with a knife at his throat; David and Jamie had stabbed and beaten up two brothers called Witham in Chislehurst: David Norris had been charged, but the CPS dropped the case six weeks before Stephen died, on the grounds of 'staleness'.

By 1994 Neville and Doreen (or Deville and Noreen, as I too often inadvertently called them) were desperately frustrated by the failings of the criminal-justice system. They felt strongly that there was a real lack of vigour and enthusiasm, and so – even if it might be considered novel and overstretching the bounds of normal practice – they both wanted to set a new agenda, with refreshed pace. It was in these circumstances, and after much soul-searching, that we decided to mount a private prosecution. This was both extraordinarily rare and risky, for while such a course had occasionally been taken before, those who had succeeded could be counted on the fingers of one hand. The principal risks were that we would have to rely on the resources of the police to help our investigation and to preserve exhibits; that witnesses might not cooperate; and that, at the end of it all, the Attorney General might step in and enter what is known as *nolle prosequi* ('no prosecution beyond this'). On top of all this was the question of public funding, which could not be assumed to be a foregone conclusion. Despite all these considerations, a private prosecution was the only option available.

The new police team seemed cooperative and keen to catch the killers, so Commander Nove authorised secret surveillance of the suspects at Gary Dobson's flat in Eltham. The subsequent Macpherson Report was to state:

As a result of the intrusive surveillance of late 1994, during the second investigation, we have confirmation that the suspects were then and certainly before that date infected and invaded by gross and revolting racism. Jamie Acourt was not subject to the surveillance, because he was in custody, charged with another offence involving violence in a night club. There is no reason to believe that he was any different from the others so far as overt racism is concerned.[13]

We, and those who attended the inquiry much later in 1998, watched an edited version of the surveillance tape, over an hour long, but only a small part of the many hours recorded. Before he played the tape, William Mellish said, 'There is no purpose in summarising these long recordings ... but a flavour of what was repeatedly said should be given. We stress that the sentences used are only part of prolonged and appalling words which sully the paper upon which they have been recorded.'

When we listened to the recording we could see what Mellish meant:

NEIL ACOURT, Sequence 11: 'I reckon that every nigger should be chopped up, mate, and they should be left with nothing but fucking stumps ...'

DAVID NORRIS, Sequence 50: 'If I was going to kill myself, do you know what I'd do? I'd go and kill every black cunt, every Paki, every copper, every mug that I know. I'd go down to Catford and places like that, I'm telling you now, with two sub-machine guns, and I'm telling you I'd take one of them, skin the black cunt alive, mate, torture him, set him alight ... I'd blow their two legs and arms off and say, go on you can swim home now ... (laughs).'

GARY DOBSON, Sequence 27: 'He said "The fucking black bastard, I am going to kill him." I cracked up laughing. I went, "What black geezer?" He went, "The Wimpy one, the fucking black nigger cunt, fucking black bastard." I went, "What, the Paki ..."'

LUKE KNIGHT, Sequence 11: 'It was Cameroon, a fucking nigger country ... Fucking our presenters saying, "Oh yeah, we want Cameroon to win this", why the fuck should he want niggers to win it when they're playing something fucking like Italy ...'

Mellish summed up the tapes when he said that they showed 'appalling racist or raving bigotry', and I referred to 'racism conjoined with an obsession to extreme violence', since on frequent occasions knives were brandished and stabbing movements and 'demonstrations' were practised by the youths.

The footage was indeed horrifying: racism at its most crude and violent. But the four used veiled language about the murder, as if they were aware they might be being bugged. They couldn't disguise their body language from the hidden cameras, however, and the resulting mock stabbings at exactly the place where the knife entered Stephen, severing a major artery, are chilling. There is Neil Acourt, raising his arm and plunging it into an imaginary body, over and over again.

I know that people argue that 'an Englishman's home is his castle' and therefore it is inviolate, but if it is possible to prosecute someone for a crime committed in the home (such as murder or rape), then why should incitement to racial hatred, so clearly manifest here, escape the long arm of the law? This also touches on the libertarian argument so often bandied around that, in a free society, you can say what you damn well like. I don't agree, as there have to be limits in order to protect the vulnerable and the freedoms that supposedly lie at the heart of our democracy, and one such basic freedom is the right to exist without being physically or verbally threatened, whether inside or outside the home.

In the run-up to the private prosecution on behalf of the Lawrences I wanted to adduce this material in the case against the five, but the evidential rules made it problematic. There were no admissions of complicity or detailed knowledge of the murder. At that time a person's behavioural 'propensity', 'disposition' or 'bad character' could not be put in by the prosecution as a matter of course. Although the tape showed extreme racist 'propensity or disposition', this in itself was insufficient. Additionally, the conduct took place well after the murder, and it could be argued that it only reflected an attitude of mind present at the moment of filming. In the end, the peg I used to argue its admissibility in evidence was the fact that it demonstrated the possession of knives similar to the murder weapon; a willingness to carry them in public; and a stabbing action strikingly similar to the one used to kill Stephen.

As a matter of interest, the legal position has been changed dramatically by the Criminal Justice Act 2003, and therefore evidence of disposition now has a much greater chance of being admitted.[14]

In December 1994, at Duwayne Brooks's trial for disorder at the BNP protest, Judge Tilling threw out the case, saying he was worried for Duwayne's health and had no intention of adding to his considerable stress. But Duwayne had waited more than a year to be cleared and was bewildered and disheartened.

He was central to the private prosecution, especially as some other crucial witnesses – including Joey Shepherd – had been so alienated by the initial police team that they wouldn't now cooperate. Joey and Royston Westbrook, travelling on a bus on the night of the murder, had failed to identify any of the suspects at parade, and they were scared of these violent men who were still at large. No one could blame them.

On Saturday 22 April 1995 – exactly two years after Stephen's death – I remember feeling extremely nervous about launching the private prosecution. A lot was at stake, and I had taken advice from a number of prosecuting barristers whom I knew well and who were kind enough to proffer their views. Whenever I get these nerves, which is more often than you may imagine, I have a habit of arriving at court desperately early, as if by doing so I can steal a march on everybody else. This time nothing could have been further from the truth, because when I arrived at Greenwich Magistrates' Court at around 7.30 a.m. it was closed, and I was forced to wander the streets to find a local café. (What I usually find is a greasy spoon, where the workers who are having their early-morning tea find someone wearing a suit, carrying a briefcase and reading the *Guardian* to be a mild cause for amusement.)

Three hours later I was able to tell the court that we had information against each of the suspects that they had murdered Stephen Lawrence. Four of them were immediately arrested, while Jamie Acourt was already in custody for stabbing Darren Giles in the heart at a Greenwich nightclub. Fortunately for the victim, this time the wound was not fatal – by a very small margin. But later Jamie walked free, claiming self-defence like Norris. These lads certainly seemed to lead a charmed life.

There followed months of legal process – conferences with the legal team, including solicitors Imran Khan and Caron Thatcher, plus Margo Boye-Anawoma, Martin Soorjoo and Steve Kamlish, all

barristers in my chambers who gave their time freely to help with
the private prosecution; hearings; committals; then more hearings –
until by the end of 1995 three of the five suspects were finally sent
for trial: Neil Acourt, Luke Knight and Gary Dobson.

Feeling apprehensive at Greenwich was nothing compared with
the first day in Court Number One at the Old Bailey. This was one
of the few times in my life I was a prosecutor, and it felt strange
to think I would effectively be introducing the case, rather than
responding as defence counsel. The suspects were older and tougher
by now, while the Lawrences were determined, but very tense. I
didn't know the judge, Mr Justice Curtis from Birmingham, and
was surprised that the case was not being heard by one of the judges
who usually sat at the Old Bailey.

Straight away the defence lawyers for the three accused said they
were going to challenge the admissibility of Duwayne's evidence. In
the normal run of things, as barrister for the prosecution, I would
have been allowed to address the jury, setting out the case against
the accused. But in the light of the objection, the judge ruled that I
could not mention Duwayne's evidence in my opening remarks, and
to try and open the case without reference to the central evidence
of identification was going to be exceptionally difficult, as well as
highly unusual. In order to provide the jury with a coherent account,
I had rapidly to reorganise the remaining material differently, and
was worried because already I could feel the case slipping away.

A jury was sworn in and heard a small amount of evidence, but
when it came to Duwayne's turn, the jury was removed and there
began a 'trial within a trial' concerning the admissibility in law of his
evidence. What that meant in this case was a challenge to its integrity
as a precondition to it being allowed to go before the jury. It was then
that attempts to discredit Duwayne rose to the surface, and sympathy
towards him on account of the trauma he had suffered was turned
against him, as if he was *too* traumatised to be reliable. But I was clear
that in his initial statement, taken only hours after the event, he had
lucidly described the circumstances and people involved. It was his
subsequent statements that had muddied the waters, for Duwayne
had changed details of his account – and the defence jumped on him
and picked him apart in front of the judge alone.

Duwayne had identified both Neil and Luke at identity parades, but a policeman named Sergeant Crowley, who had accompanied him back and forth to the crime scene, gave a statement that Duwayne said that friends had coached him in the appearances of the two, so that he could pick them out. Duwayne always denied this, but it was a young, bitter black youth's word against that of a policeman. I tried to explain the psychological impact of trauma on the memory, and how stored images can sometimes suddenly flash back when they are triggered, but Duwayne conceded under pressure that he might have confused two people as the stabber.

This blew apart our main witness, but not necessarily our whole case, for I was banking on the jury being able to piece together an accumulation of evidence: other eyewitnesses; the horrific surveillance video; a limited amount of scientific evidence about fibres from clothing; and, of course, our ability to undermine the accused through cross-examination, as back-up to Duwayne.

After over a week of legal argument the judge ruled that Duwayne's evidence was unreliable. To be perfectly honest, I had never expected that the *whole* of his evidence would be ruled inadmissible, which is a very unusual course to be adopted by a judge. As lawyers, we were all terribly aware of the shortcomings and fallibility of identification evidence, which was normally dealt with in quite a different way. Either the judge might stop the case at the end of the prosecution's evidence, if there was nothing to corroborate 'a fleeting glimpse' or shaky identification; or he would provide the jury with very careful guidelines about how to approach and treat such evidence. To have it ruled offside at the very beginning of the trial was a bolt from the blue.

There were further objections in the pipeline from the defence about the admissibility of other parts of the evidence, especially the surveillance video that had been used at the committal stage and the fibres, and I had the clear impression from the tenor of the judge's ruling that we would lose those applications as well. In any event, as a responsible prosecutor I had to consider what the chances were of obtaining a safe conviction without any of Duwayne's evidence, so we all went to a large oak-panelled room in the Old Bailey to talk through the pros and cons. I was heavy-hearted, upset at having to advise the family that on balance I could not see a realistic way forward, and it was one of the most emotionally searing moments of my entire career when I returned to court to tell the judge that I did not feel it would be right and proper to continue. It was clear from his response that he thoroughly endorsed this approach and that, had we opted to proceed, he would have stopped the case anyway at the halfway stage. Doreen collapsed and had to be taken home, exhausted and crushed.

The next day the judge instructed the jury to bring in 'not guilty' verdicts on the three in the dock – and at that time, under the double-jeopardy rule, they could not have been retried.

Doreen wasn't the only one to be deflated, for I was very angry and miserable at my failure to provide the Lawrences with the justice they deserved. To win a private prosecution would have been a historic event and we knew the odds had been stacked against us, but Imran and I felt it imperative not to give up.

The next major forum was the resumed inquest, which in February 1997 recommenced before Sir Montague Levine, a large man with a handlebar moustache. Doreen was allowed to make a statement to the court, and a powerful and important indictment of the racism of the justice system it was, as she severely criticised what she saw as the 'staged' charade of the court case the previous year and called for changes in attitudes and actions by the police, CPS and courts.

We were able to give an airing to many of the Lawrences' grievances, including the case of Detective Chief Superintendent Bill Ilsley and the folded note.

In the week following Stephen's murder, Doreen and Neville had visited the police station to hear about the progress of the investigation. Doreen had written the names of the suspects given to them by the public on a piece of paper, and handed it to Ilsley at the start of the meeting. In the course of the next half-hour or so she watched as he folded and refolded the paper into a small square, and at the end of the meeting she challenged him: 'It's going in the bin, isn't it?' Ilsley quickly unfolded the sheet and insisted that it would be treated seriously.

At the inquest four years later, Sir Montague Levine took the sheet and refolded it – it was exactly as Doreen had described. 'It *is* only the size of a postage stamp,' he declared and held it aloft. The public gallery erupted. A senior officer was caught out: uninterested in and dismissive of people in pain, and crucially of evidence which, had it been acted upon at that stage, could have changed everything.

Then the five hooligans were forced to attend, which was significant in itself – but what a farce it turned out to be. They swaggered and strutted and claimed their right under the Coroners' Rules not to incriminate themselves by answering, 'I claim privilege.'

I asked Norris his name. 'I claim privilege,' he answered, smirking, and the same reply became like a bizarre mantra to every question, however innocuous, put to each one of them: 'I claim privilege', 'I claim privilege', 'I claim privilege'.

Other issues emerged at the inquest, including the reluctance of any police officer to put Stephen into the recovery position at the roadside, and the volte-face of John Carnt, in charge of the second police investigation, who claimed that everything done first time around was professional and was only hindered by the vociferous interference of the campaign group and the family. Doreen and Neville were astonished. These officers had shown apparent support in the run-up to the private prosecution, and now they were resiling. It was reprehensible.

But, in my experience, juries are usually intelligent and perceptive, and when faced with such evidence they brought in a momentous verdict: 'Stephen Lawrence was unlawfully killed in a completely unprovoked racist attack by five white youths.' They allocated blame in a process that was denied to the jury in the private prosecution, which was hugely important.

The next day the *Daily Mail* carried the banner headline 'MURDERERS' over pictures of the five, accusing them of killing Stephen and inviting them to sue the paper if it was wrong. They never have.

Doreen was galvanised by Carnt's about-turn. Her faith in any member of the police was shattered, and Imran formally complained to the Police Complaints Authority (PCA) about the conduct of the investigation.

Meanwhile there was change in the air. The Met decided to ask a team from Kent Constabulary to look at the issues surrounding the Stephen Lawrence murder, and by May 1997 the government had changed. To its great credit, one of the first things the Labour government under Tony Blair did was to declare a judicial inquiry – not, however, without some significant prodding from the Lawrences. Jack Straw, the Home Secretary, announced that, as well as looking at the particular circumstances of Stephen's death, the terms of reference were to 'identify the lessons to be learned for the investigation and prosecution of racially motivated crimes'.

We had finally done it. At last there was to be a public forum, fully funded for the first time, where issues of ineptitude, corruption and racism had to be explored. And then the work began.

At the end of December 1997, the Kent Report found 'significant weaknesses, omissions and lost opportunities in the conduct of the case'. The wheels were turning fast and I felt a huge responsibility on my shoulders.

Then Sir William Macpherson of Cluny was appointed as Chair of the public inquiry. Initially Doreen was not happy with this choice, because in the past Macpherson had been severe on asylum-seekers, and we had a long meeting about his appointment with Jack Straw. Finally Doreen was persuaded that Macpherson would be fair in his approach, and he certainly couldn't have been in any doubt that he was being scrutinised, because her reservations were published by the press.

On Tuesday 24 March 1998 the public inquiry opened in a pink monstrosity of a building called Hannibal House, at the Elephant and Castle, where alongside Macpherson sat his panel of advisors: Ugandan-born Bishop John Sentamu, Tom Cook (former Deputy Chief Constable of Yorkshire) and Dr Richard Stone (GP and race-relations activist). The proceedings were informal, dignified and serious, with a much-respected opponent Edmund Lawson, QC (who died unexpectedly in March 2009) acting for the inquiry and a whole raft of lawyers representing all interested parties.

Taken from the transcript of the second day of the Macpherson Inquiry, 24 March 1998, my opening remarks were these:

'Nearly fifty years ago from now, namely in 1948, in the Southern States of America there was a black Baptist minister by the name of Dr Vernon Johns, and his parish was a Baptist church in Dexter Avenue, Alabama. Following a series of murders of young black men in that town by gangs of white men, those murders having gone unchecked, no sanction and in the face of enormous public disapproval and the risk of violent retribution to him, he entitled his last sermon, "It is safe to murder Negros". He was detained by the police and forced to leave. He did.

'His successor was Dr Martin Luther King, and hence the birth of the Civil Rights Movement in the United States of America. Dr Johns's point then and our point on behalf of the Lawrences now is this: Stephen's teenage killers and their close friends and relatives all felt safe in what they did and in the knowledge of what they did. We suggest that the Inquiry needs to examine closely how a climate has been created in which such obvious and overt racism can breed and wreak such appalling havoc with impunity. In part there are three answers to this: the first is that it lies with those in our community who continue to applaud and support these attitudes and activities; secondly it also lies with those who remain silent or indifferent and who are not prepared to confront such attitudes at source; thirdly, and perhaps most pertinently for this Inquiry, the climate is created by law-enforcement agencies which fail to take speedy and effective and committed action to pursue such illegality. The magnitude of the failure in this case, we say, cannot be explained by mere incompetence or a lack of direction by senior officers or a lack of execution and application by junior officers, nor by woeful under-resourcing. So much was missed by so many that deeper causes and forces must be considered.

'We suggest these forces relate to two main propositions. The first is, dealing with the facts themselves, that the victim was black and there was as a result a racism, both conscious and unconscious, that permeated the investigation; secondly, the fact that the perpetrators were white and were expecting some form of ... protection. The inordinate and extensive delays and inactions, some of which to use the phrase already applied were "crass", give rise to one plain inference and one plain question which we suggest has to be boldly addressed: was the initial investigation ever intended to result in a successful prosecution? The process being undertaken by all of us must begin from a clear and unequivocal premise that this was a racist killing. The forces that applaud and support and continue to support [such racism] go unabated up to the doors of this Inquiry.'[15]

Suffice it to say, the days in the inquiry were long, intense and demanding, generating piles of documentation, hours of cross-examination, columns of publicity and huge public interest.

We managed to get a bit nearer the truth on the Norris (father/son/police) connection. During the private prosecution the chief witness Duwayne Brooks was protected night and day by an ex-Flying Squad Officer, now a sergeant in the Met. Years before, when Clifford Norris was under surveillance by Customs and Excise for drug dealing, this very sergeant had been seen in a pub with Norris making notes, using a calculator, carrying a carrier bag containing a number of oblong slabs or packages, and on one occasion receiving a carrier bag from Norris. Soon after this Norris disappeared for more than four years.

In his evidence before the inquiry, Neville Lawrence said:

> I would say that both racism and corruption played a part in this investigation ... As to corruption I think that some police officers investigating my son's death were connected to the murderers in some way or other.' And in my closing speech I summarised Neville's allegation in this way, 'We shall be asking the inquiry to draw such inferences – namely, that there must have been collusion between members of the criminal fraternity and some police officers.[16]

Because of the serious nature of this allegation, the inquiry required a higher standard of proof than for other matters being investigated – the criminal standard of 'beyond reasonable doubt' – and this was much more difficult to achieve, especially, as we conceded, because there was no direct evidence of corruption. We were asking the inquiry to make this inference based on a large number of circumstances, in the same way that a prosecution often requires a jury to infer guilt.

I suggested that there were 'a number of stages that ultimately must be combined and viewed in a cumulative way ... Firstly, the occurrence in terms of quantity and the nature of serious basic errors made by senior and experienced officers in the investigation, which cannot be explained by accident, oversight or overwork.' Second, there were 'clear and obvious examples of senior officers at the centre of this investigation colluding to cover up the truth about vital events'.[17] Finally, there was the Norris factor.

It is fair to say that although the inquiry did not find corruption proved, there were an extraordinary number of crass, basic errors:

1 Failure to arrest by Monday 26 April 1993, or at the very least to obtain a search warrant for specific addresses.
2 Failure to consolidate eyewitness identification evidence.
3 Failure to pursue a line of enquiry relating to a possible sixth suspect who could have been the 'blond offender', and a failure properly to eliminate potential candidates.
4 Failure to develop information expeditiously and effectively in order to convert it into evidence.
5 Failure to make contemporaneous records and, where some were made, a failure to ensure their retention.
6 Failure to establish an effective surveillance operation in the two weeks after the murder and a failure to put the product that was obtained to any use.
7 Failure to ensure the completion of forensic-science examination of potential exhibits.

The inquiry lasted more than nine months, and by the end we were all exhausted – and yet exhilarated. Duwayne had been vindicated, his trauma recognised; the five suspects were, in Macpherson's words, 'arrogant and dismissive, evasive and vague'; police officers had been exposed as either ignorant of the law or downright racist, or both; the highest-ranking police officer in the land had issued an apology; and the public had had their eyes opened to a depth of racism within the police that had never before been acknowledged. It was, according to Macpherson's phrase, which will always be associated with the Stephen Lawrence murder, a case of 'institutional racism'.

We awaited Macpherson's report with anticipation, and it was finally published in February 1999, following an announcement in the House of Commons by Jack Straw, who declared, 'I want this report to act as a catalyst for fundamental and irreversible change across the whole of society.'

There were seventy far-reaching recommendations in the report, covering accountability, definitions of racist crimes, training in first aid, cultural diversity, changes to complaints procedures and the treatment of victims and witnesses. For example, it is only since Lawrence that the system has recognised that victims have a role to play, because Neville and Doreen were not sufficiently incorporated into the process.

What Macpherson suggested is that victims, whether witnesses or not, should be allowed representation, and this is important. In France in the inquisitorial system – a system that I have been accused of advocating, which I don't, although I acknowledge that elements of it are interesting – victims do have a status. They become a civil party, even in a criminal case, and are entitled to representation, advice at all stages and official police liaison. This hasn't been instigated in Britain yet, but I think it should be. I am very conscious of victims' rights because I represent them often in inquiries, so I know how strongly they feel about the fact that they are left out and not sufficiently recognised. A rape victim, someone who has suffered a serious assault or a child in the legal process should be entitled to a lawyer, in order to ensure that there is communication and protection at a time when they are at their most vulnerable. What has happened up until now is that the state says, 'We are representing you', but unless they have a particularly sympathetic prosecutor in the CPS, the individual can feel very isolated.

What else has happened since the inquiry? The Race Relations Act has been amended to cover the police and all central government bodies. These are profound changes, and ones that could not have been achieved, or even contemplated, without the commitment and resilience of the Lawrence family. There is still much to change, and racism has by no means been eradicated in our institutions, but those who perpetrate it have been issued a stern warning.

In 1999 Yvette made another compelling documentary called *Hoping for a Miracle*, taking the Lawrences back to Jamaica and to Stephen's graveside. Then in 2000 she co-produced with Granada *The Murder of Stephen Lawrence*, a powerful drama directed by Paul Greengrass and starring Marianne Jean-Baptiste and Hugh Quarshie, which won the BAFTA Best Single Drama award and is an exceptional summation of the Lawrences' experience.

In 2002 two men served nine months in jail for shouting 'nigger' and throwing a drink can at a black man, who turned out to be an off-duty detective, DC Gareth Reid, who recognised them in their flash red car, which they drove at him. It happened on Well Hall Road, exactly where Stephen died. The men were David Norris and Neil Acourt.

Doreen has gone on to open a superb centre for the education of young architects as a memorial to Stephen – though in its opening week in February 2008 someone destroyed the beautiful Chris Ofili decorative windows at the front of the new building, a despicable act.

The trauma and the aftermath of this case were to have a profound impact on us all over the following years. Here the state came up against two parents who were not going to rest until justice was done and those culpable were held to account. It was a long and bitter struggle, which had a huge influence both on society and on our institutions, but which left the murderers free. They know who they are – and we know who they are – and to date they have not been brought to justice. Yet.

I am often asked what is the most significant case I have ever undertaken, and I cite this one because I was affected by two ordinary, yet exceptional individuals who displayed remarkable courage and tenacity, changing perceptions and agendas for this and the next generation.

Their struggle continues to this day, ensuring that the achievements of the inquiry are not left to gather dust on some obscure shelf within the Home Office, the Ministry of Justice or New Scotland Yard. Questions are constantly posed by the Lawrences, harking back to Macpherson's own priority: implementation. On 24 February 2009, in the Methodist Central Hall, Westminster, senior politicians and police officers were called to account, with Doreen warning about the pernicious persistence of racism in the manner of urban policing. Within days of Doreen's exhortations a case surfaced at Belgravia police station in central London, where black community service officers (CSOs) testified that they were required to travel in a separate van to white CSOs. Apartheid appears to be operating in London.

It is of interest to note that Dr Richard Stone, one of the Macpherson panel, produced a report entitled 'The Stephen Lawrence Inquiry 10 Years On' in February 2009, in which he concluded: 'While much is made of the fact that the percentage of black officers has doubled between 1999 and 2008, in reality this was only from a relatively low starting point of 2 per cent to approximately 4 per cent. This is considerably below the national target of 7 per cent set for the police service overall.' He also added that the mentality of rank-and-file officers has not altered and that institutional racism still persists.[18] The fight goes on . . .

There are many other inquests that have left a mark on my memory, some of which are, as I write, yet to be resolved.

Ricky Reel was a young man whose body was found in the River Thames near Kingston in October 1997. His family remains convinced that Ricky was the victim of a racist attack, and at the inquest the jury returned an open verdict.

In 2003 in Gaza, James Miller, a cameraman who was making a film about Palestinian children, was shot. In the same year, less than a mile away, Tom Hurndall, a twenty-two-year-old journalist who rushed in to rescue a group of small children being fired at by Israeli soldiers, was shot in the head. In both cases the juries at St Pancras Coroner's Court in London returned verdicts of unlawful killing/ murder by soldiers in the Israeli Defence Force in Palestine, and we are still endeavouring to persuade the British Government to institute proceedings against the soldiers, both junior and senior, who have been identified. So far there has been a serious reluctance to act. As ever it is the family having to persuade, cajole and set the agenda, when you might think that the government itself would want to respond on its own initiative. In a remarkable film entitled *The Shooting of Tom Hurndall* – written by Simon Block, directed by Rowan Joffe and broadcast by Channel 4 in October 2008 – the fight by Tom's parents, Jocelyn and Anthony, was brilliantly portrayed. Tom's sister Sophie has been so affected by his death and the sacrifice he made that she is now working for the charity Medical Aid for Palestinians.

I have also represented families at inquests affected by two different, but extremely serious bombings in Ireland. The first was Dublin/ Monaghan on 17 May 1974, when car bombs killed thirty-two people – the greatest loss of life in a single day during 'The Troubles', greater even than the second atrocity, in Omagh in August 1998. In both cases there remain a large number of unanswered questions concerning the nature of the information available to the authorities and, in the case of Dublin, the extent to which the authorities themselves, north of the border, colluded with Protestant paramilitaries.

In doing all these cases I became acutely aware that many of the relatives of the victims had very little support (financial or otherwise) and were having to learn from scratch each time the lessons about procedures and institutions. In order to meet this need and provide a pool of information and support, I and others (including the tireless

Suresh Grover) established the National Civil Rights Movement (NCRM) in the mid-1990s. I was inspired by Martin Luther King, who became the symbol for the NCRM; the movement subsequently assisted the families of Michael Menson, who was torched to death by racists; Judith Alder, whose brother Christopher died while lying face down and unconscious in a pool of blood in a police custody suite in Hull; Roger Sylvester, who was manhandled by police in a mental hospital; Zahid Mubarek, murdered by a racist in Ashford Remand Centre; Harry Stanley, shot dead by police, who mistook a chair leg that he was carrying for a firearm; and many more.

The achievements in this field were undoubtedly brought about by a small team of highly committed solicitors – amongst them Imran Khan, Gareth Peirce and Louise Christian – and by thousands of ordinary people who responded to the call and helped to organise and campaign throughout the UK.

The irony of all this is that the intrinsic value of public inquiries and inquests is being threatened by legislative change, some of which has already happened. The Inquiries Act 2005 will almost certainly result in no further tribunals along the lines of the Macpherson one, and the Coroners Bill 2009 has resurrected the spectre of secret, non-jury inquests where the government considers it to be in the national interest. The battle continues, and it will probably require another family to stand on the front line and ensure the truth is publicly told.

THE TROUBLE WITH IRELAND

The Price Sisters, the Bloody Sunday Inquiry

In the English criminal-justice system you're innocent until proved Irish. And the trouble with Ireland has been the English.

For the last nine centuries Ireland has been invaded and occupied by the English, starting with the Anglo-Normans in 1171, through Oliver Cromwell's vicious repression in 1641 and the Black and Tans in the 1920s, to the British Army, until the Good Friday Agreement in 1998. British rule has been marked by massacre, death and destruction. Land has been confiscated; absentee English landlords have mercilessly exploited the indigenous population. Small wonder, therefore, that Theobald Wolfe Tone, an Irish Protestant lawyer who trained at the English Bar, had this to say at his trial before an English court martial in Dublin on 10 November 1798, when he was facing execution on charges of treason and leading an insurrection by the United Irishmen:

> To subvert the tyranny of our execrable government, to break the connection with England, the never failing source of all our political evils, and to assert the independence of my country – these were my objects. To unite the whole people of Ireland to abolish the memory of all past dissentions and to substitute the common name of Irishmen in place of the denomination of Protestant, Catholic and Dissenter – these were my means.[1]

The so-called 'Troubles' in the north of Ireland stem from the 1920–23 period, with the establishment of the Irish Free State or the Republic and the separation of the six counties of Ulster. There, Protestants outnumbered Catholics by two to one and maintained a perpetual majority in government at Stormont. This fed down into every aspect of life, where Catholics found themselves at a serious disadvantage and constantly discriminated against in employment, housing, higher education, welfare and medical facilities – and even on the High Court bench, where in the 1960s there were six Protestants and one Catholic.

Although my own upbringing in suburban Whetstone was a world away from the experiences of the young people whose civil rights had been severely oppressed in Northern Ireland – bad housing, unemployment, prohibited protest marches, internment, and so on – I have always been fascinated by Irish history, and a whole new world opened up when I started representing Irish clients.

On 8 March 1973 a rail strike forced me to drive from my home off the Archway Road to the Old Bailey. It was a miserable, damp London morning and my old car, a second-hand Triumph 2000, was having trouble getting started. By the time I had driven into central London, I was very late and took a chance on finding a parking space near the court. To my surprise, the usual parking restrictions had been waived because of the strike, so I gleefully left my car on the road outside the main court entrance and galloped up the steps into the building.

Two hours later an IRA bomb exploded in a car right in front of mine, and the Triumph was blown to smithereens. I was showered with glass while reading by the window in the library on the top floor. It was one of four bombs planted that day, two of which exploded, the other being at Whitehall army recruitment centre, injuring 180 people. I could so easily have been one of them. It was both frightening and edifying.

What remained of my car was towed home to the leafy suburbs of Highgate and left outside the house to await the loss adjuster. Late that night there was a loud knock at the front door – what now? – I opened the door (stark naked, my customary sleeping attire) to a policeman who apologised sincerely for disturbing me, but he was 'sorry to report, sir, that your car has been vandalised'. 'I think not, officer,' I replied, 'it's more a case of exploded.' Shocked, he immediately got out his notebook as if to track down the culprits.

Within hours, ten people were arrested and then charged in

connection with the bombings, and a few days later I was asked by Bernie Simons to defend two of them: Marian and Dolours Price. Because of the atmosphere surrounding the case – the first Irish bomb attack on the mainland since the 1890s – it was difficult to find anyone to represent them, but as I had been in the Angry Brigade case the year before, Bernie knew I'd be up for it. Nevertheless I was filled with trepidation about taking on a case that had generated so much public hatred. The feeling amongst colleagues and even neighbours was one of outright hostility – they really thought it was treacherous of me to represent these people. But that didn't stop me, and I was madly curious the first time I went to meet the Price sisters.

Dolours and Marian were beautiful dark-haired women from Belfast, not that much younger than me. At the time they were student teachers and were well educated, intelligent, and taught me so much about life on the edge that I have always felt indebted to them. It was impossible not to be attracted to these two passionate and committed people. I remember sitting for hours and hours in the claustrophobic, distempered gloom of Winchester Prison visiting room, as they each sat balled up on a plastic chair, with their arms wrapped around their knees; I found myself drawn more and more into their lives, slipping into their shoes. Listening to their experiences, teased out of them with skill and wry humour by David Walsh, actor turned outdoor clerk,[2] I felt a tide of rising anger on hearing how their basic human rights were being denied as Catholics. They spoke graphically of the discrimination and oppression their family encountered daily: of their homes being burned down by Protestants; the anguish they felt at witnessing civil-rights protesters ambushed and bludgeoned by Protestants while the RUC looked on in passive collusion; the loss of close friends and neighbours; the introduction of an ill-thought-out policy of internment (detention without charge or trial) in August 1971, which targeted Catholics and well-known Republicans – and the final straw was Bloody Sunday on 30 January 1972, when British soldiers killed thirteen innocent protesters on a peace march in Derry.

Hearing at first hand about all this spurred me on to represent the sisters with commitment, in recognition of their history.

The ten-week trial was held in the Old Shire Hall in Winchester beneath a replica of King Arthur's Round Table, and saw some of the strictest security precautions in British legal history. The court was heavily guarded throughout, with four rows of plain-clothes detectives sitting behind the dock while Dolours and Marian sat with their six co-conspirators surrounded by at least fifteen prison officers. All doors to the court were bolted.

The sisters were famously indomitable in court, ironically amused at pictures of my wrecked car. I was less amused to know I could have been in it. At one point during the trial the car became a matter of mild merriment. Stephen Sedley cross-examined the senior investigating officer about the time at which they thought the bomb car had been parked. The officer revealed that they had originally had reliable information about a different time. When asked for the source, he answered that it was very close to those present in court. Under a little extra pressure, he was pleased to disclose that it was Mr Mansfield who had incorrectly informed them about the time he had arrived at the Old Bailey. This was a real lesson in how witnesses may be mistaken initially and how, when confronted with what everybody else says, they may begin to change their account, as I did when I attended Snow Hill police station to make a further statement.

Despite my best efforts, the sisters were convicted on 14 November 1973, and although originally sentenced to life imprisonment, their sentence was eventually reduced to twenty years. They spent four years as Category A prisoners. Both went on to put themselves through a living hell in the fight to be transferred to a prison back in the north of Ireland. They were the first Irish hunger strikers on English soil, coming near to death in Brixton Prison before being force-fed for 200 days.

I remember visiting them with Bernie on more than one occasion, and Marian describing the process:

'Four male prison officers tie you into the chair so tightly with sheets you can't struggle. You clench your teeth to try to keep your mouth closed, but they push a metal spring device around your jaw to prise it open. They force a wooden clamp with a hole in the middle into your mouth. Then they insert a big rubber tube down that. They hold your head back. You can't move. They throw whatever they like into the food mixer – orange juice, soup, or cartons of cream if they want to beef up the calories. They take jugs of this gruel from the food mixer and pour it into a funnel attached to the tube. The force-feeding takes fifteen minutes, but it feels like for ever. You're in control of nothing. You're terrified the food will go down the wrong way and you won't be able to let them know because you can't speak or move. You're frightened you'll choke to death.'[3]

It was harrowing to see their condition, so emaciated and weak, but the sisters didn't give up and finally won their demand to be repatriated.

Yet again the clients I represented were educating me in the politics of real life in our own back yard. I repeatedly had to ask myself the simple question: what would I do in the same circumstances? Deprived of basic rights, what would I be driven to do? This was a steep learning curve – they were ordinary young people like me, brought up to believe in fairness and the power of democracy as the means of change. If this is denied or fails, what other options are available? It's a perennial dilemma: the one faced by Mahatma Gandhi in his struggle against British imperialism; by Nelson Mandela in his struggle against the apartheid regime; and by Yasser Arafat in his struggle on behalf of the Palestinian people. There is a very fine line between the collective civil disobedience espoused by Gandhi and the armed struggle espoused by the others, a line drawn between the use of force and the use of passive resistance. Both are in defence of the communities they represent, and it is recognised in international law that you are entitled to use force in self-defence. This is where the freedom fighter may, for some, become synonymous with the terrorist (see Chapter 13). For example, how do we view the founders of the Israeli state who fought the British using the tactics of the terrorist? In 2008 the situation in Zimbabwe was redolent of this dilemma. How would we view an armed insurrection by a battered, bruised and mutilated people? More to the point, given its history, how could the ANC justify its inaction on this issue?

I have thought about this long and hard, and in principle I am utterly opposed to the infliction of any harm upon innocent civilians, for whatever reason. But I recognise that I have not been on the receiving end of systemic brutality at the hands of a state, and I'm really not sure what I would be compelled to do, any more than a resistance fighter in occupied France during the Second World War.

The Price sisters' experience also brought me face to face with the problems attached to representing people who were generally regarded as subversive and undesirable. I faced open hostility, abuse and ostracism, both within the professional arena and in the community at large, and things got so bad that I received death threats – not a unique occurrence during my working life.

Yet again there are echoes from my childhood. During the war Father had been ambivalent towards the O'Learys, who lived next door in Naylor Road, and despite their having invited us into their Anderson shelter during air raids, they were only fully accepted when their son was killed in the Battle of Britain and suddenly became a war hero. Even in 1973 my mother thought it unthinkable that I should represent Irish terrorists. It was as if I had become Irish myself.

In a sense the antagonism has remained with me throughout my working life. I am aware that members of the judiciary regarded me as a dangerous radical. Such perceptions were fuelled by the fact that I did not adopt the customary surgical approach to my work; a barrister is not supposed to get close to the client, let alone identify with their feelings or beliefs. In other words, each case is seen as just another body to be operated on. I felt, in order to properly represent and reproduce the feelings and responses of my client to the circumstances in which they were placed, I had to get inside the shell of the person, which meant spending long periods of time in conferences with the client, listening very carefully to what they had to say. But listening is not enough; you have to take what they say seriously and follow it up, however bizarre that may appear. Truth can be stranger than fiction.

For fellow members of the Bar in the late 1960s and early 1970s, the habitual response to a client's claim was usually one of disbelief. Leaders at the Bar would often begin a trial without having met their client. In some cases they wouldn't even go down to the cells during the trial to discover what the latest instructions were. All of this was a matter for the solicitor to deal with. I found this was the most common complaint that lay clients had about the Bar – it was aloof, arrogant and unsympathetic. Although this has largely changed, government policy on publicly funded criminal legal aid runs the risk of returning to this somewhat prehistoric approach by not paying sufficient regard to the need for time spent with a client, building trust and understanding.

After the Price sisters' trial came a series of other alleged IRA cases, one of which involved a conspiracy to blow up the ocean liner *QE2*. Another concerned the bomb early in the morning of 12 October 1984 at the Grand Hotel in Brighton, where many politicians, including Prime Minister Margaret Thatcher, were staying for the Conservative Party conference. And I represented two more young women, Martina Anderson and Ella O'Dwyer, accused of conspiracy to bomb other seaside towns in the UK.

The defendants in all these cases were highly political and articulate. The unspoken rationale which undoubtedly underlay these conspiracies was that every other democratic means had been tried and had failed, and it is notable that since their release a number of them have played an active and constructive role in the peace process in the north of Ireland. Significant among them is Gerry Kelly, who is now a junior minister in the Stormont government.

The origins of their grievance lay in the struggle of the civil-rights movement to achieve its aims, a struggle that had its most graphic expression in 1972 with the appalling events of Bloody Sunday.

There were two investigations into what happened that day. Two days after Bloody Sunday, the then Prime Minister Edward Heath (whom I cross-examined at the inquiry) announced that the Lord Chief Justice, Lord Widgery, was to preside over a tribunal – and Widgery's swiftly produced report, published within eleven weeks of the events on 19 April, duly supported the army's account, largely clearing the soldiers and British authorities of blame, and was criticised as a whitewash. Then the Saville Inquiry (which came to be known colloquially as the Bloody Sunday Inquiry, or BSI) was established by Tony Blair in January 1998, under the chairmanship of Lord Saville of Newdigate, with John Toohey, QC, a former Justice of the High Court of Australia with an excellent reputation for his work on Aboriginal issues, and Mr Justice William Hoyt, QC, former Chief Justice of New Brunswick and a member of the Canadian Judicial Council.

Between 1999 and 2004 I represented three families who had suffered bereavement or serious injury that day, and I was immediately aware that the inquiry was a vital part of the ongoing peace process in Northern Ireland, which has recently led to the remarkable achievement of Gerry Adams and Ian Paisley – who, at the height of the Troubles, had occupied entrenched positions on opposite sides of the bitter divide between nationalists and loyalists – working together in government, and to the final withdrawal of British troops from the north of Ireland in 2007.

In my view the inquiry came close to performing the same role as the Truth and Reconciliation Commission under Archbishop Desmond Tutu in South Africa. There has been unwarranted and ill-informed criticism, mainly about the BSI cost – as if the truth can be measured in monetary terms – but it is absolutely vital for the establishment of peace that there should be a clear foundation in justice. You cannot have one without the other.

I made some very good friends in Derry during the time I stayed there. The three solicitors I got to know best were Des Doherty, Paddy McDermott and Greg McCartney, an amazing trio whose undoubted trademark was their rapid, rapier-like, withering wit. They spoke so fast most of the time I had difficulty understanding what they were on about, and their one-liners would put Bob Hope to shame. They were all steeped in political history and experience, and brought both passion and humanity to the proceedings. A regular rendezvous was on Wednesday night at The Clarendon; by the time I arrived, there was always a queue of pints of Guinness on the bar waiting for me. I couldn't down the quantities they did (save Des, who is teetotal) and to begin with even a couple of pints had me losing my wits. So much so that on one occasion I found I had been escorted to another late-night bar without realising where I was, until someone said, 'We'd best get you home before the next police raid – there's no licence here.' My two juniors, John Coyle and Kieran Mallon, both members of the Northern Ireland Bar, kept me on the straight and narrow (and their knowledge of law wasn't bad, either).

But what I found really tricky was the enduring divide that still existed in Derry, where some families would not cross the River Foyle from the Catholic Bogside to the Protestant Waterside, or vice versa. I was invited to join Alan Green, QC, and some other barristers for dinner one night at a restaurant in the Waterside; it was a lovely summer evening, so my colleague Michael Topolski, QC, and I decided to walk there. Michael took a taxi home, but I walked back alone. The next day I was given a right old dressing-down for being so stupid and tempting fate. People were still being killed for doing less.

I should have been more circumspect, because lawyers have not been immune to attack. On Sunday 12 February 1989 in Belfast two masked gunmen forcibly entered the family home of the well-known and respected civil-rights lawyer Pat Finucane, who lived there with his wife Geraldine and three young children. He was shot fourteen times in front of his wife, who was also wounded. It was a cold-blooded assassination carried out by paramilitary loyalists under the banner of the Ulster Defence Association (UDA), who were in fact British Special Branch agents. In 1982 a unit within the British Army Intelligence Corps was established, the Force Research Unit (FRU). This unit recruited members of the UDA, like Brian Nelson, a former British soldier, who stood trial in 1992 in the wake of the Stevens Inquiry into collusion, and pleaded guilty to a range of charges arising from that investigation.

I have come to know Geraldine and her family well, helping them to campaign for an independent, thorough public judicial inquiry, which has been promised and recommended, but has not yet been implemented. Such an unprecedented attack on a lawyer, with all the predictable fallout, requires an examination of who authorised it and how far up the chain of military and political command it went. In February 2009, on the twentieth anniversary of Pat's murder, Geraldine made clear to an audience of international observers in Dublin her unrelenting determination that she would never settle for anything less.

On 15 March 1999, Rosemary Nelson, another solicitor in the North, was killed at the age of forty by a car bomb outside her home in Lurgan, County Armagh. She too had three children. Another loyalist paramilitary group calling itself the Red Hand Defenders claimed responsibility, and this is being currently investigated in a judicial inquiry. One of the issues to be determined is the extent to which there was official collusion.

I was particularly affected by this murder, as I had met Rosemary in London shortly before her death to discuss yet another murder, this time not of a lawyer, but of Robert Hamill, following a violent assault in Portadown, County Armagh, on 27 April 1997. I attended Rosemary's funeral and was deeply moved by the outpouring of communal grief for her.

I also became aware of the need for protection when chairing an inquiry in Cullyhanna in 1991 into whether there was a shoot-to-kill policy being operated by the British Army in Armagh, following the shooting on 30 December 1990 of twenty-year-old Fergal Caraher by British troops. I was grateful that my hosts provided an entourage of bodyguards, who were careful to chaperone me everywhere.

The plight of lawyers and the rights of citizens affected by the Troubles has been the main concern of a charity that I have sponsored since its foundation in 1990: British Irish Rights Watch (BIRW). It is strictly non-sectarian and independent. The director Jane Winter won the Beacon award for Northern Ireland in 2007 and the Irish World Damian Gaffney award in 2008; in March 2009 BIRW became the first human-rights group to win the new and prestigious Parliamentary Assembly of the Council of Europe (PACE) Human Rights Prize for its outstanding work. In the early years we faced a good deal of scepticism and some hostility in relation to this work, because such an organisation was only thought necessary in countries abroad, not in the heart of Western democracy. There was denial and obfuscation, particularly in relation to allegations of harassment, intimidation, death threats and the murder of lawyers.

Bearing all this in mind, I took greater care about my own security in Derry by changing the places where I stayed and by regularly altering my routes. Even so, on one memorable occasion a Derry citizen walked up alongside me, grabbed my cases and marched off into the distance. Was this the start of some kind of kidnap attempt, or had I become paranoid? The latter. The man had very kindly taken my cases on ahead to the Guildhall, where the hearings were taking place.

On 30 January 1972 – Bloody Sunday – twenty-seven civil-rights protesters had been shot by members of the 1st Battalion of the Parachute Regiment, led by Lieutenant-Colonel Derek Wilford, during the Northern Ireland Civil Rights Association march in the Bogside area of Derry. Thirteen people, six of whom were minors, died immediately, while the death of John Johnson (aged fifty-nine) a few months later has been attributed to his shooting in William Street on the day. Many witnesses, including bystanders and journalists, testify that all those shot were unarmed, while five of those wounded were shot in the back; fourteen others were injured. I represented two who were killed and two who were injured.

The campaign by the Provisional Irish Republican Army (PIRA) to unite the north with the south of Ireland had begun two years prior to Bloody Sunday, but as a result of the day's events its membership was significantly boosted, and Bloody Sunday remains among the most significant events in the recent troubles of Northern Ireland because it was carried out not by paramilitaries but by the British Army, and in full view of the public and press.

Many details of the day's events are in dispute, with no agreement even on the number of marchers present that day. The organisers claimed that there were 30,000 marchers; in his tribunal Lord Widgery said there were only 3,000–5,000; in Parliament, Bernadette Devlin McAliskey, MP, estimated the crowd at 15,000. Whatever the true number, a measure of the importance of the day is the amount of material that has been produced about it – copious books and articles, as well as several documentaries and two major feature films.

The march's planned route was to the imposing Derry Guildhall, but because of army barricades it was redirected to Free Derry Corner. A small group of teenagers broke off from the main march and, throwing stones and shouting insults at the troops, tried to break through the barricades, intent on marching to the Guildhall. At this point a water cannon, tear gas and rubber bullets were used to disperse the rioters. Such confrontations between soldiers and youths were common in Northern Ireland, and at no time in the past had a civil-rights march ever been used as cover or an excuse for IRA or paramilitary activity. Observers reported that the rioting was not intense. However, two people were shot and wounded by soldiers on William Street.

At a certain point, reports of an IRA sniper operating in the area were allegedly given to the army command centre. In response, the order to fire live rounds was given, and one young man, Jackie

Duddy, while running alongside a priest named Father Edward Daly, was shot in the back as he fled down Chamberlain Street away from the advancing troops. The photograph taken that moment – of Father Daly waving a white handkerchief while trying to escort the mortally wounded Duddy to safety – is seared into my memory.

Those who died were:

John (Jackie) Duddy (17) was shot in the chest in the car park of the Rossville Flats.

Patrick Joseph Doherty (31) was shot from behind while attempting to crawl to safety in the forecourt of the Rossville Flats.

Bernard [Barney] McGuigan (41), whose family I represented at the Saville Inquiry, was shot in the back of the head when he went to help Patrick Doherty, who was lying on the ground injured. McGuigan was waving a white handkerchief at the soldiers to indicate his peaceful intentions.

Hugh Pius Gilmour (17) was shot in the chest as he ran from the paratroopers on Rossville Street.

Kevin McElhinney (17) was shot from behind while attempting to crawl to safety at the front entrance of the Rossville Flats.

Michael G. Kelly (17) was shot in the stomach while standing near what was termed the 'rubble barricade' in front of the Rossville Flats.

John Pius Young (17) was shot in the head while standing at the same barricade.

William Noel Nash (19), whose family were my clients at the inquiry, was shot in the chest near the barricade. In his case there was telling film evidence of his father, Alexander Nash (a further client of mine), waving whilst at the barricade in an attempt to get the paratroopers to stop firing. He too was shot and injured.

Michael M. McDaid (20) was shot in the face at the barricade as he was walking away from the paratroopers.

James Joseph Wray (22) was wounded and then shot again at close range while lying on the ground.

Gerald Donaghy (17) was shot in the stomach while attempting to run to safety between Glenfada Park and Abbey Park.

Gerald (James) McKinney (35) was shot just after Gerald Donaghy.

Witnesses stated that McKinney had been running behind
Donaghy.
William A. McKinney (26) was shot from behind as he left cover to
try to help the older man, Gerald McKinney (no relation).

The third family I represented was that of Danny Gillespie, whose
head was grazed by a bullet as he left Glenfada Park. He survived.
The city's coroner, retired British Army Major Hubert O'Neill,
issued a statement on 21 August 1973, at the completion of the
inquest into the killings, declaring:

It strikes me that the Army ran amok that day and shot without
thinking what they were doing. They were shooting innocent
people. These people may have been taking part in a march that
was banned, but that does not justify the troops coming in and
firing live rounds indiscriminately. I would say without hesitation
that it was sheer, unadulterated murder. It was murder.[4]

The official army position, backed by the Conservative British
Home Secretary Reginald Maudling in the House of Commons the
day after Bloody Sunday, was that the paratroopers had reacted to
the threat of gunmen and nail-bombs from suspected IRA members.
No British soldier was wounded or reported any injuries from
gunfire or nail-bombs, nor were any bullets or empty cartridge
cases or exploded nail-bombs recovered to back up their claims –
though there was one soldier who accidentally and literally shot
himself in the foot. But even he couldn't bring himself to tell the
truth about what happened, and it was agreed amongst a number of
his platoon to pretend that it had occurred when he accidentally fell
down some steps. All eyewitnesses present (apart from the soldiers),
including marchers, local residents and British and Irish journalists,
maintained that the soldiers fired into an unarmed crowd, or were
aiming at fleeing people and those tending the wounded.
The Saville Inquiry was to be more comprehensive than the
Widgery Tribunal, interviewing a wide range of witnesses, including
local residents, soldiers, journalists and politicians. The inquiry sat for
434 days, hearing over 900 witnesses, with an additional 1,555 witness
statements. Yet there were some glaring omissions. For example, more

than 1,000 army photographs and original army helicopter video footage, plus some of the guns used on the day by the soldiers, which could have been evidence in the inquiry, were lost by the Ministry of Defence, which claimed that the guns had been destroyed.

I spent four years taking a plane from Stansted to Derry at 5 a.m. every Monday morning, returning on the 6 p.m. flight every Friday evening. It was tough being away for so long from Yvette and our son Freddy, but I kept reminding myself that this was nothing compared with the hardship endured by my clients. By 2004, Mrs McGuigan, for example, had waited thirty-two years to find out what had really happened to her beloved Barney.

There is one matter upon which a large measure of agreement had been reached by the time of the inquiry: that the four individuals whose interests I represented were not terrorists and posed no threat to anyone. They were innocent Derry citizens, as were all those who suffered death and injury that day. This much had already been made clear by both John Major and Tony Blair, endorsed by William Hague, when explaining the need for a public judicial inquiry. It was also the logical inference to be drawn from the position adopted by the military at the inquiry: that they only shot at those perceived to present a lethal threat, either as gunmen or as bombers.

This gives rise to a conundrum, which no doubt Lord Saville will address in his report. I raised it in my opening and closing addresses, and with a number of senior military personnel. According to the soldiers' versions, there must be two groups – the terrorists whom they shot, and the innocent whom someone else shot. The question is, therefore, where are all the dead and injured terrorists, and who shot the innocent civilians?

I cross-examined General Ford,[5] in London, and in short form his replies came to this:

Question, MICHAEL MANSFIELD: Why were the thirteen shot at by paratroopers?
Answer, GENERAL FORD: I do not know, that is presumably what this inquiry is going to find out.
Q:.This inquiry has one duty, I suggest you have another. It has always been your duty, as Commander of Land Forces, to be able to come here where there are relatives, and in Derry now where

they are watching the screens, so that you finally would be in a position to explain why thirteen apparently unarmed people were shot by paratroopers?

A: I am not in a position to explain why thirteen apparently unarmed people were shot by paratroopers. It is obviously a long and complex question.

A small insight into the military psyche and perception on the day arrived in an anonymous brown envelope. It was a tape recording, which has subsequently been authenticated, of a conversation between two soldiers in radio communication on Bloody Sunday itself. It has not been possible to discover who recorded it or where it had been kept over the intervening years, but it was played at the inquiry; it had never been heard in public before. I have further anonymised the identified voice as 'A'; the other voice, 'B', has never been traced.

A: The whole thing's in chaos . . .

B: Obviously.

A: I think it's gone badly wrong in the Rossvilles. The doctor's just been up the hospital and they're pulling stiffs out there as fast as they can get them out.

B: There's nothing wrong with that.

A: Well, there is, 'cos they're the wrong people. Erm, there are about nine – between nine and fifteen – killed, erm, by the paratroopers in the Rossville area.

B: Yeah.

A: They are old women, children, fuck knows what and they're still going up there. I mean their – their Pigs [armoured personnel carriers] are just full of bodies, erm, there's a three-tonner up there with bodies in.

B: Yeah, we saw it. Stiffs all over the place.

Towards the end of the conversation voice B names a senior officer, General Ford, who was 'lapping it up'.

A: Was he?

B: Yeah. He thought it was the best thing he'd seen for a long time.

A: Interesting, isn't it?

B: 'Well done, First Para,' he said, 'look at them, twenty-four of them wheeled off.'

A: Good, excellent.

B: And he said, 'You know, this is what should happen.'

A: Yeah.

B: He said we are far too passive and . . . I'll tell you later.

A: Yeah. OK. Bye-bye.

B: Ciao.

When this was played to General Ford at the inquiry, he said, 'Well, quite honestly there is no truth in what they said at all. It is highly emotional and exaggerated.' Another matter for the inquiry panel to accommodate.

A classic illustration of why re-examining long-held assumptions is so important arose during the BSI. Back in 1972, once the shooting was over, there was clearly an urgency amongst the military to obtain accounts from the shooters in 1 Para. Allegations were surfacing in public about indiscriminate firing and undoubtedly questions were going to be asked in the House of Commons. In any event, the military authorities themselves would need to conduct an investigation.

A senior officer, Major Loden, said that he collated a list of engagements from shooters who attended his command vehicle in Clarence Avenue, Derry, between 17.30 and 18.30 on the day of the shooting on 30 January. This list, which became known as the 'shot list', was attached to his report dated 31 January, and then became his statement for the purposes of the Widgery Tribunal.

Although it was available to Widgery, the shot list never featured in any of the evidence, nor was it the subject of any question, nor was it referred to in Lord Widgery's report. Furthermore, neither the families nor their representatives appear to have been aware of it. Nevertheless, it was to provide the basis for the public position adopted by the army, and then by the government, later on 30 January and on subsequent days.

It was not until the BSI shifted to Westminster to hear the soldiers' evidence that it occurred to me that this list should be subjected to intimate scrutiny, which for some reason had never occurred.

Under the heading '1 Para gun battle 16.17 to 16.35' the list itemised fifteen engagements with eighteen targets by means of grid references (GR) on a military ordnance map. Each target was described as a nail or petrol bomb, or gunmen with pistol or rifle. Although the position of each shooter was given a GR, significantly there had been no attempt to identify the soldier in question by name or number.

Together with my solicitor, Des Doherty, I painstakingly translated each engagement onto maps. Once the GR for the shooter and the GR for the target were plotted, lines of trajectory could also be calculated.

Upon completion, serious discrepancies began to emerge between this version and the descriptions given by the soldiers in written statements and oral evidence to the Widgery Tribunal. Some shot lines were impossible, some engagements unattributable and, above all, there was little or no relationship to the known civilian dead and injured.

It will be for Lord Saville to grapple with the implications of these points and to make the final determinations, if possible, about the individual incidents.

One of them involved Soldier F, who was a key witness for my clients the McGuigans and was the soldier they firmly believed to be responsible for Barney's death. It was clearly going to be a highly charged and important moment for the family to be in the same room as this man. My difficulty was how to get Soldier F to admit his responsibility after all these years. I remember the day well, because before lunch 'F' was questioned by a number of other counsel before my turn came. Over lunch I disappeared to a small room on my own, in order to sort out competing thoughts. On the one hand, 'F' would have been forewarned to expect a grilling from me; on the other hand, he had already been put through the mill by others – so I had to find a different approach. I have a strong belief that everyone has the capacity to regret, to come clean and in a sense to feel compassion, given the chance, and as I was pondering, I knew that 'F' too would be sitting in another room with a certain amount of mental turmoil of his own.

What follows is an extract from the verbatim transcript of my cross-examination of Soldier F at the Bloody Sunday Inquiry. It was a remarkable ten minutes.

Question, MICHAEL MANSFIELD: Soldier F, I represent three families, and the first thing I want to mention to you is the Nash family and their father, who appeared at the time to all observers as an elderly man, went across to the barricade to try and assist his son, Willie Nash, who had already been shot dead by a paratrooper. He then got shot in the arm himself, and I suppose you cannot help about any of that?

Answer, SOLDIER F: No.

Q: I represent a second family, Gillespie. He is still alive to tell the tale, Danny Gillespie, he was in Glenfada Park, his head shaved by a bullet, as you heard yesterday; and I suppose you cannot help about that, either?

A: That is correct.

Q: I also represent the family of a man called Barney McGuigan, shot dead at the end of Block 1 of the Rossville Flats. So you appreciate what I am going to do, I am going to focus on that one because, I suggest, that is certainly one that you can help about; do you follow?

A: Yes.

I then asked a number of scene-setting, introductory questions.

Q: What I want to do – I am afraid it will take a few minutes to do it – I want to carefully take you through why you are the person who shot him, not because of anything you began to remember yesterday, but because you were seen doing it. Did you know that?

A: No, I did not.

Q: You have never been told that other people saw you do it?

A: No.

Q: Does that concern you?

A: The thing is – as far as I am concerned, in the statement I made on that day, I shot a person with a pistol and that is it.

Q: You did not make a statement on that day saying—

A: All right, on the few days afterwards or whatever.

Q: A few days afterwards, yes, quite a long time . . .

A: Whenever it was mentioned.

Q: Yes, whenever it was. Well, we will have to come to that, I am afraid. I am going to do it carefully, so there can be no misunderstanding. Do you appreciate I will not be asking you to remember anything much, because you do not?

A: That is correct.

Q: Except scenes, possible places. Before I do, can I establish this: you realise, perhaps now, that so far as we can tell you are the only soldier who has admitted firing from the corner of Glenfada Park North?

A: That is correct.

Q: All right. Could we have on the screen, please, first of all photograph 429. This is not a photograph taken on the day, but it is just to get your bearings again because your memory is so bad. This is Glenfada Park North and you will see the corner where there is a lamp post and the entry goes out on to Rossville Street with Block 1 in the distance; all right, is that fair enough?

A: Yes.

Q: Could we have another photograph, please, 431. Again, this time there are people there, the same corner, a bit closer, the same lamp post. Again you can see Block 1 in the distance and Block 2 beyond that all right, you can see the general layout if you look at the photograph. Never mind the people for the moment, just getting the feel of it, and finally, 433. This is looking back into the mouth of Glenfada Park North, taken on the day with the lamp post there on the right-hand side; do you see?

A: Yes.

Q: It is that corner, near that lamp post where you were in a kneeling position; is that right?

A: No, I do not think so.

Q: You tell us where you think you were, then?

A: According to my statement, I was over on this side (*indicating*).

Q: Just point on the screen where you say you were?

A: Just there (*indicating*).

Q: So you put yourself on the other side, or mouth, of the entry to Glenfada Park, do you?

A: According to the – um – documents I was shown yesterday that indicate where I was actually positioned.

Q: Was anybody else in a kneeling position in the mouth to Glenfada Park, so far as you know? That is not exactly the corner of Glenfada Park?

A: I do not recollect.

Q: You do not recollect. No one else has admitted being in a kneeling position there; do you follow?

A: Yes.

Q: Could we go back to that last photograph again, 433, because it was taken on the day? The lamp post at the corner of Glenfada Park North where you have indicated, or where it is indicated on the plan, is near that lamp post; do you see?

A: OK, yes.

Q: Right. So that is where you were, in a kneeling position.

A: Yes.

Q: According to you.

A: Yes.

Q: In that position you were seen by a number of soldiers; did you realise that?

A: No.

Q: Up on the walls, that is beyond the Rossville Flats, there were observation points; did you know that?

A: No.

Q: And those observation points were manned, not by paratroopers, but in the main by members of the Light Air Defence Regiment. You did not know that, obviously?

A: I did not.

Q: I am not going to go through them all, there are a number of them, but one in particular gives a graphic description of what I suggest is you firing, because you are the only one on that corner in a kneeling position, so it has to be you; do you follow?

A: I do.

Q: This is an officer; he is known as 227, in the Light Air Defence Regiment. Before I tell you what he says, you better be shown the view that he says he has of the corner, and so on. Could we have 2204.033. This is roughly the view, nothing can replicate it precisely, that he had from the walls, where you can see the end of Block 1. You can see Block 2 and you can see the corner of Glenfada Park that we have just been talking about, with the lamp post. Can you see it?

A: Yes.

Q: That is roughly the view: 2204.034 is a photograph closer; this time there is an armoured personnel carrier which is there, which I appreciate was not there when you were there. In the distance is that same lamp post with two people standing by it; all right?

A: Yes.

Q: In the foreground is the same body that you have been shown before, of Barney McGuigan. Again, he [227] has identified these photographs. Finally, 2204.035. This is a photograph, and I would like – I am sorry to put figures to you – you to bear in mind this figure is also known as EP25/17, and I have to come back to that, but this photograph he, 227, also identified. That is the general scenario. I take it, therefore, that you had never been shown what he said about these incidents at the time?

A: That is correct.

Q: He said it many times and he repeated it here last week. He is an officer. He was in charge of the observation post. Could we have 2189, please, paragraph 8. I am going to read it to you, because it may be you have not seen it before:

'I then heard two or three rapid pistol shots from the area of the Rossville Flats. The kneeling soldier [that is, I suggest, you, because he has already described that] fired two deliberate shots towards my right and downwards [he is up on the walls] aimed, I believe, in the direction of the near end of Block 1. As he did this I saw a man falling. He was a few paces out from the end of Block 1, where a small group of people were gathered. I have seen EP25/17 [that is the photograph I have just shown you, all right?] and EP25/18 [that is another one in the same series] and identify the foreground figure as the man I saw fall. I should add that the Pig [an armoured personnel carrier, otherwise known as a Saracen] appearing in the photographs was not there when the paratrooper fired. I saw nothing in the hands of the man who fell.'

That is a very clear description; is it not?

A: Yes.

Q: By someone, of officer rank, whose job it was to observe that day and nothing else much; do you follow?

A: I do.

Q: And he is not alone. This is not just civilians, but other soldiers who saw the kneeling paratrooper fire in this way. So bear that in mind. He gave evidence at Widgery, just so there is no doubt at all, can we have one passage, 2196, please. This is what he told Lord Widgery at letter A onwards, please:

'Question: When he fired [he is talking about you again] how many shots did he fire?' 'Answer: Two shots, sir.'

'Question: When he fired those two shots, did you see any man who may have been his target?' 'Answer: Yes, sir, I did.'

'Question: Where was that man?' 'Answer: By the bottom end of Block 1.'

'Question: Was that near the telephone kiosk?' 'Answer: Yes.'

'Question: What did you see?' 'Answer: I saw a man fall, sir.'

'Question: Did a small group of people gather?' 'Answer: They stood away there as soon as he was hit.'

'Question: Would you look at EP25.'

Then I will not trouble you with the rest, because he goes on to the same photographs again and he identifies the man in the photograph, in the foreground, Barney McGuigan, as being shot by the kneeling soldier, whose name he obviously did not know, but it was you. I am not for the moment going to trouble you with other soldiers who saw a very similar scene; I want to switch, if I may, to the civilians, for this purpose a series of photographs, please.

Could we have on the screen 813, please? Photograph 3 813, it is given a different number, but it is the same photograph you have already seen before, only now what we have in this sequence are photographs taken in sequence by this one photographer. 813 is EP25/17 with Mr McGuigan there in the foreground, which he [227] identified, and you will see behind there is a group of civilians by a telephone kiosk and the corner where the lamp post was and you were just off the picture, of course, in the mouth of Glenfada Park; do you follow?

A: Yes.

Q: Could we have 814, a very similar picture, again the civilians; you see more of them this time. 815 is the other photograph shown during the Widgery hearings to this soldier, and in his statement, it was EP25/18. Again, he [227] identified the man he saw you shooting as Barney McGuigan. You will see again the same people in the background. 20 816, please, the same people in the background. 21 817, a shot taken along the wall of Block 1, the gable end, towards the telephone kiosk. This Tribunal [Saville] has heard from witnesses who were there on the receiving end; do you follow?

A: Yes.

Q: 818, I suggest you can see there in the faces of these unarmed civilians the terror being inflicted, I suggest, by you; you can see it, can you not?

A: I see the picture, yes.

Q: You can see the terror, can you not?

A: I can see the picture.

Q: Come on, I am only asking for a very obvious comment, the woman on the right-hand side there. Fear, terror, upset, anguish; it is all there, is it not?

A: Yes.

Q: You could say that in the first place, and we would save a lot of time. 819, please, the same sort of scene, I do not go further. They are all in sequence. One of those – I am only going to deal with one – but there are several who have given evidence from the gable end. One of them, her name is Geraldine McBride, only she was not known by that name then, she was not married, Geraldine Richmond, provided a statement to the Inquiry of what she saw because she knew Barney McGuigan. Could we have AM45.5, please. She is one of the ones in the photograph, I will not trouble you with which one, just two paragraphs, 25 and 26. I presume you have never seen this before, either?

A: That is correct.

Q: I am going to read it with you . . . except for the second paragraph, which I am going to ask you to read to yourself – paragraph 25:

'Barney McGuigan, one of the men huddled at the wall with me, was a community man and was generally looked up to. After a short time (although I do not know how long) Mr McGuigan said that he could not stand the sound of the man calling any longer and that if he went out waving a white hanky, they would not shoot at him. We tried to dissuade him from going out. We told him they would shoot him. However, he was brave and he stepped away from us holding the white hanky in his hand. Although I cannot be certain, I think he held it in his left hand. He walked out slowly sideways in an arc towards where we thought the sound was coming from. He stepped out about ten to twelve feet away from us. All the time he was walking I could see the left-hand side of his face. We were calling to him all the time to come back. He kept looking back towards us. I could see bullets going past us and Mr McGuigan from all directions, although I did not hear automatic fire. The bullets sounded the same as those I had heard when I had been running down Rossville Street earlier.'

I do not wish to read the next paragraph out in public, it is there for you to see; would you read that to yourself, please.
(*Pause.*)
A: Yes.

Q: You will accept, I think, that the injury suffered by this man, who had no more than a handkerchief in his hand, was truly horrific; was it not?
A: Yes.

Q: I want, in this context, for you to see two photographs, and there is a reason for showing them to you, but I do not ask that they are put on the public screen, I want you to see them, however. Could we have P180? That is the entry wound at the back of the head towards the left ear; do you see?
A: Yes.

Q: Shot, I suggest, by you when his head was facing at least at an angle away from you; you follow?
A: Yes.

Q: Could we have the next photograph, 181, and that is the result of what you did. I am going to ask you because, as you fully recognise and have been informed many times, it is virtually the last occasion this family can expect from you, at least recognition of what you have done; are you prepared to make that recognition?
A: As I have said in my previous statements, the person I shot from that corner had a pistol in his hand; that was it.

Q: If you have noticed, I have not relied on a memory that does not exist; you do not have a memory, do you; do you?
A: If you say so.

Q: No, you have said so.
A: At that particular time I have no recollection of it, that is correct.

Q: If you have no recollection, there is no way that you can stand here today and suggest you did not shoot this man, Mr McGuigan, is there?
A: No.

Q: Would you, for the benefit of his wife, who is here, and his six children, finally accept and recognise – we will come to whether you meant to do it in a moment, but that is what you did; are you happy to, or are you prepared to at least accept that?
A: Yes.

(*Pause.*)

Q: I want to take you through what must have happened. When you came to make your very first statement, where you do not mention this at all, I am going to suggest clearly, but there are some reasons I want to develop, why you had left it out. You left it out, I suggest, not because you had forgotten, but because you recognised that what you had done in killing the man with no pistol, but only a handkerchief, really could not be justified; that is why it was left out, all right, was it not?

A: Not in my opinion, no.

Q: Not in your opinion. I want to just demonstrate to you why I suggest you did not forget it.

LORD SAVILLE: Just wait one moment, Mr Mansfield.

(*People crying, leaving the gallery.*)

Mrs McGuigan had collapsed on finally hearing a soldier admit to killing her husband after so many years. She was carried outside into the foyer of Central Hall, Westminster, and when she recovered she just said, 'Thank you, that's enough. I don't need to hear any more.'

The hearings were concluded in November 2004, and the family is still waiting for Lord Saville's findings.

Those findings will embrace many more and much wider issues than I've chosen to describe here, and I do not feel it would be appropriate to pre-empt the inquiry's report by elaborating any further, save to set out what the families I represented wanted to know and still want decided. Who pulled what trigger when is but a small part of the picture. The real and the central question is how this was ever allowed to happen. The planning, the decision-making and the rules of engagement are at the core of the answer. Each of the major witnesses, senior army officers and politicians, was provided with written notice by me of our basic points so that they were not caught unaware or ill prepared. The core propositions upon which witnesses were asked to comment, and upon which the inquiry has been asked for determinations by us, are: first, whether the role of 1 Para on 30 January 1972 had as its primary objective the inception of a process to reassert military authority in the Bogside no-go area in Derry – in short, to teach Bogsiders a lesson, but not to reoccupy at this stage, which would be accomplished by Operation

Motorman in July 1972; second, whether the arrest operation was merely a pretext for legitimising what was, in simple terms, a frontal assault or incursion into the no-go areas; third, whether these objectives explain why the arrested persons, the dead and the injured were all innocent civilians; fourth, whether the Parachute Regiment was selected to perform this role because of the manner in which it acted as a hard-and-fast response unit in Belfast; and finally and most importantly, whether the whole operation had been sanctioned at the highest level by the Cabinet in Whitehall, recognising that such an exercise necessarily involved an inevitable and foreseeable risk of serious injury or death to innocent civilians ... and innocent the four citizens I represented most certainly were – at least on that there was, and can be, no dispute. From the outset it was never suggested, on behalf of the soldiers, that any of them were terrorists or posed a threat of violence. My central point throughout was that if the soldiers persist in claiming they only shot persons who *were* posing a violent threat, then who shot the innocent civilians? I eagerly await the result of the inquiry's assiduous, time-consuming labours.

One of the most heartening and humbling moments for me, during the whole of the period I was involved in the Bloody Sunday Inquiry, came with an unexpected meeting organised by my solicitor, Des Doherty. We went out to dinner one night to meet a friend of his, Richard Moore. Des told me little or nothing about Richard in advance, and as the meal progressed I came to the slow realisation that he was totally blind. He was so proficient at ordering, eating and directing his conversation that his disability was not obvious to me. Far more extraordinary was the story he told, which stemmed from the year of Bloody Sunday in 1972, when, aged ten, he was blinded by a rubber bullet fired at point-blank range into his face by a British soldier in Derry. Richard was not consumed by bitterness and hatred; indeed, quite the reverse. He has devoted his life to reconciliation and education. He has gone out of his way to trace and meet the soldier who shot him; to establish an organisation called Children in Crossfire, which has raised millions of pounds to provide food, housing, schools and clean water in Ethiopia, Kenya, Tanzania, Gambia, Brazil, Colombia and Bangladesh. By going into schools across the religious divide in Northern Ireland, by showing them what is possible in environments far worse than theirs, he has brought young people together with a sense of purpose that is not infected by bigotry and prejudice: an indisputable model for integrated education. Wolfe Tone would have been proud.

10

THAT LITTLE TENT OF BLUE

Prison Riots

I never saw a man who looked
With such a wistful eye
Upon that little tent of blue
Which prisoners call the sky
And at every drifting cloud that went
With sails of silver by.

Oscar Wilde, *The Ballad
of Reading Gaol* (1898)

Over the years I have had to visit most of the prisons in the UK penal system, many of which are unremittingly depressing and oppressive. We have managed to remain at the top of the European prison population poll – at the time of writing this, more than 83,000 inmates – and the government was even considering reintroducing Dickensian prison hulks to deal with the excess.

In most prisons human rights are a non-existent concept, and for most prisoners being inside is a dehumanising and degrading experience, with prison regimes in the main attempting to control and contain, rather than educate and rehabilitate. As a lawyer I am very familiar with the frustrations of cancelled and delayed visits, sometimes missing clients altogether due to unexpected transfers. The awkwardness of the prison authorities can make life very frustrating, but every cloud . . .

I once travelled all the way to Blundeston, a prison in the Suffolk outback, only to find that my client had been transferred to London that very morning. There was no way we could get back to see him and so, it being a beautiful summer day, my legal companion and I paid a surprise visit to an artistic community she'd heard of along the coast at Southwold. It turned out to be a naturist commune (gratifyingly supported by Adnams Ale), which required visitors to strip off. I managed everything but my socks.

Prisons stop at nothing in the interests of so-called security. The indignity of frisking and strip-searching at high-security facilities; the endless delays and lack of privacy. Bugging scandals come as no surprise; I've been trading notes at conferences with my clients for years, because prison interview rooms have long had ears (as the solicitor and Labour MP Sadiq Khan discovered in 2008). Prison visiting has always been a catalogue of aggravation. But if it's like that for a QC, what must it be like for the prisoners and their families? Far worse.

In 1983 I became involved in a siege at Parkhurst High Security Prison on the Isle of Wight, and it was like a nightmare come true.

My connection was through a prisoner named John Bowden, a South Wales lad turned bad by drink and unemployment, who had come to London, where he sold newspapers on the street for the Socialist Workers' Party. I had defended him at the Old Bailey in relation to what had become known as the Camberwell Murders, a series of particularly grotesque and gruesome killings, which had involved carving up homosexuals or winos while they were still alive and freezing the cuts. Bowden had been convicted about a year before the events that erupted at Parkhurst.

I had gone away for the weekend with my family to a hotel in Norfolk and had left no forwarding telephone number because I wanted a few days away undisturbed. After an enjoyable break I was about to drive back to London with a car load of children when the hotel receptionist ran out and said that somebody wanted me urgently on the telephone. Wondering how anyone could have found me, I went back to the hotel lobby and took the call. It was a *Daily Mirror* journalist, who told me that there was a major prison siege at Parkhurst, and that my client Bowden had the Assistant Governor in his office at knife-point and was threatening to kill him unless I went down to speak to him.

The *Mirror* had arranged a helicopter to take me immediately to the Isle of Wight, but I refused the offer as I didn't want to get tied up with a newspaper. Instead I drove home as fast as I could, to find the house surrounded by journalists waiting to speak to me. I took the family in, settled them down and considered what I should do next, deciding that I wouldn't rush into anything. I telephoned the prison to say that I was willing to help, but they declined my offer and said that there was no need, and under those circumstances there was no point in going if they were not willing to let me in. So I told the press to go away while I awaited any other official requests. In the middle of the night I was telephoned by somebody in the Home Office, asking if I would be prepared to go down. I agreed, explaining that I had been waiting for the past four hours or so.

To my amazement, they didn't send round a fast car immediately, but said that a police car would pick me up at dawn, another five hours away. It did indeed come at the allotted time and rushed me through the deserted London streets at a rate that would have got us to the Isle of Wight in an hour. But then, even more to my astonishment, it swept into Waterloo Station, where the driver handed me a ticket for the milk train to Portsmouth.

Between the Home Secretary phoning and the police car arriving, the *Daily Mirror* had been on the phone regularly, but I had declined the use of their resources. However, they then told me that a young reporter was going to go to Parkhurst with me, because Bowden had asked to speak to someone from the *Mirror* as well. In addition, my solicitor, Michael Fisher, and my junior counsel at trial, Dora Belford, agreed to come.

We all arrived at the prison at about the same time on a rather cold morning, and again the press was waiting. We were ushered into a conference room with the prison psychiatrist, the Governor and many more, all of them trying to dissuade me from doing anything, on the basis that Bowden was a known psychopath who would carve me up in front of the press, and they could not guarantee my safety. I asked for a private line to Bowden because I felt that if I could speak to him, I could probably get through to him psychologically and discover what the real problem was, but the authorities refused. Eventually, as there was no progress and the Assistant Governor still had a knife at his throat, they agreed, though I suspected that the line they'd provided was being listened to.

In our first phone conversation, just as he had been at his trial, Bowden was perfectly reasonable, indicating – as in so many of these prison siege and riot cases – that the real problem was to do with conditions: solitary confinement, punishment blocks and so on, but mainly interference with mail and telephone calls, access to lawyers, and the fact that the prisoners were always being moved from one prison to another at a moment's notice. He went on to say that in order to release the Assistant Governor, he wanted me – and me alone – to go to meet him, where he would make a statement that had to go on the front page of the *Daily Mirror* the next day, and he would then release his prisoner.

I asked him, 'What guarantee do I have that you will keep your word?' He replied that he would throw all of his weapons out of the office window on the ground floor as he saw me walking across the prison yard, and that in turn *he* would have to trust that I wasn't coming with guns on me, or supported by hidden prison officers.

Funnily enough, I did trust him, and having sorted out this bizarre strategy, I then had the difficult task of trying to persuade the prison authorities that I didn't want any kind of armed guard. I asked that all the sharp-shooters be taken off the roof, and wanted no prison officers whatsoever within sight of Bowden, along with a promise that they would not storm the wing where the office was – at which point they said that if they were to do what I asked, then whatever happened to me would be my own responsibility. I replied that as far as my own safety was concerned, the only people I wanted with me were the young *Mirror* journalist (who by this time was quite shaken at the prospect of going across the yard without any protection) and my junior, Dora, who was extremely courageous in agreeing to accompany me.

I shall never forget that walk from the office to the prison wing. It was one of those occasions when there was a great stillness – not a leaf moved, not a bird fluttered, no sound anywhere – and I sensed that every single prisoner was at a window watching me. And it was even more terrifying as I had recently seen the dramatic reconstruction of a prison siege at Attica jail in the USA, which had ended in disaster. Clearly there must have been prison officers hidden away, but also watching, so all eyes were on this apparently empty yard.

Each pace was like a mile, and with each stride I wondered whether

I'd been completely mad to agree, but there was no turning back. I hardly dared look up from the ground, for fear that any untoward movement might be misinterpreted by the onlookers. After what seemed an eternity we got close to the window and, true to Bowden's word, various weapons *were* thrown out – though they turned out to be an adapted pair of scissors and a sharpened comb. I hoped, of course, that he hadn't kept any back. He then dictated to the reporter, through the window, the statement that he wanted put in the press. Every word seemed to take a painfully long time, which I trusted would not push the patience of the prison authorities beyond the limit.

I then had to go round and into the office to ensure that the Assistant Governor was released unharmed as part of the bargain. The ultimate phase was in a way the worst, because I had to wait while Bowden unlocked the door and I couldn't be sure what I was going to find. I had a kaleidoscope of thoughts. Suppose my trust was misplaced and Bowden had kept back a proper knife? Suppose he rushed me? Suppose he wanted to take the Assistant Governor with him in order to secure his release? How would I react?

When just seconds later the door opened, my panicky fears were unjustified – but I was surprised to see Bowden not only with the Assistant Governor, but also with another prisoner. I asked Bowden to let the hostage come out first, so that I could see he was unharmed. Thankfully, he was.

The feeling of relief was immense, but I insisted that I accompany Bowden to make sure that he wasn't beaten up before being taken to the hospital wing.

I then had an interview with the Governor, and tried to extract a promise that there would be no prosecution of Bowden, otherwise it would make the resolution without bloodshed of sieges of this kind impossible in the future. If in fact Bowden was punished within the prison system, prosecuted or beaten up by prison officers, he wouldn't be as cooperative, should there be a next time. At that stage he was indeed treated properly and was not harmed, but eventually he was prosecuted, and I gave evidence on his behalf at his trial. He got extra time.

Our dramatic negotiations with Bowden were regarded as a success and lives had been saved, but it didn't end there. The young journalist spoke to the night editor of the *Daily Mirror*, who initially refused to print the statement in its entirety on the front page because it named certain prison officers. I spoke to the editor myself and said that if he didn't put it on the front page in an unedited form, I would make it known that the *Daily Mirror* had reneged on the deal and had put other lives in jeopardy. The article *was* printed on the front page.

While I didn't expect any particular gratitude for the role I'd played in getting the Assistant Governor released, I did find it odd that when I bumped into him at the main gate on a subsequent visit to Parkhurst, he didn't say a word, but just walked on by. As for the Home Secretary of the day, I received a most perfunctory acknowledgement. *Tant pis!*

Although the brutal manner in which he drew attention to his grievances can in no way be condoned, John Bowden had just cause to protest, for the 1980s saw a massive increase in prison overcrowding, especially in local prisons and remand centres where innocent or as-yet-unconvicted people awaited trial. And there was no greater example of the malaise at the heart of the prison system than Risley Remand Centre, near Warrington in Cheshire.

Opened in 1964, Risley was a modern facility built to hold 608 prisoners: 514 men and 94 women. Just over twenty years later it was holding 956 prisoners – 831 men and 125 women – and physical conditions were as bad as they were in the crumbling Victorian prisons such as Strangeways in nearby Manchester.

At Risley, prisoners were in their cells for more than twenty hours a day, while the food was revolting, prepared and served in unhygienic conditions. Before the 'riot' in 1989 there had been three suicides in the space of five weeks, yet none of the suicide-prevention measures supposedly functioning across the prison system had been activated. No wonder that in 1988 the Chief Inspector of Prisons, Stephen Tumim, described Risley as 'barbarous and squalid', 'appalling and totally unacceptable', 'dirty and dilapidated'.

On 1 May 1989 Risley erupted, in a protest led by an articulate black man called Wadi Williams, who had originally sprung to prominence with his involvement in the Spaghetti House siege in Knightsbridge in 1975. Rough breaks and poor education had led him down a criminal path, but he came to realise his disadvantage and was eventually one of those prisoners who used his time wisely, becoming an Open University graduate.

That May Day, 120 prisoners from D wing at Risley assembled in the exercise yard, planning to stage a symbolic sit-down protest to draw attention to the horrendous conditions in which they were kept. However, a separate protest the night before on B wing had been put down by the 'MUFTI' squad – Minimum Use of Force Tactical Intervention squads were the prison officers' equivalent of riot police, later replaced by Control and Restraint teams – and it seemed unlikely that the D-wing protest would even be able to begin before there was violent intervention. The D-wing men therefore changed tactics and decided to occupy a landing inside the prison. Wadi Williams described the events that followed:

> With the MUFTI on the ground floor corridor rushing up the stairs we had a serious head-on confrontation. We were seriously concerned for our safety, given the squad's reputation for gross violence and brutality ... We quickly fashioned a barricade and the struggle for control of the wing was on. We were obliged to confront the staves and shields of the MUFTI with whatever was to hand. This included pouring concentrated liquid soap down the stairs to stop them rushing up the stairwell; doors were taken off their hinges and used to barricade the main access area ... After 10–15 minutes we gained control of landing 5 and turned our attention to landing 6 ... There was a race between us and the MUFTI as to who would gain control of the flat roof connecting the wing ... There then ensued a brief but fierce struggle, after which they retreated and we were able to establish our defensive line and take control of the main roof and effectively take control of D wing ... The uprising was now in full swing![1]

Fifty-four protesters stayed on the roof of D wing for three days. They held up banners and shouted down demands to the media for an inquiry and for improvements to conditions, and for no reprisals against them when they came down. As they staged their rooftop protest, many supporters watched from outside the prison walls.

Among the protesters, the level of political awareness was high.

Prison officers taunted the white prisoners, shouting, 'Throw the niggers off the roof!' and 'How can you be led by niggers?', but the protesters refused to be divided along racial lines. The men made democratic decisions and finally gave themselves up as a united group, having negotiated for solicitors to be present and for photographs to be taken of themselves, in case they were beaten up later on.

I represented Wadi when he and the other fifty-three were charged with riot, and although riot is defined as 'unlawful violence for a common purpose', we mounted a case on the grounds of self-defence against an inhumane system. This was a first, in which I was supported by prison law expert Tim Owen and solicitor Jeremy Hawthorne, manic Liverpool FC fan and an everlasting fount of hilarious political anecdotes; we argued that the inmates were using 'reasonable force' in a situation where they were effectively falsely imprisoned. Much of the 'riot' was on CCTV, so when the seventy prison officers began to give evidence, it soon became clear that some of them were lying. Under pressure they admitted racism, hosing the prisoners on the roof, scant knowledge of suicide precautions, and the use of force. Some also admitted that Risley was a dump.

Suddenly some new evidence was sprung on us. It emerged that a course tutor in Hull Prison (where Wadi had been transferred from Risley) thought it his moral duty to hand over to the prosecution an article written by Wadi that was graphic in its description of events during the 'uprising', as the prisoner called it. (The account above is an excerpt from this article.) The idea of this manoeuvre was to try to discredit Wadi, destroy confidence in the protest and divide the defendants, but it failed, and the public gallery certainly enjoyed the more lyrical elements of the article. When it was time for the course tutor to explain his rationale, I had barely begun my cross-examination when I turned to find that he had fainted and collapsed over the side of the witness box. The very same thing had happened to the first witness in the first trial I ever did. What is it about me?

The trial had its diverting moments. One of the inmates, who was defending himself, would occasionally begin the morning's proceedings by producing his breakfast on a plate, turning it upside down to show how it had congealed and stuck to the dish. Another diversion came when graffiti appeared on the outside walls of Walton jail in Liverpool, where the defendants were held, announcing in true theatrical-poster style: 'COMING SOON – KEN DODD!' The entertainer was facing tax-evasion charges at the time, but he was acquitted and never did make an appearance in Walton jail.

When the jury heard the defendants' serious catalogue of grievances, they were understandably horrified and were convinced that things had to change, but the judge was unsympathetic towards the prisoners and directed the jury to ignore our arguments of justified protest. The jury, however, chose to ignore *him* and acquitted all of them – and the Risley protesters celebrated, in Wadi's words, 'the awesome creative strength . . . released in people whom society had for so long dismissed as irrelevant'.[2]

After his release, Wadi was subsequently nabbed burrowing into a bank in Norfolk, a region where his colour rather marked him out – and so it was back to jail for him. I hope that by now he is free and rebuilding a life that better uses his charismatic powers, though I shouldn't wonder if he still signs his letters with the acronym 'RITS' – 'Revolution Is The Solution'. The prosecution never did work it out. They thought it was like 'SWALK' – 'Sealed With A Loving Kiss' – a term of endearment!

(I later used Wadi's name for the boy hero in a children's book entitled *Whale Boy*,[3] for which my teenage daughter Anna created some charming drawings. These inspired our friend Maggie Raynor, a professional illustrator, to provide beautiful illustrations for the published version. I donated my royalties to Friends of the Earth and the Whale and Dolphin Conservation Society, and hope they saved a few – and I'm delighted that the book is still set reading in some London schools.)

Risley was rebuilt after the uprising, and the men's remand centre was converted to take category-C prisoners, serving medium-length sentences. Conditions in the refurbished blocks were much improved by an end to slopping-out, more visits, less censorship and greater access to telephones, while staff attitudes became less aggressive. However, by 1993 the increasing remand population in the north-west was once again being housed at Risley, with unconvicted prisoners being put in the old, condemned wings of the prison.

The 'women's side' of Risley remained unremittingly dire: overcrowded, uncaring and unsanitary. When the new Chief

Inspector of Prisons, Sir David Ramsbotham, visited in 1996, women told him that the previous weekend they had been locked up the whole time, except for meals; that there had been no access to the phone; that there were inadequate bathing facilities and nits and fleas were spreading; that staff treated the women like children and assumed all prisoners were drug-takers, but there was no assistance for those who were; that male officers were looking into women's cells; that the food was disgusting; that prisoners were being arbitrarily transferred across the country; and that visitors had long waits to get in. And so the age-old problems resurface and are perpetuated. When will this merry-go-round finally come to a stop?

The Risley verdict was a public humiliation for the government, and one it would take major steps to avoid in future: in the wake of the massive revolt that spread from Strangeways Prison through the entire system the following April, criminal charges were deliberately rephrased so as to render a political defence virtually impossible.

The Strangeways riot on Sunday 1 April 1990 involved a notorious rooftop protest led by Paul Taylor, whom I subsequently represented, and former prisoner Eric Allison wrote an important summary of the conditions there in a book entitled *Strangeways 1990: A Serious Disturbance*, for which I wrote the foreword. Eric is an ex-con, so his experiences are first-hand and therefore entirely authentic.

To the outsider, Strangeways – before April Fool's Day 1990 – was just another dustbin of a local prison. The sort to be found in most major cities. Old, though far from crumbling, the squalid Victorian relic was grim, overcrowded and crawling with cockroaches. Two or three men were sharing cells designed in the 19th century as the minimum space that one man could live in. Within that space (12ft × 8ft) the men would eat, sleep and perform all their bodily functions. When they needed to piss or crap after the last 'slop-out', they would do so in open buckets, or wrap their excrement in newspaper, to hurl out of the barred window. Each and every morning, the 'shit parcel patrol' would collect hundreds of these offerings from the floor of the exercise yards. Small wonder the cockroaches and rats prospered. The food was lousy, as was access to showers or baths (once a week), and communication with the outside world severely limited – one letter a week and a visit once a month. But as bad as the conditions were, they served only to annoy, inconvenience and humiliate the prisoners. The factor that engendered the rage and hate among the jail's population was the brutal, sadistic and savage behaviour of a sizeable section of the staff.

You see, above all else, Strangeways was a 'screws' nick'; it was the staff's writ that ran, not the rules supposedly put in place by the Home Office. And they were proud of it. They took pleasure in letting you know in no uncertain terms that it was their jail. The general attitude was epitomised by the 'heavy mob', the bullies who handed out the beatings and were far from ashamed of it. These men strutted the wings and landings in their steel toe-capped boots and slashed peaked caps. In the 1960s, many of this group wore National Front badges on their uniform – in a prison with a large black and ethnic minority population.

The segregation unit at Strangeways – known as 'the block' – was where the worst of the treatment was dished out. I spent many months there, in that prison within a prison, in the two decades that preceded the uprising. I heard the screams and saw the blood-spattered walls that evidenced the torture. So confident were my keepers that they made no attempt to hide the nature of the regime from the priests, doctors and governors who, supposedly, went down the block to monitor the welfare of those segregated.

That is why, on that April Fool's Day in 1990, during a period when I was at liberty, I went down to Strangeways to express my solidarity with the generation who had said enough was enough and rioted.[4]

The eruption at Strangeways should not have been a surprise to anyone, as it followed years of tension and frustration within British jails: in 1990 alone, there were major disturbances at over twenty prisons. Conditions were dehumanising and prisoners' complaints rejected by the authorites, while families' needs were neglected as well.

Shortly after 10.25 a.m. that Sunday, the Reverend Noel Proctor found himself facing an unusually large and restless congregation at his morning service. As he delivered his sermon, one of his 300-strong audience, twenty-eight-year-old Liverpudlian Paul Taylor, snatched the microphone and, sparking the events that would cause more than £55 million-worth of damage, declared: 'This man has just talked about the blessings of the heart and about how a hardened heart can be delivered. No, it cannot, not with resentment, anger and bitterness being instilled in people.'

Minutes later vital keys were in the hands of the prisoners and being used to release everyone, and with only 100 guards to control up to 1,647 inmates, the struggle was one-sided. The officers soon deserted the prison.

In any prison, sex offenders are the 'beasts', 'monsters' or 'nonces', and before long the Strangeways prisoners had turned on unconvicted sex offenders on remand in C and E wings. The paedophiles were beaten and kicked, and one remand prisoner, forty-six-year-old Derek White, later died from his injuries.

Fires were started in parts of the building as dozens of prisoners scrambled onto the roof, and as a helicopter hovered overhead, police reinforcements were met with a bombardment of slates. On the Monday, as the world's press gathered outside, prisoners returned to the roof in makeshift balaclavas, continuing to hurl both missiles and abuse as, below, MUFTI officers in riot gear fought to gain control of four of the nine accommodation wings.

By the third day many inmates were beginning to feel the pressure, and violence gave way to negotiation, but as the days progressed the protest became a siege. The authorities responded by cutting off the electricity supply, spraying the roof with cold water and playing loud pop music non-stop, to wear down the prisoners' resolve. A steady trickle of prisoners gave themselves up, until only a hard core of protesters remained.

Taylor, the ringleader, used a traffic-cone as a megaphone to transmit his messages to the press, blaming the 'arrogant and ignorant attitudes' of the staff and maintaining that the prisoners had only planned a peaceful sit-in. He also sent a message of condolence to the family of Walter Scott, a prison officer with a history of heart disease, who had unfortunately died of cardiac failure.

On 25 April, after three and a half weeks of protest, which had made headlines around the world, the last five men to surrender were carried from the roof in a hydraulic 'cherry picker', with Taylor, the last man down, raising a clenched fist in a final gesture of defiance.

The Strangeways riot was the biggest protest in British penal history. When it was over, this Victorian fortress – a symbol of state power at the heart of Manchester city centre – lay in ruins, and when the dust had settled two men were dead, 194 inmates and staff had been injured and the gutted prison needed total rebuilding.

To defend Paul Taylor at the subsequent trial I was briefed by solicitor Mary Monson, who put me up when I was in Manchester and was endlessly generous and frenetically fearless. Unfortunately, when it comes to dogs I am not, and her two Rottweilers terrified the life out of me on a regular basis, but I thoroughly enjoyed playing football with her sons at the end of a court day.

The protesters were put on trial in groups, and on 14 January 1992 nine of the core 'ringleaders' went before a jury in Manchester Crown Court: it must have been intimidating for them as there was heavy security, with armed police, a bulletproof dock and screening of all lawyers and relatives. The men had all been charged with riot and some with the murder of Derek White, the alleged sex offender on remand, but before long the murder charges were dropped for lack of adequate evidence, combined with the fact that White had a pre-existing thrombotic condition.

Unlike the Risley trial, we were unable to run a 'self-defence' case, but were forced to concentrate on the minutiae of who did what to whom, because larger issues of social policy were disallowed.

This was the only time in my career where during trial I was obliged to withdraw my representation, because my position had been compromised by my client's change of instructions. (For reasons of client confidentiality, I am not permitted to reveal what the change was.) Taylor defended himself, was convicted of riot and spent an extra ten years in prison – but it is my understanding that he received sackloads of fan mail, particularly from women who had seen him bare-chested on the roof at Strangeways and were offering proposals of marriage. Despite having parted company, we remained on good terms.

The Strangeways riot made a difference. The prison was rebuilt and renamed HMP Manchester. Slopping out was ended; phones were installed on the landings; showers could be taken daily; and the men were out of their cells longer than they were in them. But as at Risley, the biggest difference was the staff's attitude: the arrogance was gone.

Risley was in many senses a precursor to Strangeways. Both protests exposed appalling conditions and the brutality of prison officers; both destroyed the myth that only long-term prisoners would protest; both wrecked large sections of the prisons, forcing closure and refurbishment. In other ways Risley was very different from Strangeways: the protesters there were far more organised, and although it was easier for the state to contain the riot physically, it was much harder to deal with politically. The new offence of prison mutiny in the Prison Security Act, introduced in 1992, was as much a response to the deliberate political protest at Risley as to the largely spontaneous uprising at Strangeways. It states that 'any prisoner who takes part in a prison mutiny where two or more prisoners, while on the premises of any prison, engage in conduct which is intended to further a common purpose of overthrowing lawful authority in that prison shall be guilty of an offence'.[5] It attracts a maximum ten-year prison sentence. This is equivalent to the repeated attacks on the right to strike. If nobody listens, as they clearly don't, then prisoners may be driven to stage protests – which of course should not endanger life, but which should not be categorised as mutiny.

The protests in the 1980s and 1990s did at least accelerate the speed of change throughout the prison system.

David Waddington, Home Secretary at the time of the Strangeways riot, invited Lord Justice Woolf (later Lord Chief Justice) to report on the cause of the protests, and the results of his investigation were published in February 1991, calling for root-and-branch reform of the prison system and roundly condemning those in authority, who for decades had resisted all moves to extend even the most basic human rights to prisoners. Woolf envisaged smaller jails of 400 inmates, divided into units of fifty to seventy prisoners, where respect and trust could be built up between staff and inmates. But he rejected calls for legally enforceable minimum standards, and instead opted for a voluntary setting of standards resulting in a system of 'accreditation' of prisons, which has never really worked. There was no specific proposal to banish the institutionalised brutality of so many regimes, and the use of medicines for the control of prisoners is still widespread.

Unfortunately, almost twenty years after the Woolf Report, there is an abundance of evidence to show that, across the penal estate, inmates are still forced to endure atrocious conditions.

In January 2008, our outspoken Chief Inspector of Prisons, Anne Owers, published her sixth annual report, which stated:

> Our prison system is at a crossroads. There are signs of a more effective and measured approach to policy and strategy, some new initiatives, and plenty of good operational practice to build on. But, on the other hand, the risk is that we will move towards large-scale penal containment, spending more to accomplish less, losing hard-won gains and stifling innovation.

Owers predicted a prison-population crisis:

> During the year, the prison population went from one all-time high to another, staving off disaster only by a series of short-term, often expensive, emergency measures, together with the crisis management skills of those working within the prison system.[6]

At the same time there had been a dramatic rise in self-inflicted deaths (suicides) in custody, which rose by 40 per cent during 2007. Many suicides were among some of the most vulnerable – foreign nationals, indeterminate-sentenced remand prisoners, and women – and at the most critical time, in the early days of imprisonment. The report noted delays in replacing poor accommodation, building workshops and fully rolling out the new drug treatment system.

I believe the refusal to initiate far-reaching change has its roots in our attitude to convicted prisoners – a disregard, an ability to forget those who are out of sight, as if they barely exist. And in so many of the regimes I have witnessed over the years they hardly do. There is something about the aridity of these places, the lack of stimulus and care of the intellect and soul, that really offends me. I believe that each individual has the capacity to change, given the right help and encouragement. Even the simplest of things can open up locked personalities – such as the chance to learn an instrument in a brass band, or write and act in a theatre group – the positive effects of which I saw in Wandsworth Prison, for example. Some institutions take an enlightened approach to their inmates, while others are stuck in a custodial psyche that prevents any prospect of rehabilitation or personal development.

Anne Owers warned of the dangers of investing in prison building at the expense of sufficient funding in regimes and called for full implementation of the report on vulnerable women and innovative proposals to reduce reoffending and to deal with underlying problems in probation, mental healthcare and social and voluntary services. 'At a time of severely restricted public funding, there is now a real risk that we will get worse, as well as more, prisons.' Finally, the Chief Inspector called for a Royal Commission or major public inquiry to develop a blueprint for a coherent and sustainable penal policy for the future.

I'm not holding my breath.

THE MAGIC BULLET?

The Challenge of DNA

Saturday-morning cinema at the Gaumont, Tally Ho Corner, North Finchley, was always a moment of light relief in the school week. Not so much for the films – *Champion the Wonder Horse, The Lone Ranger* ('Hi ho, Silver!') and *Tom and Jerry* cartoons – but for all the other elusive attractions, such as girls. It was also a period when cinemas had projection rooms at the back, of the kind featured in *Cinema Paradiso*, when reels of film might slip a little or need an inconvenient break for a change of reel, or inexplicably show a sequence of a black background with white stars and dots flickering past. It was at moments like these that I would become absorbed by the beam of light cast by the projector through the darkened auditorium towards the screen. (This might well explain why I remained celibate for so long.) The beam contained, or so it seemed, millions of tiny specks or motes floating in frenzied random motion, none of them visible once the lights came up, or in ordinary daylight. So crowded was the beam that I wondered how the picture could penetrate such density. Then I wondered how much of the area surrounding me was saturated with this space debris, which presumably got sucked in by my nose and mouth. Since the film did get shown, and no one died from speck suffocation, I relegated my thoughts to the zone in my brain reserved for trivial pursuits.

Over the last four or five years these thoughts have been resurrected and, I hope, put to good use. I have been encouraged to join a circuit of speakers in performances called *An Audience with...*, which have included such luminaries as Tony Benn and the late John Mortimer, and which enable me to address audiences I would not normally reach, in a variety of places and venues throughout the country – sometimes theatres, at other times cinemas. I do it Dave Allen-style on a stool, with minimal props – part talk, part questions – and my hope is that I can give the law a human face and demystify some of its quaint habits. The audiences are incredibly well informed and always ask highly pertinent questions about up-to-the-minute topics. DNA is one of them: 'Do Not Ask,' I respond! They want to know about the process, its reliability and whether it's safe for all of us to contribute to a national databank.

I assume that they, like me – and like jurors, for that matter – are pretty down-to-earth and far from stupid, but in need of visualising what lies at the heart of it all. In comes the projector beam and all the unseen particles. I ask each member of the audience to start by considering the seat on which they sit. Once they leave, it is highly likely that a part of them remains on that seat. Beside traces from the fibres of their clothes, particles deposited by their bodies may end up on the surface of the seat, as well as on the surrounding surfaces, including the floor. Those particles could emanate from blood, sweat or tears; from combing or stroking hair; from scratching or rubbing the skin; from licking, spitting or kissing; from nose-blowing or sneezing. The list is endless – and there is always some bright spark in the audience who can think of an activity that I haven't mentioned. Once a chain of transference is envisaged, this can extend to people sitting nearby, who in turn may inadvertently carry your trace to a completely different place; or you may do so yourself, or the trace may become airborne. The longer the chain, from primary contact through secondary onwards, the smaller the amount being transferred. Therefore the presence of your DNA at a particular scene may have significance, and equally it may not.

Suppose a crime is committed in the vicinity of your seat shortly after you've gone. Your DNA – either alone or mixed with another person's – may be recovered. The other DNA trace could have come from the perpetrator of the crime, or it could have come from someone who'd sat in the seat before you, or from someone who had carried the trace from somewhere else. Scientists sometimes refer to a prior deposit as 'incidental'.

A further complication arises once the crime scene is investigated, and while much of this may seem obvious, all too often the ramifications have not been thought through carefully enough. The individuals who examine the scene bring with them a potential array of DNA (both theirs and other people's), which they have picked up accidentally. It comes with their own bodies, their clothes, the tools of their trade – the equipment they use for detecting, collecting and packaging samples. Is the scene-of-crime kit they are using DNA-free? Has there been a control test in order to assess this? This may seem unnecessarily laborious, but when we come to consider the size of the particles we're dealing with, and the sensitivity of the tests now being employed, its relevance will become apparent.

In one of the early cases in which DNA played a major part, I sought to demonstrate the practical difficulties facing any crime-scene examiner.

Question to witness: What do you wear?

Answer: Overalls.

Question: Are they new or laundered? Where have they been stored? Where did you put them on? What clothes were you wearing underneath?

The same questions were repeated in relation to gloves and shoe covers, and the interesting bit came at the end of the witness's examination of the scene. I asked where he had taken off his protective clothing. He replied that he had done so outside the premises, after the exhibits had been packaged, and that he took everything off, leaving the gloves till last. However, he accepted that the gloves may have touched surfaces contaminated with the DNA, and that in doing so the outside of the gloves may have retained DNA particles. The witness went on to point out that he had thrown the gloves away.

But, I asked, how did you take the gloves off?

And as he demonstrated in the witness box exactly what he did, he suddenly realised that he had used a bare hand to remove the second glove. He knew very well what was coming, because the next question was: What did you touch with that hand before you washed it (if he did), before leaving the scene? The risks are that DNA particles on his hands might then be transferred to other surfaces, including central exhibits in the case (even though they may have been packaged), because a particle on the outside may end up on the inside.

Since that first case, protocols and procedures have been tightened considerably, but creating any contamination-free zone is a huge mountain to climb, and the best you can do – short of eliminating DNA evidence altogether – is to ensure that contamination is reduced to a minimum.

So far I have not even got beyond the scene of the crime, because obviously any collected sample has to be transported and stored at the laboratory. Then it has to be unpacked and examined, and the DNA extracted, amplified and analysed. At each stage the risk of contamination has to be contemplated; in other words, there is the danger of a spurious or a false-positive finding.

The magnitude of the challenge facing forensic science is compounded by the pressure to derive a DNA match from ever-decreasing trace amounts recovered from the scene, which requires employing ultra-sensitive techniques. To understand how sensitive these methods have become, it helps to know what it is these scientists are looking for, once the swab with a sample on it arrives in the laboratory.

The human cell, most of which is water, is the basic unit of life. At the centre of the cell is a nucleus containing forty-six chromosomes (in twenty-three pairs), which carry hereditary information, or the genetic code. The chromosomes themselves are made up primarily of proteins and nucleic acids, specifically DNA (deoxyribonucleic acid), which is structured like a twisted ladder or helix, with something in the region of three billion rungs. You might imagine that a cell housing a mind-bogglingly big ladder could be seen by the naked eye or even spotted in a projector beam, let alone by some hugely perceptive microscope, but the fact is that we are dealing with dimensions at the other end of the universe or infinity spectrum, and we have moved from the inconceivably grand scale to the incomprehensibly petite. Since 1999 1ng of DNA – one billionth of a gram, equivalent to somewhere between 150 and 160 cells of DNA – has been the standard starting template for the purposes of obtaining a profile. To get a handle on this, imagine you are looking at a minute speck of blood, yet what is currently being contemplated in the laboratory is a process that recovers a DNA profile from an even smaller quantity, namely less than 200 picograms: a picogram is one million millionth of a gram.[1]

If you're still reading this, just try to imagine what it's like trying to write it – and it doesn't get any easier with what comes next, because scientists (like lawyers) love appearing inscrutable by using in-house vocabulary, in this instance acronyms. If I said, 'MM is an OAP who would need GM before running faster than a BMW', you would probably be able to translate most of it, but in case you ever run across any of this DNA stuff again, I've inserted the most commonly used acronyms alongside the explanations.

Having established the amount, what is the comparison you are trying to make? The majority of the human genetic code is the same in all individuals, which explains why we all have a head, arms and legs, and so forth. There is less than 1 per cent of each individual's DNA that is different, and interestingly it's the stretches of DNA on the ladder for which there is no known purpose that provided the key to understanding this. In 1984 British geneticist Dr Alec Jeffreys (now a Professor and a Sir) identified locations or *loci* on the ladder where there were hyper-variable repeat patterns of DNA. Currently in the UK the Forensic Science Service (FSS) uses ten *loci*, where the variability is described as Short Tandem Repeats (STR). This was at one time misleadingly compared to a fingerprint; rather, it is a profile, and by no means the whole of it.

From the beginning it has been recognised that the whole business would be easier if a bigger sample could be obtained, and this was achieved by the introduction of a method capable of copying the original sample millions of times, which then enables the scientist to run tests on the copies: it uses a substance called polymerase, which causes a chain reaction (PCR) that reproduces the DNA. The amplification process (called a cycle) is undertaken twenty-eight times using a pre-prepared kit (SGM Plus). In the drive for greater detection, the number of amplification steps has been increased from twenty-eight to thirty-four, and this is where we encounter amounts smaller than 200 picograms. At these levels, described as 'touch DNA' or low-template/low-copy number (LT/LCN DNA) analysis, the sensitivity is such that the test may reveal DNA not related to the alleged incident – in other words, the DNA already referred to as either 'incidental prior deposit' or deposit due to contamination. Alleles (the name of a variant of a gene) may 'drop out' and by chance not get amplified; alternatively, one may 'drop in' (stochastic effect – statistically random).

Sounds like some sort of glorious genetic tea party, doesn't it? Therefore, if you're going to be sure who's at the party you have to keep going back in the room, as it were (or rerunning the test), and maintain a high degree of caution when interpreting what you see.

It may be that the test itself is at fault if it is unable to achieve reliable reproducibility, which is precisely the issue I have raised, under the heading of inter-verifiability. Unless the test is validated and accepted by the scientific community, its admissibility in court is questionable.

I represent one of the families who were victims of the Omagh bombing in August 1998, and it was the judgment in the trial of Sean Hoey, charged with involvement in that bombing, that addressed this problem in a very public way. In December 2007 Mr Justice Weir delivered a scathing critique of the evidence, which resulted in the acquittal of the defendant,[2] and part of that critique revolved around the alleged finding of the defendant's DNA on a number of devices. The judge was particularly concerned at the wide variance in expert opinions, not only between the prosecution and the defence, but also between the two experts called by the prosecution. The defence case was that the LCN system had not been validated by the international scientific community. For example, it has only been adopted for evidential purposes in two other countries in the world, the Netherlands and New Zealand, whereas in the United States it is used only for intelligence purposes. During the trial it was revealed that the amplification process had produced a DNA match not only with the defendant, but also with a fifteen-year-old boy from Sussex who had never been to Northern Ireland.[3]

Much play was made by the FSS that this was a technique that had in fact been used in the Peter Falconio murder trial in Australia, where the defendant's 'touch DNA' had been recovered from the gearstick of the van in which Falconio and his girlfriend Joanne Lees had been travelling. Bradley Murdoch was a mechanic who approached the couple's van in the outback and, based largely on the DNA evidence, was convicted in 2006 of shooting Falconio and assaulting Lees.

However, in the light of Mr Justice Weir's observations on Omagh, a full review was carried out by independent scientists headed by Professor Brian Caddy, whose work in relation to the Birmingham Six I describe in Chapter 17. His report in the spring of 2008[4] accepted the thrust of the judge's points about validation, especially the need to assess the ability of a procedure to obtain reliable results, and outlined twenty-one proposed recommendations, foremost among which is the need for a 'national education programme setting out the advantages and limitations of Low Template DNA in order to establish a conformity of approach to crime scene work'.

One of the particular problems in the Omagh case was that no one in 1998 appears to have thought about the possibility that items being recovered, transported and stored from the scene might be susceptible to DNA examination and analysis and the hazards of contamination. The older the incident, the more likely that this will be the case.

That was one of a number of grounds of appeal I put forward on behalf of James Hanratty's family at a posthumous appeal in 2002. Hanratty had been hanged in 1962 for the notorious A6 murder of Michael Gregsten and the rape and shooting of Valerie Storie in a Bedfordshire lay-by, and a small sample of her underwear had been retained by the police. Hanratty's body was exhumed and a match of his DNA was made with DNA on the sample. A similar result was achieved in relation to a handkerchief found with the murder weapon at the back of a double-decker bus. We argued, unsuccessfully in this instance, that continuity and integrity had been compromised throughout the significant lapse of time the sample had been stored. Besides the risk of contamination, a sample of DNA may degrade, depending upon the atmospheric conditions under which it is kept. Prior to the development of DNA techniques in the mid-1980s, exhibits officers and others would have been unaware of the potential for cross-contamination – for example, with regard to the storage of Hanratty's clothes when they were taken to court for the trial in 1961.

Despite the dismissal of the appeal, doubts remain and were best expressed by investigative journalist Paul Foot[5] before his untimely death. He had researched and campaigned in relation to this case over many years, and in the late 1960s had carefully interviewed over fourteen witnesses who in various ways were able to corroborate the alibi evidence that James Hanratty gave for the first time at his trial. It included fine detail with regard to the Ingledene boarding house in Rhyl where Hanratty had stayed and the evidence of Margaret Walker, a landlady in a neighbouring guest house, who was certain of the date when a young man matching Hanratty's description came to her house looking for lodgings, the night of the A6 murder. This evidence was not seriously undermined in the Court of Appeal. Paul Foot's view was that if there was DNA to show that a man staying in Rhyl committed a murder 200 miles away, then there was something seriously wrong with the DNA.

DNA works both ways. It may exonerate or exclude someone just as easily as it may assist in the proof of guilt.

In 1992, after sixteen years in prison, Stefan Kiszko was released after it was demonstrated that semen on the dead victim could not have been his. In 2007 the real killer – Ronald Castree – was convicted on DNA evidence. Also in 1992 the Cardiff Three had their convictions for murder quashed, and in 2003 Jeffrey Gafoor was convicted as a result of DNA analysis. Colin Stagg was originally charged and put on trial for the notorious murder of Rachel Nickell on Wimbledon Common in July 1992, but the trial judge stopped the case in 1994. Fourteen years later DNA evidence led to Robert Napper, Rachel's real killer.

The implications of these results go far beyond just convicting the guilty; they expose the real risks of convicting the innocent, who may have confessed falsely, been vulnerable or mentally unstable, or been erroneously targeted by over-zealous investigative methods. These are serious fault lines in our system of criminal justice and no area is sacrosanct.

A striking example of this relates to the role of circumstantial evidence – that is to say, indirect evidence inculpating a suspect in the commission of crime. More often than not there is no direct evidence, no eyewitnesses, no admissions or confessions, no contemporaneous audio-visual recordings. Instead what is relied on is a combination of circumstances, a spectrum which may range from forensic science at one end through to opportunity and motive at the other.

The traditional approach to such material has tended to be for the defence to underplay its significance and for the prosecution to overplay it. All too often, the trial judge has been prone to remind juries that, whilst care is required, circumstantial evidence can provide the most compelling form of proof. Analogies are drawn with links in the chain of guilt, but more commonly with strands in a length of rope. Even if one strand falls away, the rope does not necessarily break; much depends on where in the spectrum the strand lies.

No jury should convict unless it can be *sure* – this is known as the 'standard of proof', sometimes described by the words 'beyond reasonable doubt'. Inevitably these are highly subjective terms of art, not science. It is absolutely essential for a jury to appreciate the meaning and significance of these seemingly simple concepts, which are not always easy to apply. In addressing a jury about the critical nature of this test, I like to employ phrases such as 'driven to the conclusion' or 'as certain as is humanly possible'. It is not the mathematical certainty of the slide rule, but it is the certainty that each of us expects whenever a life-changing decision in human affairs is undertaken. Nothing less is acceptable where the liberty of the subject is at stake.

What this entails, so far as circumstantial evidence is concerned, is that the inference of guilt must be unequivocal and inexorable. The circumstances must point in one direction only. If there's more than one explanation, or more than one possibility – such that the defendant *might* be guilty, but on the other hand might *not* – the necessary standard of proof has not been reached.

The dangers that lie just below the surface of this extremely delicate exercise were graphically illustrated by the intervention of DNA in the case of Michael Shirley – a true victim of circumstance.

In 1986 Michael was an eighteen-year-old able seaman in the Royal Navy, whose ship HMS *Apollo* had docked at Portsmouth. While on shore-leave he went to Joanna's nightclub, where he met a woman called Deena Fogg. He left the club with her in a taxi between midnight and 12.30 a.m. on the night of 8/9 December. They parted company after arriving near Deena's home address.

Not far away, between 12.30 and 1 a.m. on the same night in December, another young woman, Linda Cooke, was raped and killed by a man stamping on her head and neck, on waste ground at Merry Row. Michael was charged and convicted of her murder at Winchester Crown Court on 28 January 1988. The basis of the case against him rested on four circumstances. The first was semen found on intimate swabs taken from the victim, which came from the same blood group as Michael (a group he shared with almost 25 per cent of the British adult male population); the second related to injuries on Michael's face, arms and back, which could have been inflicted by the victim; the third was a right shoe impression with the word 'Flash' in the heel, which was discernible on the abdomen of the victim (Michael possessed a pair of shoes bearing this word in the heel, which he admitted he could have been wearing that night); the fourth was the fact that he was in the general area at about the time of the attack.

Whilst any one of these strands alone would have been insufficient, their combination provided the jury with a rope upon which they hung a verdict of guilty. Therein lies the danger: the infusion or cross-transference of the stronger strands into the weaker. In a nutshell, it's like adding two and two and making five. My argument has always been that if an individual strand has little or no probative value, then it cannot and should not be enhanced by adding to it one that has.

Michael remained in prison for sixteen years, maintaining his innocence, forgoing parole and serving an extra eighteen months beyond his tariff or earliest day of release; he went on hunger strike five times (one lasting forty-two days, which nearly ended in an irreversible coma). He told the *Daily Mirror* after his release in July 2003, 'I'd rather have died in jail than admit a murder I didn't do.'[6]

Earlier that year I came on board for the first time to represent Michael at a renewed appeal. His first application had been turned down in 1989. Over the intervening years both the Criminal Cases Review Commission and my instructing solicitors, Nelsons, had pursued further lines of enquiry. One of them followed an insistent request from Michael for a DNA test to be carried out, something that had not been available at the time of his arrest and trial. (This was hardly the reaction of a guilty conscience.) Enough material had been retained for this to be done, and the result opened the prison gates.

The profile of the crime-scene DNA obtained from the victim's swabs was 'mixed' (as might arise in the theatre-seat example I've already mentioned). The profile in this case may be visualised as akin to a barcode on a supermarket product – a series of parallel straight lines. These are called 'bands'. Some of the bands were attributable only to the victim; some were common to both the victim's DNA profile and Michael's. There was, however, an array of 'foreign' DNA bands which could not have come from either the victim or Michael, save one band consistent only with Michael. This single band, however, occurs in the profile of approximately one in three unrelated individuals among the population at large.

When this was discovered, it put an entirely different complexion on the prosecution case. It had never been suggested that there were two male attackers, and there was no evidence of any prior intercourse between the victim and anyone else that night. There was only speculation. Therefore the killer could well have been the person who deposited the array of 'foreign' bands. No reasonable jury, properly directed by the judge, could safely have convicted Michael if it had known all this. It cast each of the four original circumstances in a far less sinister light.

The blood grouping was large and inconclusive; the defendant's injuries could not be forensically linked to the victim, let alone accurately dated; the shoe mark was similar to any one of 1,058 pairs sold by Marks Shoes in 1986, or to 1,721 shoes manufactured by Melkrose. It had been estimated, conservatively, that fifty-one pairs had been sold in Portsmouth alone. By the time of the appeal, further evidence had been uncovered about timings and movements, especially the taxi log. This enabled us to restrict the window of opportunity in such a way that there was no missing time within which the murder could have been committed by Michael.

All well and good, but his young life (like that of Linda Cooke) had been shattered, albeit (unlike Linda's) not ended. His mother barely recognised the serious man on his release as the same carefree son who had been imprisoned sixteen years before.

Michael summed up his experience: 'It's like crying in the dark when there's nobody there to hear you. You just sit there knowing you are innocent, asking why people don't believe you . . . I would love to meet the jury now and very gently ask them what convinced them to convict me and whether they would do so now.'[7]

This all bears an uncanny resemblance to the case of Sean Hodgson, who served twenty-seven years before DNA finally supported his long-standing refutation of confessions he made at the time, to the rape and murder of a part-time barmaid in Southampton.[8]

Having now examined all the DNA stages from deposit through to final analysis, there is one more hurdle to clear.

Assuming that a reliable match is achieved on analysis, and given the enhanced specificity of the test, there is a further question relating to the chance that it may have come from someone else, unrelated to the matched person. This probability used to be expressed in thousands, but is now expressed in millions. Herein lies the pitfall – not so common now – which became known as 'The Prosecutor's Fallacy'. Having brushed up against logic and semantics as part of my philosophy degree, this was a little easier for me to fathom than the minutiae of the science, although not without considerable assistance from expert statisticians.

Suppose there's a murder and my DNA is found on the murder weapon, and suppose that this match is calculated to have a probability of one in a million out of a population of fifty million. The probability that my DNA would match that of the murderer is one in a million, and therefore the probability that I didn't do the murder is one in a million. Or is it? The probability of it matching me is one in a million if I'm a randomly selected person. But this also means that there are another forty-nine people out of the population of fifty million who also match the DNA. So the probability that I did the murder is actually only 2 per cent. Everything depends on what is called 'conditional probability', encapsulated by the phrase GIVEN THAT.

So question A, GIVEN THAT *I am innocent, what is the probability that my DNA will match the DNA profile from the crime sample?* is not the same as question B, GIVEN THAT *my DNA matches the DNA profile from the crime sample, what is the probability that I am innocent?* It is an easy elision to make, whereby the answer to the first question is given as the answer to the second.[9] This was canvassed in an appeal I did in 1994 before the Lord Chief Justice Lord Taylor, where there had been an allegation of sexual offences against women students in Manchester, and a retrial was ordered.

The elevation of DNA science to the status of some kind of Magic Bullet is understandable. In one of its first applications in 1986 it helped to exculpate a young man who had falsely confessed to the rape and murder of Dawn Ashworth. There have been many similar cases since. The danger – as ever – is the assumption of infallibility, and recently this has had the effect of reviving both the arguments in favour of a national databank containing the DNA of every UK resident and the arguments in favour of the return of capital punishment. This is why I have felt it necessary to trespass upon the detail in this sphere, lest these arguments should prevail in the absence of the shortcomings I've attempted to identify. At least one member of the higher judiciary, Lord Justice Sedley, has already publicly supported the databank proposal. On the other hand, Professor Sir Alec Jeffreys has opposed the retention of thousands of innocent people's DNA, saying it raises 'significant ethical and social issues'.

English and Welsh police already have wider sampling powers than the police of any other country, and per capita we have the world's largest database, holding the DNA profiles of 4.5 million people, including some 24,000 samples from young persons aged between ten and seventeen who were arrested but never convicted, plus a disproportionate number of Afro-Caribbeans: 40 per cent of black men in England and Wales have their DNA stored on the database, compared with 9 per cent of white men, and there are real concerns that it could be open to abuse. The President of the National Black Police Association, Commander Ali Dizaei, has declared: 'Black men are disproportionately targeted right across the criminal-justice system where there is no evidence whatsoever that they disproportionately commit crime. We see the current data as a classic example of institutional racism.'[10]

The Criminal Justice Act 2003 provided for the indefinite retention of fingerprints and biological samples from all persons arrested for recordable offences in England and Wales, even if those persons had been acquitted. In 2007 the government proposed an extension so that bio-information can be kept from anyone who has been arrested, whether they were charged or prosecuted or not. Professor Sir Bob Hepple, ex-Chair of the Nuffield Council on Bioethics, considers: 'The establishment of a population-wide forensic DNA database cannot be justified at the current time. The potential benefits would not be great enough to justify the cost and intrusion to privacy.'[11]

Reassuringly in December 2008 the European Court of Human Rights in Strasbourg ruled that keeping innocent people's DNA records on a criminal register breached Article 8 of the Human Rights Convention, covering the right to respect for private and family life. As a consequence,* police forces in England and Wales could be forced to destroy the DNA details of hundreds of thousands of people with no criminal convictions.[12]

The public has been treated to the spectacle of numerous government departments managing to leave important files in railway carriages or on office desks for inexplicable periods of time, or relying on pigeons to convey super-sensitive personal information from north to south. With security like this, goodness knows where my DNA might end up. And that is exactly the problem. If the police are going to be allowed to trawl through the databank following a serious crime, I am then going to have to prove why and how my DNA might have arrived at a particular crime scene, and why I am not the perpetrator. Since it may have got there merely by sitting in a cinema seat, and because the match comparisons may have occurred a long time after the crime, this is going to pose considerable difficulty for the innocent citizen, leaving aside the fact that it reverses the normal burden of proof in criminal cases.

DNA is undoubtedly a remarkable discovery, but like any scientific advance it should be treated with respect, and we should all be vigilant about its limitations.

---

* It took the Home Secretary five months (to May 2009) to propose very modest measures which barely satisfy the ruling. In short, the DNA profiles of the unconvicted can still be retained for between six and twelve years depending on the gravity of the allegation.

COPS AND ROBBERS

Carl Bridgewater and the Travesty of Confessions

I have gained a reputation for taking on police malpractice. I am feared – or so I am told – by police officers who have to face my rigorous cross-examination, one of whose number once stepped into a lift at the Old Bailey with a colleague of mine. Noticing that this officer was shaking and had a ghostly pallor, my colleague asked him what was the matter; tremulously, he replied: 'I've just been Mansfielded.'

One of my first-ever cross-examinations of a police officer was on an unusually hot, sultry day in summer 1968, in a converted church hall in Gypsy Hill, south London. The judge sat on a bench near the rafters, the jurors were ranged in pews, and the witness box was the old pulpit with a number of steps leading up to a small door. Very much a 'rookie' barrister, I was defending a man involved in a chemist-shop burglary and, anxious to experiment with my new-found skills in cross-examination, I wanted to use the ploy of turning away from the witness box towards the jury while asking my questions, thereby unnerving the witness.

First up was the policeman who had apprehended the alleged burglar and who was now going to be revealed as a liar by my stunning ruse. But at the critical moment I lost my nerve and asked him a really crass opening question: 'What is your name and number, please?' This produced nil response. Undaunted, and cheered on by my ability so rapidly to destabilise a witness, I kept looking at the jury and asked the question again. This time there was not only no response, but consternation appeared on the faces of the jury. I turned round to see the cause of their disquiet – there was no one in the witness box. The policeman had completely disappeared. Slightly flummoxed, I turned to the judge, who had been dozing and who now, startled by the interruption, asked what had happened to the witness. The usher was outside having a quick fag, so the prosecution barrister asked a court official to open the door of the witness box – and the policeman rolled out of the box down the stairs and landed on the floor. He had fainted. Before I had gathered my wits, St John Ambulance attendants appeared with a stretcher and carried him off. A police inspector assured me later that his collapse had had nothing whatever to do with the power of my cross-examination, but with the mundane fact that the officer had not eaten while on duty all night . . .

I am not sorry to have upset some police officers, and have been very happy to do so if they needed to be exposed for misconduct or even corruption. However, my motivation has always been to improve the way in which policing is conducted, for the benefit of clients, citizens and the police service alike. Nowadays I am asked to address the main police training colleges to try and develop correct policing methods and allied evidential matters, and as a consequence one of the best-known Commissioners of the Metropolitan Police, John Grieve (at one time head of the Met's Racial and Violent Crime Task Force, now retired), has become a respected academic associate of mine.

Many of my cases have involved serious miscarriages of justice, and often they've been surrounded by a poisonous atmosphere where the presumption is of guilt rather than, as it should be, of innocence, and the police and prosecution are under enormous public and political pressure to secure convictions. At such times counsel for the defence can quickly become a hate figure: I have been regularly subjected to death threats, and the problem is trying to work out the likely source. I have always felt the best defence is keeping a high profile, but at one stage I was made really afraid for my life and for my family, with all sorts of threats coming over the phone and to my door. When my junior found a suspicious package under my car, I called in a favour and John Grieve lent me his personal bomb detection kit, a mirror on a stick. The offending

package turned out to be a discarded bag of vegetables – but heigh-
ho, I am a veggie . . .

Maybe because I'm tall, I don't often feel physically intimidated,
but I'm sure that every time I have a row with someone at a football
match or in a cab over some racist remark I put myself at risk. I do
at times feel anxious about not performing well and letting my client
down, but the day I walk into a court not feeling that fear will be the
day I stop practising: if you're not worried, you get lazy and take
things for granted. Whenever there's a temptation to stand by and do
nothing, I remind myself of the words of Pastor Martin Niemöller,
who was imprisoned by the Nazis – in a poem that became central
to his penance and reconciliation initiative after the war:

> In Germany, they came first for the Communists,
> And I didn't speak up because I was not a Communist;
> And then they came for the trade unionists,
> And I didn't speak up because I was not a trade unionist;
> Then they came for the Jews,
> And I didn't speak up because I was not a Jew;
> And then they came for me . . . and by that time there was no one
>   left to speak up.

Of all my cases involving police malpractice, few were more
disturbing than that of Carl Bridgewater, which became known as
the case of the Bridgewater Four.

It was a fine autumn afternoon on Tuesday 19 September 1978
when young Carl, aged thirteen, was finishing off his newspaper
round by delivering the evening paper to Yew Tree Farm in Wordsley,
near Dudley in the West Midlands. Yew Tree Farm was a cosy home
full of valuable antiques, and when at about 4.20 p.m. Carl went
inside, he would have been expecting to see retired farmer Fred
Jones and his frail old cousin Mary Poole. But they weren't there,
and instead Carl encountered someone who shot him brutally in the
head. A local doctor on his rounds, Angus Macdonald, found Carl
in the living room, his head on a bolster on the settee surrounded
by blood, his feet on the ground and his newspaper bag still on his
back. The farm was in chaos, and it was clear that Carl Bridgewater
must have disturbed an armed robber. He paid with his young life.

This horrific murder stunned the local community, and despite the huge response from the public and many hundreds of potential witnesses being interviewed by the investigating officers, only fourteen people had seen a pale-blue car parked in the driveway to the farm at the time of the shooting. But the makes of vehicle were not consistent among the witnesses, ranging from a Vauxhall Viva to a Ford estate to a van – nothing conclusive; and there were only seven sightings of people in the vicinity at the right time. Then a single shotgun cartridge case was found not far from the farm – and that was all.

On 30 November the same year there was an armed robbery at a remote farmhouse, Chapel Farm, not far from Yew Tree Farm: the elderly inhabitants were frightened, pushed about and bruised, and the robbers went off with £300. The getaway car had been seen and it led to Vincent Hickey, a local thief known to the police, and three men were arrested in December: Vincent Hickey, Jimmy Robinson and an Irish carpenter named Pat Molloy, whom I later came to represent on his final appeal. These men were by no means angels – but they were not murderers. There followed a long and complicated chain of events, with confessions, admissions of guilt for the Chapel Farm robbery and denials of involvement in the Yew Tree Farm murder.

On 21 December, Vincent's seventeen-year-old cousin Michael Hickey was picked up. Initially he couldn't remember where he was on the afternoon of the Yew Tree Farm murder four months earlier, but he denied being at the farm. Then he and Vincent remembered that they had been at his girlfriend's flat, where a new sofa was being delivered. The delivery note showed this was the date of the murder, and at the time of the actual gunshot they claimed to have been at a garage buying a car.

Pat Molloy was arrested on 8 December. He was subjected to an intensive period of interrogation, prior to an alleged oral and written confession on Sunday 10 December. He was in custody for 55¼ hours, during which there were five interviews lasting about ten hours, all in the absence of a solicitor.

The oral and written confessions became the fulcrum for the whole case. In them Molloy accepted that he was at Yew Tree Farm, engaged in a burglary with the others, when Carl was shot by Jimmy

Robinson. Molloy stated he was upstairs at the time searching through drawers when he heard a bang. He went downstairs and witnessed the murder scene and then ran outside.

The police claimed that at 15.40 on 10 December, having in earlier interviews denied involvement, Molloy was seen alone in his cell at Wombourne police station by DC Perkins, with DC Leeke listening outside in the corridor and DS Robbins making contemporaneous notes. Over the course of twenty minutes the officers asserted that Molloy gave them details of his presence at the farm. They went on to claim that he then dictated his confession in a written statement (Exhibit 54), which was taken down by DC Perkins between 16.00 and 16.20.

When Pat Molloy eventually got to see a solicitor, ten days later, his account of what happened was very different:

> I have been questioned here for about four days and nights. One of the men concerned is Vince Hickey. The detectives here brought a statement to me, signed by Vince Hickey admitting that he'd been involved. He named me as being there. He also named Robinson as being there. I was very upset over this. He also has a brother or cousin, I'm not sure, called Mickey Hickey. A few weeks ago, these two Hickeys called for Jim. I don't know the details until afterwards. They went to this farmhouse and held up three old people and robbed them of £300. I felt mad about this man putting my name up. As far as I can say I was not there, but I made a statement saying I was there but I wasn't there.[1]

Some months later, he added this:

> I agree that these statements are a correct account of the interviews with these officers. What I said however is not the truth. The details came from what had been said to me by the police. Also, I was knocked about by the police. I was hit in the face by an officer DC Perkins. I think the plate of my false teeth was broken with one blow. I was punched. I was also under continual questioning night and day and even when they left me the door was hammered every half an hour. I was given nothing to drink and had to drink water out of the toilet bowl. I was given food that was heavily salted. I

was told by the police that if I admitted to burgling the place then they would be satisfied. With regard to stacking the drawers in the bedroom I never used to do this. I was not that tidy.[2]

These were the instructions that the solicitor had written down at the time, and which I produced at the final appeal.

The four men stood trial at Stafford Crown Court between 8 October and 9 November 1979. Molloy and his legal team faced a serious dilemma. If he put forward the account described in his instructions, which necessarily involved suggesting deceit, fabrication and violence by the police, then his own bad character could go before the jury. If he were disbelieved on oath, then he ran the risk of a conviction for murder. If, on the other hand, he did not give evidence, did not challenge the confession or how it was obtained, then he might at best be convicted of burglary and at worst of manslaughter. Molloy remained silent at his trial and was convicted of manslaughter; the others were convicted of murder.

The rules of evidence are very clear. What one defendant says about another in an out-of-court statement cannot be used as evidence against another defendant, unless it is adopted, on oath in the witness box, as the truth by the defendant who made it. Molloy did not give evidence, so technically his confession was not evidence against the others, but in reality – as everyone appreciates – the prejudicial damage had been done by Exhibit 54.

As soon as Pat Molloy began his sentence, he started his campaign to clear himself of Carl's manslaughter, of being a terrible 'grass', and to prove the other men's innocence. If he'd been guilty, he could just have kept his head down and got out in eight years, whereas he began to help Ann and Fred Whelan, the dogged and determined parents of Michael Hickey, to clear the men's names, and in February 1980 Ann enlisted the equally resolute Paul Foot, campaigning journalist and columnist on the *Daily Mirror*.

A friend and a fellow socialist, Paul was a fantastic intellect. He died far too young in 2004, and I am constantly troubled by the misfortune of losing family and friends in their prime. I remember sitting at Paul's hospital bed a few years ago when he was very ill indeed from a stroke. We managed a laugh together, and I told him that he had to get up and get going again, as he was one of a kind –

and, remarkably, Paul did recover his ability to walk and speak. He was so utterly indomitable and is sorely missed.

Pat Molloy was missed too, because in June 1981 he died in prison from a brain haemorrhage. By this time he had convinced his co-convicted that he was extremely remorseful for his false confession (Exhibit 54), but that something else had happened at the police station which had made him give it.

In December 1981 there was an application for leave to appeal in front of the top judge, Lord Chief Justice Lane, but it was clear that their Lordships were not persuaded by the new evidence as they denied the application.

Michael Hickey then embarked on what no other prisoner has endured: the longest ever rooftop protest, lasting eighty-nine days in 1983–4, and through a freezing winter he was sustained by fellow inmates throwing him up food or sending parcels via Michael's 'fishing hook'. It was incredible and, being four years after his conviction, added to the power of his claims of innocence: he was not going to yield. Michael's protest generated immense publicity for the case, but he had to serve an extra two months in solitary confinement as a result, and was so worn down by the physical and mental strain of it all that he spent the next ten years in Ashworth mental hospital.

There followed other police enquiries, until by 1985 Jim Nichol, who became my instructing solicitor for Pat Molloy, had taken over the case of Michael Hickey as well, and it was Jim's tenacity and diligence which eventually led to the revelations that freed the men – though that was to take another twelve years.

Things started to unravel when new forensic methods came into play. DC John Perkins, who had taken down Molloy's 'confession' in Wombourne police station on 10 December 1978, had always maintained that Molloy had dictated every word to him. But Reverend Andrew Morton, an expert in language patterns, had tested Molloy's confession against his letters from prison, and concluded that Exhibit 54 had been made up by more than one person – and other experts concurred. Jim Nichol sent this information – together with new allegations from three other prisoners, that DC Perkins had forced them to confess by the use of violence – to the Home Secretary as the basis of an appeal.

The campaign to free the three men and clear Molloy's name posthumously was so long and protracted that it defies belief. There was one unsuccessful appeal in 1989 and many refusals to refer back; new and botched police enquiries; further rooftop protests by the accused, one by Jimmy Robinson in 1993, when he spent eighty-two days on the roof of Gartree Prison in Leicestershire; and meanwhile Paul Foot lost his job on the *Mirror*. There were TV documentaries and articles; more evidence trawled through by a persistent Jim Nichol, revealing a lack of disclosure of important documents by police and the prosecution; a succession of reluctant Home Secretaries; judicial reviews and heartbreaking delays and disappointments, and so on and so on – until in 1993 a powerful film by Don Shaw called *Bad Company* exposed the effect on the families and the incredible struggle by Ann Whelan to clear Mickey's name.

The film had an enormous impact on public opinion, and on one of the country's top forensic psychologists, Dr Eric Shepherd, who came forward to agree with the other experts on the Molloy 'confession'. I went public and endorsed Shepherd on a news programme, and then the foreman of the jury at the original trial let it be known that he felt the convictions were unsound – and he mentioned in particular the effect of Molloy's confession. He'd begun to have doubts some time before, and when he went public it added to the momentum for change.

But it wasn't until 1996, after two petitions and a judicial review threatening Home Secretary Michael Howard with court if he didn't thoroughly review the evidence, that Howard grudgingly sent the case back to the Appeal Court. Jim was finally given evidence by the prosecution that had been denied to the defence for eighteen years. There were 17,000 police messages and 260 undisclosed files, and he trawled through the lot.

This detailed process of re-examination began to reveal the truth. Jim Nichol asked his determined forensic handwriting expert Robert Radley to look at the original notorious Exhibit 54. As is so often the case, it was the tiniest quirk of fate, the tiniest unturned stone, beneath which lurked a massive mountain of lies.

There is a technique for paper and handwriting analysis called ESDA (electro-static deposition analysis). Every time you lean on, press on or write on a piece of paper, some form of impression can be made upon any paper beneath. Occasionally, if you hold a subsequent page up to the light, you can see this with the naked eye, but more often than not you have to treat the page with a chemical and then examine it under an intense low-angle light. (All this is now a bit passé in the electronic age of emails.)

What Mr Radley found, still attached to the top of the original statement, was an exhibit label. Quite unwittingly this label had protected the underlying paper. When he applied the ESDA technique to this area, it disclosed impressions which had been made before Exhibit 54 had been written. They were words from another statement purporting to have been made and signed by Vincent Hickey. The paper used was from Wombourne police station, not from Redditch, where Hickey was being questioned.

Mr Radley and another expert, Dr Hardcastle, both thought that the impressions of words were similar to DC Leeke's known writing, and that there were no significant differences. The signature was not Hickey's and had been forged; this time, the similarities were with the writing of DC Perkins.

The Court of Appeal, in July 1997, said that this evidence led them to two conclusions:

> First it supports Patrick Molloy's statement through his solicitor that immediately before he confessed and the reason for his confession was the showing to him of a statement apparently made by Vincent Hickey, stating that he and James Robinson were present at Yew Tree Farm. Secondly, it is evidence that police officers who were questioning Patrick Molloy were prepared to employ deceit to obtain a confession from him.[3]

There were other disturbing features, which Dr Hardcastle accepted when I cross-examined him. The oral interview could not have happened as the police suggested. There were two reasons, partly based on further research by Mr Butterworth, a Reader in Psychology at University College, London. First, there was an abnormally high coincidence between clauses used in the oral interview and identical clauses appearing in a written statement. There were sixty-eight relevant clauses in Exhibit 54, and twenty-three were identical to clauses in the record of the oral interview.

In experimental conditions, the ratio was never more than 2.7 per cent, nowhere near the 33.3 per cent in this case. Second, the writing speeds were also improbable to impossible, when calculating the number of individual characters with the number of minutes said to have been occupied by writing them. Put shortly therefore, it was well-nigh impossible for Patrick Molloy to have repeated his oral confession so precisely in its written form, and it was well-nigh impossible for a police officer standing outside in a cell corridor to have written it down in the time available. All in all, it stretched credulity beyond breaking point.

If more were needed, the final straw was the disappearance of the contemporaneous notes themselves. DS Robbins was ill at the time of the trial, so the notes were never produced then, or as it happens at any time since. When questioned about this later, he said that he hadn't transferred the notes to his pocketbook (that too wasn't available) and in any event the original notes had not been verbatim, and he only managed to get down about 70 per cent of what was said ... or should I say, *not* said! Without those 'confessions', the Appeal Court said that Molloy would not have been prosecuted for the Yew Tree Farm offences.[4]

After this, all the convictions began to unravel, contaminated by this rotten core document, and on 21 February 1997 the appeal of the Bridgewater Four was allowed. Ann Whelan, Jim Nichol and Paul Foot's huge endeavours had finally paid off, and Vincent Hickey, Michael Hickey and Jimmy Robinson stepped out into the daylight onto the Strand. From the day Pat Molloy had had the security of legal advice, he had always maintained his innocence, but sadly only his son Nick was alive to see his father finally vindicated that day.

The released men suffered terrible depression after their long years in jail, but whatever the personal pain, the campaign had shown that truth cannot be hidden for ever. It must be remembered, of course, that there is another family equally affected and distressed – that of Carl Bridgewater, because no one has ever been brought to justice for his murder.

The West Midlands Serious Crime Squad, which included the detective who falsified Vincent Hickey's signature, was wound up in 1989 after evidence came to light of other fabricated confessions and planted evidence in twenty-three cases during the 1980s.

*   *   *

There were lessons to be learned by us all from the Carl Bridgewater case, as it highlighted the need for a thorough reappraisal of professional attitudes. When Julia Dick, then a pupil in my chambers, asked me what I thought was the most important point in the Bridgewater appeal, I advised her: 'Always listen to the client's account and follow through the instructions you're given.' During my early career frequent assertions were made by defendants about police malpractice. They embraced the obvious 'verballing' – the drainpipe admission: 'You got me bang to rights, guv' – through to 'I *did* make a written confession, but it was beaten out of me.' Both the courts and the Bar looked upon such claims with a large measure of disbelief, which meant that barristers were prone to preface their questions in cross-examination of police officers with, 'Officer, I'm sorry, but I have to put it to you that this was not said . . .' or 'Is it possible that you laid hands upon my client?' In other words, what the barrister was saying publicly was: 'I don't believe a word my client has told me, but I have this unpalatable duty to put it to you.' Small wonder that juries also found the allegations against police incredible.

There was another consideration: if the defendant had any 'previous', then he would almost certainly be advised not to make any allegations against the police, in order to avoid his own bad character being made known to the jury.

The Bridgewater appeal clearly supported not only my client, but many of the other hapless defendants who for years had been complaining about similar police corruption.

My own approach was quite different. In the midst of all this there is a very fine balance to be struck. Defendants do lie and the police can be honest. Therefore the barrister must subject the client's instructions to the most careful scrutiny and critical analysis. But if the client steadfastly maintains his or her plea of innocence, then the case must be fought strongly and convincingly on that basis, whatever the risks. I have been proved wrong on many occasions, with people I secretly thought might be guilty being found not guilty by a jury, and vice versa. You just don't know. The evidence of innocence could be somewhere and, if you delve deeper, it will reveal itself. So I start off with a set of beliefs from somebody who wants me to represent them, where there is usually a bigger issue at stake, and that causes me then to investigate the case very thoroughly. Making an assessment of who is telling the truth is one of the most difficult exercises.

As a matter of interest, when I was a panellist on BBC Radio 4's *Any Questions* in Hastings in 2007, in response to a question put to me by a senior uniformed police officer I asked the assembled audience of around 200 whether there was anyone who could honestly say that they had never told a lie. No one put their hand up (including me). The tests of truth that are commonly employed in the courts relate to demeanour, consistency and background. However, professional liars can sometimes satisfy all these criteria, whereas vulnerable and innocent defendants may satisfy none.

All of this is quite different to the extremely rare situation of someone insisting on pleading *not* guilty when they have admitted their guilt to me. In essence, this is what lies behind the hoary old question, 'do you represent the guilty?' No problem – they plead guilty! However, it's not quite as straightforward as that. I have to be sure their admissions are reliable, relate to the specific offence(s) charged and are freely given. Provided they are and they understand the repercussions, then they enter a plea of guilty. I then present the mitigating factors to the court such as 'he (or she's) very sorry'; 'he's just a beginner'; 'he'll not do it again'; or 'he's been watching too much *Life on Mars*'. This is just what I would normally do for somebody who wants to plead guilty from the start.

More importantly these days, I can conduct a mini-trial (a Newton Hearing) on a plea of guilty and challenge the prosecution version of events in order to establish the defendant's account: 'I did it my way'. Witnesses can be called and cross-examined and this process preserves any credit that may accrue for a plea of guilty.

Should my client refuse to plead guilty when he's told me he really is, I am obliged to point out how little I can do. On the whole, not much. I am entitled to 'put the prosecution to proof' (meaning I require them to call their evidence since it's for them to prove guilt). This is a fairly hollow exercise and a waste of time and money because in these circumstances I cannot put forward a positive case suggesting innocence, cross-examine prosecution witnesses to suggest they are wrong and least of all call the defendant to say he didn't do it – effectively to lie. I have never done this and I know of no other member of the Bar who would contemplate it. So, back to reality . . .

In all cases barristers are supposed to be like surgeons, objectifying the patient/client; remaining impartial; not identifying with the client – otherwise they can't do the job. That's what I was told when I started, and that's what I have always ignored. I'm sorry, Lord Chancellor, but the fact of the matter is that for me to do the job I have to feel committed, to understand where my client is coming from and why he or she has got there. Interestingly, because most people know the way I operate, I do not have to choose my clients; they choose me. Some don't want to come under my intense scrutiny, so stay away, while others who do want that kind of involvement are keen to have my representation. This has led to my *not* representing big corporations, the state and major tyrants, and throughout I have attempted to be true to an inner conscience. Although emotional responses can be very difficult to handle, I believe that to deny them in your working life is as ridiculous as denying them in your personal one.

Until recently barristers were supposed to take the next case that came along, just like taxis picking up the next fare. In practice, however, the taxi-rank principle never really worked like that: some barristers only did private work, some specialised in specific areas (like tax or fraud), and others chose only to prosecute. I chose to defend. In a multicultural society choices have to be made, and barristers should be entitled to make them without being brought to book by the profession. It's important that principles are applied, as long as they are openly and honestly canvassed.

If a member of the British National Party came to me, I'd feel obliged to point out that I do not appreciate anything they stand for. Would they really want me to represent them under these circumstances, as I would be extremely uncomfortable? I would never assume their guilt, but I wouldn't be able to get close enough to represent them properly; neither would I want them to be convicted and then blame me for not pulling out all the stops on their behalf. This is what I would say in those circumstances, but fortunately I have never had to say it. Somehow BNP defendants haven't come knocking on my door.

In any case, in my early days the taxi-rank principle never seemed to apply to 'political' cases – and it was therefore often extremely difficult to gain representation for clients in the most challenging ones. Interestingly, the policy has now been ameliorated: but not for some high-flown ethical consideration, but because of the government's legal aid changes, which require barristers to sign contracts with the legal aid authorities. The Bar recognises, as it had to do in privately funded work, that a barrister may refuse a case if he thinks it is not properly remunerated. In private work, it means that if you don't get the fee you ask for, you can say you're not doing it, and the same sort of thing now applies to publicly funded work. Funny how money can speak louder than words . . .

The problems that beset the West Midlands Serious Crime Squad were not limited to that force. Systemic problems were exposed in the Metropolitan Police with the arrests of the so-called Tottenham Three, arising out of the Broadwater Farm disturbances and the murder of PC Keith Blakelock on 6 October 1985, and in the South Wales Police over the Cardiff Three (one of whom, Stephen Miller, was my client), and the murder of Lynette White on 14 February 1988.

I was very familiar with Broadwater Farm and Tottenham, in north London, having lived nearby and having helped to establish the Tottenham Neighbourhood Law Centre. Following the disturbances I represented fourteen-year-old schoolboy Mark Lambie, who stood trial in 1987 for riot and participation in the murder of PC Blakelock. His acquittal was partly due to my cross-examination of a prosecution witness who was an accomplice charged and convicted of minor offences. There is no transcript, but I do remember the gist of what happened.

Danny Simpson, my instructing solicitor in the Tottenham case, was an intrepid investigator and skilful lawyer who had obtained correspondence sent by the witness to a friend. The letters were incomplete, but none the less revealing about himself and events on Broadwater Farm that tragic night, and proved invaluable in cross-examination. The witness was shocked to know I had them, and could not work out how many letters were in my possession. My recollection is that as I went forward, the witness became increasingly nervous, as he'd forgotten exactly what he'd written.

The tension grew and eventually he asked for a convenience break. After an inordinately long interval he returned and announced that he had something he wanted to say. He accepted that he had not told the whole truth, and it was a turning point for Mark Lambie. The trial judge withdrew the charge and the jury acquitted him of riot and affray.

Whilst the present government's new proposals for anonymity of witnesses may be necessary in extreme cases, informers could have a licence to lie and inculpate others in order to settle old scores; it could also mean that the type of cross-examination I undertook in that trial would become severely constrained, because the content of the letters might reveal the identities of both writer and recipient.

Many years later, I discovered to my dismay that despite strong advice to leave Broadwater Farm following his acquittal, Mark Lambie had stayed on and was convicted of being the super-boss, dubbed 'The Prince of Darkness', who operated a drugs and extortion racket in the area. When failures like this occur, I not only feel upset for the victims, but deeply frustrated at such a squandering of time and the waste of a life.

Other defendants including Winston Silcott were convicted in the Tottenham case, and I came to represent one of them on appeal, Engin Raghip. His family were Turkish Cypriot; he was born in London and lived with his girlfriend and three-year-old son. At the time of the Broadwater disturbances he was nineteen. He had suffered serious learning difficulties as a child and was illiterate.

After his arrest he was interviewed ten times over four days, lasting a total of fourteen and a half hours in the absence of either a solicitor or an independent person. He was not permitted any contact or visits until after his confessions in the seventh and eighth interviews. His conviction rested entirely on these admissions.

The obvious and key question was the extent to which the confessions were reliable. There are two aspects to this. Reliability may be assessed by examining the internal and intrinsic quality of what has been said: how does it look, how does it sound, how does it compare with what is known about what actually happened? These are relatively superficial markers, and someone may acquire information from many different sources about an incident in which they took no part. Reliability may also be assessed by examining the nature of the speaker. This is even more difficult because there are learned responses, and the vulnerable or disadvantaged often manage to devise mechanisms to disguise their underlying problems.

Prior to the mid-1980s, and in particular the 1984 Police and Criminal Evidence Act (PACE), the police and the courts both approached these matters in a fairly rudimentary manner. On the whole a confession would not be ruled inadmissible unless you were able to demonstrate that it had been extracted by force or the threat of force. This was a threshold that could rarely be achieved. There was a glimmer of recognition that lesser factors could produce unreliable confessions, and these were encapsulated in informal guidelines known as the Judges' Rules. Unfortunately these were honoured more in their breach than in compliance. A school of judicial thought went along the lines that, provided a confession had not been beaten out of you, why on earth would anyone make what was termed 'a statement against interest'?

During these years there was a gradual recognition and appreciation that there were a multitude of subtle forces at work that might result in a false confession. These forces might not be obvious and could easily be missed by judges, juries and interrogators alike. There were three outstanding experts who pioneered advances and moved the frontiers of understanding, often in the face of scepticism, disbelief and even hostility. They were Gisli Gudjonsson, James MacKeith and Olive Tunstall. Together they embraced psychology and psychiatry, with particular regard to social and educational development. They were able to demonstrate the myriad of different mental, social and educational factors that have a diffuse and subtle effect upon the person being questioned. Even an interview being conducted in seemingly proper conditions, with contemporaneous recording, access to legal advice and the presence of a solicitor or appropriate adult where necessary, could not be guaranteed to produce reliable statements.

Although PACE introduced a number of marked improvements and protections for those detained in a police station, it was far from watertight. Interestingly, it was having a dry run in 1985 in the Broadwater Farm investigation, and yet people still fell through the safety net. A young person with an unstable background and with impaired educational development may not fall within the broad definition of mental illness, but may be quite unable to follow a simple line of questioning. That person may also be unduly willing to accept forceful suggestions to please the questioner. Gisli developed a series of tests that could be objectively applied by different psychologists, and these are now widely accepted: for example, he was able to measure susceptibility and suggestibility. Many of the tests are set out in his authoritative work, *The Psychology of Interrogations, Confessions and Testimony.*[5]

At the beginning, however, some felt that this was a 'soft-soap' option for heavy-duty dudes who should really be locked up. Others felt there was no need for this kind of expertise, because we can all make our own assessments about whether somebody meant what they said or had been forced to say something they didn't mean. It was this latter approach which led to the failure of Engin Raghip's first appeal in December 1988. Evidence of the kind described above was ruled to be inadmissible by Lord Lane, because Engin had registered an IQ rating of sixty-nine, just above the cut-off borderline laid down by the courts. In these circumstances Lord Lane declared that the jury had ample opportunity to gauge the degree of intelligence and susceptibility of Engin when he gave evidence without the assistance of experts.

By the time of the second appeal in 1991 there had been a sea-change in attitude. Two experts from the time of the original trial changed their minds in the light of Gisli's work and accepted that Engin was impaired to a significant extent in his intelligence and social functioning, which placed him in the borderline subnormal range of intelligence. Gisli himself described Engin as being at 'the bottom end of the borderline range of 70 to 79, within the lowest 4% of the population, giving a mental age of between 10 and 11 years'.[6] This also demonstrated that while the IQ cut-off point for normality/abnormality was a useful tool, it was in fact somewhat arbitrary and should not be a determinative factor.

There was, however, another powerful argument on the second appeal; enter stage left once more handwriting expert Mr Robert Radley. Six years before the Bridgewater appeal he'd been called in to examine the notes relating to Winston Silcott's interviews.

Winston had been arrested on Saturday 12 October 1985 and interviewed five times by Detective Chief Superintendent Melvin and Detective Inspector Dingle, who said he took contemporaneous notes. They were not signed by Winston, who refused to do so, and no solicitor had been allowed to attend. Once again the only basis for the conviction in relation to the murder of PC Keith Blakelock was primarily the content of the fifth interview. This comprised innuendo and ambiguity in the face of strong assertions of guilt being made by the interviewer, derived from unnamed sources – for example it was claimed that Silcott said: 'You ain't got enough evidence. Those kids will never go to court. You wait and see. Nobody else will talk to you. You can't keep me away from them.'

Some of the most damaging remarks occurred on page 5 of the notes. What Mr Radley found, however, by examining indentations on page 1 of the notes, was that there had been another version of page 5, which did not contain any of the damaging comments recorded in the existing page 5. And there were other discoveries, like a missing page 7. Mr Radley's opinion was endorsed by Dr David Baxendale, another expert document examiner who had been employed by the Home Office. Roy Amlot, QC, on behalf of the Crown, accepted both the evidence and the necessary inferences to be drawn. The court held that it destroyed the basis of the Crown case. It went on to observe that 'The notes were said to be taken contemporaneously and so far as page 5 is concerned they plainly were not. This conclusion had a knock-on effect for the whole appeal.'[7]

Mr Amlot made this very fair concession:

It seems to the Crown that the proper way to view it is to look at the broad picture. That picture is Melvin was the officer in charge of the case. He was the senior officer in the case. He was the officer who had close control of the whole murder enquiry and he was the officer to whom all junior officers looked in respect of any significant decision. I say that because Mr Mansfield has asked the question: would the Crown have gone on against the other defendants knowing what everyone does know of the apparent misbehaviour of the officer in charge of the case? It seems to us that this is an appropriate question for Mr Mansfield to ask in the circumstances and the answer that we have of course considered carefully is unequivocally we would not have gone against Raghip or Braithwaite or any of the other defendants having learned of the apparent dishonesty of the officer in charge of the case.[8]

Both Melvin and Dingle faced charges in relation to the fabrication of the notes, and were acquitted in 1994.

That was the year in which one of the most hallowed principles underpinning the criminal-justice system was effectively abolished – the right to silence. This was an age-old and highly valued principle, which the judiciary themselves had termed 'the golden thread of British justice'. It had been broken by a Thatcher regime that was not only bent on decimating 'society', which she said didn't exist, but also bent on eliminating legal safeguards that had been enshrined in our common law for centuries.

The Criminal Justice and Public Order Act 1994, sections 34 to 39, allows courts and juries to draw inferences from a suspect's silence in custody or in court. The legislation explicitly states that the court or jury can draw whatever inferences they see fit from a suspect's silence, when determining whether the accused is guilty of a charge. The anomaly is this: whilst the right to silence still exists, technically, if you choose to exercise it you run the risk of adverse inferences being drawn from your silence. This doesn't seem like much of a right to me. As for the argument that this provision was protecting the guilty, one only needs to reflect upon the cases cited in this chapter to realise that had the right been exercised, or had the preconditions for its exercise been strengthened and enforced, this might have circumvented the disastrous consequences of wrongful conviction for Pat Molloy, Engin Raghip and Stephen Miller.

Another of the most common complaints that I came across in my early days – but not now – was the tendency of Establishment mainstream barristers, faced with a seemingly strong case and a defendant claiming mistreatment by the police, to advise such a client to plead guilty. This was not confined to the Bar – some firms of solicitors succumbed to the same temptation. It meant less aggravation, less investigation and time for more cases. The Labour government's criminal legal aid policy enshrined in the Carter Review is likely to resurrect the same situation. This review was an attempt to introduce market-force economies, especially economies of scale, so that large conglomerates of lawyers would be awarded franchises or block finance, and smaller firms would be squeezed out. For example, there will be more money to be earned from a morning of guilty pleas than from weeks spent preparing one case of not guilty. The government's real objective can be aptly summarised by the acronym OCOF – One Case, One Fee. To which there is an obvious riposte!

The case of the Cardiff Three (Yusef Abdelahi, Tony Paris and Stephen Miller), involving the murder of a prostitute named Lynette White, was a massive miscarriage of justice in South Wales, and it was not the first of its kind. Nearly forty years earlier, in November 1949, twenty-five-year-old Timothy Evans had walked into Merthyr police station and confessed to disposing of his wife's body down a drain outside his home at 10 Rillington Place in the Notting Hill area of London. When the drain was inspected, which involved a number of police officers lifting a heavy manhole cover with difficulty, nothing was found. Evans was re-interviewed and implicated his landlord, John Christie. There was a further search at the address, where the bodies of Evans's wife and daughter were found in an outside washhouse. Evans then confessed to both murders and stood trial at the Old Bailey, where – despite claiming once again that Christie had murdered both victims – he was found guilty of murdering his daughter and sentenced to death. He was hanged at Pentonville Prison on 9 March 1950, but was subsequently vindicated when Christie himself was arrested in 1953 and confessed to killing seven women, including Mrs Evans. Christie himself was hanged in July 1953, but it was not until 1966, following publication in 1961 of *10 Rillington Place*, Ludovic Kennedy's seminal book on the case, that Timothy Evans was granted a posthumous pardon. I first read *10 Rillington Place* during my final years at Keele, when it was highly influential in forming my thinking about the deep inadequacies of the British legal system and the enormous struggle that has to be undertaken by anyone to put things right. Kennedy's account is still on my bookshelves today.

Back in Cardiff during the 1980s, a series of cases in which I was involved gave rise to evidence of disquieting police practices relating to interviews: the Welsh arson conspiracy in 1983, when my client David Burns was acquitted; the Cardiff Three case in 1988, when on appeal my black client Stephen Miller was released; and the murder of newsagent Phillip Saunders in the same year, known as the Cardiff

Newsagent case, with my client Michael O'Brien being released on appeal many years later.

There have been some remarkable developments in the Cardiff Three case since the appeal in 1992. DNA evidence emerged that led to a *white* man, Jeffrey Gafoor, admitting to and being convicted in 2003 of Lynette's murder. Then in 2008 three civilian prosecution witnesses from the original trial were convicted of perjury. In March 2009 Assistant Chief Constable Collette Paul, of South Wales Police, announced that fifteen people would face charges in relation to the investigation – twelve of them either retired or serving police officers. In the light of this announcement, it is improper for me to comment further on the Cardiff Three until these charges are resolved.

What has been at stake in all these cases, whether West Midlands, Metropolitan or South Wales police, has been the extent to which the basic requirements of due process have been respected.

The approach of our system has always been: better one guilty person going free than a whole host of innocent people being wrongly locked up. I still think, despite the threats that we are subjected to on a daily basis (escalating knife crime, for example) that, in order to get convictions, we should not be tempted to lower the threshold of proof or do without juries – and I have no doubt at all that lowering the threshold is what successive Home Secretaries have been trying to achieve for the majority of cases.

In the documentary film *Presumed Guilty*, directed by Yvette for *Inside Story* for the BBC, and in my book of the same name co-authored with Tony Wardle,[9] I argued strongly that one measure that would help to prevent miscarriages of justice arising from false confessions was audio and video recording of police interviews. This has become obligatory, and remarkably there are now very few confessions . . .

Unfortunately, government policy raises the spectre of false confessions all over again. Both Tony Blair and Gordon Brown originally wanted ninety days to hold a suspect, which is equivalent to a prison sentence without trial: no other country, even Spain after the Madrid bombings, saw fit to introduce such a draconian measure. The police rationale in the briefing provided to the Home Secretary, Charles Clarke, by Assistant Commissioner Andy Hayman was flawed, based as it was in part on a case in which I was intimately involved: the 'Ricin' case (see Chapter 20). This was the same officer who was roundly criticised for his handling of the misinformation put out by the police about the shooting of Jean Charles de Menezes at Stockwell Underground station in July 2005 (see Chapter 21), and who subsequently resigned in the wake of personal allegations surfacing in the press.

Part of the police rationale was that the existing period of detention of fourteen days did not provide them with long enough to employ in-depth interrogation techniques, but it is the use of such techniques during extended detention that runs the risk of false confessions. So far as general investigation is concerned (for example, decrypting computers, tracing mobiles and bank accounts) this commonly continues after an initial arrest and charge. In the Ricin case, my client Sihali had to wait two years for trial during which further evidence was served and additional charges were laid. An extended period of detention would have made no difference to the eventual outcome.

I was (and remain) so incensed by these proposals that I argued both publicly and behind closed doors with Charles Clarke. I briefed Members of Parliament to oppose the extension of detention – it is notable that this is the only occasion upon which a defeat was inflicted on Tony Blair's government – and a compromise of twenty-eight days was reached. That was all the more remarkable because this issue concerns principles of natural justice in the face of the perennial argument about the 'war on terror', and it also shows what it is possible to achieve by collective opposition on a large scale. However, the extension of the twenty-eight days to forty-two remains a very real government objective.

Why on earth Gordon Brown, who prior to becoming Prime Minister had no experience of or responsibility for criminal justice, should have persisted with the proposal beggars belief. Predictably it ran into enormous opposition from a previous Lord Chancellor (Charlie Falconer), a former Attorney General (Peter Goldsmith), a former Director of Public Prosecutions (Ken Macdonald) and even from Baroness Manningham-Buller, ex-Head of MI5 – and finally the Shadow Home Secretary David Davis was driven to resign on this issue. Should it ever become law, there is a strong case that it would be incompatible with the European Convention on Human Rights.

Rather than wasting time with anti-terrorist legislation of this kind, which since 1973 has done little or nothing to prevent terrorist acts, the police and security services should concentrate their efforts on thorough, accurate and responsible intelligence-gathering and collation, as they have enormous powers under RIPA (the Regulation and Investigation of Prosecutions Act). A series of recent cases concerned with bombings and conspiracies in London have shown one of two things: either that both the police and security services are hopeless at doing their job of collecting information where they should, or that they are collecting information, but are failing hopelessly to make connections and realise its significance. If either of these two situations led to the reported 'intelligence vacuum', then the victims and their families plainly deserve a full independent public inquiry once the various trials are completed.*

Due process and reliability of evidence are fundamental to a just legal system. But what exactly is 'due process'? It trips off the tongue quite easily and its convenience may overshadow its significance. It is not an adjunct or an accessory, or some kind of bureaucratic and perfunctory formality. It is simply a way of describing essential procedural and protective provisions which enable an individual, confronting the might of the state and its statutory powers, to receive a fair trial. It counterbalances the resources, research and investigation employed by state agencies.

There is nothing technical or mystical about the rules of due process. Ordinarily, if you're faced with an accusation of misconduct or misbehaviour you would have some pretty natural responses and questions. Who says? When? What? Why? How? Where's the evidence? Who can help? Anyway, you prove it!

---

* It now appears, from the Parliamentary Intelligence and Security Committee Report published on 19 May 2009, that in fact both these points have some validity. There was information on a 'ringleader' of the 7/7 bombings, who had been photographed in 2001, was later filmed at a training camp in Yorkshire and who then appeared on the fringes of the 'Fertiliser Conspiracy' (see Chapter 20). This information was not properly collated, assessed and fully identified until after 7/7. (c.f. Jean Charles de Menezes investigation, see Chapter 21). There was also a lack of communication between agencies – police and security services. These failings are now explained away on the basis of a shortage of resources, which wasn't exactly what was being argued at the time.

These questions translate into principles of natural justice, or 'due process', such as: access to free legal advice and representation at all stages; a clear and precise exposition of the charges; ready access to independent and impartial judicial scrutiny; proportionate access to all evidence and information; a fair trial before an independent and impartial tribunal on tested and reliable evidence; and above all, according to a presumption of innocence which can only be displaced by the state discharging its obligation to prove guilt 'beyond reasonable doubt' (the onus and standard of proof). This is intended to be a system, as far as is humanly possible, for safely convicting the guilty and not the innocent.

There is no point in having these rules unless there is an appropriate sanction should they be broken by the authorities. Minor infringements may not matter but major ones could and should be capable of putting an end to a case either at trial or on appeal.

On the rare occasions that this happens, it is commonplace for senior police officers to characterise the rules as arcane and part of an elaborate game played by tricksy lawyers to extricate guilty clients. At the same time the government of the day portrays the rules as a hindrance to expeditious, efficient and economic conviction. So, out go: the right to silence, rules against second-hand or hearsay evidence; and in come: limits on disclosure, extended detention for questioning, and shifts in the onus of proof from the prosecution to the defence for some offences. This is known in academic circles as the 'crime control model'.[10]

By these means the 'due' in 'due process' is slowly being diluted on the basis that the pendulum has swung too far in favour of the so-called hardened, professional criminal who is 'playing the system'.

These sentiments are predicated on the belief that we, police and government, know who are guilty and if we can't prove it we will have to get them, the defendants, to do it for us. I have represented enough of these so-called hardened criminals – most of whom do not feature in this book – to know that the real risk in these cases is one of 'noble cause corruption' by the police. The unspoken rationale behind this contention runs along the following lines: 'well, he may not have committed *this* crime, but he's probably done others in the past, and may do more in the future – so we'll nab him now'. If you like, it's a form of 'preventative detention' and punishment all in one. That's not justice either and I have resisted it for over forty years.

Interestingly when police officers themselves become defendants, their complete conversion to the tenets of due process is both swift and touching!

On a cold winter night in February 2009 at a petrol station in Wandsworth I was approached by a man who claimed to remember me from a court case in 1972. I thought he meant I had represented him, and as I couldn't remember any details I merely acknowledged him. He then surprised me by explaining that he was an ex-member of the Flying Squad whom I had cross-examined. 'You were a nasty bastard,' he said, 'but you did a good job.'

13

THE SWITCH

Freedom Fighter or Terrorist?

When I was born in October 1941 the Second World War was well under way, and my eldest brother Gerald was just sixteen, one year older than my other brother Ken. They both volunteered for the services as soon as they could, Gerald in the Second Battalion Scots Guards in July 1943 and Ken in the Fleet Air Arm: a baptism of fire for both, to live through the Blitz as teenagers in London and then to enter the conflict itself when so young. For Gerald it was the start of a traumatic life laden with anguish and adversity, which he faced with quiet fortitude and resignation.

Fascism, as embodied by Adolf Hitler, provided an obvious and identifiable enemy to be fought with Churchillian resolve, for it was a just war against a dictatorship of manic proportions, which practised eugenics, genocide and torture. Having crossed the Rhine with the Guards Armoured Division, Gerald was billeted with a German family. He was still a teenager, but despite the tangible hatred engendered by all things German, he experienced generosity and kindness that fuelled conflicting emotions. He learned to speak German, engaged in correspondence with German war veterans, and formed a strong attachment to a young German woman whose friendship he retained until he died, more than sixty years later. It was not just the Rhine he had crossed, but also the divide between ordinary people caught up in a tide of events not of their making, but orchestrated by political forces far beyond their control.

Gerald had barely returned from being part of a victorious army in Europe, adjusted to peacetime and acclimatised to the hopes and visions of a utopian Labour government, when he was suddenly drafted into a nightmare from which he never truly recovered: another war, this time in Malaya. He was still only twenty-three when in August 1948 he came down to Ventnor on the Isle of Wight, where I was on holiday with my parents, and sat on the beach with us, keeping his uniform on the whole time. He had come to say goodbye prior to his imminent embarkation on the troopship *Empire Trooper* on 6 September, and whereas he was usually laconic, cryptic and funny, that day on the beach he was quiet, withdrawn and overshadowed by a sense of foreboding. He knew, although I didn't, that he was facing an entirely different war, to be fought in an entirely different way. The enemy had changed to one less readily identifiable and more insidious, but considered to be ideologically far more threatening: communism.

Great Britain had fought alongside the communists during the war. They were our allies, but once the war was drawing to a close, the Soviet Union – which had sacrificed millions of fighters for freedom – was cast in a different light, no doubt due in large measure to the Machiavellian oppression wrought by Stalin on the back of a violent revolution thirty years before. Hence the race for Berlin. The communist threat became the rationale for a great deal of Western foreign policy (besides the wars in Malaya, Korea and Vietnam) until the end of the Cold War and the collapse of the Berlin Wall on 9 November 1989.

Since then an equally global 'ism' as personified by Osama bin Laden – Islamic fundamentalism – has taken the place of the ones that preceded it, and once again the wars that are being fought are against an enemy that was at one time an ally. Both the USA and the UK supported Saddam Hussein against Iran, and the USA in particular supported the Taliban against the Russian invasion of Afghanistan: hence the expression 'the Switch'. Much of the time of course this has little to do with democracy, let alone freedom, which are merely useful mantras for masking political and economic greed, currently epitomised by consumerism and the need for oil.

The Switch is also a useful mechanism for demonising opposition by employing the aphorism that 'One man's freedom fighter is another man's terrorist', and it attempts to minimise and marginalise the genuine and legitimate struggles of people for their civil rights and existence. Once this has happened, those who are being demonised run the risk of becoming more and more desperate until their cause finds support in movements that have a bigger political or religious objective, and such movements can manifest just as much megalomania and perpetrate just as many atrocities as the governments that have characterised them as terrorists. One feeds on the other, in a never-ending cycle. As Lord Acton wrote in 1904, 'Power tends to corrupt, and absolute power corrupts absolutely'[1]; and the losers, inevitably, are the weak, the vulnerable and the impoverished. That is why, in my view, the instruments of international law have such an important part to play in developing concepts of accountability, the rule of law, equitable dispute resolution, justice and peace. (See chapter 22.)

My brother's tour of duty in Malaya lasted two years. For him it was hell on Earth, while for me it was the other end of the Earth. He sent a monthly aerogram bearing strange stamps, which I collected; and he told of deathly experiences on jungle patrol. This was guerrilla warfare, in which the enemy was rarely glimpsed and even more rarely encountered, and he lived at the end of and on the edge of his nerves, never knowing what to expect. Most of the time he was wet and hot in an unbearably humid environment, wading through swamp or hacking through undergrowth. If a bullet didn't get him, then leeches, snakes or mosquitoes would, while malaria, dysentery and diarrhoea were commonplace. Sitting in the comfort of North Finchley, I thought that anyone who could endure and survive these gargantuan odds must be made of heroic stuff close to that of a Greek god.

The British campaign was successful on its own terms by moving and isolating large numbers of civilians, and at the same time winning their hearts and minds by the provision of food and accommodation. Nevertheless the origins of this crisis are instructive. Vested economic interests in the rubber and tin-mining industries, which were important to Britain's own recovery, insisted on the term 'State of Emergency': otherwise their losses would not be covered by Lloyd's insurance. In fact, of course, it was a full-scale war between the Malayan National Liberation Army (MNLA), the military arm of the Malayan Communist Party (MCP) and the British authorities.

From 1946 to 1948 there were a series of strikes and industrial disruption in Malaya, which culminated in increasing militancy and violence and, in 1948, in the murder of European plantation managers. The British Government, as it was to do over the years in other jurisdictions, imposed severe measures that curtailed civil rights. Political parties on the left, especially the MCP, were banned, and the police were given the power to arrest and detain without trial those who were members of such parties, or were suspected of being members or of assisting members. The MCP had considerable support among the Chinese population, who were deprived of voting and land rights and were extremely poor. Ironically, the MNLA was based on the Malayan People's Anti-Japanese Army, which had fought against the Japanese during the war and was trained and equipped by the British. The Switch. If the British Government had in the first place recognised the legitimate grievances expressed by the working population – which was not terrorist by nature, but merely wanted some basic rights – my brother might not have had to suffer as he did. It was the use of force and deportation in order to protect British economic interests that led to a dramatic escalation in the unrest; and, unbelievably, the State of Emergency declared by the British colonial authorities in 1948 was not lifted until 1960.

Everyday and ubiquitous struggles of this kind have been a theme of my working life, encountered in the many cases where individuals have found themselves facing terrorist or allied charges in British courts.

In 1996 a group of Iraqi professionals – doctors, lawyers and their families – tried every way imaginable to escape the vicious regime of Saddam Hussein. My client Mustafa Shakir Abdul-Hussain and his wife had been tortured because they were Shiites opposed to Saddam's regime, and death warrants had been issued against them both. They tried to bribe their way out; to fly out via Lebanon; to cross the border into the Sudan by car. Eventually they were successful and made it to the Sudan, but that country soon became regarded as a haven for terrorists and all flights to and from it were due to be suspended. They were desperate for a new start in Europe, and one night in August they were watching a film on television about a hijacking. Taking over an aircraft all looked fairly straightforward, so they decided this was a possible new option, and after a couple of attempts at boarding international flights to Germany without valid passports, they and two other families in a similar position were forced back towards Iraq on a domestic Sudan Airways flight to Jordan.

They arrived early in order to board first and occupy seats near the cockpit. By now they were recognisable as a group, but as it was a local flight, they hoped that security would not be so tight. Like the amateurs they were, the six men of the group stood in line with their families, including children, carrying a motley array of makeshift weapons such as scissors and balsa-wood model craft knives hidden amongst the kids' toys. They were asked to stand back while a larger group of passengers was checked through security, and watched while these people were being searched – and, to their shock and horror, a series of large, lethal-looking knives were discovered. Dismayed, my Iraqis thought they had been usurped by another band of hijackers and, by now in complete disarray, waited in trepidation to see the fate of the people in front. But nothing happened. The group ahead of them was ushered through security – and turned out to be butchers destined for the annual Jordanian Butchers' Convention.

Buoyed up with fresh determination, the Iraqis climbed on board, but by this time they had been allocated seats at the back of the plane, which was not a good position from which to enter the cockpit. Uncoordinated and leaderless, one of the group decided to act as soon as the plane was airborne and the stewardess came down the aisle offering tea. Armed with a squeezy, tomato-shaped ketchup dispenser (as found in Wimpy Bars) bound up with black tape to look like a grenade and filled with salt to give it weight, he leaped onto his seat and demanded that the stewardess open the door to the cockpit. Unfazed, she took no notice, and told him politely but firmly to sit down and have a cup of tea. He refused, and in the course of the hubbub dropped the 'grenade', spilling the salt all over the floor – at which point the stewardess imperiously told him to clear it up. Following this humiliation, further threats were made with plastic knives and other imitation grenades, until access was gained to the cockpit and the pilot.

For some reason the butchers' knives had been placed for safe keeping in the cockpit, and these were distributed among some of the group. The Iraqis took control of the plane, which had to refuel in Cyprus before landing successfully in Britain at Stansted. There the men were detained, and as the 197 passengers disembarked, a number of them wanted to thank the hijackers for their safe arrival and treatment while on board.

The trial of the six men, which took place at the Old Bailey in 1997, was arduous and highly charged at every stage. The defence that I, together with Keir Starmer (now Director of Public Prosecutions), mounted for Mustafa (as for the others) against the charge of hijacking was not a denial that they'd done it, but that it had been carried out under duress, an unusual and untested defence known as 'duress of circumstances or necessity'. The ordinary defence of duress has very strict conditions, in order to prevent those committing serious crime from escaping justice by claiming that they have been forced to participate by the threats of a co-conspirator: there has to be a clear and immediate nexus between the criminal act and the threat of substantial physical injury (such as a gun to the temple).

We argued that the law should be given a broader interpretation in cases of this kind. The gun may not be there pointing directly at you, but it may be only a matter of a few hours away. Saddam's agents had tracked the men to the Sudan, and they knew that time was limited before their inevitable torture and death. As this was an integral part of the defence, the Saddam regime had to be exposed to the jury, and beside the spoken evidence of witnesses, the judge permitted the showing of a film of some of the atrocities perpetrated, particularly against the Marsh Arabs in the south and the Kurds in the north. These descriptions and accounts were heart-rending and extremely distressing to watch, and by way of analogy we compared the necessity of the hijack to some of the essential and life-threatening activities carried out by the civilian resistance in France during the German occupation and the Vichy regime.

At one stage in the proceedings the pilot of the hijacked plane was called to give evidence. As is usual, the court usher went outside and asked the witness, who was in full uniform, to follow her into the court. He was sworn in and then asked by the prosecution, through an interpreter, the routine opening questions:

'Are you such-and-such a name?'

This was translated into Arabic for the witness, who replied in Arabic, which was then translated back into English for the court.

'No' was the one-word reply. The prosecutor looked puzzled, but carried on: perhaps the interpreter wasn't up to much?

'Do you live at such and such an address?'

This time the translation took a little longer.

'No' came back the answer. The prosecutor riffled through his papers: obviously something was odd, but he carried on regardless; maybe the man had moved.

'Were you the pilot on flight number such-and-such between Khartoum and Amman in 1998?'

'No' was the swift response. By now the judge, jury, prosecutor and I were very bewildered.

'Well, who *are* you?'

'I was the pilot on flight number such-and-such between Abu Dhabi and Beirut in 1999.'

He was appearing as a witness in the court next door![2]

Sometimes dealing with this kind of case is unbearable, and the stress and strain on everyone, clients and defence alike, is immense. People may have waited months or even years on remand, finally to reach the courtroom; they may have endured oppression and possibly torture back home and a kind of psychological torture here; then the trial day finally arrives. There are long days in court listening to interminably detailed evidence; cramped journeys back and forth to prison; witnesses stoking the case against you; the anticipation of a dynamic defence, and perhaps getting a pathetic one; anxious scrutiny of the impassive faces of the jury; waiting in dingy cells in the bowels of the court, relieved only by the daily visit of your counsel.

I liked my client Mustafa immensely. He was intelligent and cultured, but spoke limited English – most of our conferences were conducted via an interpreter, and no matter how professional and sympathetic the interpreter, this can prove very tiring and inhibiting. We decided to dispense with her services on several occasions and communicate in 'pidgin', and struck up a very cordial relationship. The trial had been demanding, and as it drew to a close it became extremely tense. One morning when I nipped down to the cells for my customary check, to see how Mustafa was and what questions he might have, I could sense that he was very on edge and nervous. I was in a wicked mood and, with a completely straight face, I told him I had been discussing the case overnight with the judge, who had said that the trial had been taking far too long and that he was anxious to get on to sentencing, as this was international terrorism and an example had to be set. I was so sorry, there was nothing I could do; he – Mustafa – was due for execution the following day. For a split second he looked aghast, then he burst into peals of laughter. This was a man whose own family had experienced summary execution, but despite that he got the joke. Difficult times can produce ridiculous situations.

At the close of the evidence and before final submissions to the jury, the judge, Mr Justice Wright (who later became the coroner in the Stockwell inquest: see Chapter 21), ruled that we had not established our duress defence in law, and therefore he had no alternative other than to withdraw it. He was intending to direct the jury that there was no defence; effectively the direction was tantamount to a finding of guilt. This put all the barristers, including me, into a predicament because if there was no defence we could not make final speeches to the jury, and other than remaining in court to keep an eye on the judge's summing-up, there wasn't much else to do. We discussed the various limited options with the defendants and decided unanimously that we should withdraw. Such a decision is exceptional and wasn't entered upon lightly, but it did leave the way open for the defendants to address the jury directly, from the dock if they so wished. The judge permitted this, and their impassioned pleas had a tremendous impact both on the jury and on the judge.

The jury was immensely sympathetic, especially as it was clear that the Iraqis had no intention of blowing up a plane with their children on board; the jury sent a note to the judge saying they had difficulty in reaching a decision and that they felt 'great compassion' for the defendants. But although the jury kept refusing to convict them, and begged the judge to be lenient if they did, he insisted that they had to bring in a guilty verdict 'on the facts'. Mr Justice Wright told the six defendants that although he had paid 'close attention' to the jurors' plea for compassion, 'I must pass sentences which reflect society's condemnation of what you did' – adding that in the last seven years there had been 225 hijacks, or attempted hijacks, worldwide. The Iraqis were jailed for terms ranging from four to nine years: not long, given the sentencing in comparable cases.

Afterwards an appeal was lodged against the judge's ruling, and that ruling was overturned by the Court of Appeal in 1998.[3] In doing so, Lord Justice Rose said that the law was imprecise, but the trial judge had interpreted it too strictly. 'If Anne Frank had stolen a car to escape from Amsterdam and had been charged with theft, the tenets of English law would not have denied her the defence of duress of circumstances on the ground that she should have awaited the Gestapo's knock at the door.'[4]

Mustafa and the five others were released. There was no retrial and eventually my client was granted asylum.

Just suppose that, once domiciled in the UK, Mustafa had decided to continue his struggle against Saddam Hussein by raising money for armed insurgents in Iraq, by attending meetings in London to get political support and by possessing literature along the same lines: he could have been arrested by the British police under anti-terrorist laws. The Switch.

When I first started to practise in 1967, Archbold's *Criminal Pleading, Evidence and Practice*, the main textbook for practitioners, had no reference to terrorism. Now it's stuffed full of it. Terrorism is defined as:

> 'the use or threat of action designed to influence the government or an international governmental organisation or to intimidate the public or a section of the public, and made for the purpose of advancing a political, religious or ideological cause'.

'Action' embraces 'serious violence against a person, serious damage to property, endangering life and creating a serious risk to the health or safety of the public or serious interference with an electronic system'.[5] This definition is extremely wide because it is capable of covering both individual and group action as well as actions undertaken by states: for example, the invasion of Iraq was plainly unlawful and was intended to accomplish regime change and not to recover weapons of mass destruction, which did not pose any form of immediate threat and did not even exist.

In the light of this, internationally there is no consensus about the definition of terrorism. So when the International Criminal Court (ICC) was established in The Hague in 2000, war crimes and genocide could be tried (having already been defined), but not terrorism. The reason for this is obvious: too many governments realised they could end up in the dock. It is against this background that acts of terrorism, for whatever cause, have to be approached with caution. I have probably acted in more terrorist cases than anyone else at the Bar – starting in 1973 with my own car-bomb incident – but nevertheless have always been implacably opposed to the use of violence to promote a political objective (other than in circumstances of an immediate need for self-defence). That is why I think that Mahatma Gandhi's employment of non-violent collective means to shock the authorities into dialogue is entirely appropriate. However, even he would be likely to be prosecuted in the UK today, particularly if he protested within a mile of the Houses of Parliament, like Brian Haw and his anti-Iraq war tented encampment.

This is not an idle debate, because similar observations were made about the African National Congress (ANC). Whereas Nelson Mandela is rightly lauded as an international hero and his statue has been placed in Parliament Square, there was a time when Margaret Thatcher regarded him as a terrorist and was unwilling to welcome him to the UK upon his release – unlike, of course, General Pinochet, whom she obviously thought had played such a prominent part in promoting justice and human rights in Chile that she fêted and welcomed him with open arms.

I had attended a fundraising auction at the Arts Theatre in London for the benefit of the ANC and its programme of reconstruction after Mandela's release, and one of the photographs I bought was rare: it showed all the defendants who had stood trial with Mandela, accused of treason in 1956. Subsequently I was invited to a reception for him in London and decided to take this rather large photo, wrapped in brown paper, tucked under my arm. When I arrived, Mandela was predictably surrounded by the great and the good, and I began to have cold feet about interrupting him with this brown-paper package, when he had no idea who I was. Still, I really wanted to meet him, and so, mindful that he who hesitates is lost, I plunged straight in. Mandela was entirely gracious, unwrapped the photograph and took time there and then eloquently to recount the fates of the many people in it: so many had died, and so many had suffered imprisonment alongside him. He kindly signed the back of the photograph for me and dated it: 12 October, my birthday. It's a closely guarded possession.

A number of years before this I had represented an Armenian charged with conspiracy to kidnap the Turkish Ambassador in London. He and the other defendant denied any such conspiracy, but admitted that they wished to expose the way the Turkish state had maltreated the Armenian community. As with the Iraqi hijack case, it was necessary to present as much evidence as possible about the history of this abuse. The high point was the genocide carried out between 1915 and 1923, when up to 1.5 million Armenians died in death camps and on death marches at the hands of the Turks. Not only has this always been denied by the Turkish Government, but the very existence of Armenian villages and place names within the borders of Turkey has been airbrushed out of history.

At this time I was still married to Melian and had five gorgeous but mightily energetic children, and weekends were a hectic round of different activities. Jonathan was a successful table-tennis player; Anna and Louise were both accomplished horse-riders and swimmers, and in addition Anna was an award-winning ice skater; Leo was wicked at tennis and wildly funny; and then there was young Kieran, who was four, independent and adventurous.

We lived in an unwieldy Victorian house in Crouch End, north London, and keeping tabs on the needs of a large, lively family while in the middle of this high-profile case involving the Armenians was demanding. I was aware that there were ongoing squabbles over sweets and crisps, so to try and exercise a modicum of control, these were hidden in a larder in the kitchen. One of my sons took a keen interest in these treats, and early one morning I heard footsteps padding past our bedroom and down the stairs. I guessed the motivation and silently followed him down, and as I approached the kitchen I could hear rustling from the cupboard. Always believing that patience is the better part of valour, I sat myself quietly down on a kitchen chair and waited. The rummaging continued, but eventually he emerged, his dungarees stuffed with packets of biscuits, crisps and whatever else he had been able to reach – and his surprise at seeing his father sitting opposite the cupboard door led him hurriedly to try and hide his cache of goodies. In his haste to pull up the long zip of his all-in-ones he did the inevitable and caught his penis in the zip. Ouch! The poor boy was in agony.

This being a new experience in my catalogue of childish mishaps, I decided to try and rescue the trapped body part with a pair of kitchen scissors, but only succeeded in cutting the dungarees to shreds and leaving the zip still firmly attached. So the next step had to be the local hospital, and I woke the family to get them started for the school day, before wrapping my dear son in a towel and putting him in the car. Chaos reigned in the house, and in the midst of it all I telephoned the Old Bailey. Always believing it is best to be straightforward, I asked a bemused telephonist to let the judge know about my son's trapped penis and that I would be late, but please to continue the case without me, as my junior would stand in until I could be there later in the morning.

Arriving at Casualty, I jumped the inevitable queue and, when the nurse took a look, she exclaimed, 'Oh no, not another one!' It turned out that my son's predicament was so common that they had a special pair of tailor's scissors, which did the trick in a trice.

His penis intact, I drove him home, then high-tailed it to the Old Bailey – to be greeted by a barrage of waiting photographers taking shots in the direction of my trousers. Like a Chinese whisper, the message to the court had been distorted: the trial had been stopped, and word got out that Mansfield had his penis trapped in his zip. I went to see the judge in his room in order to apologise for the confusion, only to find that he too had thought it was my own predicament, for he opened the conversation by asking, sotto voce, if I was OK. The headline in the *Sun* next day read: 'Fly Boy Stops Terror Trial!'

My client was acquitted and I subsequently attended his wonderful Armenian wedding, with son in fine fettle.

I had a personal reason for sympathising with that client's cause, as I was only too well aware that it wasn't just the Armenians who had suffered during the First World War at the hands of the Turks. My father's left leg had been demolished by Turkish machine-gun bullets on 27 October 1917, while he was serving on horseback with the Third City of London Yeomanry Eighth Mounted Brigade in

Palestine, as part of General Allenby's campaign with the Egyptian Expeditionary Force across Sinai, which ended with his entry into Jerusalem on 11 December 1917. The amputation of my father's leg was carried out at the 70th General Hospital in Abbasia, Cairo, when he was only twenty-one. He had joined up at the same time as his elder brother Kenneth, who remained in the Middle East with his family throughout what became known as the British Mandate of Palestine between 1919 and 1948. It was during this time that the British Army became targets for the Zionist paramilitary organisations Haganah, Irgun and the Stern Gang, whose activities were regarded as terrorist by the British authorities, although a number of their members went on to become the founding fathers of the Israeli state.

As a child I had been vaguely aware of all this, partly because my father was very sympathetic to the plight of the Arab population and was angry about the violence meted out by the Stern Gang, but also because our tiny, suburban semi-detached housed an intriguing and romantic watercolour by the renowned Scottish painter favoured by Queen Victoria, David Roberts. It hung above a neat black upright piano, at which I spent many frustrating hours trying to learn Strauss when I would have preferred Scott Joplin, and to bring matters to a head I stabbed middle C with a kitchen knife. No more lessons for me with Miss Cross – who undoubtedly was! Meanwhile I had tried to imagine where the place depicted in the painting could be: it was a desert scene with tiny figures alongside camels resting in the heat of the day, and with two huge statues in the middle distance. It wasn't until Easter 2001, when I paid a visit to Cairo for a conference about the Lockerbie case, that I realised how significant David Roberts was, and what was the probable inspiration for the painting. It appears that the two huge statues are the Colossi of Memnon in the plain of Thebes, and the artist is highly revered in Egypt because he captured the original hues and pastel colours – palest lime-green, yellow, violet – revealed when the sand that had covered the columns of the many temples for centuries was removed.[6]

The history of the inter-war years is crucial to an understanding of the ongoing crisis in the Middle East and to one of the most emotionally intense trials I have undertaken. The British expedition in Egypt through to Palestine was motivated less by the need to defeat the Germans than by the desire to begin preparations for the post-war era – similar to the manoeuvring that took place at the end of the Second World War. In 1916 there was a secret agreement between the British and the French (the Sykes-Picot Pact), by which they proposed to carve up the Middle East into spheres of influence. There was a fear that the Turkish Caliph might order a military jihad, thus bringing into the war other Muslim nations on the side of the Central Powers. If this were to happen, the Suez Canal would become a critical transport artery. Essentially the League of Nations and proposals for partition were merely vehicles for dividing up the spoils of war and ensuring control over, and access to, various resources thought necessary for the maintenance of colonial influence. The British took responsibility for Palestine, and the French for Lebanon and Syria. If these territories had been ceded to them instead of being mandated, the level of war reparations being sought by the Allies would have been diminished. On the one hand, the British – through the intermediary T. E. Lawrence (of Arabia) – promised the local Arab population independence for a united country that covered most of the Arab Middle East, in exchange for support of the British during the war. On the other hand, in 1917 the Balfour Declaration promised to create a Jewish national home in Palestine. Land and territory were being used as pawns in a political power game, and not for the first time. The empires of the Greeks, the Romans, the Crusaders and finally the Ottomans had all done the same. Small wonder that the people who actually lived there resorted in the end to force to protect their very existence. It is an irony beyond measure that the Israeli state, born out of discrimination and extermination against Jews, should now be practising those very same policies against the Palestinians.

In 1994 Jawad Botmeh, a thirty-one-year-old Palestinian, and Samar Alami, a thirty-three-year-old Lebanese banker's daughter, were accused with others of planting car bombs outside the Israeli Embassy in Kensington Gardens, London, and at the offices of a Jewish philanthropic institute in north London: no one was killed, but there were many injured. Strangely, the Israeli Embassy security cameras ran out of film at the critical time of the attack, and no senior figure was present in the embassy when the bomb went off.

Botmeh and Alami had been students in London for some years, active in Palestinian student politics, and they both admitted their support for the Palestinian cause against illegal Israeli occupation of Palestinian land. In 1996 Ben Emmerson and I were instructed by Gareth Peirce and we worked hard on their defence. They absolutely denied being involved in the bombings in London, but did admit dabbling amateurishly in assembling explosive materials for the defence of Palestinian civilians in Palestine, devices which they believed could be flown by civilians in model aircraft over the heads of Israeli aggressors.

Knowing that I like to get a better understanding of what life on the ground is like, Jawad suggested that Gareth and I should pay a weekend visit to Palestine. It was supposed to be clandestine so as not to jeopardise the safety of Botmeh's family, so Yvette came along too as 'cover': this was to look like just another holiday weekend. We stayed in Jerusalem at a large anonymous hotel, and various Palestinian relatives of Botmeh took considerable risks to come and meet us, one even travelling in the boot of a car. Late the same night we were escorted to the home of an Israeli woman lawyer who had been courageously defending Palestinians on the West Bank, and met intellectuals and campaigners who had seen the situation deteriorate over the years. They were pretty despondent but, amazingly, still committed to fighting for change. (How they must be feeling now, following the utter and indiscriminate destruction in Gaza, of which I became acutely aware on a delegation in March 2009, is not difficult to imagine. There could be little doubt that this was sheer retribution on a civilian population that had dared to elect Hamas. It may be time for all concerned to reflect on Milton's epic poem 'Samson Agonistes' with its memorable line 'Eyeless in Gaza, at the mill with slaves'.)

We took a very early-morning trip to Botmeh's home, on the way seeing large groups of Palestinian men waiting desperately to be chosen by a handful of Israeli employers for the chance of a day's work across the divide, while Israeli helicopters circled overhead. Perversely, it reminded me of those powerful photographs by Bert Hardy of cloth-capped English workers in the 1930s Depression in Jarrow, also waiting for a handout, in another era on the other side of the world.

Botmeh's family was so welcoming and generous it was overwhelming. Breakfast had been lovingly prepared by Jawad's mother – a large, comforting woman whose soft smile and generous spirit no doubt belied the anxiety she was feeling – and we sat down to a feast, aware that it must have left them hungry for a week. The meal was peppered with disquieting stories of the lengths they had to go to in order to maintain some kind of normality and the hardships they had to endure: a ten-minute walk transformed into a three-hour journey for Botmeh's sister to reach school every day; the Roman water supply, which had irrigated their land for literally thousands of years, now diverted to Israeli land; the destruction of the olive groves that were their main source of income; the hut by the railway line used by Israeli police to interrogate and sometimes torture young Palestinians – which was especially poignant for me, as I believe my uncle helped build that very railway line.

We left amid embraces, small gifts of sweet delicacies and hopes for success for the trial; this kind of responsibility 'goes with the territory', as they say, but it is never easy to bear, and in this case I felt a heavy burden. How was I to secure the freedom of these young people when prejudice is so weighted against them?

Being escorted everywhere (for our security and enlightenment) by Palestinians who had clearly kept their humanity, despite the hardships they faced, was a salutary lesson. Yvette and I were guided round a school in a rambling, ramshackle refugee camp, packed with eager faces that I was asked to address. Holding the microphone, looking out over hundreds of uniformed girls and boys, as in any school, I asked myself: what do I say to children with such a bleak future? I spoke of strength, dignity, human rights. The children were positive and open, like all children everywhere, but were my words merely hollow rhetoric?

The refugee camp is one of many that were a legacy of 1948, when thousands of Palestinians were dispossessed, and some refugees have remained there ever since in appalling conditions, while the remainder have been exiled abroad without the right of return.

The nearby hospital was clean and modern and appeared well equipped, but it was stretched to capacity, with young men and civilians suffering horrendous injuries inflicted by Israeli troops. A group of them, some almost ready for release, sat in chairs around an airy but clinical room, many with head bandages or the obvious loss of limbs. The strange thing was the atmosphere of eerie calm. Was it our presence that silenced them, or a kind of resignation? Maybe they resented our visit. The doctors said these young men would probably either take up arms or be dead within months; a very few, with help, might escape to a quieter environment; others might end up in jail, like my clients back in London. The director of the hospital, a warm and obviously dedicated soul, was desperate for us to communicate their plight to the wider world, but I suspect he knew, as I did, that it is hard to get people to listen when it comes to Palestine. We managed to call the director as a witness in the trial, despite dogged obstruction by the Israeli authorities.

Leaving the West Bank to cross back into Israel was akin to passing through Checkpoint Charlie in East Berlin. Yvette and I had to get out of the car, say goodbye to our friendly Palestinian guide and, alone and very tense, walk the couple of hundred yards across 'no-man's-land' scrutinised by Israeli armed guards. It felt a very long way across the dusty ground in a kind of heightened reality, until the same barren land became Israel.

Before our departure I had an appointment with a Professor Zitrin, a world expert on explosives. A very unusual substance, TATP (or Triacetone Triperoxide, one of the most sensitive explosives known, being extremely reactive to impact, temperature change and friction), had been used in the London bombs, and he knew a lot about its properties. When we arrived for the meeting we walked straight past him, because I hadn't realised that he was also a senior Israeli police officer and was therefore dressed in uniform. We had a very pleasant lunch together, but he was circumspect as well as friendly, and it was clear that he knew exactly why we were there and was aware of our movements. Realising that the time for our return flight was fast approaching, he offered a police car to take us to the airport – a kind but highly embarrassing gesture, and Gareth sat grim-faced in the back of the car. As we approached the airport, Zitrin asked me to return one day to give a lecture at Haifa University, and casually let slip that I must answer truthfully all questions by security at the airport. All three of us were totally unprepared for this eventuality. There were long queues. We were separated and asked a series of penetrating questions. In my case,

they knew right down to the breakfast menu that day what I had
been up to. I also had in my bag the incriminating special Palestinian
delicacies from Botmeh's mother. Gareth, in true solicitor mode, was
inscrutable. Yvette successfully deflected their interest by admiring
the female Israeli soldier's hairstyle (so close-shaven she was almost
bald), while I gave a long and detailed account of lunch with one of
their police chiefs. We only just made the flight.

The trial lasted weeks and the judge allowed much disturbing
evidence about the state of Palestinian life, but the jury found both
Botmeh and Alami guilty, and they were sent down for twenty
years. We appealed against the conviction, but leave wasn't granted
until 2000.

In 1997 ex-MI5 agent David Shayler had revealed that shortly after
the bombing he became aware that there had been a prior warning,
by an organisation not linked to the accused, of a terrorist attack on
the Israeli Embassy. Ministers, led by Home Secretary Jack Straw,
accused Shayler of being a traitor and ridiculed his assertion that
any such warning had been received by the security services.

At the appeal, I accused the Crown Prosecution Service and the Home
Office of wrongly throwing a blanket of secrecy over intelligence-agency
information, which we believed could clear the pair. I argued that this
suppression of evidence rendered their trial unfair and their convictions
unsafe. What is more, non-disclosure of relevant information was a
breach of Article Six of the Human Rights Convention.

It eventually emerged in court that Shayler was telling the truth.
After months of prevarication, the security services finally admitted
that there was such a warning about a terrorist attack and that it had
nothing whatever to do with Samar Alami or Jawad Botmeh.

As Paul Foot wrote in the *Guardian* on 31 October 2000:

Why hasn't anyone heard about this before? The answer is simple.
The security services and the Metropolitan Police Special Branch
were struck down with a terrible attack of HE – Human Error –
an attack that rendered them quite incapable of carrying out their
most elementary duties in the course of criminal justice.

The terrorist-organisation warning was 'disseminated' by a
document within the security services, but 'for reasons of human

Frank and Marjorie, 14 June 1924, Exeter.

'A clear desk reflects a clear mind': my father, Deputy Chief Controller, GNER.

Blitz baby takes a break during bombing.

Me and father – I'm in there somewhere! – the back garden of 73 Naylor Road.

Ken, Fleet Air Arm

Frank, Marjorie, Gerald and me, Ventor, Isle of Wight. On the eve of Gerald's departure for the Malayan Campaign, 1948.

Gerald, Scots Guards

The label in the larder.

An early holiday in Exmouth, Devon, in 1948 – paternal advice about sartorial deportment.

A preparatory 'maiden' over!

Me and Jeremy, two of three Musketeers in our training ground near Dollis Brook.

Highgate School Combined Cadet Force – learning to point out the obvious!

My mother, Marjorie

Me, Ken, Gerald and Nora, his first wife, Tilbury
Docks, London. Ken en route back to South Africa.

Keele University – a student union committee
meeting with Maureen Ritchie.

Melian,
Anna, me &
Jonathan

My Triumph 2000 that got blown away – the Old Bailey Bombing of 1973.

My 'antique' wig that also got blown away
– in October 1987.

Angela Weir, the Angry Brigade
trial, 1972.

From left to right: Freddy, Yvette, Anna, me in full-bottom wig, Keiran, Leo and Louise. Taking Silk, House of Lords, 1989.

Tooks Court Chambers with daughter Louise.

More clerks who keep an eye on me! Sandra, Lennox, Philippa and Carol B.

A cluster of clerks. *Back*: Simon, David, Kieran, Alistair; *middle*: Carol T, Lee, me, Martin, Diana, Natasha; *and front*: Milla.

The long shield brigade at Orgreave, Miners' Strike, 1984: defending the indefensible, Margaret's Marionettes!

Topside holding area prior to the three-stage clearance. 'There were about 5,000 to 6,000 in front of us,' said Asst. Chief Constable Clements, 'and the sky was black with missiles.'

Bernard Jackson's arrest   Eric Newbiggin

Yvette's parents,
Sally and Paul
Vanson, 1985.

Yvette and I on the first anniversary
of Orgreave, 18 June 1985, during
the trial at Sheffield Crown Court.

Acquittal: the end of the Orgreave Trial, 1985.

The Birmingham Six
after their successful
appeal. *From left to right*:
Johnnie, Paddy, Hughie,
Chris Mullin MP, Dick,
Gerry, Billy.

In chambers preparing for
the appeal, the wall behind
dominated by a map of
Birmingham city centre.

**Mirror
man
helps
to end
jail
siege**

Reporter Boam

THE siege of Parkhurst
jail was over yesterday
— and Mirrorman
Roger Boam helped to
end it.

Assistant governor Gerry
Schofield, pale and
shaken, but unharmed,
was freed by two
prisoners who had held
him hostage at knife-
point for 28 hours.

The siege at

Helped to solve prison siege

by Lorraine Anam

HORNSEY barrister
Michael Mansfield was
at the centre of the
Parkhurst Prison siege
last week.

Mr Mansfield (41), of
Weston Park, Cruch End
called in to talk to two
prisoners who had taken
Assistant Prison Governor
Gerry Schofield hostage at
knifepoint.

After 15 minutes with Mr
Mansfield and a newspaper
reporter, convicted killer
John Bowden and robbery
Jimmy McCraig released Mr

Schofield and gave them-
selves up.

This week father-of-five
Mr Mansfield said: "Bowden
wanted to bring his grievances to light in the outside
world.

"I felt from the moment I
spoke to him on the phone
that he wouldn't harm anyone, and my feeling was confirmed when I actually saw
him at the prison.

"At no time did I feel I was
in any danger for that reason.
Obviously the main object of
the exercise for me was to act
as a mediator between Bowden and the authorities."

● Michael Mansfield.

Press coverage of
the Parkhurst Seige,
January 1983.

TOLD WE
WILL DIE

Strangeways rooftop
protest, 1990.

With Doreen Lawrence at a fundraising dinner.

Free at last: Kevin Callan steps out of the Court of Appeal victorious, flanked by his mother and father.

I carry a copy of this photo of Angela Cannings and Jade, a gift from Angela, in my wig box.

Judith Ward

Freddy, Vincenzo and Eileen Dallaglio: after the trauma, tickets to the England–Argentina rugby match at Twickenham as a thank you from the Dallaglios.

'Pigs' advancing down
Rossville Street

Advancing 'Pigs' scatter Derry peace protesters on Bloody Sunday 1972.

As chairman of the Cullyhanna Inquiry I question an eye-witness to the shooting, with colleague Michael Topolski.

The trauma of an eye-witness after the shooting of Barney McGuigan by the telephone box.

Gable End (Block 1)
Rossville Flats

Lamp post

'Pig'
Saracen

Rossville
Street

Glenfada
Park North

The Aftermath (see p.163)

Barney McGuigan
lies dead

I arrive at Jill Dando's address for the jury view.

Mouloud Sihali, acquitted of the Ricin Conspiracy, 8 April 2005.

The day of Nabeel's acquittal in the Fertiliser Conspiracy, 30 April 2007.

Gareth Peirce and I with Jawad Botmeh at his wedding to Eliza after his release in 2008.

Fatmir Limaj:
return to
Kosovo in
triumph.

Me with Tony Benn and Helena Kennedy at Tony's
medal presentation by the Cuban Government, May
2009.

Ludo Kennedy and I at an Amicus event.

Benjamin Zephaniah,
Pam Ferris and I at a
Viva! fundraising event:
nodding acquaintances!

Diana and Dodi: an intimate moment before departure from the rear of the Ritz, Paris.

A 'brief' word at the Inquest.

Jury view of the Alma tunnel, 2007.

The grieving parents of Jean Charles de Menezes at home in Brazil.

The mother of Jean Charles de Menezes with a photograph of her son.

Rucksack photograph of Hussain Osman, July 21 attempted suicide bomber.

Relatives of Jean Charles de Menezes make their feelings clear about which verdict should have been available to the jury.

With some of those wayward files . . .

error' it was not placed on the files shown to the prosecution counsel in the Botmeh and Alami case. A copy of the document about the warning was passed by MI5 to MI6, but this didn't get to the judge in the case during the disclosure hearing; instead it was filed by an MI6 desk officer. They said it was an oversight. The document was also passed to the Metropolitan Police Special Branch, whose officers were hunting the bombers. It was 'placed in a file germane to the main thread of the information received but was not placed in the file connected to the Israeli embassy or one which would have fallen within the Crown disclosure'. More human error?

From this grotesque catalogue there were only two possible conclusions. The first was that both sections of the security services are so hopelessly disorganised that they cannot follow elementary rules of disclosure, and that even in cases involving terrorism and bombing they are incapable of making good use of any information they receive. Or second, that MI5, MI6 and Special Branch conspired not to disclose information that might damage the prosecution of Samar and Jawad.

The appeal was adjourned while we investigated yet more evidence that the police knew of another suspect, but had kept quiet about him. On 1 November 2001 I remember Yvette and Jawad's mother sitting in the corridor outside the courtroom waiting for the result: we were desolate when the appeal was finally rejected. Jawad's mother graciously sent me a beautiful Palestinian glass bowl, which I cherish.

While in prison Jawad had taken up painting, and in 2003 the Kufa Gallery in Bayswater, west London, staged an exhibition of his work. They are powerful paintings. One shows a settlers' road cutting through the mountain behind Battir village – a village that in 1949 the painter's grandfather negotiated with Israelis to keep on the Palestinian side of the 'green line', the line that has since turned into a vast, illegal concrete wall, which snakes through Palestinian land on the outskirts of Bethlehem. Another large 'canvas' was actually painted on a prison sheet, a violent collage of headlines and imagery from attacks on Palestine and its people, with splatters of 'blood' suffusing the whole image. It hangs in my room in chambers. Jawad also makes wonderful pots. We have one in our living room, a constant reminder.

Jawad was finally released on parole in August 2008, and shortly afterwards Yvette and I had the immense pleasure of attending his and Eliza's wedding, where we had a chance to meet his family again, this time under happier circumstances. I have recently learned that their first child is due very soon. At last a happy ending?

In the late 1980s I undertook another political trial, in which a group of Sikhs were charged with a plot to assassinate Rajiv Gandhi in London because of their treatment at the hands of the Indian state. The trial was in Birmingham, and Yvette came with me as she was filming *The Birmingham Wives* (see Chapter 17) for the BBC's *Everyman* programme. We were asleep in a hotel in the centre of the city when we were rudely awakened by a fire alarm. Looking out of the window, I saw flames leaping out of a shop window opposite, too close for comfort. Without stopping for anything, I rushed out half-naked, but halfway down the stairs I remembered something very important. Yvette was still in the room, dazed but relieved I had come back for her – but as I grabbed my briefcase stuffed with court papers, she truly discovered my priorities, and has never quite forgiven me. As we stood in the dark outside the evacuated hotel we learned that the seat of the fire was in a stamp shop: it was a case of arson. Apparently a vicious philatelist war was being waged in Birmingham at the time.

Now there is the newly designated 'war on terror', and cases involving Islamic fundamentalism bring the arguments about 'terrorists' or 'freedom fighters' into the sharpest relief. They do so because the defendants are largely 'home-grown martyrs', bombing their adopted homeland in retribution for the unending civilian casualties being inflicted in distant Muslim lands in the Middle and Far East. Over the last few years I've been briefed in a string of these trials. The defendants cannot be dismissed as mindless self-seekers: they are without exception intelligent, well educated and articulate. Their discussions recorded by covert police surveillance, and the chilling suicide videos recovered in their possession, need to be scrutinised carefully and then directly addressed.

The essence of their claim is that the civilian population in the aggressor nations bears a share of the responsibility for what has been happening to their counterparts in Iraq, Afghanistan,

Palestine, the Balkans, Chechnya and Kashmir. While there may be a grain of truth in this, it cannot possibly be a justification for the random reciprocal killing of non-combatants on buses, trains or in skyscrapers, any more than the carpet, blitz and atomic bombing in the Second World War or the so-called 'collateral damage' in the Balkans, and most significantly the whole of the unlawful invasion of Iraq and its aftermath. None of this is a defence of freedom by anyone's definition. 'An eye for an eye and we will all end up blind.'[7]

Tahira Tabassum was the wife of Omar Sharif, the first British-born suicide bomber in Israel. In April 2003 Sharif and fellow Briton Asif Hanif, from London, walked into a Tel Aviv bar with explosives strapped to their bodies. The explosion from Hanif's bomb killed three people and injured sixty-five. Sharif tried to detonate his device, but it failed to go off. He was found dead a fortnight later in the sea off Israel.

Tahira had met Sharif while at King's College London, in 1996, and by the time of his death was twenty-eight years old. She was charged with withholding information by failing to tell the authorities that her husband was planning a suicide bombing. The key evidence against Tahira was Omar's email eight days before the attack, in which he wrote: 'We did not spend a long time together in this world but I hope through Allah's mercy and your patience we can spend eternity together.'[8] When she read this she was shocked, not because she believed he meant to become a suicide bomber, but because she thought he was going to leave her and stay in Syria on his own, abandoning her with three small children.

In fact, she learned of the attack from a television report, and heard of her husband's death from television too – and far from being treated as a grieving widow, she became 'an enemy of the state'. Tahira was removed from her small children, aged six and five, and from the two-month-old baby whom she had been breastfeeding when arrested, and was locked up for twenty-two hours a day, without the support of family and friends, while being held in Belmarsh jail in south-east London. She was devastated: she loved her husband and didn't understand how this middle-class, public-school-educated man had become a murderer. She was very depressed when I met her, but resolute in insisting that she never knew what was going to happen. Soon after, I managed to get her released on strict bail conditions.

At the trial in April 2004 we produced evidence that Tahira was completely unaware of what her husband was planning, and the jury heard how she had every intention of joining him in Syria. She had filled out visa applications for their children on 8 April, two days before Omar flew to Damascus, and on 15 April had gone to a gynaecologist to have a contraceptive device fitted.

Tahira was a devout Muslim and told the jury that she believed Islam forbade suicide. During the trial we canvassed a number of issues concerning the right in England to debate the status and role of various tenets of the Islamic faith. What was of particular concern was whether these codes of belief condone the use of bombing (particularly suicide bombing) in furtherance of that faith and the belief in the Caliphate (an international Islamic super-state).

Fortunately the jury believed in Tahira's innocence and she was acquitted.

In contrast to Tahira, Saajid Badat never denied his complicity in terrorist offences, and at his trial pleaded guilty. He was a twenty-five-year-old British man accused of being allied to Richard Reid, the British shoe bomber arrested in the USA in December 2001. Saajid had withdrawn from the conspiracy to blow up a US-bound aircraft, but accepted that he had been part of it at one time. They had apparently been plotting the attacks since 1999, but Saajid was uneasy about the plan.

Reid was caught trying unsuccessfully to light a fuse in his shoes connected to plastic explosives, while on a flight from Paris to Miami on 22 December 2001. He was overcome by passengers and the crew, who gave him sedatives, and in January 2003 was jailed for life by a US court.

An unactivated device similar to Reid's had been discovered in Saajid's home in Gloucester. He had booked a ticket to fly from Manchester to Amsterdam before boarding an onward flight to the USA, but changed his mind and returned to the UK on 10 December 2001, with the device still in his possession. Clearly in turmoil, four days after his return Saajid had sent an email to his 'handlers', indicating that he might withdraw.

I gave a detailed mitigation on Saajid's behalf about his

politicisation. He was an intelligent, grammar-school-educated boy who left home at eighteen as a result of tensions with his father. Working in London as a kitchen porter and security guard, he was moved by accounts of the suffering and victimisation of Muslims in the Balkans, Chechnya and Kashmir, and particularly by the ethnic cleansing in the former Yugoslavia. In 1998 he went to Sarajevo, the capital of Bosnia, where thousands of Muslims had been killed. I argued that this wasn't an academic anger, but that 'he saw for himself, heard for himself, what had happened to Muslim families'. In January 1999 the nineteen-year-old Saajid travelled to Afghanistan and attended camps for military training, as he wanted to help 'defend' Muslim communities against attack: I compared him with those who had gone to fight Fascism in the Spanish civil war in the 1930s, and whose burning sense of solidarity was captured so compellingly in Ken Loach's film *Land and Freedom*. He left to travel around Europe, and met Reid in Amsterdam. Saajid returned to Afghanistan following the 11 September 2001 attacks and was recruited by the Islamic organisation Abu Hafs for the plot.

I felt it was important for the court to understand the pressures some of these young people experience: how Saajid faced 'moral blackmail' to carry out the bombing, and how he was going through a turbulent time in Afghanistan. In a letter to his family he wrote: 'I have a sincere desire to sell my soul to Allah in return for paradise.' Saajid Badat had clearly crossed the line between defending the integrity of indigenous communities and inflicting aggressive injury and death upon innocent civilians.

By December 2001 Saajid had returned to Britain and showed clear signs of renouncing violence. He told his handler in an email dated 14 December, which was recovered by police, that he was ill: 'I will keep you informed, but you will have to tell Van Damme [Reid's cover name] he could be on his own.'

In 2007 I told the court in mitigation that Saajid had resolved to return to a normal life: he had resumed his studies at an Islamic college in Blackburn and had abandoned terrorism. Saajid's faith, which according to most Islamic scholars condemns violence, had led him to pull out of the mass-murder plot, and I contended that, 'It was faith that in one sense took him to the very brink of disaster, and at the same time it was the same faith that pulled him back.'

The judge, Mr Justice Fulford, told Saajid that he would have faced a fifty-year sentence, but gave him credit for pulling out of the plot, for pleading guilty at the first reasonable opportunity and for renouncing terrorism. He was sentenced to thirteen years in prison, where he remains.

14

LIFTING THE LID

Judith Ward and Disclosure

You would assume that all parties in a case automatically get to see all the relevant evidence. Well, you'd be wrong. Non-disclosure has been at the heart of a series of miscarriages of justice dating back to the 1970s. The police did not tell the defence that Gerry Conlon, one of the Guildford Four imprisoned for pub bombings in October 1974, had an alibi in London that night; or that Stefan Kiszko[1] was physically unable to commit the sex crime for which he was convicted. It has been a constant struggle to get the laws on disclosure changed. For years it has been an uneven playing field, with police and prosecution only disclosing what they believe to be relevant to their case.

Transparency is one of the most fundamental tenets of natural justice, part of what is known as the 'equality of arms'. The state has accrued all the powers and resources for investigating crime on our behalf, and it is only fair that the product of such researches, paid for by us as taxpayers, should be made available to all parties if a trial ensues. Individual defendants cannot possibly be expected to compete with such investigative facilities but, subject to Public Interest Immunity (PII), they should be entitled to examine the whole picture, which in one sense has been obtained on their behalf. It is this aspect of the French inquisitorial system, as I have described in my book *Presumed Guilty*,[2] that theoretically provides for full disclosure of the dossier assembled by the investigating *juge d'instruction*, the Examining Magistrate. Without access of this kind, it is extremely difficult to ascertain what lines of enquiry have been overlooked or not completed; what potential exhibits have been mislaid or mislabelled; what information has been mishandled; and what scientific results have been misreported. On this last point a negative finding – often considered irrelevant by prosecuting authorities because it does not carry their case forward – may be as important as the positive finding on which they do rely.

Take fingerprints. A defendant could be charged with murder based on an accumulation of circumstantial evidence showing a motive, opportunity, presence near the scene shortly after the murder, and a fingerprint on a chair near the body and on the knife used for the killing. A number of queries come to mind. How many surfaces other than the chair were examined? Were any prints belonging to people without legitimate access discovered? Were there any unidentified prints? Was the fingerprint relating to the defendant examined for his or her DNA? Was the victim's blood associated with the prints, and if so, is it possible to tell whether the print was on the surface before the blood or vice versa? The answers to any one of these queries could lend an entirely different perspective to the case. They may appear to be rather obvious and commonplace, but it is far from guaranteed that this sort of material will be readily forthcoming before or during a trial.

It was not until 1996, when Michael Chance, who had had responsibility for the prosecution of the Carl Bridgewater murder case (see Chapter 12), wrote to my solicitor Jim Nichol prior to the appeal, conscientiously expressing concerns about the possible non-disclosure of prints found on Carl's bicycle which were *not* those of the convicted men, that the defence became aware of their existence. The paltry justification put forward by the Home Office at the time is typical of the thinking that has pervaded this area far too long: the prints were considered irrelevant because it was believed that the intruders wore gloves. Anyway, the bike could have been touched by anyone at any time. All of this is possible, but that's not the point. Before this revelation, the Home Secretary Michael Howard had been minded to refuse an application to refer this case back to the Court of Appeal, which eventually exonerated the men. Overturning the smallest stone can reveal the biggest truth.

It is alarming to note that this sort of non-disclosure was still continuing, even after the major exposure of systemic failure revealed in the tragic conviction of Judith Ward.

The Judith Ward appeal was a watershed case demonstrating intellectual corruption across a broad spectrum of prosecution agencies well beyond the police themselves, and each agency had displayed selectivity in disclosure based on their prejudices, preconceptions and assumptions.

Judith was born in Stockport, Cheshire, in 1949. She had an unhappy childhood dominated by a violent, alcoholic father who eventually disappeared, leaving her mother to work long hours cleaning when she wasn't beset by illness. Despite her best efforts, Judith's mother was often not around to give her six kids support, which left Judith at a young age as sole carer for her younger siblings. As a result she missed a great deal of schooling and became a troubled young woman, tiny in stature and timid by nature. She did odd jobs and trained as a stable girl, then at seventeen suddenly left home for a job in Ireland on a farm in Dundalk, near the border with Northern Ireland.

This was 1968–9 – the 'Swinging Sixties' for some, but in reality a time of soul-searching and agitation. The Vietnam war engendered massive protests; militant French students provoked aggressive state intervention; there were civil-rights marches in Alabama; and nearer home in Ireland campaigns for civil rights by the Catholic minority in the North led to battles with loyalists, the British Army moving in and the Provisional IRA being formed. Judith wasn't politically active at this time, but she was interested in Irish history. Things got tricky at the farm with an unexpected marriage proposal to this emotionally and sexually naive girl: frightened, she ran away and joined the British Army.

They trained Judith at Catterick in Yorkshire, as a 'communications centre operator', using phones and telex machines. Keen to experience new places, she applied to be posted to Cyprus, but got no further than Aldershot. She hated it there and once more, when faced with a difficult situation, went AWOL – this time to Dublin, where she ended up sharing a flat with a bunch of anarchists, socialists and Republicans. Afraid that the army might come after her, she adopted a false name, but that didn't help. Picked up by the Royal Ulster

Constabulary one day, she was sent back to England, where she was discharged from the army. In 1973 she ended up in London and met a guy in Kilburn who was active in Sinn Fein. This was the period of the IRA bombing campaigns when my car was exploded by the Price sisters, and Judith was one of those on the vigil outside the prison where they were on hunger strike. She worked in hotels, in Woolworths, in bars: any old job to keep a few pence in her pocket.

On 10 September 1973 she and her friend Elaine were coming out of the cinema when they heard that a bomb had been detonated in Euston station, and stupidly went to 'look see' out of curiosity. They were sitting in the pub on the station when they got talking to some men, one of whom was from Belfast, sharing a pint – and suddenly they were all surrounded by plain-clothes police and taken away for questioning.

The two girls' alibis were checked out and, crucially, the time when the bomb exploded was when Judith and Elaine had been seen leaving the hotel where they were working. The police took swabs of their hands six times, and Judith discovered much later that she had four negatives and two faint traces of explosives, while Elaine had five traces and one negative. The Belfast man had four positives and two traces: he could have been handling explosives and contaminated Judith's hand when he shook it and she shared his pint. They were all released.

Seeking new adventures, Judith ended up in Chipperfield's Circus, in a huge arena called Belle Vue in Manchester. She enjoyed looking after the horses, but when the circus folded in the winter she upped sticks and this time went on the road, starting in London. By now Judith had lost what little stability and self-esteem she had had in her life and took to dossing around, sleeping rough on goods trains and taking off wherever the newest friend led her. In February 1974 one such fellow landed her in Cardiff and then disappeared, and so – fatefully – Judith decided to hitch to Liverpool, city of the Beatles.

On 4 February 1974 a bomb exploded in an army coach on the M62 motorway in Yorkshire, killing twelve people, and on 18 February Judith was charged with conspiracy to cause the explosion. Within a few weeks she had also had laid at her door the bombing in 1973 at Euston station and another at Latimer College in Buckinghamshire, and she pleaded not guilty to all the charges. Still only twenty-five,

Judith was alone, without legal help and was put in isolation in the notoriously foul remand centre known as 'Grisly Risley' (some of the grimmer details of which can be found in Chapter 10).

By the time of her trial in October 1974 Judith was completely disoriented. She had been hospitalised for acute appendicitis; had made a 'confession' and withdrawn it; had been heavily sedated; had made up a marriage to a non-existent IRA man; and was generally in a terrible state, self-harming and contemplating suicide. The doctors' reports of her 'acute psychotic depression' were never presented in court, but then neither was most of the evidence that could have saved her from conviction.

If you had to pick a time to be tried for a 'terrorist' offence, this wouldn't be the ideal one, as the early to mid-1970s was a turbulent era. There was the Angry Brigade; the IRA, which had begun its mainland campaign; the Red Brigade in Italy; the Red Army Faction; the Baader-Meinhof Group in Germany and the PLO hijacking planes. No wonder the public was afraid of what was coming next. It was not unlike the climate of fear following 11 September 2001 or 7 July 2005.

So when the jury arrived every day at Wakefield Crown Court to try Judith Ward, who had been dubbed 'the motorway bus bomber', they saw a huge police presence surrounding the building, armed marksmen on the roof, visitor searches, security passes – all in all, an atmosphere of intense paranoia. There were bomb hoaxes and then came the real thing: the Guildford pub bombs went off during the case, and a few weeks later the Birmingham pub bombs were detonated (see Chapter 17). In this understandable heightened state of hysteria, it was hardly surprising that Judith got thirty years and twelve life sentences.

Fast forward the fifteen and a half years that Judith spent under perpetual surveillance in the cold, drab, top-security H wing for women in Durham Prison with nine other 'Cat. A' inmates and an array of drug dealers, murderers and others. At the beginning Judith was in a state of apathy: she trusted no one and sank into depression, becoming thin and ill. Later she started studying, learning skills such as computing, and found ways to accommodate her situation. But she had little support other than regular visits from her family – no friends and no outside campaign. She was the forgotten miscarriage of justice.

In 1988 Judith finally left Durham for Cookham Wood in Kent, and then in 1990 she was moved to Holloway, where conditions were more relaxed as she was no longer a Category-A prisoner. She even set up a desktop printing business, making cards and posters for inmates and units in the prison. When the Birmingham Six were released and Billy Power asked publicly, 'Why is Judy Ward still in prison?', she allowed herself almost for the first time to think that some day she might have a chance of freedom, and not long after their release Billy and the Six's support group chairman, Paul May, went to visit Judith. She changed her solicitor and her cause was taken up by Gareth Peirce, whose determination, allied to the group's new campaigning focus, meant that in September 1991 Judith's case was referred to the Court of Appeal.

I was brought on board with Nick Blake as my junior, and we began the long sift through the original 1974 trial papers. On 27 April 1992 the appeal was due to start, but the prosecution suddenly asked for a three-month delay on the grounds that they 'weren't ready'. They'd only had eighteen years to prepare, and even the judges thought this was a bit strong: they gave the prosecution not three months, but one week.

Our defence team had discovered many new things about Judith's case: for example that there had been three secret Home Office-initiated independent reviews in 1985, 1987 and 1989. And once the digging began, it uncovered a veritable Pandora's box. Without question it was the worst case of non-disclosure in my whole career, and one which exemplifies the magnitude of risk that is run when the pressure is on to convict those considered to be culpable. No one is immune, and everyone needs to be vigilant at all times.

Judith had spilled confessions and admissions like beans. They were all over the place, in every sense of the phrase – bizarre and random. Spread over different occasions between February and March 1974, she confessed to carrying explosives, to planting the bomb on the coach, to gun-running in Ireland and to planting the bomb at Euston. Some confessions she retracted, others she did not.

Added to this, it was claimed, she had made the bombs because she tested positive for Ng (nitroglycerine) under her fingernails; positive on swabs taken from her hands and duffle bag; and because positive traces of Ng were found in the caravan where she had stayed for a time. A persuasive picture when put in short form, but one which – unbeknown to the defence – was far from complete. It was the tip of an iceberg that had remained submerged for years.

The West Yorkshire Police had failed to hand over to the DPP 1,700 witness statements. Many of them were immaterial, but a number were entirely supportive of the thrust of the defence at trial: that Judith was a pathological liar and an attention-seeking fantasist. Between March 1972 and June 1974 there had been seven interviews by different police authorities which displayed a propensity to admit activity that could be shown to be fictitious. A member of the DPP's staff as well as a barrister were criticised by the Court of Appeal for their role in the non-disclosure.

The scientific non-disclosure was monumental. It is rare indeed for the court to use strong (let alone strident) language, but their Lordships – Lord Justices Glidewell, Nolan and Steyn – quite legitimately took three senior scientists and two medical doctors to task. The doctors' reports concerning Judith's mental state and her attempts to commit suicide were not disclosed in full and crucial incidents were omitted. When I asked about them in the Court of Appeal the answers were regarded by the court as 'astonishing'. The doctors either could not remember or were not especially concerned, because they quite often encountered this kind of thing in a large remand prison.

But this was nothing compared to the forensic science. Disclosure was 'woefully deficient'. Three senior scientists from the Royal Armament Research and Development Establishment took the law into their own hands and concealed from the prosecution, the defence and the court matters that might have changed the course of the trial. The catalogue of 'lamentable' omissions I summarise as:

i. A failure to reveal actual test results for Ng, which had been misleadingly described as positive.

ii. A failure to reveal discrepant Rf values on TLC (thin-layer chromatography) tests for Ng – meaning that the range of variation in reading undermined their reliability.

iii. A failure to reveal that other substances (not Ng) might produce a similar reading on a TLC test where a suspect sample and a control are spotted onto a plate dipped into solution [it's like watching ink rise up a sheet of blotting paper. The other, non Ng substance was boot polish!]. The three senior scientists, Mr Higgs, Mr Elliott and Mr Berryman, suppressed this during the trial.

iv. Misrepresentation and concealment of firing cell test results [experiments which showed how anyone might quite innocently become contaminated with explosives by touching debris or other secondary sources].

Most concerning of all during the oral evidence of the three scientists at the trial, they 'knowingly placed a false and distorted scientific picture before the jury'.[3]

After almost nineteen terrible years Judith was free. She had paid a heavy penalty for the frailties of our legal system. Lord Justice Glidewell did not just identify what these were, but how they may have come about:

> For lawyers, juror and judges, a forensic scientist conjures up the image of a man in a white coat working in a laboratory approaching his task with cold neutrality and dedicated only to the pursuit of scientific truth. It is a sombre thought that the reality is sometimes different. Forensic scientists may become partisan. That is what must have happened in this case.[4]

Quite apart from all this, there is another sombre and salutary thought. Confession evidence should not be accorded the status of the Holy Grail. In one case after another we have seen how it isn't worth the paper it's written on. In this case it was uncovered by the benefits, ultimately, of full disclosure; for Stephen Miller by DNA evidence, for Engin Raghip by forensic psychology, for Pat Molloy, the Birmingham Six and Winston Silcott by the searching eye of ESDA (electro-static deposition analysis). These examples are the reason I have argued for more than twenty years that there should be no confession-only convictions. Even pleas of guilty are suspect on this basis alone. What is fascinating is the sharp decline in confessions and confession-only cases in the face of regulative and protective measures that have been introduced. This clearly suggests that their frequent occurrence for so many years was both suspicious and artificial.

It was deeply disturbing therefore to discover a criminal justice system entirely dependent on confession evidence. During the spring of 2009 I was part of an independent delegation of British lawyers examining the operation of the Israeli military court system in the Occupied Territories of Palestine (OTP). In any one year up to 7,000 Palestinian defendants, mostly in custody, await trial on a variety of allegations ranging from stone throwing to bombing. Ironically these courts are a remnant of the British Mandate and even more ironically their reliance on confession evidence is a legacy of the historic British approach. The vast majority of defendants confess and well over 90 per cent of them plead guilty. No military court judge we met seemed to bat an eyelid at this unreal situation. In fact, confessions are described as the 'queen of evidence' requiring no more than 'feather-light corroboration', which predictably comes from yet more confessions provided by accomplices. No legitimate criminal justice system ever devised by mankind has achieved such a level of success.

The delegation report will have to assess what factors contribute to these results – obvious candidates are: the age and vulnerability of defendants; oppression exercised at the point of detention through to interview; extensive delay; the conditions of custody and increased sentences for contested cases.

I was thrilled when the Ward judgment brought about the prospect of real change. The police and prosecution were no longer to be the only ones to make decisions about the relevance of unused evidence; from now on, the defence was to be granted access to the complete pool of material.

Any police investigation generates a lot of information, such as witness statements, scientific reports, notes of conversations with potential witnesses, and so on. The police and the Crown Prosecution Service (CPS) then decide what will be used as prosecution evidence, and the rest becomes 'unused material'. Of course this rejected data may not be of interest to the prosecution, but it could really help the accused. The prosecution was now required to provide the defence with all relevant evidence, unless the trial judge ruled that it could be held back on grounds of public interest. And for a few years following the Judith Ward case the defence could go and inspect any material they liked. Not any more . . .

After a while there was a backlash from police and prosecutors, who complained that they had to spend vast amounts of time and money supplying the defence with material, much of it 'irrelevant'. So in 1997 the government introduced the Criminal Procedure and Investigations Act (CPIA), a dangerous piece of legislation which created two tiers of disclosure, putting the onus on the prosecution to decide what unused information should be disclosed.

It is left to a police disclosure officer (who is not legally trained) to list unused, non-sensitive material, and anything that might undermine the prosecution's case is supposed to be disclosed to the defence. If it wants further disclosure, the defence must first supply a defence statement (a synopsis of the main points of the defence case in advance of the trial). The prosecuting authority is then supposed to supply any unused data that helps the defence case.

Of course this can lead to further miscarriages of justice. For example, the disclosure officer in one case was the very same police officer who was the subject of a formal complaint of assault by the accused. It came as no surprise when it emerged that a record of a telephone call to the police station from a member of the public at the scene, claiming that the police were assaulting people, was withheld.

The problems with the police acting as guardians of disclosure is that they are not trained to raise doubts about the guilt of those accused of crime, and they often display prejudice because they instinctively believe that the accused is guilty. The new rules depend entirely on the judgement, assiduousness and honesty of the police officer who assembles the information and on the impartiality of the CPS lawyer who assesses whether the material may assist the defence. It's all too disturbingly frequent that evidence which contradicts the prosecution case fails to reach the defence – a case of back to the bad old days . . .

The outcome has been that major trials have collapsed, at huge expense. Unworthy defendants have had their cases dropped when a judge's patience with a failure to disclose has finally run out, while those wrongly accused have come very close to going on trial without knowing about crucial evidence that would secure their acquittal. More disquietingly, how many innocent people are still going to prison because the disclosure regime is so inadequate?

The CPS needs to be told that it has to inspect the unused material itself, not just glance at the list produced by the police, even though it may need extra funds to do so. And defence lawyers should be allowed, once again, to go and look at whatever material the police have got.

The risks of non-disclosure continue to be a matter of concern well after the Ward judgment in 1992. In that same year thirty-two-year-old Paula Gilfoyle was found hanged in the garage at the home she shared with her husband Eddie, in Upton on the Wirral. She was eight and a half months pregnant. On the day of her death Eddie was at work at a hospital between 11.30 a.m. and 4.30 p.m. and returned home to find a suicide note. When she wasn't in the house, he went round to his relatives to try and find her. Paula's body was found later in the evening by Eddie's brother-in-law, Paul Caddick, an off-duty police sergeant.

At the start the whole affair was treated as a non-suspicious death. As a consequence, the crime scene and potential exhibits were not preserved as they should have been. Four days later Eddie was arrested for murder and convicted at Liverpool Crown Court in 1993. He protested his innocence from the beginning.

Factors that undoubtedly had a bearing on his conviction were the unlikelihood of a woman at that stage of pregnancy taking her own and her baby's life; the difficulty of achieving it on her own, given her condition, her height and the beam involved; her non-suicidal state of mind, according to friends; and the existence of other suicide notes in her handwriting, which it was suggested had been obtained by Eddie for a first-aid course at work.

I represented Eddie at his first appeal in 1995 and at his second in 2000. The first centred on a sighting by a witness at a time when the prosecution claimed Paula had already been killed by Eddie before he went to work. The second focused on expert evidence concerning ligatures and the mechanics of hanging. Both appeals were dismissed.

A determined journalist, Dominic Kennedy, persisted with enquiries for many years. On 20 February 2009 *The Times* revealed that it had recovered, under the Freedom of Information Act (FOI), important police notes describing what witnesses attending the scene had said and done.[5] According to Kennedy, the police had variously claimed that these notes didn't exist or had been destroyed. What has to be ascertained now is whether they were in possession of information that was not disclosed to the defence at trial. A doctor who attended the scene had estimated contemporaneously that the time of death was approximately six hours prior to his examination of Paula's body. If this estimate were to be correct, then Eddie was still at work. It is anticipated that the CCRC (Criminal Cases Review Commission) will be asked to follow this up.[6]

In December 1988 there was a series of burglaries and murders close to London's orbital motorway, the M25. First came the bizarre murder of a homosexual in a field, and much depended on confused sightings of a red MG sports car, on the timings of various television programmes that witnesses used as reference points, and on evidence given by accomplices whom I described as 'The Job Lot', because one of them was called Jobbins. Relevant information about them was not disclosed. At the trial I represented Michael Davis, one of a number of defendants, and later both Davis and Raphael Rowe, a young Rastafarian, at appeal.

Randolph Johnson, Michael Davis and Raphael Rowe were jailed for life in 1990. The men's first appeal in 1993 was unsuccessful, but later it emerged that the prosecution had failed to disclose that an associate of the three defendants told police that another man – not Randolph Johnson – had taken part in the crimes. This key prosecution witness also turned out to be a police informer who had received a £10,000 reward. The three men continued to fight to clear their names, and finally the European Court of Human Rights ruled unanimously that their trial had been unfair and the CCRC referred their case back to court. The M25 appellants were eventually successful and walked free on 17 July 2000. Raphael Rowe is now an occasional presenter and researcher for BBC Radio 4 and for *Panorama* on BBC television.

The case became the leading authority on a completely new procedure for disclosure, which I suggested to Lord Chief Justice Taylor, in relation to Public Interest Immunity (PII) hearings. The type of material which is covered by public interest can be quite wide-ranging, from official secrets at one end to the modus operandi of covert police surveillance at the other. This involves a crucial ethical question for defence counsel in particular.

For many years the English convention had been that counsel might be shown confidential information, on the understanding that the information would not be communicated to the client. I objected to this procedure because I felt that proper representation required my client knowing as much about his own case as I did, and he might well have important observations to make about the accuracy of the sensitive material. My objection entailed being excluded from the court while it considered whether the material should be disclosed to the defence for the purposes of the trial or appeal. I felt so strongly about my professional duty that I went to the Bar Council for their approval for the stand that I had taken, which I duly obtained. The Lord Chief Justice accepted that I was right in principle, but a procedure had to be devised in order to allow some representation and input from the defendant. At the hearing I suggested a league table for disclosure, dependent upon the degree of sensitivity involved, but unfortunately this has evolved into a completely different system, whereby special counsel is appointed for the defendant to deal with the PII hearing.

This has become a major feature of a singularly unhealthy part of our system in the Special Immigration Appeals Commission (SIAC). These are tribunals dealing with immigration issues, and if the immigrant is considered to be a 'terrorist', the hearings are in camera. While the individual may be represented generally by his own barrister, that barrister is not allowed to be present at the secret hearings, where only a special counsel can appear; and once he does so, that special counsel is in 'purdah' (Hindu for the screen that protects Indian women from public view) and can no longer speak – even to the client's barrister – about what is happening in the hearings.

These issues surfaced in the notorious Belmarsh case in which the House of Lords denounced in robust terms the Labour government's SIAC scheme, where detainees were locked up indefinitely without charge and without knowing the nature or detail of the allegations against them. I have always refused to participate in SIAC hearings save for one instance, and a number of special advocates publicly resigned after the Belmarsh case because of the injustice of the system. Yet another example of the scant regard successive Labour governments have had for the rule of law.

The dilemma posed by how to deal with the disclosure or non-disclosure of sensitive information, yet at the same time meet the requirements for a fair trial – especially for a defendant under Article Six of the European Convention on Human Rights – has become more acute over the last few years, and the current conundrum concerns intercept evidence or telephone tapping. This is so sensitive that you cannot even ask if it has happened, let alone what has been heard or recorded. It's a bizarre anachronism, because almost all other forms of covert surveillance can be adduced. If the security services, Special Branch or the anti-terrorist squad have employed an eavesdropping device, which might be in a nearby house or vehicle, although the exact location may not be revealed, the conversations can be. If a hidden camera is used to take still or moving images, these too can be produced. So it's difficult to see why a telephone conversation is any different. Provided the provenance, continuity, integrity and context of the recording can be established, it is clearly capable of providing the best evidence of what was in the minds of those planning a crime. Where there are complications about audibility and intelligibility, these are all matters that the trial judge would have to take into account in deciding whether it was sufficiently reliable to put before a jury. The security services have been exercised about this for years, but everyone in the real world is aware that telephones are tapped – and probably tapped more often than we imagine, given the expanding surveillance society within which we live. So it isn't exactly a state secret that needs to be shrouded in mystery.

I represented two defendants in separate major terrorist conspiracy trials, both of which ended in 2007. One was alleged to be a central figure, the other on the fringes, and in both cases there was intense and extensive surveillance by both the police and the security services. In both cases the defendants, the solicitors and I were quite sure that telephone tapping had taken place, and the defendants were adamant that any record of their telephone conversations would prove their innocence.

All I could do was request that the trial judge ensured that the prosecution (which is also precluded from using the content of the tapes) did not make assertions about a defendant that conflicted with any information they had about what had been said on an intercept. In order to get round this tricky situation for a prosecutor, it was decided that the tapes of any recording (or the notes relating to any such tapes) would be destroyed before trial. It was argued that the tapes were only used for intelligence purposes and not for prosecution and trial. I think that even Charles Dickens's bureaucratic government office in *Little Dorrit* would have been proud of this level of circumlocution.

Both defendants, who were at risk of thirty-year prison sentences, were fortunately acquitted, but without the benefit of the telephone-tap disclosure.

Telephone and computer evidence are now central features of most major criminal trials. The prosecution takes delight in constructing multicoloured and complex telephone graphics to demonstrate association by conspirators, but jurors are not stupid, and they will also be asking themselves why they haven't heard about the content of the calls depicted in the graphics: something we all know is there, but is never referred to.

It may be getting worse. When the government set up a Privy Council Review in 2007 chaired by Sir John Chilcot, I gave evidence of my experiences and my misgivings. The Privy Counsellors plainly had to grapple with two diametrically opposed forces: one favouring the logic of inclusion, the other security. The result is a compromise that may be unworkable, in which the ban on intercept evidence will be lifted subject to a raft of preconditions and, most worryingly, the increased use of special counsel in a new PII Plus regime. This really is *Alice Through the Looking-Glass* territory, and is anathema to the concept of a fair trial.

15

SHARED EXPERIENCE

The Deptford Fire, the Bradford Twelve,
the Mangrove and Spike Milligan . . .

Anyone who drives north out of central London heading for the M1 or the A1 (the Great North Road) is likely to go along the Archway Road corridor that runs between Dick Whittington's Highgate Hill on the one side and Hornsey on the other. En route you pass, largely unnoticed, a solid red-brick monolith of a building, unwieldy and unprepossessing. It had been a Methodist church, but with dwindling congregations during the post-war period it had stood empty, bordering on the derelict, for a number of years by the time I moved nearby with my young family.

I have always shunned mainstream party politics because it inevitably becomes bogged down in territorial power games and personality squabbles. Instead I have found it far more satisfying and productive to concentrate my energy on single-issue campaigns, which tend to transcend the usual political boundaries, and for me this begins with the place and community where I live. It is often all too easy to pontificate about how others should organise their lives in foreign lands and ignore what is going on in your own back yard or outside your own front door.

Sharing a local common goal brings people together in a way that little else does, and often helps to strip away embedded prejudices that we all carry around. Although the church, the pub and the post office can provide a focal point of contact, none of them can be as effective as a community centre with no strings attached. Whereas the village hall performs this role in rural areas, for the urban dweller there is nothing similar. Of course local authorities sometimes fund and establish purpose-built community centres on inner-city estates, but they are usually soulless caverns, which become an excuse for graffiti and general desecration by idle hands.

Given the chance, though, people often have extremely constructive ideas about their own environment; and the problem is getting your voice heard and then translating the voice into action. Standing together with a collective and unified message can generate remarkable changes, and in the early 1970s a number of volunteers came together to transform the empty shell of this church into a local amenity. It took a great deal of commitment and stamina to persuade various funding bodies and Haringey local authority to permit this development, but the obvious benefits spoke for themselves, and in the end a highly successful centre known as Jacksons Lane was established. Both Melian and I helped as much as we could – as did Nicky Gavron, Labour Deputy Mayor of London until 2008 – and gradually a concrete wilderness gave way to a comfortable place for the older generation to pass the time of day; for young people to meet to exercise or party; for all sorts of groups to hold their meetings; and for others merely to have a drink and a bite to eat. Nothing extraordinary, indeed quite the opposite, but then that was the whole point.

Jacksons Lane began to get a reputation beyond the locality when a theatre space was created. This was initially intended to encourage local aspiring talent, but it also attracted professional theatre companies who wished to have a testing ground for sometimes very experimental work. One such company was Shared Experience, run by Mike Alfreds. I was particularly taken by its performances, which reminded me strongly of another experiment that had occurred in the Potteries while I was at university: theatre in the round at the Victoria Theatre in Stoke, inspired by Stephen Joseph. Never having visited the theatre in my youth other than to see the Crazy Gang or – unbelievably now – *The Black and White Minstrel Show* with my father, this experience opened my eyes and my mind to a completely different and intimate world, from Arnold Bennett to Shakespeare. More recently, Northern Broadsides, under the dynamic direction of Barrie Rutter, has continued to keep me hooked with lively, intelligible and novel interpretations of 'The Bard', the latest featuring Lenny Henry as a powerful and emotional Othello.

One of the earliest productions by Shared Experience at Jacksons Lane was *Bleak House* by Charles Dickens. The idea that this 900-page novel could be turned into a manageable stage play seemed a bridge too far, but it was performed over three consecutive nights by a small company whose members took on several different parts, extemporised their own sound effects, had no special costumes and no props or stage scenery. Everything was communicated through words and actions alone, and it was completely compelling from start to finish: I didn't miss a minute of it. Mind you, the content contained a cutting analysis of the wheels of justice grinding amazingly slow. What I didn't appreciate then was that, ten years after watching this, I was to break away from mainstream chambers to set up my own at number 14, in a small cobbled street with Georgian lamp standards called Tooks Court off Cursitor Street. The next-door house had a small sign outside it indicating that Dickens had lived there. I'm not entirely sure whether that is correct, but given the steady flow of camera-wielding tourists, it was clear that many others believed that he had. What is certain is that when writing *Bleak House*, Dickens did draw upon this tiny street for locating Mr and Mrs Snagsby:

> On the eastern borders of Chancery Lane, that is to say, more particularly in Cook's Court, Cursitor Street, Mr Snagsby, a law stationer, pursues his lawful calling. In the shade of Cook's Court, at most times a shady place, Mr Snagsby has dealt in all sorts of blank forms of legal process; in the skins and rolls of parchment; in paper-foolscap, brief, draft, brown, white, whitey brown, and blotting; in stamps; in office quills, pens . . .[1]

A little later Dickens describes a scene that could be contemplated now:

> The day is closing in, the gas is lighted, but it is not yet fully effective, for it is not quite dark. Mr Snagsby standing at his shop door looking up at the clouds, sees a crow, who is out late, skim westward over the slice of sky belonging to Cook's Court. The

crow flies straight across Chancery Lane and Lincoln's Inn Garden into Lincoln's Inn Fields . . . to the house of Mr Tulkinghorn.[2]

All very evocative.

Meanwhile, back on the Archway Road, efforts continued to raise money. One memorable occasion involved Spike Milligan and his wife Patricia Ridgeway, an accomplished classical pianist, entertaining a packed house. I had been a long-standing *Goons* fan, listening avidly on a large, fake-mahogany wireless with three black plastic knobs (for long, medium and short wave) to nearly every single episode of their zany humour – a sort of humour that no one has matched since, except possibly John Cleese in *Monty Python's Flying Circus*. (I love the fact that when Spike first proposed the idea to the BBC, they thought it was going to be called *The Go-on Show*.) In Jacksons Lane, Spike was in a particularly anarchic and disruptive mood, appearing at completely unscheduled moments and from utterly unpredictable places while Patricia was playing, preceded by a silent, rapidly moving trombone slide! Many years later, when I happened to be addressing an environmental campaign meeting in Trafalgar Square, I had the unenviable task of following Spike. There was a ladder by the side of Nelson's Column enabling speakers to mount the plinth to deliver their speech, and I held the ladder to let Spike come down before I went up. As I did so, I introduced myself by saying, 'I don't suppose you'll remember me . . .' – but before I could get any further, quick as a flash Spike replied, 'As long as *you* do, you'll be fine!'

No sooner had Jacksons Lane got itself on the map than the Department of Transport wanted to take it off, with a widening scheme that would have transformed the Archway Road into a motorway. All the usual claptrap was wheeled out about bottlenecks, traffic flow and freight costs, just as it is today, not only in relation to roads, but also to airports – as short-sighted a view then as it is now. The never-ending rush to get more people more quickly to more destinations is a self-defeating objective, never mind the disastrous toll inflicted upon the environment and the guzzling demand for oil.

I chaired a campaign named ARC 73 to oppose the road development, and ultimately to take the fight to a planning inquiry, and we endeavoured to present an integrated transport policy that paid much greater regard to rail, canal and river modes of transport. If there had to be road expansion of this kind, then stick it underground, which coincidentally was what had been done with the Northern Line on the Tube. In the end, thankfully, the main proposals of the scheme were not carried out and Jacksons Lane survives to this day, a tribute to the tenacity of local people rather than the drive for profit.

Throughout this period – as well as my days at school and university, my early upbringing in Finchley, my married life in Belsize Park and Highgate, and my first years at the Bar – I was barely conscious of the trials and tribulations faced by the post-war black immigrant population symbolised by the arrival of the *Empire Windrush* at Tilbury docks in London thirty years earlier. None of my friends, neighbours or colleagues were black. It was only after the 1961 Commonwealth Immigration Act, which, paradoxically, led to a rush to get in under the wire and an increase in the number of immigrants, that classrooms across the UK began to reflect the new complexion and composition of our society. Those children's parents had been subjected to a very British form of apartheid whereby, although it was not government policy, large swathes of Middle England were bitterly opposed to the influx, and – notoriously – landlords put up signs saying: 'No Irish, No Dogs, No Blacks'. Tension spilled over into clashes and riots in Nottingham and in Notting Hill during the 1950s, and I should have been far more aware of these developments than I was. I glimpsed some of this when Bernie Simons asked me to represent Darcus Howe, one of the so-called Mangrove Nine who were charged following a showdown between police and protesters at the Mangrove restaurant in Notting Hill in 1971. At that stage I only met Darcus briefly, but both he and the Mangrove were to become critical factors in awakening me to what had been going on.

One after the other, I became involved in the cases of people who were no longer going to put up with, or ignore, wholesale discrimination and who were immersed in the politics of resistance.

Fifteen thousand people marched through London with demands for recognition and civil rights in the wake of a dramatic fire in Deptford, south London, in 1981. A house full of black teenagers had gone up in flames, resulting in the deaths of thirteen of them, while twenty others were injured in the blaze that engulfed the house. The fire started on the ground floor and quickly spread, the young people being trapped upstairs by the smoke and flames. Police launched a murder inquiry after survivors described how they had seen a car being driven away from the incident as the fire broke out; the police also said they had found evidence of a liquid substance that may have assisted the spread and intensity of the fire. It later transpired there was a potential device found under a dustbin lid below the front window. Officers had been called to the house earlier in the evening after receiving complaints about noise levels; they suggested someone may have started the fire because they were angry about the loud music, or because they had been excluded from the party.

There were different theories about the cause – one of which was that it was a racist attack – and I represented a number of the families at the inquest.

Darcus Howe had helped to organise the demonstration together with John Le Rose, who ran the New Beacon book shop in Stroud Green, and one Sunday shortly before the inquest began they unexpectedly came round to my house in Crouch End. They were two very different characters – Darcus was larger than life, ebullient and assertive, while John was more retiring, gentle and calm – but together they formed a holy alliance, a partnership to be revered. They had realised, quite rightly, that if I were to understand the predicament and feelings of the families I was representing, it was essential that I should have a strong working knowledge of the background of the black community. Three hours later I certainly did.

There have been two inquests into the Deptford fire tragedy, both of which concluded with an open verdict.

Following close on the heels of the Deptford fire were the trials of the Bradford Twelve and the Newham Seven, which gave rise to the slogan 'Self-defence is no offence'. In both cases, at different ends of the country, Asian youths assembled petrol bombs in order to defend themselves against impending attacks by members of the National Front.

First-generation black and Asian immigrants were concerned about political equality; they recognised common causes and struggles with whites – for jobs, housing and education – and were less worried about preserving cultural differences. Police brutality and racist attacks, culminating in the inner-city riots of the late 1970s and early 1980s, produced the Scarman Report.[3]

In April 1976, twenty-four people were arrested in pitched battles in the Manningham area of Bradford, as Asian youths confronted a National Front march and fought the police protecting it. These were young radicals taking on the traditionalists within their communities, who were seeking to deny women equal rights and keep different religious and ethnic sects apart.

The next few years brought further conflict between Asian youths and the police, culminating in the trial of the Bradford Twelve in 1982. Twelve young Asians faced conspiracy charges for making petrol bombs to use against racists, and before their trial I was briefed by Ruth Bundy, one of a rare breed of no-nonsense, intelligent and committed solicitors.

I represented a young man called Tarlochan Aura, who was mild-mannered and deeply political. He and the other eleven had got wind of the imminent arrival of coachloads of members of the National Front from London via the M1, and when they realised the venomous nature of what was in store, it was decided to prepare defensive materials in the form of milk bottles adapted to become Molotov cocktails. Each bottle was one-third filled with petrol and had a rag stuck in the neck that could then be lit and thrown, and the bottles were stored in crates. However, the police arrived before the National Front, and the defendants were arrested for possessing explosive substances. The question at the trial was whether a petrol bomb was truly an explosive substance or merely a pyrotechnic.

This led to two moments of light relief. One came when co-defending counsel the late Edmund Alexander (a member of Tooks) attempted to demonstrate – in court! – how easy it was to assemble a petrol bomb, and how its effect did not constitute an explosion. At the point at which Edmund lit the rag, the judge ducked and made a rapid exit. The other was when all defending counsel went to a nearby courtyard with an expert, Dr Keith Borer, who was again to demonstrate the relatively innocuous nature of petrol bombs. He produced a crate of milk bottles, half-filled them with petrol, lit the rags and suggested we throw them at a wall to see what happened.

This was undertaken enthusiastically by all, and the meagre result was just a blackened wall. Well, not quite the only result. A window was suddenly flung open and an extremely irate man leaned out, shouting abuse at us: our target had turned out to be the rear wall of the Conservative Party offices in Leeds. The police were summoned and leading counsel had some testing questions to answer . . .

As Ruth Bundy so clearly remembers:

The thing that the police and the prosecution believed until the very beginning of the case was that the defence was going to be based on denial of any involvement in any activity to do with the making of petrol bombs . . . the actual defence being, 'Yes, we did this; yes, we were proud to do it; we believe we had to do it. It was a defence of necessity, and when the National Front never came to Bradford, fine, we never had to use these preparations that we had got together' . . . that element of surprise I think was tremendously important because the defendants then just took the courtroom by storm really, and the jury listened very, very, very carefully.[4]

So we argued that the Bradford Twelve were acting in self-defence, and we won. They were all acquitted of every charge – a remarkable victory.

It was a long trial and it was one of the many times in my career when I had to 'camp' with a solicitor or live in digs during the week – rushing home to see the kids and try and pick up family life again for a day and a half at the weekend. It was hard for Melian with five children and a career of her own to pursue, and these periodic separations began to take their toll on our relationship. I have made sacrifices for my work and beliefs, which have given me a fulfilling and stimulating career, but that commitment wreaks havoc with domestic bliss and I really don't know how you achieve a 'work–life balance', as they now call it. I failed in that respect and am sorry for the effect on my family, but I cannot deny the satisfaction I have derived from seeing so many defendants walk free after enduring the stress of being tried for an injustice.

As a result of the continuing frustrations felt by the Asian community, Bradford council drew up a new anti-racist strategy, based on a model pioneered by Ken Livingstone's Greater London Council.

It declared that every section of the 'multiracial, multicultural city' had 'an equal right to maintain its own identity, culture, language, religion and customs', championing both equal rights and the right to be different. Bradford established race-relations units, drew up equal-opportunities policies, and gave millions of pounds in grants to black and Asian community organisations, the aim being to encourage groups to express their distinctiveness, discern their own pasts and pursue their own values and lifestyles. Multiculturalism was born, but was not to mature without the people of many communities being driven into pockets of segregation.

Much the same issues arose in the two cases of the Newham Eight and the Newham Seven in London, when young Asians were faced with threats from white racists and the National Front. Sadly, the events of these two cases were repeated thirty years later when another generation of Asian youths were once again defending their community in Manningham against an incursion, but this time by the BNP. Unfortunately a number of these young individuals pleaded guilty when they had a perfectly legitimate defence. Some first-time offenders were given seven years for stone-throwing, and I was brought in on appeal to try and reduce these heavy sentences, which had been passed by the Crown Court. Some were reduced, others weren't.

Running alongside all of the events in Deptford, Bradford and Newham was the systematic targeting of the Mangrove restaurant on the All Saints Road in Notting Hill, run by Frank Critchlow. Frank was a charming, laid-back, but quietly authoritative man from Trinidad, and all he really wanted to do in life was cook, entertain people in a cheerful environment and at the same time provide a refuge for the unemployed. So he started with a small café called El Rio in Brixton and then graduated to the Mangrove in 1969. It was a low-key success from the start, as there were few Caribbean-run establishments serving good West Indian food.

Times were hard for Frank's community. Rising unemployment fuelled competition for jobs and heightened the tension between black and white communities; racial discrimination was the norm; stringent immigration controls were being introduced; and the 'Rivers of Blood' speech by Tory MP Enoch Powell in 1968 had painted scenes of Britain being torn apart by racial violence and further stoked the engines.

It wasn't long before Notting Hill became a cauldron for black culture, and oddly the Mangrove restaurant became its focus – I'm told the food was very good – and attracted intellectuals like C. L. R. James, Richard Neville and the *Oz* pack, musicians, radical lawyers and even John Profumo. Everyone, it seems, but me . . .

The early 1970s was a period of enormous racial tension, and Notting Hill was not immune to the gathering political storms: it was right on the front line, and the Mangrove came to symbolise resistance by a generation ready to reject racist oppression. Frank didn't invite it, but he attracted the attention of a local senior police officer named Pearman. There were heavy-handed and repeated police raids on the restaurant. The police just did not like Frank Critchlow, and no one ever really understood why. He had moved upmarket from the Rio to a proper, well-run restaurant, and maybe they couldn't bear to see an ordinary black guy making a go of something. Or maybe they resented the fact that the Mangrove became an unofficial centre for young black people in Notting Hill, providing a more constructive haven than street corners. Or perhaps it was because Frank lived with a white woman, Lucy, and was enjoying a happy family life. The Mangrove wasn't a drugs den – far from it: Frank was determined to keep drugs out and was always personally 'clean', but the police seemed intent on closing it down, and time and again they raided it for drugs.

This in turn provoked discontent and unrest within the black community. Constant hostile policing and harassment meant the Mangrove inadvertently became a meeting place for community activists, and things started getting heavy after a demonstration was organised by the Action Committee for the Defence of the Mangrove, which began as a peaceful protest of about 150 people sporting rather graphic anti-police placards (such as 'Kill the Pigs'), then escalated into a violent clash between local police and protesters. Of the nineteen people arrested, nine, including Frank Critchlow, were later charged and tried at the Old Bailey as the Mangrove Nine, described as 'black-power conspirators'.

The trial lasted for fifty-five days and highlighted the oppressive treatment and policing of black people in Britain – and in December 1971, Frank, Darcus Howe and seven others walked out of the Old Bailey, freed by a jury following multiple charges of conspiracy to riot, affray and assaults on police.

Frank was immensely supportive of his community, but suddenly found himself thrust into the forefront of the 'struggle'. Unexpectedly his local restaurant had become the focus for community mobilisation and resistance and – more up his street – the meeting place for the organisers, performers and musicians of the Notting Hill Carnival. The police of course didn't let up, and it never really ended for Frank, who was constantly harassed and accused of providing a front for drug dealing. In a further trial in the late 1970s, this time of the Mangrove Six, Frank was again acquitted.

In 1989 I represented Frank when he was falsely accused of dealing in heroin following another raid on the Mangrove, and the trial took place at the Knightsbridge Crown Court behind Harrods (which is now owned and used as offices by Mohamed Al Fayed). It was at the time of the Critchlow case that I began to cycle to court, partly for health and environmental reasons, but also because with continuing death threats I felt that it would be more difficult to conceal a bomb on a bike.

Thirty-six police officers testified against Frank in a drawn-out court case but the jury chose to believe him and Frank was cleared of all charges. He eventually won a case in 1992 against the Home Office for false imprisonment, battery and malicious prosecution. Frank won £50,000 in damages, but it was small comfort as the Mangrove had been closed down while he was awaiting trial, and his personal life was decimated.

The Notting Hill police commander, one Paul Condon, was rewarded for his assiduity over the Mangrove operation and went on to higher things as the top man at New Scotland Yard. We were to clash later in a significant exchange at a rather high-profile inquest: into the deaths of Princess Diana and Dodi Fayed.

In a sense, all Frank had wanted to do was exactly what I had got myself involved in at Jacksons Lane, and I have maintained my belief in the community with other projects intended to provide across-the-board help and advice. One was the establishment of the first neighbourhood law centre to give free advice in Tottenham, and the other was the Acre Lane neighbourhood set of barristers' chambers, an idea that turned out to have been ahead of its time by trying to directly serve the community in Brixton, instead of being remotely situated in the Inns of Court.

The draconian measures which are being taken within public funding, particularly with criminal legal aid, mean that in the future barristers will have to consider completely different ways of working, one of which will be within the community.

Ironically, the economic wind of change may force barristers to relinquish lavish and expensive premises in city centres in favour of much smaller administrative and collectively resourced offices. This will permit the growth of satellite branches at a local level within the community. Back to the grass roots.

THE EXECUTION

Ruth Ellis, Mahmoud Mattan

The sun was going down at the end of a sultry summer afternoon in New Orleans. Throughout the day the crowds had been growing, quietly anticipating the appearance of the main men, and just before 6 p.m. the stream of people flowed towards the principal arena, and you would have to take life and limb in both hands if you wanted to be in pole position near the stage to see the action. Freddy was nine and pretty lively, and he became our passport to paradise by racing ahead and scrambling between the legs of the adults until he was in the front row. Yvette and I apologised profusely as we pushed our way forward because we had to retrieve our wayward son – and of course once at the front there was no way back, so we were forced to stay put and listen to the very reason we had come to the 1996 New Orleans Jazz Festival: the Neville Brothers. Their distinctive voices, pulsating rhythms and gospel influence create the sort of music that has everyone moving. 'Brother Jake' is one of those numbers: you come away from listening to it with every limb loosened and every mental muscle laid-back.

The New Orleans visit happened quite by chance. I was chairing a debate in London about the iniquities of capital punishment, when my physical appearance must have betrayed the inner strains and stresses I was trying to contain. For me, there are always a number of competing pressures besides the case of the moment (at the time, that of the Stephen Lawrence family): other trials in the pipeline which require constant preparation and end-of-day conferences, sometimes at a prison some distance from London; one or two public speaking engagements per week; and the management of an evolving set of chambers. As Head of the set, this last responsibility can be both invigorating and debilitating, for in a way chambers is not dissimilar to an overgrown family: you love every member, but there lies the rub. It's unpredictable, and I never know from day to day who may be facing insurmountable problems or even who may decide without forewarning that they need to move on. There is no contract of employment, no partnership between the members; at best, chambers is a loose collective, bound together by a common purpose and understanding; at worst, it is a marriage of convenience – and as far as I am aware, this is unique in the business world. I try to be available, accessible, fair-minded and relaxed, but it is no easy task. Yet when the system works, chambers can provide an incomparably supportive and creative environment at all levels. Achieving this in an undemonstrative, affable and effective manner has been Patrick Roche, for many years deputy head and now co-head, assisted by the diplomacy of Elizabeth Woodcraft. Together they bolt the nuts and turn the screws!

In the midst of this maelstrom of events I have received steady support from successive PAs: Breda, Susie, Emily, and for the last decade, Camilla Cameron. With close family ties to the law and a passionate feel for fairness, Camilla has fielded a stream of endless enquiries from prisoners, journalists, researchers, academics and politicians. The most challenging and time-consuming are the stalkers – in person, on the phone or by email. The patience of Job is a prerequisite, especially when dealing with incessant demands ranging from offers of marriage to threats of arson to chambers.

Most of the time I try to dissipate and absorb feelings of stress, otherwise I'd become an emotional wreck, quite unable to do the job. Since anger and injustice have been two of the predominant and most powerful forces driving me, it needs quite a lot of handling to ensure that I don't explode at the wrong moment. None the less, there has to be a safety-release mechanism, and mine is having a go at other issues not directly related to the one in hand.

Luckily for me, at the London debate my stressful state was recognised by another participant, a man I had never met before. Clive Stafford-Smith is an English lawyer who had worked and lived in the United States for over twenty years, concentrating on death-row cases, and he was only too aware of the daily pressures faced by criminal lawyers who take their work seriously. At the end of the meeting he was nothing less than forthright: 'You look drained, Michael,' he observed, then asked if I needed to get away – and within minutes he had generously offered me his house in New Orleans and mentioned the Jazz Festival. This invitation had come just at the right time, for I was overdue a break. Before long Clive and I became friends and colleagues, and lately he has campaigned tirelessly against the outrageous excesses and illegality of Guantanamo Bay.

While the events affecting the black communities in Notting Hill, Deptford and Bradford were unfolding in the UK, a young man called Andrew Lee Jones was growing up in rural Louisiana, not far from New Orleans. He was the fifth son of a black sharecropping family, and when his father died in 1973 and his family were evicted from their home, he took to the road and to petty crime. In 1984 he was charged with the murder of the daughter of his ex-girlfriend.

The trial took place in Baton Rouge, in front of an all-white jury because black people were traditionally excluded. It lasted less than one day and, with no scientific evidence to link him to the crime – the main connection appeared to be the fact that he did, of course, know the victim – he was found guilty and sentenced to death. On appeal (which was not concerned with conviction, only sentence) in 1991, his court-appointed lawyer admitted that he had not been able to provide a fair defence for Andrew: he'd only received the papers a short time before the trial began; and anyway he hadn't had enough experience to conduct capital trials of which this was his first. Worst of all, he had not been aware that throughout the trial Andrew had been medicated with Thorazine, prescribed as a tranquilliser, far in excess of the normal amounts. Andrew spent seven years on death row and was given nine execution dates.

Over the fifteen months leading up to his execution Andrew had corresponded with an English woman named Jane Officer, whom he had met through Lifelines, an organisation founded in 1987 by Jan Arriens as a 'pen-pal' initiative: it began with a solitary letter and grew to 2,500-plus people writing to prisoners on death row. As a result of her correspondence, Jane Officer went to the USA for the first time in her life to plead for Andrew's life at the Parole

Board hearing, and spent the remaining hours of Andrew's life with him and his family. But despite all that effort and the support of his ex-girlfriend (the mother of the victim), Andrew was executed on 22 July 1991.

In order to offer support to others on death row, the Andrew Lee Jones Fund was established in 1992. Jane published his letters and diaries in a book entitled *If I Should Die*,[1] for which I wrote an introduction that compared the contents with the dramatised work of Sister Helen Prejean in the remarkable film *Dead Man Walking*, produced by Working Title and starring Susan Sarandon and Sean Penn.

I was invited to a preview of the film, after which there was an interesting and informative discussion. One of the contributors was a woman whose son had been murdered, but who had no wish to see the murderer executed: she argued that execution would not bring back her son and it would not deter others; all it would mean was that there would be another bereft mother like herself. The film depicted a particularly brutal killing and you were left in little doubt that the Sean Penn character was guilty, but this is at the sharp end of the debate, and for me there can be no morality in retributive justice. If you want to make a point about the undesirability of taking life, you do not do so by committing the very same act, even though it bears judicial legitimacy. In the words of Andre Sakharov, a prisoner of conscience in the USSR: 'I regard the death penalty as a savage and immoral institution which undermines the moral and legal foundations of a society . . . and that savagery begets only savagery.'[2]

My visit to Louisiana brought home to me how serious the situation was. Clive was fighting a lone battle, with the odds stacked well against him, and death-row work was not attractive – let alone remunerative so far as American lawyers were concerned, for the majority of death-row inmates were black, poor and badly represented. For example, in the 1992 trial of George McFarland, his lawyer was asleep for most of the hearing, missing important prosecution witnesses. No one seems to have bothered to wake him up, and the trial judge, while accepting that there was a constitutional right to a defendant having the services of a lawyer, added, 'The constitution doesn't say the lawyer has to be awake.' The Court of Appeal upheld the judge's view.

It seemed to me that back in Britain we could increase our practical assistance to Clive and others, but I was in two minds about raising money and awareness for these issues when the United States, one of the richest countries in the world and supposedly at the heart of democratic values, should have remedied the situation itself. The vast majority of states in the USA practise the death penalty, and the main debate appears to be primarily about how it is carried out. Currently that debate centres on the use of a three-drug cocktail delivered by lethal injection: the first one is supposed to sedate, the second to paralyse all parts of the body except the heart, and the third stops the heart, finally causing death. There are occasions when sedation is not effective.

A terrible example of the inhumanity of the system is the case of Michael Richard, who was executed in Texas on 25 September 2007 after a state courthouse refused to stay open an extra fifteen minutes to allow the filing of an appeal based on the constitutionality of lethal injection. Richard's attorneys had been unable to file the appeal on time because of computer problems – problems that they had already brought to the court's attention. The US Supreme Court then refused to stop the execution. Earlier in the day, however, it had agreed in a Kentucky case to review the lethal-injection issue, a decision that led to a *de facto* moratorium on all other lethal-injection executions around the country. The Supreme Court's ruling on 16 April 2008 held that the use of lethal injection does *not* violate the American constitution's ban on 'cruel and unusual punishment'.

It doesn't really matter which form of execution is considered: firing squad, electrocution, gas chamber, hanging or, in some countries, stoning. The whole process is cruel and inhumane.

Amnesty International's yearly statistics[3] suggest that in 2007 at least 1,252 people were executed in twenty-four countries. Up to 27,500 people are estimated to be on death row across the world, while 88 per cent of all known executions took place in five countries: China, Iran, Saudi Arabia, Pakistan and the USA. Saudi Arabia had the highest number of executions per capita. China, which the report refers to as the world's top executioner, classifies the death penalty as a state secret. As the world and Olympic guests were left guessing in August 2008, only the Chinese authorities knew exactly how many people were being killed with state authorisation. And so it remains. By the time of the 2009 Amnesty report (for the year 2008) the number of recorded executions worldwide had nearly doubled to 2,390. Fifty-nine countries were involved but China again led the way with 1,718 executions. The most chilling aspect of this increase is China's deployment of ten mobile death chambers masquerading as ordinary coaches but with the seats removed and the windows darkened. Inside a lethal injection is delivered.[4]

Given these serious breaches of human rights, one has to ask how the British Government justifies its economic links with and staunch support for regimes in Saudi Arabia, China and the USA itself, and it seems to me and to others that in these circumstances we should at least begin the campaign in the West before tackling the Middle East and the Far East.

Building on the experiences of the Andrew Lee Jones Fund and the work of Clive Stafford-Smith, I felt it important to broaden our ambit of activity and the constituency of support in the UK. With that in mind, we began an enlarged intern scheme under the name of Amicus[5] to train young lawyers to undertake death-row cases, initially in the USA.

The stated objects of Amicus are:

to promote the relief of suffering and distress to those persons and families of those persons who are awaiting execution in any state of the United States of America and who, for reasons of their poverty, are in need of legal or other assistance to ensure the preservation of their rights of appeal and to ensure that their imprisonment is administered, so far as is possible, humanely.[6]

For more than twelve years Amicus has been extremely successful, and up to 2009 had helped to fund or place over 250 interns. Sister Helen Prejean has become an active patron of fundraising events in the UK, and the charity has saved lives. For example, in the case of Bobby Purcell in Arizona the defendant was sixteen years old at the time of the offence, and after he was found guilty the judge adjourned the sentencing part of the hearing to another date. His lawyer alerted Amnesty International to the potential breach of international standards, and Amnesty contacted Amicus. Lawyers Owen Williams and Fiona Elder, both from Bristol, drafted an *amicus curiae* brief for the sentencing hearing, explaining the position in international law, as part of the overall strategy for the mitigation – and the judge was persuaded by Bobby's attorney to pass a life sentence. Similar work has been successfully undertaken by Tooks member, Hugh Southey, on behalf of the Bar Human Rights Committee, in seeking to persuade the US Supreme Court to stay executions which violate basic human rights.

There was a glimmer of hope about the death penalty in 2007, when the United Nations General Assembly voted, by 104 to 54 with 29 abstentions, to end its use. All that remains is for the resolution to be implemented . . .

Now that Amicus is well established in the USA, it is hoped that it will be able to extend its services to other parts of the globe – for example, the Caribbean and Africa, which are often forgotten. There is now a remarkable project initiated by a young barrister named Alexander McLean, who has been personally tending to the needs of prisoners in Uganda, Sierra Leone and Kenya by raising money and helping with medical facilities, libraries and farming schemes. Some of the prisoners – particularly in Uganda – are teenagers on death row imprisoned for minor crimes.[7]

I find it a sobering thought that the death penalty was only abolished[8] in the UK two years before I began to practise in 1967, and – remarkably – continued for some offences right up until 1998. The last hangings took place on 13 August 1964, when Gwynne Evans was executed at Strangeways and Robert Stewart at Walton jail. Had the penalty not been abolished in 1965, a large number of the innocent people whom I have represented and who are mentioned in this book would now be dead – most notably the Birmingham Six, the Bridgewater Four, Judith Ward, the Tottenham Three, the Cardiff Three and Barry George – and that is one of the most compelling arguments against the use of an irreversible and final sentence of death when the criminal-justice system itself is fallible.

I can only imagine what it must have been like to conduct a murder trial under the shadow of the noose: it's bad enough at the moment, when defendants receive extraordinarily long sentences of thirty years or more. The nearest I have come to it, however, is in relation to cases from other parts of the world where the death penalty persists, and in appeals in domestic cases from the period when it was still in operation. When I first started there were a large number of such appeals in capital cases, from the West Indies to the Privy Council in Downing Street, London, as the last Court of Appeal. The convicted person often had no money, and on many occasions had not even been represented at his trial. Senior members of the Bar were reluctant to undertake this unpaid work as it entailed a fair amount of research and preparation, and therefore it was thought to be an appropriate experience for young entrants who had to learn on the job. I found this a trifle odd and very worrying, realising that somebody's life – a person whom I would never meet, but had only read about – depended on my getting it right.

The initial stages would be completed on paper only, and if I didn't proceed successfully there wouldn't even be a hearing; if I did succeed in getting a hearing, it might be extremely short and not very sweet. I cannot now remember just how many of these cases I did, but it was well into double figures – and, sadly, mostly I failed.

Several of those executed before 1964 have subsequently been exonerated, including Timothy Evans for two of the 10 Rillington Place murders and Derek Bentley for his part in the shooting of a police constable in November 1952. A lesser-known instance was Mahmoud Hussein Mattan, whom I represented in the Court of Appeal on 24 February 1998 and who had been executed on 3 September 1952, after Evans in 1950 and before Bentley in 1953.

A merchant seaman originally from Somalia, Mattan settled in Cardiff in the late 1940s, but such was the level of racism against him that he and his Welsh wife were forced for a while to live in separate houses on the same street. He became a steel worker, but was made redundant in 1952, and on 6 March that year a shopkeeper named Lily Volpert was found murdered with her throat cut at her shop at 203–4 Bute Street, in the Butetown area of Cardiff docks. The key evidence at Mattan's trial came from an eyewitness called Harold Cover, who claimed to have seen him coming out of the doorway of the shop at about the time the murder must have been committed. Mattan's defence was one of alibi: he said he'd been at the cinema and then gone home, never having been in Bute Street, let alone in the shop.

But what had not been disclosed to the defence at the time of Mattan's trial was a statement made by Cover on 7 March 1952, the day after the murder, a significant element of which had been that the person he described coming out of the doorway of the shop had a gold tooth. This was not a feature he described in his trial evidence before the jury that convicted Mattan, and anyway Mattan did not have a gold tooth. The defence were also unaware that Cover had received a reward in the region of £200 – which in 1952 would have bought a house in Cardiff – and that another Somali called Taher Gass had been interviewed by Cardiff police on 10 March. He lived at 196 Bute Street, and admitted that he had been past the shop three times on the evening of the murder.

The story took a sinister turn when in May 1969 Harold Cover was convicted of the attempted murder of his daughter by cutting her throat with a razor: he was sentenced to life imprisonment.

Just before the start of the appeal in 1998 there was a dramatic development, which gloriously illustrates the fundamental technique I've always propounded of going back to the drawing board and starting all over again. The day before the appeal was due to be heard, my junior Anne Shamash from my chambers, at my request was trawling through unused documents for a second time in the back room of a South Wales police station when there fell out of a notebook a small slip of paper bearing the faint traces of pencilled copperplate handwriting. It had been written by the senior investigating officer, DI Roberts, by then deceased, and the assiduous researches made by Anne and my solicitor Bernard de Maid revealed an explosively important observation by the Inspector: 'The man seen by Cover was traced – Gass (Taher) . . . useless? Cover left Cory's Rest, 7:50 p.m., identifies the Somali in the porch as Gass.' What we then discovered was that Gass had been tried for murder in 1954 and committed to Broadmoor on the grounds of insanity: it was thought he had been deported later to Somalia and was no longer alive. At the time of his trial a telex had been circulated giving a description of Gass, which was consistent with the eyewitness evidence about the man in the doorway – most crucially, he had a gold tooth in his left upper jaw.

In quashing the conviction for Mahmoud Mattan, the Vice President of the Court of Appeal, Lord Justice Rose, went on to comment that the case had a wider significance:

First, capital punishment was not perhaps a prudent culmination for a criminal justice system which is human and therefore fallible. Secondly, in important areas, to some of which we have alluded, criminal law and practice have, since Mattan was tried, undergone major changes for the better. Thirdly, the Criminal Cases Review Commission is a necessary and welcome body without whose work the injustice in this case might never have been identified. Fourthly, no one associated with the criminal justice system can afford to be complacent. Fifthly, injustices of this kind can only be avoided if all concerned in the investigation of crime and the preparation and presentation of criminal prosecutions observe the very highest standards of integrity, conscientiousness and professional skill.[9]

Mattan's name was cleared, but he had paid for this injustice with his life.

The last woman to be hanged in Britain was Ruth Ellis on 13 July 1955. Her appeal in September 2003, which I also undertook with Anne Shamash and Bernard de Maid before a court led by Lord Justice Kay, received very different treatment from Mattan's. There was palpable hostility from start to finish and the court, when dismissing the appeal, questioned whether it had been a sensible exercise and use of court time to consider an appeal so long after the event – especially when Ruth Ellis herself had consciously and deliberately chosen not to appeal at the time – and urged the Criminal Cases Review Commission to consider these factors in future before referring a case back to the court.[10]

What the court did not know was that the family and friends of Ruth Ellis were so upset by the court's approach to the appeal that they wished to withdraw at the beginning of the second day's hearing. I persuaded them to remain, believing that it is always important for the full picture to be deployed and examined, in the hope that something positive will prevail, but on reflection perhaps they should have left when they wanted to.

The original trial of Ruth Ellis had taken place at the Old Bailey in June 1955 and had lasted a mere two days. There was no question that she had shot her lover David Blakely outside a public house near Hampstead Heath,[11] and her defence throughout was that she was guilty of manslaughter by reason of provocation, rather than guilty of murder. She gave evidence about the considerable abuse that she had suffered from Blakely over a long period of time, but before Melford Stevenson, QC, came to make his final speech to the jury, the judge, Mr Justice Havers, ruled that her evidence did not amount to a defence in law as it then stood. There was therefore no closing speech for the defence, and after the summing-up the jury took barely twenty minutes to return its verdict of guilty.

The kernel of the argument revolved around whether the undoubted cumulative effect of months of abuse and violence contained a sufficient and immediate nexus to the shooting, which occurred after a lapse of time and a journey from Ruth's home to the pub, carrying a gun, with which she intended to inflict serious injury. Put another way, for the claim of provocation to succeed there had to be evidence from which a jury could infer that there was an impulsive loss of self-control flowing immediately from some incident of provocation. Interestingly, at the time of Ruth's execution, changes to the law were being contemplated (and were eventually brought about by Section 3 of the Homicide Act 1957), in which the ambit was expressly stated to include 'things done, as well as things said'. The jury had to determine whether these things were enough to make a 'reasonable man' do as the defendant did. It was that same statute (at Section 2) that provided a defence of diminished responsibility for someone who killed another, but was suffering from such an abnormality of the mind (meaning arrested or retarded development, inherent cause, or disease or injury) that it substantially impaired their mental responsibility.

The difficulties and complexities thrown up by these definitions has been canvassed a number of times since Ruth Ellis's trial and appeal, most notably in the cases of Kiranjit Ahluwalia and Sara Thornton, both of whom had killed their abusive husbands. I represented Sara at her second appeal against a murder conviction in 1995 and during her retrial in 1996 at Oxford Crown Court. This time she was convicted of manslaughter and was subsequently released.

The most obvious difficulty is that while the Homicide Act 1957 does *not* require the loss of control to be 'sudden and temporary' (derived from the words of Lord Devlin in 1949), that still tends to be the benchmark. For women the moment of violent and fatal reaction may be delayed, either because they are physically unable to use force at the time of the worst abuse or because the provocation which finally unleashes the violence is triggered by a very minor occurrence. Often this received an extraordinarily hostile reception from judges of the old order, who came out with all the usual clichés about women being free to leave their battering partners. But gradually the courts have begun to recognise what is variously described as 'the slow burn', 'the last straw' or cumulative provocation. At the centre of this is a woman battered physically and psychologically, and unless she can place herself within the confines of the two very limited defences of provocation and diminished responsibility which result in manslaughter, then she will be convicted alongside serial killers, contract murderers and multiple bombers. It is partly for these reasons that members of the higher judiciary and others have wanted a change in the mandatory sentence of life incurred by a murder conviction in these cases. The Southall Black Sisters have provided inestimable support for women defendants and their families, as well as campaigning effectively to get both law and practice changed.

In the first major review and re-examination of the law on murder since the abolition of hanging more than forty years ago, the government proposes to abolish the existing law on provocation and replace it with new partial defences, tailored to those who kill as a response to 'a fear of serious violence; and/or in exceptional circumstances, a justified sense of being seriously wronged'. The rationale for this is 'a concern that the current partial defence of provocation is too easy to access by those who kill after losing their tempers, but that it does not provide a sufficiently tailored response to those who kill out of fear of serious violence'.[12]

All this is too late for Ruth Ellis, but thankfully Sara Thornton did not have to face execution after her first trial and failed appeal.

In 1974, nineteen years after the execution of Ruth Ellis, her sister Muriel made contact with the executioner Albert Pierrepoint, who had also been responsible for the hangings of Timothy Evans and Derek Bentley. Not only did she meet him, but a number of letters passed between them, and it is clear from her book, *My Sister's*

Secret Life, that she was less than impressed with the description he gave of Ruth's last moments. None the less, also in 1974 Pierrepoint published his autobiography in which he wrote: 'I've come to the conclusion that executions solve nothing and are only an antiquated relic of a primitive desire for revenge which takes the easy way and hands over the responsibility for revenge to other people.' Interestingly, Muriel cites the words of another executioner, H. W. Critchell of Brixton:

> There were at least ten people waiting to witness or carry out the execution of Ruth Ellis. There was the governor, the padre, the sheriff, a hangman, the death watch – all would have been greatly relieved had a reprieve been granted. No such miracle happened as Ruth Ellis hit the road. These ten or more people looking down at the pit at that ghastly spectacle suspended from that rope received a severe shock to their systems. It is the living that suffered by this devilish, uncivilised practice. I write this in good faith. I have entered that pit and shamed myself many times. I am thoroughly ashamed. No medicine can ever help me. I still suffer.[13]

Peter Aitken (now Adams) was the first man *not* to be hanged after the abolition of capital punishment. I didn't represent him at trial or on appeal, but I knew Shirley Cooklin, who was his prison visitor for many years and with whom he corresponded.[14] I helped her campaign to secure his release, and when that was successful she held a celebratory party at her home in Gospel Oak, north London. At this event she spoke, I spoke and then the novelist Beryl Bainbridge spoke.

Either Beryl was overcome with excitement or the effect of champagne, because as she finished her speech she began to fall backwards. I saved her from hitting the floor, and we carried her to a bedroom upstairs and wrapped her in a coat that happened to be on the bed. A taxi was ordered and she was duly dispatched to her terraced house in Camden Town. Some time later a woman at the party became distraught and then nearly hysterical: her coat, which had been on the bed upstairs and contained her money and keys, had disappeared.

This was a double trauma because the woman was going through an acrimonious divorce and did not want to contact her husband for help, so she pleaded for someone to track down Beryl and the coat – and as I happened to know the road where Beryl lived, I offered to take her to the address.

When we arrived, all was in darkness. I knocked on a neighbour's door to see if she knew if Beryl was in, or if there was any way of gaining access. Meanwhile the coat owner was growing ever more distressed, and the neighbour, seeing this, told me that I could get into Beryl's house if I wanted – the preferred point of entry being a large Georgian sash window on the first floor that was permanently unlocked.

To reach this window you had to get onto a small wrought-iron balcony, climb over railings onto a narrow ledge, and then over more railings onto the balcony in front of the said window. The neighbour offered me a large screwdriver to lever up the sash, but as I had had a drink myself and am hopeless at heights, I declined the offer (in addition to which, I wasn't sure this was going to be a good career move). But by now the damsel in distress was going berserk: there was no alternative, and I caved in.

I have little memory of how I arrived at the window, but I do starkly recollect a moment of extreme hesitation on Beryl's balcony. If apprehended by the law, how on earth was I going to explain breaking into a house with a screwdriver on behalf of a woman I didn't know, to retrieve a coat from another woman I didn't know? But having got this far there was no going back, so I used the screwdriver to ease up the sash window and entered what appeared to be an upstairs living room. As I edged my way across to the door, I looked back towards the window where a street light was illuminating the room – and to my horror, silhouetted against it, was a man sitting at a grand piano. Seemingly I had been caught in the act, and as always in such circumstances I tend to blurt out rather banal observations. 'Terribly sorry to disturb you . . . just passing through . . . forgot my coat,' I muttered. But the man was not impressed and remained resolutely silent. So, switching to a more personal approach, I went up to the piano, stood behind the man and touched him on his shoulder – only to find that it was stiff! A momentary frisson of fear gripped me, until I realised that he was a dummy.

With a sense of relief, but feeling extremely stupid, I proceeded downstairs to the ground floor, where I could hear Beryl snoring, but my progress along the hall was barred by a rather large stuffed moose, which doubled as a coatstand. The desired coat not being on the unfortunate moose's head, I made my way tentatively into the front room, where I found Beryl fast asleep on the couch, still wearing the blessed apparel.

This was a bridge too far. How would I explain to Beryl, if she was roused from her slumbers, that while wielding a screwdriver I was merely retrieving a coat for a stranger? I rushed out of the front door and told the stranger, 'Over to you', but she was in such a state by now that she could scarcely move a muscle. So once again this naive soul capitulated and went back in to do the deed.

If you've ever tried to get a garment off a limp body you'll know how difficult it is, especially if you don't want them to know that you're disrobing them – and in this case I certainly didn't want a National Treasure being dropped unceremoniously on the floor. But somehow I managed to slip the coat off Beryl and return it to its rightful – and grateful – owner, whom I then drove back to her car in Gospel Oak.

By this time, sadly, the party was over.

17

NO EXSKUSE

The Birmingham Six

How do we know what we know? How do we know that the sun will rise tomorrow? How do we know, as in the well-known verse by Ronald Knox – 'That this tree I see / Should continue to be / When there's no one around in the Quad'?

As philosophical conundrums, these questions doubtless seem excessively scholastic and airy-fairy, far removed from the issues of liberty and freedom – and too often of life and death – that concern the courtroom. But in reality they lie at the very heart of the legal process. These epistemological queries, raised for argument purposes by A. J. Ayer and Antony Flew back in Keele days, are important starting blocks.

Just because events have always followed a certain course in the past, that does not necessarily mean that this pattern is immutable or contains some golden law governing all eventualities – and the assumption that the pattern is unchangeable invites serious dangers in the field of forensic science, on which so many criminal cases hinge.

A jury in such a case has to be sure, driven to the conclusion – in fact, certain – of guilt before it convicts, in order to displace the presumption of innocence. This high standard is essential to prevent the deprivation of liberty on a whim or a fancy, but at the same time it may entice witnesses to harden their evidence in order to satisfy it. Science itself can rarely, if ever, achieve a mathematical certainty, but there's always a risk that individual scientists may feel impelled to cross the Rubicon from uncertainty to certainty in order to meet the test set by the law. In practice what happens is the easy elision of workaday assumptions with a state of mind that entertains no reasonable doubt, and in the witness box that often translates into: not 100 per cent sure, but 99.9 per cent sure. Comforting, but dangerous.

A positive scientific finding expressed in this way can misleadingly set the tone for the whole case and therefore have far-reaching effects. It begins with interrogators being convinced they have the right person in custody, and this then affects the nature of the questioning, which is couched in unequivocal language. Your prints and DNA have been found at the scene, so how can you explain them, unless you are guilty? The innocent interviewee is lost for words; the duty solicitor may also feel the evidence is compelling and incontrovertible. End result? Sometimes a false confession, and then wrongful conviction.

A classic example of these propensities arose with the Birmingham Six, a renowned miscarriage of justice and one that set a new agenda for the criminal-justice system as to how such cases should be handled in future. A Royal Commission on Criminal Justice was appointed in 1991, which led to a new Criminal Appeal Act in 1995, and another Commission to identify and investigate miscarriages was established in 1997: the Criminal Cases Review Commission (CCRC).

What has to be remembered is the enormous struggle by the Birmingham Six to clear their names, a fight that was long and arduous, lasting from 1974 until 1991,[1] and played out against a backdrop of mostly hostile (and sometimes venomous) opposition. Being a convicted Irish bomber in that period was almost synonymous with the stigma attached to leprosy, and as I represented more defendants facing these allegations than anyone else, I was often tarred with the same brush. Tabloid newspapers trade only in simple equations.

The tireless insistence of the Six on proving their innocence was reminiscent of the sterling pioneering work done by Ludovic Kennedy in relation to the conviction of Timothy Evans, for murders that had in fact been carried out by John Christie at 10 Rillington Place in the 1950s (see Chapter 12). Against the odds and against established legal opinion, Ludovic fought a solitary battle in his search for the truth. When the fallibility of confession evidence was established, Evans's name was cleared – too late to save him from the gallows, but not too late to be granted a posthumous Royal Pardon in 1966.

Both Ludovic's book[2] and the 1971 film starring Richard Attenborough were inspirational for me, and it was both an honour and a thrill to be able to meet Ludovic when he turned his attention to the case of the Birmingham Six.

The Birmingham Six – Hugh Callaghan, Patrick Hill, Gerard Hunter, Richard McIlkenny, William Power and John Walker – were all Belfast-born, but had lived in Birmingham since the 1960s.

Walker, a crane driver, was a kind, sociable grafter who had six daughters and a son, while McIlkenny, a father of five, was a millwright at a local forging factory. They were both Republicans – Walker because his father had been tear-gassed by the British in Derry, and he believed that this had precipitated his father's death in 1972. He was also deeply disturbed by the Bloody Sunday killings of thirteen innocent civilians in the same year (see Chapter 9), but he demonstrated his beliefs only by collecting money for the Prisoners' Dependents' Relief Fund, and was not a member of the IRA or Sinn Fein. Nor were Kate and Richard McIlkenny, who were from Ardoyne, although Kate's cousin and Richard's brothers were interned there, and money was raised for their families via raffles. Hunter and Hill also helped out with the fundraising.

Fatefully, on Thursday 21 November 1974, Billy Power and four of the others decided to attend the Belfast funeral of their acquaintance James McDade, who to their surprise had turned out to be a member of the IRA and had blown himself up in Coventry earlier that week while planting a bomb. It was a casual decision by the men to go to Belfast, and probably partly an excuse to visit home. Hill's aged aunt had just had a stroke, so he thought this was the golden opportunity to visit her, while Hunter wanted to see his recently widowed mother.

Three of the men had been unemployed for a while and didn't have the cash for the fare, but by dint of borrowing and betting they raised enough to go. Billy's wife Nora lent him £4; his brother-in-law agreed to loan him £10; and Billy won the rest on a horse, which he thought was great good fortune. It turned out to be the worst luck of his life.

The five eventually set off, armed with a pile of Mass cards for the deceased, a change of clothes and a sandwich or two. Their friend Hugh Callaghan, a timid man who suffered from ulcers and had been out of regular work for three years, had no intention of going to Belfast, but on the spur of the moment decided to see the others off at Birmingham's New Street station. At 7.55 p.m. they boarded the train and he waved them goodbye.

The Birmingham bombs were detonated at 10.25 and 10.27 on the evening of 21 November – the first in the Mulberry Bush pub at the foot of the Rotunda and the second in the Tavern in the Town, a basement pub on New Street – and the resulting explosions were collectively at that time the most serious terrorist blasts in mainland Britain: twenty-one civilians, many of them Irish, were killed and 162 people injured. It was carnage. A third device, outside a bank on Hagley Road, failed to detonate. The explosions were immediately credited to the Provisional IRA, although the group was to deny this two days later.

Oblivious to the impending horrors in their adopted home city, the five men had changed trains at Crewe and by 9.15 p.m. were on the connecting service to Heysham Harbour. They were almost alone in the carriage and started to play cards to while away the journey, and when they got off the train at the ferry terminal, Hill walked ahead of the others and, having no luggage, got on the ferry to Belfast without any problems. Meanwhile the other four went through the Special Branch bag check, where they were approached by police and interviewed about the reason for their journey.

They did not tell the police the true purpose of their visit to Belfast, afraid they would be stopped from going – a fact that was later held against them – and while the questioning was in progress they were informed of the Birmingham pub bombings. The four men were horrified at the news, but being reassured that the questioning was just to eliminate them from police enquiries, they agreed to be taken to Morecambe police station for forensic tests. They were worried about Paddy Hill and asked where their mate was – with the result that, unfortunately for him, he was taken off the ferry to join them.

Meanwhile, back in Birmingham, Hugh Callaghan had not arrived home and his wife Eileen was in turn angry (it was her birthday) and worried (the scenes of the bombings were all over the news). When he did turn up he was very upset, having been near the Tavern soon after the explosion. He'd spent the rest of the evening with various friends in various pubs, talking about the outrages and feeling glad to be alive.

Later in Morecambe, at 3 a.m., forensic tests were conducted by Frank Skuse of the North West Forensic Science Laboratory of Chorley, who checked each man's hands in turn over the next few hours, using the relatively simple Greiss test for detecting nitroglycerine. McIlkenny's and Hunter's results were negative, but Power's and Hill's right hands proved positive, and Walker showed minute traces of ammonium and nitrate. From then on the lives of the five men were never to be the same again.

Around the same time as Skuse was carrying out his experiments, Superintendent George Reade, a senior CID officer from Walsall who had been put in charge of the interrogation of the five, arrived in Morecambe with three CID crews and Detective Inspector John Moore of West Midlands Serious Crime Squad. At least five of the police contingent were carrying revolvers.

The Birmingham CID officers later said that they hadn't seen the five until 9.30 a.m. the next morning, but they had been made aware of the forensic results and were convinced they had the Birmingham pub bombers. According to the men, from roughly 6 a.m. on the Friday morning onwards they were beaten up in turn by a number of officers – hit and punched around the head and face; kicked in all parts of the body; subjected to verbal and physical abuse; and threatened with death. None of these allegations were accepted by the police and were hotly contested at the original trial. The various narratives that follow are derived from the trial testimony of the men, set out in detail by Chris Mullin in his authoritative and seminal book *Error of Judgement*.[3]

Each of the men was told that their wives and children would be harmed unless they confessed. They could hear the others screaming in nearby rooms and knew they were in serious trouble unless they cooperated. By 10.30 a.m. Billy Power was so scared and hurt that, against his will, he agreed to say anything the police wanted, and was forced to sign a six-page statement confessing to planting the bombs.

Hill received the same treatment from the police, but stubbornly refused to confess – and despite terrible threats and later, on the journey to Birmingham, a gun being repeatedly put in his mouth and the trigger pulled (to great laughter), he never did confess.

Walker was booted in the spine and punched repeatedly on scars from an operation for ulcers; he had cigarettes stubbed out on a blister on his right foot and was kicked in the genitals. One officer produced a revolver and put a blanket over his head, then held the gun to his temple. Walker heard a loud clap and thought he'd been shot, and then the officers started laughing. In the end he became disorientated, lost consciousness and was in no state to confess.

Hunter was slapped and punched by Reade and Moore; McIlkenny got off 'lightly' with a ferocious kick to the right shoulder and Moore jumping on top of him and holding a blanket over his face until he couldn't breathe. Neither Hunter nor McIlkenny confessed in Morecambe, but by the following day they were back in Birmingham and things got infinitely worse. At Queen's Road police station there were more beatings, and the men were kept awake all night, often standing, so they became very confused.

In the early hours following the bombings, the houses of the five men had been raided and searched, but none of their wives were told they had been apprehended.

Seven weeks earlier a bomb in Guildford had exploded, and shortly afterwards another one in Woolwich, in both cases killing British soldiers from nearby barracks and a number of civilians. In the preceding month seven other explosive devices had been planted in Birmingham. There was already a nationwide wave of anti-Irish sentiment, but by the morning after the 21 November pub bombs things had turned very ugly. Irish people were afraid to go onto the streets; Irish pubs, clubs and homes were petrol-bombed; there were vociferous demonstrations at northern airports; and at the British Leyland car plant banners proclaimed, 'Hang IRA Bombers'. The police knew they had to get results quickly to avoid an escalation of violence. The pressure was on to arrest someone – *anyone*.

Eileen Callaghan came back from work on the Friday at about four o'clock to find four armed police in her home: they said that if she didn't act normally someone would get shot. She was terrified, as was her daughter Geraldine when she arrived home, and when Hugh rolled in after ten, he was grabbed by the arm and had a gun pointed at his head, before being taken into custody.

Callaghan was interviewed and was distraught to find not only that he himself had been arrested, but that the police had detained the others too, and in the police station in Solihull he was subjected to much the same treatment that the five had suffered in Morecambe, with the added bonus of an Alsatian for company outside his cell.

The Six maintained that the maltreatment continued over the weekend, with sustained beatings, mock executions and threats to their families finally making five of them cave in. All but Hill 'confessed', but the discrepancies in their statements were many, either because they'd had to make it all up or because the police had told them what to say. Thus Power 'confessed' that there had been six bombs, whereas Walker said three and Callaghan only one; while the actual bombs had been planted in holdalls, their confessions spoke only of plastic bags; they each placed the others at different pubs, so that some of them were in two places at once; and so on. And when Callaghan tried to withdraw his confession, he had a gun stuck in his stomach.

The Six's families had first heard of their arrest by watching the news. They rushed around searching for their husbands and finally went to the court, but were too scared of the mob outside to go in. They eventually saw them in prison in Birmingham on Tuesday afternoon, where they found all six men in an appalling state.

It wasn't long before the Walker and Hunter families left for Ireland, though the McIlkennys and Eileen Callaghan stuck it out in Birmingham, protected by their neighbours. Pat Hill also stayed put, while Nora Power went to live in London. But wherever they were, they always stuck by their men.

The Six first appeared in court on Monday 25 November, when they were remanded in custody and taken to HMP Winson Green, where they have described how they were subjected to terrible ill-treatment by both prison officers and inmates, running the gauntlet before being thrown into baths whose water became red with blood. When they reappeared in court on the 28th they all showed visible signs of bruising and violence. (In June 1975 fourteen prison officers were charged with varying degrees of assault, but were found not guilty, and in 1977 the six men pressed charges against the West Midlands Police. These charges were dismissed.)

On 12 May 1975 the Six were charged with murder and conspiracy to cause explosions. Three other men, James Kelly, Michael Murray and Michael Sheehan, were charged with conspiracy, and Kelly and Sheehan also faced charges of unlawful possession of explosives. It was most unfortunate that these three were in the dock with the six innocent men, because unlike the Six they did have links with the IRA.

The trial began on 9 June 1975 in Shire Hall, Lancaster Castle, and lasted forty-five days, with Mr Justice Bridge presiding. I got to know that court much later: it's a huge panelled room, like a Gothic cathedral, with the judge sitting away in the distance from both jury and witnesses. It is a very intimidating place.

After legal arguments in a 'trial within a trial' lasting eight days, the statements that the men had made in November were deemed admissible as evidence. The accused were furious and repudiated their confessions at the trial, while the other evidence against them was largely circumstantial, through their association with IRA members.

As always, a persuasive factor for the jury was the scientific evidence, which – though supposedly objective, non-partisan and provable – always carries enormous weight.

Dr Skuse described the test he had used on the night of the bombings to detect the presence of nitroglycerine (Ng). It was called the Greiss test, after the scientist who discovered it. Dr Skuse told the jury that, on the basis of these tests alone, he was 'quite happy' to conclude that both Power and Hill had had contact with commercial explosives. Asked to define exactly what he meant, he went the extra mile and said he was 99.9 per cent certain. 'Quite happy' in the sense of 'fairly happy' might have been nearer the mark, but in the sense of 'completely happy' it was ultimately his undoing. In fact, although Hill and Power had tested positive by the Greiss test for handling explosives, no traces of any explosives were found at any of the Six's homes.

During the trial Eileen Callaghan attended the summing-up and visited Hugh regularly, though Pat Hill and Theresa Walker weren't present; Sandra Hunter, Kate McIlkenny and Nora Power stayed in Lancaster throughout – their children were by this time with relatives in Ireland – and they were so sure of their husbands' innocence (none but Paddy Hill had any 'previous') that they mounted a campaign of their own, little dreaming that it was to last for sixteen years.

There isn't the space here to rehearse all the evidence again, but when presented with the police's word against that of the Six, and in the light of Mr Justice Bridge's direction – 'Many of the allegations made against the police are of the most bizarre and grotesque character ... If the defendants were telling the truth I would have to suppose that a team of some fifteen officers ... had conspired among themselves to use violence on the prisoners and to fabricate evidence' – the jury had a stark choice.

The jury found all the men guilty of murder, and on 15 August 1975 they were sentenced to twenty-one life sentences.

The wives continued their campaign, but to no avail. Despite serious threats to himself and his family, John Walker wrote to the Home Secretary naming those he thought were involved in the bombings, from information that he'd gleaned from Michael Murray, his co-defendant. Murray was a self-acknowledged IRA member (already serving twelve years for the offence of conspiracy to cause explosions).

In March 1976, in front of Lord Chief Justice Widgery, the Six had their appeal dismissed; and in 1980, following long legal wrangles, Lord Denning, Master of the Rolls, gave judgment on the six men's application for a civil action against the police and Home Office for their injuries in custody. He denied them the right to proceed to trial, stating:

> If the six men win it will mean that the police were guilty of perjury, that they were guilty of violence and threats, that the confessions were involuntary and were improperly admitted in evidence and that the convictions were erroneous. This would mean the Home Secretary would either have to recommend they be pardoned or he would have to admit the case to the Court of Appeal. This is such an appalling vista that every sensible person in the land would say: it cannot be right that these actions go any further.[4]

In November 1981 the House of Lords upheld Denning's judgment. This was the end of the legal road for the men to prove their innocence.

The next years were bleak, as the men adjusted to prison life. But the women never gave up, and despite harassment, poverty and the stress of long journeys to visit the men in prison, they continued to fight. Over the years their daughters joined in too, and when I first met Breda Power and Maggie McIlkenny I found them two of the most loyal, feisty young women I have ever known.

Fresh hope arrived when in 1985 journalist (and later MP) Chris Mullin and researcher Charles Tremayne began to investigate the case for Granada Television's *World in Action*. They re-examined the false confessions, reassessed the forensic science and tried to track down those really responsible for the bombings. Mullins managed to do so, speaking to the perpetrators in Ireland, and senior IRA commander Joe Cahill admitted that those who were to blame were walking around free.

However, the most significant development triggered by Granada's investigation was the research carried out by two reputable scientists: David Baldock and Dr Brian Caddy.

Brian Caddy was approachable, enthusiastic and a great communicator. His whole approach was one of efficiency, and because of this I was able to obtain a quicker grasp of the intricacies of the science than would otherwise have been the case, which was a great relief. He is now Emeritus Professor of Forensic Science at the University of Strathclyde, regularly called in as a troubleshooter when there are questions over the reliability of forensic science, and in 2008 he was commissioned by the government to perform a review of DNA procedures following the acquittal in the Omagh bombing case (see Chapter 11).

At the very point of compiling the materials for this chapter, I was passing through Gatwick airport en route to Montpellier when someone called out my name – and I was delighted to see that it was Brian, also on his way to Montpellier with his wife. This was the first time that I had met him in the twenty years since the Birmingham Six appeal, and by coincidence I was carrying in my briefcase a freshly obtained copy of his DNA review to read on the plane.

I always find these so-called coincidences a little bizarre and unnerving. I don't know whether I experience them more or less than anyone else, but it's almost as though they were meant to happen and contain some inner force. I'm not remotely religious and have no metaphysical beliefs in divine existence, but maybe – as Arthur Koestler has explored in *The Roots of Coincidence*[5] – such happenings may not be coincidence after all. The odd experience I can cope with, but their alarming regularity and poignancy are disturbing. Perhaps they occur all the time, but you only see the ones you want to see.

The objective of Brian's experiments for *World in Action* was to ascertain whether any substance other than nitroglycerine could give a positive reading – that is, a false positive for Ng, but obviously not for the other substance itself: astonishingly, no one had done this in order to validate the specificity of the Greiss test. Thirty-five samples of everyday objects were examined, especially ones that the defendants might have had contact with: cigarettes, meat pies, playing cards, the nitrocellulose lacquer used on railway-carriage woodwork, and so on.

The discoveries were startling. Some nitrocellulose-based products such as the lacquer proved positive, but so did a cigarette packet, a postcard and an old used pack of playing cards. Greiss could therefore only be regarded as a presumptive field test and not as a definitive conclusion. The substance might be Ng, but equally it might not. If the police and the jury in the Birmingham Six trial had been told this, a whole needless chain of events might have been curtailed.

On 20 January 1987 Douglas Hurd, then Home Secretary, referred the case back for appeal, and this time the Six really thought their side would be heard.

By now I had been briefed by Gareth Peirce, who was representing some of the Six. I have already paid tribute in these pages to Gareth's quiet persistence, but nothing better illustrates her resolve than the occasion when she suddenly appeared, fully kitted out in surgical mask and doctor's gown, in the labour ward at the birth of my youngest son Freddy in September 1987. For a moment I thought she was a doctor, but then she produced a sheaf of important papers for me to sign for the appeal. Fortunately Yvette was otherwise occupied at the time or she might have had something to say about the apparition – and, ever thoughtful, Gareth returned in a few days to visit Yvette in hospital, bringing Freddy a huge, fluffy, brown toy dog which Paddy Hill had made in prison for him. It sat proudly on Freddy's bed for many years.

For month after month I was up to my ears in files. In our tiny flat in Battersea the pile of paperwork competed with Freddy's nappies, and it seemed like a mountain to climb to unravel the police cover-up and dispel the prejudice that had built up over so many years. So I looked forward to my weekly game of tennis with my solicitor friend James Saunders, a small, wiry terrier of a man, dapper, highly intelligent and a robust risk-taker. Coming out of Queen's Club in Barons Court one evening following an excellent game and a pint, we found ourselves buffeted by a howling wind and surrounded by swirling leaves and debris: it was the night of the big storm in October 1987.

I rushed to get home safely, and the next day I was in the middle of a lawyers' conference preparing the appeal when I received a call from a west London police station. 'Is that Mr Mansfield? We have something of yours. It looks like a drowned rat!' Unbeknown to me, in my haste I had not noticed that my brown leather case with my robes, wig and some Birmingham Six papers had disappeared from my car the night before. Someone had forced the lock, taken the case and run across the outside grass courts at Queen's, and on the baseline where many a Stella Artois champion has stood, whoever it was had opened the case to check the contents – and, clearly disappointed, had dumped the lot. The ensuing gale blew most of it into neighbouring gardens, including my ancient, century-old horsehair wig, which ended up a tree and was initially mistaken by a householder for a squirrel.

I retrieved the wig from the police the next day, and my sister-in-law Louise kindly made it over, using the bristles of a scrubbing brush as a substitute for horsehair at her and my brother-in-law Keir's prop workshop, Keir Lusby at Shepperton Studios – the professional suppliers at Ede & Ravenscroft having declined to touch such a mangy old wig for health-and-safety reasons. Sadly the made-over wig was stolen some years later from the robing room at Manchester Crown Court. There was a spate of such thefts and the police thoughtfully informed me that wigs were the preferred adornment for strippers to cover the parts others can't reach! I now have a nasty new, synthetic wig.

Before the appeal hearing itself, and in order to help me to get my head round what on earth was involved in the science, Gareth sensibly proposed that we all visit a laboratory to witness the tests being carried out. I'd never come across any of these tests before and had little idea what would be involved, but I was confident that, as with my handwriting and fingerprint experiences, once I saw things on the ground the veil would drop from my eyes. I may be a bear of very little brain, but observing I can manage, and in the end the whole issue of forensics boils down to a large dollop of human perception along with significant margins of appreciation of subjectivity.

There were in fact not one but three tests: Greiss, TLC (sadly not Tender Loving Care but thin-layer chromatography) and GC-MS (gas chromatography-mass spectrometry).

For Greiss you need to collect the samples from the surface, in this case the hand, by swabbing, which is not as grand as it sounds. You take something like a cotton-wool bud, moisten it with an uncontaminated pure liquid like ether, and then rub it over the fingers and under the nails. Once collected, the sample is then extracted, using more ether, into a crucible or small white bowl (hopefully clean and uncontaminated). This is then divided into two more white bowls so that you have three roughly equal quantities of the sample. To find out if Ng or any other organic compound is present, you first add some caustic soda, then a Greiss reagent (something that provokes a reaction) to the first bowl. If it turns pink within ten seconds you may be onto a winner. You then turn to the second bowl, leave out the caustic soda and just use the Greiss. If it stays clear, you've got Ng. The last bowl is simply an extra one for further tests back in the laboratory.

All sorts of variables come into play, which are not difficult to imagine. There was a formula. What was it? Was it followed? Was ether or ethanol used? What percentage of caustic soda: 0.1 per cent or 1.0 per cent? What shade of pink was the pink? Did the sample go pink after nine seconds? Or ten seconds? What was the ambient temperature of the room where the test was done? (If heated, nitrocellulose, which is found on lots of domestic surfaces, could be confused with nitroglycerine.)

The next test is TLC, basically another colour test. You have a piece of test paper similar to blotting paper, and you watch how far the sample travels up the paper in relation to a known control sample of Ng: a bit like the old litmus tests that we did at school.

Finally there's GC-MS, where the sample is injected into a machine and its atomic mass is measured by a graph, like the results on a TV screen or oscilloscope. Once again, time is of the essence.

What is surprising about the original results, and should have given everyone food for thought, was that the two positive samples from Hill and Power taken at Morecambe police station were not confirmed by the subsequent laboratory tests – surprising particularly because GC-MS was reputedly a hundred times more sensitive and could therefore detect much smaller quantities. However, Dr Skuse had carried out a GC-MS test on Hill's left hand, which had not been subjected to Greiss, and this did prove positive.

The appeal began on 2 November 1987 in Court Number 12 at the Old Bailey and lasted thirty-two days. It attracted huge media attention, with many notable names joining the cause as willing observers. This time it wasn't just Nora, Sandra and Kate, but also Sister Sarah Clarke, a dedicated nun who had visited the Six in prison for years; the Irish ex-Foreign Minister and an Ambassador; the Bishop of Derry, Dr Edward Daly; the Irish Primate; former Labour leader Michael Foot; even an American Congressman: they were there to scrutinise British justice, and the pressure was on. Gareth represented her clients with humanity and tenacity, determined that they would get justice, while the six men looked older after thirteen years in jail and were probably wiser, but their spirits were high. The legal line-up was impressive: Lord Tony Gifford, QC, Richard Ferguson, QC, and myself as Leaders, with James Wood, Nick Blake and Paddy O'Connor as our juniors. We were all close friends as well as colleagues, making quite significantly different contributions to the appeal. The three juniors provided the brain powerhouse and could equally have led: Nick, for instance, is now a high-court judge. According to Chris Mullin in *Error of Judgement*,[6] we all 'had a reputation for fearlessness in the face of judicial intimidation', but 'Mansfield had one other advantage: he was that rare phenomenon, a lawyer who understood forensic science.' I'm glad that he had faith, because we faced an awesome task.

I cross-examined Superintendent George Reade about his schedule, which was designed to detail the order and times of the interviews of the men. This, I suggested when pressed by the Lord Chief Justice, Lord Lane, amounted to a 'blueprint' for a conspiracy to pervert the course of justice. I was not pursuing this lightly, or without due consideration of the evidence supporting such an assertion, but it was pretty audacious, and it goes without saying that it didn't find favour with his Lordship. A product of the old school, he said little, but his body language spoke volumes. Mostly it was his impatient, jack-in-the-box eyebrows and his rhythmic finger-tapping that were supposed to remind me I was not addressing a jury: in other words, fewer histrionics, less flair, less passion – stay cool and calm, and collect your papers on the way out.

However, it was the expert evidence I was anticipating more eagerly, in the rotund form of Dr Skuse. As Chris Mullin describes: 'thirteen years earlier he had been elevated virtually to the status of sainthood by the trial judge Lord Bridge, but by the time of the second appeal he had been retired on the grounds of limited effectiveness'.[7]

Once my cross-examination got under way, the shortcomings to which I had become accustomed over the years rose slowly to the surface: a lack of reliable working papers showing what he did and when he did it, in particular the formula for Greiss, all accompanied by an unrelenting obduracy about his own conclusions.

Question, MICHAEL MANSFIELD: When did you first commit to paper the details of the Greiss tests you had done in 1974?
Answer, DR SKUSE: October 1987.
Q. About two weeks before the hearing began?
A. Yes, it might have been a bit earlier.

Thirteen years too late. He didn't write it down at the time because he didn't think it was necessary. Even worse, he claimed it was government laboratory policy. This gargantuan lapse meant there was real doubt about the detail of what he said he'd done, especially how much caustic soda he had used and whether any ethanol had been incorporated. With regard to the non-confirmation of Greiss by the subsequent laboratory tests, he explained this by evaporation of the samples. But what he couldn't explain was why the evaporation had occurred. You're supposed to preserve the samples by refrigeration.

> *Question*, MICHAEL MANSFIELD: You knew that in 1974?
> *Answer*, DR SKUSE: I did.
> Q. So if you knew that, why not put it in a fridge?
> A. It was an omission.[8]

In any event, for the non-sensitive Greiss test to have produced at least one strong positive result there must have been a sizeable quantity of nitroglycerine in the first place, and this could not have evaporated in the time available.

As for the one positive GC-MS test done on a non-Greiss sample: surprise, surprise, there was no documentation; no trace print-out (like graph paper) from the oscilloscope; and therefore no record to verify Dr Skuse's memory that there had been a minute blip, at precisely 4.2 seconds, lasting about 0.3 of a second, sufficient to constitute a discrete peak of mass 46 representing Ng.

I walked home past news vendors' placards pronouncing Dr Skuse's failings, and we all thought we had done enough to secure freedom for the Six. Gareth was so pleased with the job I'd done on Skuse that she procured a *London Evening Standard* billboard which read, BOMB TRIAL DOCTOR'S HUGE BLUNDERS, and framed it for me. I still have it.

The evening before the appeal decision, the families decided to hold a private gathering in a hotel in Shepherd's Hill, Highgate. They wanted to thank their legal teams, and despite their apprehension and the knowledge that their men were still behind bars, they needed to be together. It was such a good idea to pre-empt the judgment with a spirit of solidarity before the fateful day. It was a typical Irish night, boozy and lively. Yvette was invited too and we took Freddy, then a little over three months old. As we came through the door, the baby was whisked away by Billy Power's wife Nora, and the women handed him from one pair of welcoming arms to another: he got more cuddles that night, from complete strangers who were so keen to show him (and us) their gratitude and affection, than in the whole of his little life to date. It was wonderful.

The next day, 28 January 1988, speaking at the end of the appeal, Lord Lane summed up: 'The longer this hearing has gone on, the more convinced this court has become that the verdict of the jury was correct.'

In my job you get inured to adverse judgments, but this was a particular monster of a travesty. The scientific evidence had been demolished. That alone should have rendered the convictions unsafe. I've learned to contain my anger – but only just. I had a habit of drawing words and images of the day in pencil on the skin of a snare drum that was part of my drum kit at home. I would then beat the living daylights out of it, drumming along to a recording of the Rolling Stones' 'I Can't Get No Satisfaction'.

The work, the dedication, the emotional commitment by the whole team, the Six and their families had come to naught. They had suffered – but so had British justice, apparently irreparably.

Despite the feelings of devastation experienced by the men and their families, by now a kind of unstoppable momentum had begun, and the calls for justice from MPs, Amnesty International and many, many members of the public drove the impetus for further investigations. There were two not unconnected events in 1989 that were the straws that finally broke the camel's back.

First, in August the Chief Constable of the West Midlands Police, Geoffrey Dear, announced the disbanding of the whole of his Serious Crime Squad. This was unprecedented: fifty detectives, many of senior rank, were transferred to non-operational duties, and several of these had been involved in the Birmingham pub bombings investigation. The Squad was accused by no fewer than ninety-one people of fabrication of confessions, falsifying statements, violence and intimidation. Nevertheless, three years after another police inquiry, the DPP decided to take no action.

The second straw was the release in October 1989 of the Guildford Four. Both cases relied on false confessions, allegations of violence by the police, and fraud and perjury to cover it up, all in a climate of anti-IRA hysteria.

By the time of the third appeal in 1991 we had matters sewn up and watertight, and it would have taken intellectual dishonesty on a monumental scale not to allow the appeal this time. The prosecution, or respondents as they're called on appeal, notified everyone in advance that there was no contest, although it was still a matter for the court to decide.

Some pretty damning evidence had come to light. First, an instance of almighty non-disclosure. This in itself was to become a thematic blot on the landscape for years to come. Institutional reluctance and reticence to reveal all, epitomised the following year in the Judith Ward appeal that I worked on with Gareth (see Chapter 14), was the high point.

It transpired that all along the Home Office laboratory in Chorley, Lancashire, whence Dr Skuse hailed, had relevant and potentially exculpatory material relating to the specificity of the Greiss test. A colleague of Skuse's in the lab, Dr Bamford, had on the night of the pub bombings swabbed ferry passengers in Liverpool and obtained positive results on two people. They were not prosecuted, let alone convicted, because it was discovered that they'd been handling adhesive tape, the constituents of which gave a positive Greiss reaction. So much for Skuse. There's never been any official explanation by any of the responsible agencies as to how this could have been overlooked throughout the trial, the first appeal and the second appeal.

Besides this, Gareth had approached Dr John Lloyd to re-examine the science. John is pre-eminent in his field, being ex-Home Office with unrivalled experience and expertise in the analysis of explosives. He looked the part to boot – monocle, slight stoop, well-worn jacket and measured delivery – and had calculated that the quantity of Ng required for the Skuse results was an absurdity, not quite a stick of 'gelly', but an amount beyond belief. Then he discovered that if the bowls had been cleaned before use with the sort of liquid soap available in the labs, this too could produce a false positive or what is sometimes termed a spurious or adventitious result.

The single GC-MS test was the subject of further reservations and qualifications. The ion said to produce the blip on the graph can also occur on swabs from hands that have not handled explosives. Additionally, a background test done on the same day as Hill's, but not taken from a suspect, had also indicated the presence of the same ion. There should have been at least three runs through the machine before anyone started talking about Ng being present on Hill's hands.

The appliance of science was not limited to explosives analysis, although the results were explosive in quite another sense.

A different police authority (Devon and Cornwall) had been engaged to re-examine the actions of the original Reade squad. Their reinvestigation was thorough and unremitting, and they uncovered a disturbing picture.

Every surviving police document was subjected to intense scrutiny. An evolving technique named ESDA (electro-static deposition analysis) was being honed to detect whether police officers had originally written something different from the version they presented in their notebooks at court. Inks were examined for subtle changes, as was the paper itself.

The result was stark. Tests showed that some of the notes of interviews claimed to be contemporaneous cannot have been, and therefore their integrity was demolished. In particular those relating to Richard McIlkenny had been written at different times, some with different inks and with paper from four different notepads. The ESDA impressions also revealed earlier versions. The findings were not limited to McIlkenny, as there were others relating to Gerry Hunter and Hugh Callaghan. It was their case in the Court of Appeal that the primary responsibility for what had happened must rest with the officer in charge of the case – Superintendent Reade. He and two other officers faced charges of perjury and conspiracy to pervert the course of justice. This prosecution was halted in 1993 by Mr Justice Garland for 'exceptional circumstances'. These were due to a combination of high-profile adverse publicity and delay.[9]

Sixteen years after the bombings, the Six walked free from the court into the street outside the Old Bailey, where a huge crowd of well-wishers was assembled, including builders from a nearby site. I rushed downstairs because it's not often possible to witness the overflow of emotion after a success like this, and as I reached the bottom of the stairs, still in wig and gown, I thought to myself: this is their day, not mine. So I stood in the shadow of a doorway to watch their elation. For me it was as though there was no emotion left to express, because I had exhausted all of it over the previous six years. When the adrenalin that has kept you afloat for so long is no longer required, you experience a quiet and slow deflation. So I stood there like an empty shell.

Freedom they had, but not a lot more. Only the clothes they stood up in. It took ten years, until 2001, before the six men were finally awarded compensation – ranging from £840,000 to £1.2 million – but the experience had demolished their lives.[10] They had no post-prison counselling; their wives had to readjust to having husbands again; their daughters and sons had to adjust to the strangers who were their fathers. It wasn't easy for any of them, and I was only too pleased to play a small part by employing Breda Power as my first PA.

Gerry and Sandra Hunter's marriage ended, as did Theresa and John Walker's. Richard McIlkenny died of cancer in 2006. Billy Power and Paddy Hill campaigned tirelessly on behalf of others claiming miscarriages of justice – and still do.

This case demonstrates the tenacity and courage of the six men falsely incarcerated for sixteen years, their families, and their champions at Granada Television's *World in Action*, who made hard-hitting, investigative documentaries that helped to publicise their situation. In 1989 *The Birmingham Wives*, produced by Yvette's company Vanson Wardle Productions for the BBC's *Everyman*, finally revealed the persistence of the men's families and the anguish they had experienced. Other programmes in a similar vein were produced over many years by *Rough Justice* for the BBC and *Trial and Error* for Channel 4 (I was an advisor on the board of the company that made the latter) systematically unravelling cases of injustice.

Unfortunately Lord Taylor, when he was Lord Chief Justice, severely criticised this kind of film-making, which was unfair. While I agree that trial by television is to be strongly deprecated in normal circumstances, Lord Taylor failed to recognise that without investigative journalism the prison gates of those wrongly convicted may never be unlocked. In those days, once the initial appeal (which had to be launched within twenty-eight days) had been exhausted, there was no further legal aid, and very few solicitors or barristers were willing or able to undertake the mammoth and often thankless task of retrieving old trial papers and briefs, visiting prisons, finding witnesses and experts and obtaining court transcripts of evidence.

For many years I tried to do this myself, unaided and unfunded.

A week would not go by – and still does not – without the familiar letter: the prison number on the envelope, the green ink, the writing giving the appearance of a ruler having been placed underneath each word: cries from the heart, desperate pleas. They cannot go unattended, because you can never tell whether that letter might be the beginning of another Birmingham Six appeal.

BIG BROTHER

Princess Diana and Dodi Fayed

George was right. Not Galloway, but Orwell. Big Brother *is* watching you. And Orwell clearly knew what he was talking about, because at the very time his last book *Nineteen Eighty-Four* was published in 1949, he was secretly passing a list of 'subversives' to a seemingly anodyne government department, the IRD – an acronym that stood for an innocuous-sounding, but clandestine part of the Foreign Office that conducted 'Information Research'. The 'subversives' were contained on a list of thirty-eight people (well-known writers, actors, academics and campaigners), which had been compiled by Orwell over a period of time – people whom he considered to be 'crypto-communists, fellow travellers or inclined that way and not to be trusted as propagandists'.[1]

The object of the exercise was purportedly to warn the authorities who not to employ in order to promote their version of the truth during the Cold War, though looking at some of the names, it is difficult to imagine many of them entertaining such an approach in any event. Nonetheless, such collaboration sits uncomfortably with Orwell's searing critique of a totalitarian world in which Winston Smith, a gnome in the Ministry of Truth, spends his time airbrushing 'inconvenient' people and events out of history.

It was this nightmare, echoing Franz Kafka, that dominated the post-war years in which I was brought up. Both *Animal Farm* and *Nineteen Eighty-Four* were groundbreaking, prophetic allegories of a society that could envelop all of us within our own lifetimes – in my case it was the threat posed by nuclear weapons and the prospect of a third world war.

I am not suggesting for a moment that my teenage waking moments were consumed with these dire warnings, or that I withdrew into some kind of bunkered existence, but these were the prevailing subliminal preoccupations of that period, and the momentous occasions when they would erupt onto the world stage remain etched on my memory: Russian tanks crushing the civilian uprising in Budapest in 1956, for example, and most frightening of all, the Cuban missile crisis of October 1962. These are the occasions when you are so affected that you can remember where you were and what you were doing at specific points in time. The first coincided with a history lesson when the master concerned was so angry about events in Hungary that he could barely speak; the second found me anxiously glued to a television set at the start of my second year at university.

Against such a backdrop it is easy to be diverted from the machinations of our own state and from what is being done in the name of national security: even Orwell's list had been withheld until 2003, when the government finally relented and allowed it to be published, partly because the *Guardian* had revealed its existence in 1996.[2]

We now have the Freedom of Information Act, but there are still provisions that exempt the security services from it, and exclude items required for 'administrative' or other 'special reasons'.

No one should underestimate the extent and powers of the secret British state. Some of its organs surface above the ground, and I have encountered them in a large number of the cases that I have handled involving MI5 (SS), MI6 (SIS), GCHQ (Cheltenham), SO15 (incorporating what was SO12, or Special Branch), armed services intelligence units and the JIC (Joint Intelligence Committee). And I have little doubt that there are others which are never identified and whose existence is never admitted.

In 1985, one year after the setting for Orwell's book, the discreet and insidious way in which such shadowy organisations can work was publicly exposed.

Even more sinister than Orwell's text, and reminiscent of the McCarthyite era in the United States, two *Observer* journalists,

David Leigh and Paul Lashmar,[3] revealed a system of blacklisting inside the BBC, located in what became known as Room 105. Here files collated on targeted individuals were marked with a Christmas-tree symbol stamped on the outside. Why the Christmas tree? Because 'O Tannenbaum' was sung by Nazi troops and sympathisers during the Third Reich, and the title translates as 'O Christmas Tree'.[4] For a time it was of interest to note that the new secret-service building on the south side of the Thames at Vauxhall sported a line of Christmas trees, a feature that has mysteriously disappeared.

The BBC files contained the names of reporters, journalists, producers and directors, and among them was Yvette. The information amassed was tenuous, amorphous, low-level political activist-type material, gathered in order to block appointments and job opportunities for those considered some form of 'risk'. Careers and lives were marred and individuals stigmatised without their knowing why, which was especially iniquitous when the information was erroneous.

The information was passed to Brigadier Ronnie Stoneham in Room 105 on the first floor of Broadcasting House behind a door marked 'Special Duties Management', and the process was called 'colleging'.

I remember when David Leigh came to see Yvette to persuade her to be named in the article. She had shown remarkable courage during the aggressive policing of the miners' strike, which she had filmed for the BBC at close quarters, but the article posed a serious risk of resurrecting a pernicious prejudice which she had successfully challenged. For the sake of bringing malpractice to book, however, she agreed, and the following appeared in the *Observer*:

> Things did not work out for Yvette Vanson. In 1979 she was considered of sufficient talent and integrity to be hired to help make 'access' films in the BBC's Community Programmes Unit. But days before she was to start, an embarrassed executive told her the job had been withdrawn. In a series of letters now held by the Observer, the BBC wrote telling her that 'the job should have gone to an internal candidate.' She was told she could apply for other jobs and offered £500 for her 'inconvenience'. We traced one of the senior officials concerned who admitted that the BBC had been

telling lies. She had been blacklisted by MI5 as 'an organiser of the Workers' Revolutionary Party'. Indeed, she had been a member of the WRP when, five years earlier, she was an actress. Although she had subsequently left the party, she made no bones about her left-wing opinions. The blacklisting is intended to be permanent. Last year, 10 years since Yvette Vanson stopped being a member of any political group, another BBC producer wished to hire her. An executive told us: 'Personnel said: "But wasn't she in the WRP?" ' This time there were protests, the blacklisting was withdrawn and she successfully worked for the BBC.[5]

But only once, on a short-term contract, and in fact on the programme through which we met.

This state interference was a nightmare for Yvette. Her career had been stalled and she had to fight her way back into the BBC, following years of working for charities and making training videos for a social-services department – none of which she regrets, although it could have been very different had she not been politically vetted and blacklisted, and for what? Being a socialist. Yvette never was employed as a full-time staff member of a British broadcasting company, but she went on to be a multi-award-winning independent producer/director, and her films are now held in the British Film Institute's prestigious archive.

The salutary point arising out of this episode is that what was done took place not only without the knowledge of the victimised, but also without the knowledge of the BBC Governors, let alone the public. Whatever machinery is in place to provide some kind of protection, like the Security Commission, there are always ways of ducking and diving, ultimately issuing the usual 'We cannot confirm or deny' statement.[6]

Cathy Massiter, who was a junior officer at MI5 in the mid-1970s, confirmed that lists of BBC candidates would pass across her desk for approval. She also appeared in a Channel 4 documentary[7] which highlighted improper surveillance, including the phone-tapping of CND and trade-union activists. The film was banned and she was threatened with prosecution under the Official Secrets Act.

I had my own extraordinary experience of the Workers' Revolutionary Party (WRP) at the same time as Yvette was experiencing her problems at the BBC – although we had not yet met.

I had finally been persuaded by Comrade Wilf to attend a WRP meeting addressed by the party's leader, Gerry Healey, at the City University on the topic of the dialectic – and I say 'persuaded' because I found the WRP's politics as outlined in its paper *The Newsline*, which was delivered to me personally on a weekly basis by Wilf, to be a little bit off my radar. Nevertheless, having studied philosophy I thought I'd give it a go, and went straight from court dressed in a dark suit and sat at the back of a crowded lecture hall. I took out my pen in order to make some notes but, finding Gerry Healey's thought processes quite impenetrable, hardly wrote a thing. At the end of his address a forest of hands shot up to ask erudite and esoteric questions, but I was none the wiser.

As the crowds filtered out of the hall I remained seated, only to find myself suddenly surrounded by a number of 'heavies' who demanded to know who I was, why I was there and why in particular my pen had hardly touched the paper. They suggested that it contained a recording device and that I was some form of spy, who would therefore have to be removed from the hall and strip-searched. I couldn't believe that someone who'd supported freedom of speech as I had was being turned on in this way, but I was clearly no match for this lot. The only thing I could do was sit tight and protest loudly. Suddenly, out of nowhere, a man appeared and with a very authoritative voice demanded, 'Leave him alone!' I had no idea who he was, but he took me by the arm and led me out, and as we left I thanked him profusely and asked him why he'd intervened. Apparently he'd recognised me from one of my trials, in which he had been a juror.

In December 2008, thirty years after Cathy Massiter, Big Brother was still operating when the Conservative MP Damian Green was arrested on charges of conspiracy and aiding and abetting in relation to alleged misconduct in public office, common-law offences which carry a maximum penalty of life imprisonment and circumvent the public-interest defence available under Section 5 of the Official Secrets Act 1989. If used, the prosecution would have to prove that the confidential information (supposed leaks about Home

Office internal policy), allegedly received from a civil servant, was damaging to the interests of the United Kingdom. What was even more astounding was the way in which the police failed to obtain the Speaker's consent, without which even the Queen cannot enter the House of Commons. Nor did the police think it necessary to obtain a search warrant for Mr Green's parliamentary office containing his papers and computers. It now turns out, according to a statement by the Director of Public Prosecutions, Keir Starmer, in April 2009, that 'the Home Office papers undoubtedly touched on matters of legitimate public interest ... and that the information contained in the documents was not secret or information affecting national security: it did not relate to military, policing or intelligence matters. It did not expose anyone to risk of injury or death. Nor in many respects was it highly confidential.'[8]

That the Home Secretary, Jacqui Smith, knew nothing of this begs the question. The issue is not one of immunity or of MPs being above the law; rather, it concerns an assumption and an arrogance of power about which all of us need to be constantly alert. If the state within a state can march into the heart of our democracy without so much as a by-your-leave, or little more than a raised eyebrow, then there is trouble in store for us all.

Bearing all this in mind, it came as no surprise to me to learn from Annie Machon's book[9] that when she and her partner David Shayler worked for the secret services, I too was (and probably still am) in the frame. Not all the time; not every phone call; not every meeting; just when it suits them. So, as with bomb threats, I've worked on the basis that it is safer for me to keep my head above the parapet – making it clear to all and sundry which side of the wall I'm on. It's more difficult to rub me out if I'm reasonably well known, but in general the level of risk depends on the level of threat that you present.

Take, for example, Colin Wallace, whom I represented on appeal when his conviction for murder was overturned by the Lord Chief Justice – and subsequently he appeared as a witness at the Bloody Sunday Inquiry. He had served in a special unit of the Ministry of Defence in Northern Ireland described as 'Psy-ops' (Psychological Operations), and his work had taken him to Derry. There has been an aura of denial and obfuscation by the authorities about the work itself and his role in it – namely, 'black propaganda' intended to destabilise and disorientate terrorists – and even more controversial was the manner of his removal from this work by the Ministry of Defence, which alleged misconduct in handling official documents, a charge roundly rebuffed by Colin. The whole saga is eloquently chronicled by Paul Foot in his definitive book *Who Framed Colin Wallace?* When Paul turned his investigative searchlight on the conviction for murder, many of the unanswered questions in the trial found a rationale in the hypothesis that Colin had been set up in order to discredit and silence someone who had become a conscientious thorn in the side of the security services.

Another example is that of Dr David Kelly, the government scientist whose death was clearly connected to the war in Iraq. It is the nature of that connection that is the big question: whether he took his own life or whether it was taken by others, the unseen forces and pressures that lay behind his death have not so far been satisfactorily explored or resolved, either by an inquest or by the Hutton Inquiry.[10]

For me there are similar unresolved questions arising from what happened in Paris on 31 August 1997. Like Budapest and Cuba, it's another of those occasions when most people can remember exactly what they were doing when they heard the news.

In my case I was staying with my family and some close friends in a remote Tuscan village where there was no television. We drove to Florence to see some of our party back off to London by air, and decided to spend one night in a hotel before returning to the village. The following morning ten-year-old Freddy raced down the corridor to our room as urgently as if the hotel had been on fire. (Which reminds me of an experience some years earlier, when I rushed to Freddy's rescue through thick smoke in a hotel on the banks of a Scottish loch, only to find that his bed was empty and there was no trace of him. I was desperate – but thankfully he had been whisked down the fire escape by a quick-thinking young girl from a neighbouring room.)

This time there was no fire, but Freddy was urging us to see something on the television in his room, and as he led us down the corridor he kept saying, 'Diana is dead.' I could not quite get a grip on what he meant, or even who he meant. In his room we all sat in front of the screen, like millions of others around the world, mesmerised, transfixed into stunned silence. The crushed Mercedes was so finite a message, and it was not long before the questions started forming. How could this be? An accident on this scale? Not only Diana dead, but two others, Dodi Fayed and Henri Paul, the driver.

At that moment it did not occur to me that I would ever become immersed in the world of Diana and the Royal Family, or that I would end up representing Mohamed Al Fayed.

For one thing, I am a republican. I have been a member of the campaigning organisation Republic[11] for years, arguing against unaccountability, inherited property and privilege and for a democratically elected head of state – and I certainly had not followed the social cavorting of various members of 'The Firm'. In the early 1990s I presented the case for change in a groundbreaking BBC televised debate, which apparently ended a long-standing, unspoken convention and taboo that prevented any serious criticism of the Queen, or of the institution of the monarchy, being ventilated.

Earlier still was the uncomfortable business of 'taking Silk'. I am sure those outside the profession think it's some kind of medieval medicinal cure for elderly ailing barristers, but 'taking Silk' is the term used to describe the tortuous process whereby, in those days, you 'let it be known' that you were ready for the call to become Queen's Counsel, and mysteriously a divine finger alighted upon your shoulder if 'they' were ready for you. I put off engaging in such an anachronistic set-up for as long as possible, and part of my reservation was having to swear an oath of allegiance to the Queen. Nothing personal, Your Majesty, but this went against the grain, so colleagues advised me to do it with my eyes closed.

Despite all these misgivings, when I returned home from Italy I couldn't help becoming fascinated by the 'back story' of Diana, most of which I had missed. A young woman at one moment hated and derided by a sizeable proportion of the media for her association with Dodi and the Fayeds, at the next suddenly transformed Cinderella-like into the 'People's Princess' at the hands of the very same critics. All is forgiven or forgotten, or both, at least until her brother unleashes a broadside during the funeral service in Westminster Abbey.

I was keen to discover more about this woman, who had clearly engendered love and hatred in almost equal measure, and the more I read, the more I appreciated her deeply felt commitment to raising awareness about major human tragedies – literally touching the lives of those affected and gaining recognition in her own right, rather than as some regal appendage.

It was in these circumstances that I found it difficult simply to accept that what happened in the Alma Tunnel in Paris was 'just one of those tragic things'. Of course it might have been, but then that's what 'they' always hope we will think. Judging whether a hidden hand is at work is always difficult, but I prefer a healthy and inquisitive assessment of the authorised version, and for me it was mere serendipity to be approached a year after the crash and asked to represent Mohamed Al Fayed for the purposes of an inquest.

Barristers are not allowed to tout for work: they have to wait to be asked, and some have wondered why I should have wanted to be involved in this case at all, supposing that it must have been for the money. Nothing could be further from the truth. The vast majority of my work has been publicly funded, with a proportion being pro bono, so money wasn't the object. But prior interest certainly was, along with a real sympathy for Mohamed Al Fayed, who had been unceasingly and erroneously attacked for wanting what any parent would have wanted: answers to why and how their loved one had died. The vitriol poured upon Mohamed's head constantly misses the point that he is a grieving father, entitled to an inquest – which, as the coroner pointed out, is obligatory in the circumstances. Furthermore, Mohamed's main concern, relating to the fears expressed by Princess Diana, would have required investigation even if he had played no part at all in the inquest.

In many of the criminal cases I've handled it sometimes helps to start at the end rather than the beginning, especially where death is involved. Ask the question: who does it benefit? If it benefits no one, that might suggest one scenario. On the other hand, if there are some obvious beneficiaries – and, more importantly, some less obvious ones – it may be productive to trace the chain of causation backwards, a bit like those kids' maze puzzles where there is only one route to the treasure at the bottom of the page, with several entrances at the top. I start with the treasure.

In the case of Diana and Dodi, I have always believed that whatever had caused the crash, it was not an accident. And, as it transpired, that belief was shared by the jury at the inquest.

Given the welter of publicity, the wealth of books, films and pundits, it is hardly surprising that the jury's verdict was not reported in full, or was misreported or misinterpreted. There is still a widespread belief that the inquest was a waste of time and money and came to no different conclusion than previous investigations and enquiries. This is a serious misconception.

The Assistant Deputy Coroner for Inner West London was the Right Honourable Lord Justice Scott Baker, brought in for the purpose after an earlier High Court judge withdrew. Such an appointment is becoming more commonplace in the wake of the Human Rights Act, as inquests broaden in scope and embrace an increasing number of legal problems. One of them is the form of the verdict contained within what is called the Inquisition.

As already outlined in relation to the *Marchioness* inquest (see Chapter 8), at an inquest there is no indictment and no defendant, nor a simple verdict of guilty or not guilty. There are four basic questions to be answered. Who was the deceased? Where? When? And how did he or she die?

The first three usually pose no difficulty, but it is the fourth that gives rise to complications – and in the case of Diana and Dodi, merely to record injuries received as a result of the car hitting the wall of the Alma Tunnel would be somewhat trite. The bigger question is: how did it come about that the car hit the wall? The courts have been resistant to this sort of extension for many years, until it was recognised that in order to comply with Article 2 of the European Convention on Human Rights, the 'how?' question would have to be enlarged. An integral part of Article 2, 'the right to life', involves an effective and independent investigation whereby the family of a victim may be able to ask the broader questions relating to the general circumstances around, and before, the death.

The High Court therefore decided[12] that the 'how?' question should mean not only 'by what means?' but also 'in what circumstances?' This decision came before the Diana inquest itself (held in 2007 and 2008), but the deaths occurred before the Human Rights Act 1998, incorporating Article 2 into domestic law, came into force. Therefore on one view the inquest could have been narrowly confined, but it was recognised that this would not be in the public interest, nor would it satisfy another purpose of an inquest, to allay rumours and suspicion.[13]

In the event, Lord Justice Scott Baker outlined a number of far-reaching questions at the beginning of the inquest and then distilled a number of options open to the jury at the end. Nevertheless, the over-arching scene was set for the jury by the coroner at the start: 'Over the coming weeks you will be hearing a great deal of evidence about the issues and events I have described, and as I have mentioned, some issues may fall away and new ones may arise. At the end of it all, you will be faced with the overriding question of whether what happened was anything more than a tragic road accident.'[14]

This, of course, represented one of the main views being constantly rehearsed in the media. Quite remarkably, just before the original start date for the main inquest hearings set for January 2007, Lord Stevens, who had been tasked to investigate allegations made by Mohamed Al Fayed, published both his research and his conclusions. This was done amid massive publicity at a press conference held in the Queen Elizabeth Centre in Parliament Square, Westminster, on Thursday 14 December 2006, and was managed in such a way that only a few people had advance notice of his report's general conclusions, while virtually no one had had time to read it in detail. Such a move was unprecedented, and there was absolutely no need for it to have occurred at this point. The Paget Report, as it was known, could have been provided to the coroner for the purposes of the inquest without the attendant publicity. Given its official status, such a step was potentially prejudicial to the fact-finding role of the jury at the inquest. Although Lord Stevens reserved issues relating to what happened in the tunnel for resolution by the inquest, he nevertheless made his view abundantly clear: 'Our conclusion is that on all the evidence available at this time, there was no conspiracy to murder any of the occupants of the car. This was a tragic accident.'[15]

It does not require a great deal of imagination to work out the headlines the next day. As a result, the jury had to be warned by the coroner at the beginning of the inquest to ignore this report and its conclusions.

Unlike most proceedings, an inquest is organic and has a life of its own. It is difficult to predict precisely how the evidence will unfold, what will become relevant and what will have less significance. Preparation as ever is the key, but much has to be done as the process develops, and over the six-month period from October 2007 to April 2008 when the coroner's court was sitting, fourteen-hour days were the norm for me. I would get up at 5.30 a.m. in our Putney flat and take the early river boat down the Thames to Blackfriars, relishing the quiet and stately journey past the dark silhouette of the forbidding chimneys of Battersea Power Station, and as the sun rose over St Thomas's Hospital I'd think of Freddy's birth all those years ago in the maternity unit overlooking the Houses of Parliament. I'd walk up from the quay to a café on the Strand opposite the Appeal Court to grab a coffee before making my way to Court 73, where the inquest was being held. Invariably I'd meet John, an avid member of the public gallery whose enthusiasm was emblazoned all over his forehead, where he had the names 'Di' and 'Dodi' inscribed in blue dye. His good humour, and that of the other 'regulars' during the inquest, provided a necessary humanising element to the proceedings.

However, the most crucial support came from my legal team: Tom Coates, my solicitor, and my juniors Henrietta Hill and later Alison McDonald. Since everything is now digital, electronic and diskified, my slow-moving pen is no match for the daily flood coming down the information highway, but they had it all at their fingertips, turning round emails, opinions and statements on their portable fruit machines – Blueberries? BlackBerries? – probably while sitting in the bath or, in Henrietta's case, while giving birth to baby Reggie. Talk about multitasking. At least this meant that I could concentrate (usually at the end of a long day on my feet and after a conference with my client) on the central issues being presented.

At the end of the inquest Lord Justice Scott Baker had to sum up to the jury and present them with various verdict options. The original version was as follows:

1 Unlawful killing (grossly negligent driving of the paparazzi pursuing the Mercedes in which Diana and Dodi were being driven).

2 Unlawful killing (grossly negligent driving of the Mercedes).

3 Unlawful killing (grossly negligent, a combination of both 1 and 2).

4 Accidental death.

5 Open verdict.

This was amended in one important respect before finally being given to the jury: the phrase 'following vehicles' was substituted for the word 'paparazzi' in option 1.

On 7 April 2008[16] the jury did not decide it was just a tragic accident (option 4), but returned a verdict of unlawful killing by the drivers of both the Mercedes and the following vehicles (option 3).

The 'following vehicles' element in the verdict was an aspect that very few commentators picked up on, or bothered with, and mostly its implications were not understood. In so far as anyone took any notice, they thought it was merely a reference to the chasing pack of paparazzi. It wasn't: there were other vehicles clearly present, but never traced and not driven by members of the paparazzi.

Even finding the paparazzi partially responsible was a different conclusion from both the French investigation and the subsequent Stevens Inquiry contained in the Paget Report.

Initially, the French authorities arrested ten members of the paparazzi for involuntary manslaughter and failing to render assistance, but they were eventually released and not prosecuted. The *juge d'instruction* essentially concluded that there was insufficient evidence against any person for involuntary manslaughter. At the inquest, none of the paparazzi was prepared to testify, even by video link from studios in Paris, and despite overtures from the coroner and the British authorities, the French Government could not secure their attendance. The only person willing to come forward was Monsieur Darmon, the driver of a motorcycle carrying a member of the pack called Mr Rat.

During the inquest it became clear that the assiduous research by DI Paul Carpenter of the British police had managed to identify every single paparazzo, together with their mode of transport. This was accomplished by marrying up descriptions, statements and hundreds of photographs, and in this way it was possible to distil from the following vehicles which were paparazzi and which were not. Upon entry to the tunnel, the majority were not – and the other vehicles include the infamous white Fiat, the ownership of which has never been satisfactorily established and which had no more than glancing contact with the Mercedes. In any event, it was not a following vehicle, as it had been overtaken just inside the entrance to the tunnel.

Surprisingly, there had been witnesses in the tunnel who had what might be termed a ringside seat, even though the whole event happened very quickly. The importance of such witnesses was recognised by the French police on the night, and they were placed under *'garde à vue'* (detention to secure evidence) and gave written statements shortly after the crash in the early hours of 31 August, together with completed diagrams of the various positions of vehicles.

Two of these witnesses were Benoit Boura and Gaelle L'Hostis, who saw the Mercedes sandwiched between a dark blocking vehicle immediately in front – with which the Mercedes had collided before it hit the thirteenth pillar and skewed across the road, impacting on the far wall of the tunnel – and a large motorcycle right behind.[17]

Boura was driving a Renault 5 on the opposite carriageway, travelling in the other direction, but he arrived at the thirteenth pillar at about the moment of the crash. He thought that the car in front of the Mercedes was larger than his own and dark-coloured, and that the motorcycle was 350 or 500cc. Gaelle L'Hostis, his passenger, thought the dark vehicle driving rather slowly in front of the Mercedes was a Renault Clio or a Super 5-type, although she did not think the car was deliberately hindering the Mercedes.[18] Both witnesses gave evidence and both were unimpeachable.

Neither the dark car in front nor the motorcycle behind has ever been traced, either by DI Carpenter or by Commander Mules or Lieutenant Gigou, who were leading the French police investigation. No paparazzo ever got in front of the Mercedes, and the motorcycle cannot be attributed to any paparazzi, because none claimed to have been that close: Darmon was the first into the tunnel with Mr Rat as passenger, whereas Boura and L'Hostis did not recall any pillion passenger on the motorcycle they saw.

There were two other witnesses placed under *'garde à vue'*: Clifford Gooroovadoo and Olivier Partouche, who were on foot near the entrance to the tunnel. Partouche stated that the Mercedes was preceded by a car 'driving at a speed – well, to apparently slow down the Mercedes that was following. I could not tell you what type of vehicle it was. Maybe a Ford Mondeo. It was of a dark colour. Clearly this car was trying to make the Mercedes slow down.'[19] In his early statements on the night, Partouche also described a powerful motorcycle 'tailgating' the Mercedes[20] and thought he saw flashes of light before the vehicles disappeared into the underpass. Clifford Gooroovadoo confirmed both the presence of a vehicle travelling more slowly in front of the Mercedes and of a motorcycle behind it.[21]

Another witness, Thierry Hackett, also gave a graphic account that was clear and unimpugned. A short distance from the tunnel entrance he saw a car being pursued by four or five motorcycles. He had drawn a plan for the French police depicting such a group, with motorcycles very close to the rear of the Mercedes. He had thought the driver of the car was being hindered by the motorbikes.[22]

At this point only one paparazzi motorcycle could have been in contention – Darmon – and he denied being part of any group as described by Hackett. Therefore the unresolved question relates to those other unidentified vehicles that were not paparazzi, but which nevertheless contributed to the unlawful killing by grossly negligent driving.

Two years before her death, at a meeting on 30 October 1995, Diana had expressed a disturbing premonition to her solicitor Lord Mishcon, who recorded: 'Efforts would be made if not to get rid of her (be it by some accident in her car such as a pre-prepared brake failure or whatever) ... at least to see that she was so injured or damaged as to be declared unbalanced.'[23]

This premonition was kept secret until after the crash, when on 18 September 1997 Lord Mishcon revealed his note to the then Metropolitan Police Commissioner Paul Condon in the presence of David Veness, a senior officer. Despite its obvious 'potential relevance', as admitted by Veness during my questioning,[24] it was disclosed neither to the French *juge* nor to the English coroner Dr Burton, who at that time was seized of the matter (the legal term for dealing with it). The crucial memorandum remained a state secret locked in a safe at New Scotland Yard.

On 20 October 2003 the *Daily Mirror* published extracts from a book by Paul Burrell, Diana's butler, in which he disclosed a note, written by Diana, which he maintained she wrote in 1996: 'This particular phase in my life is the most dangerous – my husband is planning "an accident" in my car. Brake failure and serious head injury in order to make the path clear for him to marry . . .'[25]

Two months later the Mishcon note was made known to the new coroner, Dr Burgess.

Diana's fear had been expressed to several others, among whom was Mohamed Al Fayed. This occurred when she went to stay with his family in France in July 1997. His evidence on this point was not challenged at the inquest.[26] Until the publication of the Paget Report in December 2006 it was not known to the public, let alone to Mohamed, that she had also confided this fear to her solicitor eleven years before its publication.

Plainly no inquest into her death could ignore this chain of events, for at the heart of it lay the recurring belief that she would meet her death, or incur serious injury, while travelling without her children in a small form of transport, be it car, helicopter or light aircraft: in this way fewer people would be involved. These were the genuine concerns of an intelligent woman, and not – as is often portrayed – a fevered fantasy from the brow of Mohamed Al Fayed.

Beyond this was a further concern about the extent to which her life was being monitored, not just by the press, but by the state itself. These were not far-fetched or outlandish thoughts, and no one who knew her well – like Diana's private secretary Patrick Jephson, who had been present for the Mishcon meeting in 1995 – considered her paranoid or mentally unstable in any way.

It is easy to forget just how much of a threat Diana presented to the established order. Her clandestine contribution to a searingly honest biography by Andrew Morton in 1992 was closely followed by the publication in August that year of the 'Squidgygate' tape: intimate conversations between Diana and her lover James Gilbey, in which he called her 'Squidgy', intercepted on 31 December 1989. Then in November 1995 (a month after the Mishcon meeting) came the famous *Panorama* interview[27] with Martin Bashir, in which Diana graphically described her own predicament and how she was viewed by the Royal Household.

BASHIR: Once the separation had occurred, moving to 1993, what happened during that period?

DIANA: People's agendas changed overnight. I was now the separated wife of the Prince of Wales, I was a problem, I was a liability (seen as), and how are we going to deal with her? This hasn't happened before.

BASHIR: Who was asking those questions?

DIANA: People around me, people in this environment, and . . .

BASHIR: The Royal Household?

DIANA: People in my environment, yes, yes.

BASHIR: And they began to see you as a problem?

DIANA: Yes, very much so, uh, uh.

BASHIR: Do you really believe that a campaign was being waged against you?

DIANA: Yes, I did, absolutely, yeah.

BASHIR: Why?

DIANA: I was the separated wife of the Prince of Wales, I was a problem, full stop. Never happened before, what do we do with her?

BASHIR: Can't we pack her off to somewhere quietly rather than campaign against her?

DIANA: She won't go quietly, that's the problem. I'll fight to the end, because I believe that I have a role to fulfil, and I've got two children to bring up. But I was doing good things, and I wanted to do good things. I was never going to hurt anyone, I was never going to let anyone down.

BASHIR: But you really believe that it was out of jealousy that they wanted to undermine you?

DIANA: I think it was out of fear, because here was a strong woman doing her bit, and where was she getting her strength from to continue? I don't see myself being Queen of this country. I don't think many people will want me to be Queen. Actually, when I say many people I mean the establishment that I married into, because they have decided that I'm a non-starter.

BASHIR: Why do you think they've decided that?

DIANA: Because I do things differently, because I don't go by a rule book, because I lead from the heart, not the head, and albeit that's got me into trouble in my work, I understand that. But someone's got to go out there and love people and show it.

BASHIR: Do you think that because of the way you behave that's precluded you effectively from becoming Queen?

DIANA: Yes, well, not precluded me. I wouldn't say that. I just don't think I have as many supporters in that environment as I did.

BASHIR: You mean within the Royal Household?

DIANA: Uh, uh. They see me as a threat of some kind, and I'm here to do good: I'm not a destructive person.

BASHIR: Why do they see you as a threat?

DIANA: I think every strong woman in history has had to walk down a similar path, and I think it's the strength that causes the confusion and the fear. Why is she strong? Where does she get it from? Where is she taking it? Where is she going to use it? Why do the public still support her? When I say public, you go and do an engagement and there's a great many people there.

What rattled the cage far more than all this was Diana's highly publicised visit to Angola in January 1997 in order to highlight the inhumanity and destruction caused by landmines. It is an understatement to say that this did not endear her to various vested interests, and she was criticised for interfering in political affairs and accused of being a 'loose cannon'. But she was not deterred, and went on to develop her commitment to this issue in a lecture at the Royal Geographical Society in June 1997, on a visit to Bosnia between 8 and 10 August 1997, and in an interview in *Le Monde* published on 28 August 1997, three days before her death. A trip similar to the Angolan visit was planned for autumn 1997, this time to Cambodia, along with the possibility of establishing an international hospice with the financial support of Mohamed Al Fayed.

Although there had been a change of government in spring 1997 with Tony Blair's first term in office, the Ottawa Agreement on the restriction of landmine manufacture and use was still at a sensitive stage of negotiations. According to one witness, Simone Simmons, a close friend and confidante of Diana, the Princess was undertaking a great deal of research and had:

compiled a dossier which she claimed would prove that the British government and many high-ranking public figures were profiting from their [landmines] proliferation in countries like Angola and Bosnia. The names and companies were well known. It was explosive, and top of her list of culprits behind the squalid trade was the Secret Intelligence Service, the SIS, which she believed was behind the sale of so many British-made landmines that were causing so much misery to so many people. 'I'm going to go public with this and name names,' she declared. She intended to call her report *Profiting out of Misery*.[28]

There has been a recent decision by the Information Commissioner that Diana's correspondence with John Major and Tony Blair is too private to publish under the Freedom of Information Act.[29] It is known that she wrote letters about the possibility of becoming an ambassador or emissary in relation to landmines, and the inquest heard evidence that she had attended an informal dinner with Tony Blair and Alastair Campbell at the beginning of 1997 when this possibility had been discussed. What is not known is whether any of the private correspondence deals with this or other matters relevant to her death.

To cap it all, Diana had had a long-standing friendship with Mohamed Al Fayed, who had supported a number of her other projects and causes, for which she expressed her gratitude in moving letters produced by him at the inquest; and she finally struck up a loving and intimate relationship with his son Dodi, which was equally spelled out in letters produced at the inquest. Dodi had been depicted by the tabloids as a playboy, and reputedly by the Duke of Edinburgh as 'an oily bed-hopper', but what became abundantly clear during the inquest was a completely contrary view. Witness after witness, save one (his jilted girlfriend), described Dodi as a gentle, caring and generous individual, sensitive to the needs of others, but as this was not a particularly sensational portrait, needless to say it didn't hit the headlines.

Against this background it was utterly reasonable for Diana to suppose that Big Brother was looking over her shoulder, that her telephone communications were being tapped and her movements by car were being tracked. It was only by persistent pursuit of these issues at the inquest that material came to light which had not surfaced before, even though part of the remit for the Stevens Inquiry had been to investigate Princess Diana's fears.

Records relating to the police Royal Protection Unit were

disclosed, which revealed an important meeting on 18 October 1994. The head of the unit, DAC David Meynell, recorded: 'She then told me that she knew her telephone was being tapped and that she was certain the same applied to her vehicle. She stated that she had proof that her phones were being tapped . . .'[30]

The reaction to this material provoked interestingly diverse and conflicting responses. On the one hand, the by now Lord Condon, Sir David Veness and Colin Haywood-Trimming, a Royal Protection officer, all claimed nothing was done beyond informing the Home Secretary, because they said Diana had refused to co-operate with them. On the other hand, DAC Meynell told Diana that he would look into the matter, and that her apartments and her car were searched by the team from the Palace of Westminster, with negative results.[31] There is no record of any search. Later in the inquest Meynell attempted to qualify his evidence by saying that in fact he was referring to a previous incident a year earlier.

Whatever the true position adopted by the police, Diana had a credible and understandable basis for her belief, given the circumstances surrounding the original recording of her private telephone call on 31 December 1989 [Squidgygate], and by the time of the inquest it had become clear that the initial interception could not have been carried out by the 'radio hams' who claimed to have provided the tapes to the newspapers. John Nelson, an expert originally engaged by the *Sunday Times*, provided a report to this effect to the inquest. His conclusion was that the interception 'can only have been made by means of a direct or possibly inductive pick-up tapping of the telephone line itself and the local exchange'.[32]

These two forms of bugging both involved physical interference with the handset or telephone line on royal property on the Sandringham estate where Diana was staying, and it is unlikely that this was achieved by the press, let alone by an amateur.

Matters were made worse during the inquest when I was pressing for answers about all this, and about whether it had been properly investigated. A document was revealed for the first time which showed that fixed telephone lines had also been tampered with where the Prince of Wales had been staying on the night of the alleged 'Camillagate' conversation. (A controversial recording in December 1989 of an agonisingly intimate hour-long late-night conversation,

featuring talk of tampons, between Charles and Camilla Parker
Bowles (as she then was) was made public in 1993.)[33]

The Queen had expressed disquiet and requested an investigation,
but despite denials by the security agencies, once again there was
no satisfactory explanation or documentary audit demonstrating
that such an investigation was carried out. This might provide an
interesting insight into Paul Burrell's account of his conversation
with Her Majesty on 19 December 1997: 'Be careful Paul, no one
has been as close to a member of my family as you have. There are
powers at work in the country about which we have no knowledge.
Do you understand?'[34]

While Burrell's credibility on many topics did not survive the
inquest, the fact of this meeting has been admitted in a press release
from Buckingham Palace, and at no time has the content (which
mostly related to Diana's belongings) been denied. Indeed, when
in 2002 Burrell was on trial at the Old Bailey accused of stealing
a quantity of those belongings, it was Her Majesty's sudden
recollection of being told by him that he had taken some of Diana's
items for safekeeping that brought proceedings to an abrupt end,
before Burrell himself or any defence witnesses could be called.

There were many other issues touched on during the wide-ranging
inquest hearings, which I have not explored in detail here: the box of
missing personal papers belonging to Diana, described as the 'Crown
Jewels' in the light of their potential significance; the missing Fiat
driver; the missing three hours on the evening of 30 August 1997
during which Dodi's chauffeur Henri Paul's movements could not
be traced; and the unexplained regular and sizeable sums of money
going into Henri Paul's several bank accounts over the three months
before the crash. None of these could be resolved by evidence, or
reflected in the verdict.

But Diana's fears for her safety and her preoccupation with
surveillance were thoroughly canvassed, and in my view were
found to be entirely justified. Unfortunately her predictions came
to pass – and span the very period of our history that was the focus
of Orwell's attention.

We have seamlessly passed 1984 with all its ominous prophecies,
and almost without realising it we have slid rapidly towards
the very surveillance society that could be barely imagined as a

reality in 1949: CCTV on every corner; traffic cameras tracking car registration numbers; credit and debit cards reflecting patterns of movement and use; satellites tracking mobile phones; vast databases recording medical details, welfare benefits, and so forth. The latest proposal – on hold in the light of the more pressing economic and fiscal exigencies – is the Communications Data Bill, enabling government to extend its powers under the Regulation of Investigatory Powers Act,[35] which seeks to establish a centralised database that will monitor every call we make, every website we access, every text and email we send. There is now the prospect of a cashless, chequeless society in which the mobile phone alone will be used as the mechanism of payment for goods, so every purchase will be monitored. And then we have the 'toolkit' issued to teachers for the purpose of the 'prevent agenda', by which pupils' behaviour and thinking are to be reported to the authorities, should it disclose Islamic radicalisation. And don't forget the ID card.

That these surreal proposals should even be contemplated shows how far beyond Orwell's worst fears we have travelled. The whole idea of Big Brother is now part of mainstream cheap light entertainment, in which people like the other George volunteer to have their thoughts scrutinised in greenhouse conditions and commentated upon by a disembodied voice while anonymous millions watch enthralled. This is both sinister and symbolic, for twenty-first-century Western popular culture has been traduced. It's Jim Carrey's film *The Truman Show* for real.

MILK, MUCK AND METHANE

The McLibel Two

Sunday lunch in the front room of Naylor Road in 1951.

Mother sits opposite Father, who has his back to the bay window, and I, aged nine, sit next to her, from where I can see over the privet hedge bearing that perfectly carved topiary '73', my father's pride and joy, to the road beyond.

As usual there is complete silence, except for the occasional sound of chewing or slurping (mine). Today I am rather relieved that the strict 'No speaking at mealtimes' rule is being enforced, as I won't have to explain my awful school report: at Holmewood Primary School, regularly banging shut my desk lid from a great height has been deemed enough to warrant a repeat of the whole year.

The slices of bread and butter have been consumed. (It is mandatory to eat it first, though I am never sure whether this is some kind of penance or to fill me up.) Next comes cream-of-tomato soup from a familiar tin. Father has a bottle of Whitbread's pale ale, Mother and I have water. I am day-dreaming about my fine wicket against the corrugated-iron shed door in the garden, or the next picnic with cousin Gillian, with the fun of travelling on the open boot lid of the Ford with the picnic basket wedged between us.

I glance out of the window and see the milkman and his horse and cart stopping at the houses up the hill to deliver their pintas. A slice of beef, two roast potatoes and a small round Yorkshire pudding. Not a word breaks the quiet. I think back to the trip to Edinburgh to see my brother Gerald play at the Tattoo, and of my 'guardian angel', the outrider who gallops alongside the train traversing all the obstacles: station platforms, hedges, rivers . . .

Now the milk cart has reached the cul-de-sac at the top of the hill, and the milkman leaves it in the circular turnaround as he delivers his bottles to the next doorstep. Mother starts clearing the table for pudding, and takes the plates out into the kitchen.

And then I witness a fearful sight. The horse has got bored with waiting and has begun descending the hill alone. He is gathering speed. I spontaneously blurt out, 'Dad! Dad! There's a—'

Father is adamant: 'No talking at mealtimes, Michael.'

'But, Dad! . . .'

The horse is now into a brisk canter, propelled along by the weight of the milk crates behind him. The milkman is rushing after the cart, but cannot catch up. Father is in direct line of fire.

'Dad! Please listen.'

'No. No! No! Michael!' – and as he sternly speaks those words there is an almighty crash as the horse ploughs through our privet hedge with its proud number 73, slams across the small front garden, smashes into the glass of the dining-room window and lands at my father's feet. The horse is in obvious pain and distress, and my father is amazed, shocked, incredibly upset. The last time he saw a horse fall like this was in the war in Palestine. It had trapped him by the leg – the left leg. The horse had been shot. Father had been disabled – and that instant in the dining room in Naylor Road he is transported back thirty-four years. Mother ushers me out of the room to spare me the sight of the flailing horse amid the debris of harness, wooden shafts and milk bottles, but I creep back and watch through a crack in the door. I see the poor horse writhing in panic and agony on our dining-room floor. I see my father too, completely distraught. But I daren't look as the horse is shot.

My lifelong concern for animal welfare has its roots in those few appalling minutes, and thirty years later in 1981 that concern took on a fresh focus on the very first day of Channel 4.

This was a breathtaking experiment in television, and Jeremy Isaacs, the first Chief Executive of Channel 4, wanted an innovative approach to distinguish it from the established format of British broadcasting. Instead of a melange of different programmes following hot on the heels of each other, much as they do now, there were to be themed periods of viewing, which demanded levels of concentration not previously contemplated. This was a brave and exciting challenge, especially since one of the opening gambits in the first week was *The Animals Film*, a documentary directed by Victor Schonfeld and lasting over two and a half hours.[1]

The idea was as controversial as the content, and the programme stirred up considerable advance publicity. The film contained a poignantly clear and single message: the extensive and damaging exploitation by humankind of the animal kingdom and of the environment in which we all live. It was a deeply moving, political documentary, which I have no doubt would never surface in the current climate of soap suds and self-censorship. Yvette painfully discovered this over the ensuing years, with many of her political programme proposals on which I had lent a helping hand being rejected. Even back in 1981 I believe there was some last-minute editing of material thought to be too strong for the stomachs of Middle England, and someone felt that interviews with animal-liberation activists should not be afforded airtime.

To be honest, for me the real attraction of this powerful exposé was its narrator: Julie Christie, who had been mesmeric in *Dr Zhivago* and now had me riveted to the spot, overcome and shocked. Her narration was not an unadulterated rant but a sophisticated and carefully structured journey across terrain that we take for granted: our environment, and especially the animals with which we share it; how we farm with methods that treat life as conveyor-belt, caged cargo; how we contrive mutant breeds of pig which can barely stand; how we pack poultry in dark barns with barely enough space to lift the wing, while standing in a bed of shit. In short, factory food churned out by the processes of industrial mass production.

This was just one message. There were others relating to the fur trade, animal testing in the cosmetic industries and medical research. The experiments being conducted on live animals must have caused (and still do cause) suffering beyond quantification and beyond imagination, and I found it impossible to sit through this experience without wanting to take action, without wanting to change the habits of a lifetime straight away – and the main habit is consumerism.

In one sense this film was truly revolutionary, because without propagandising some dogma, mantra or diatribe, it highlighted in one go the excesses of corporate greed and the way in which we collude with it on a daily basis. It also made me think about what right we have, as some kind of master race, to experiment with animal life as if we owned it. If this were applied to human beings – as of course was done in Nazi Germany through the application of eugenics – we would all be appalled. On one occasion, when appearing on *Any Questions?* on BBC Radio 4, I was asked whether I deprecated the use of animals to develop cures for human illness, and therefore whether I would rather die in their absence. I answered that there were other ways of developing such cures, for example through computer models or in Petri dishes, but my main point was made by asking whether any member of the audience was happy to volunteer for such experiments on themselves.

Eight years after *The Animals Film* was shown I was being interviewed by the journalist Duncan Campbell for his book about the changing face of professional crime[2] when I mentioned the film and freely extolled the virtues of Julie Christie – without being aware of his long-term relationship with her. As I rhapsodised about her, Duncan sat studiously silent: holes only get deeper. Shortly after this, I met Julie at a mutual friend's wedding, where she explained that the film had had the same profound effect on her as it had on me. Stranger still, and quite by chance, I ended up renting the very same remote summer house near Monemvasia on the Mani in southern Greece, just after she and Duncan had stayed there. It was situated in a dried-up river bed known as Butterfly Valley: there was no electricity and no running water, just a self-sustaining eco-wonder world – now, I suspect, obliterated by a concrete jungle of hotels, the foundations of which were under construction at the time we were there.

This is a fine example of the ever-expanding consumption of which we have all been a part. Can it really be said to be progress, let alone necessary? Can it really be justified in the context of a world in which a roof, a bowl of rice and a cup of water are denied to the people living in two-thirds of it? Even more fundamental is whether the planet's resources can possibly support this expansion. In 2008 we were confronted by an economic meltdown, which both symbolically and actually could be directly linked to the environmental meltdown. What are we to do about it? Spend, spend, spend? I think not.

The feelings *The Animals Film* had generated in me highlighted the need to reappraise my way of life. I don't tend to use much lipstick, eye-liner or foundation cream, but there was plenty of room for improvement on other fronts: diet, clothing, energy consumption, car use, plastic packaging such as bags and bottles, waste recycling and disposal. I had already thought that dustbins, and more recently the ubiquitous black sacks, were a seriously antiquated and unhealthy way of rubbish clearance, particularly as I had worked 'on the dust' as a student for a short time. In idle moments I had dreamed up a scheme whereby every home would be connected by subterranean pipes like mains water drainage, which would separate the different types of waste, and one pipe would lead to a municipal compost heap. Much to my amazement, I discovered recently that such a system has been put into practice in Scandinavia, and for the first time is being employed on a new, privately owned housing estate in Britain.

These thoughts also influenced the work and campaigns with which I wanted to get involved, and there was one case at this time that epitomised and encapsulated all these issues, especially corporate responsibility. Two young people took on the mighty McDonald's Corporation, and they took it on not for personal gain – for although they had very little themselves, they would gain nothing and, indeed, were liable to lose everything. Neither was it a question of personal aggrandisement, but they withstood the legal assault upon them by McDonald's where many others had not.[3] In similar circumstances, the media and newspapers had backed down when confronted by the legal might of McDonald's and apologised, but Dave Morris, a former postman, and Helen Steel, a gardener, did not.

Beginning in 1986 as members of London Greenpeace, a small environmental campaigning group (not to be confused with Greenpeace International), Helen and Dave had been circulating a pamphlet entitled 'What's Wrong With McDonald's? Everything they don't want you to know'.

The publication made claims about the effects of fast-food production on, among other things, the rainforests in South America, about the conditions of the corporation's workforce, factory farming, hygiene, health and nutrition. Some of the allegations against McDonald's were that the corporation sold unhealthy food; exploited its workforce; practised unethical marketing of its products; was cruel to animals; needlessly used up resources; and created pollution with its packaging. Few cases could be said to embrace more important issues or such essential environmental ones.

Ironically, before McDonald's responded, the pamphlet had been read by a mere handful of people who were given it while out shopping in London; now the pamphlet has been translated into more than twenty-six languages and distributed worldwide.

The court action for libel filed by the McDonald's Corporation against these two environmental activists began in 1990 – and bear in mind that under our libel laws the burden of proof (on balance of probability) of each and every derogatory statement is on the defendant.

Helen and Dave conducted their own case, and the whole proceedings went on for 313 days in court over two and a half years, making it the longest trial in British legal history.[4] Yet they did it without legal aid, and with just the free advice of committed lawyers – outstandingly from Kier Starmer, now Director of Public Prosecutions, and from me and others whenever we could. The pair did enormous amounts of research and eventually called 180 witnesses to help prove their assertions. McDonald's spent millions of pounds on the action, while the protesters had just £30,000 donated by the public, but it didn't look good for the corporation when top McDonald's executives were forced to take the stand and be questioned by two non-lawyers, who did a fantastic job.

The travesty of the case was that none of the evidence was heard by a jury, because no jury, it was thought, would understand the many complicated points of scientific interest involved and only a judge was deemed able to deal with the amount of complex material. I totally disagree: the proper adjudication of issues of such public importance should be by the public's representatives, a jury sitting in a court. Public debate can only be sparked by public involvement, and the whole 'McLibel' trial was heard by a single judge, Mr Justice Bell, whose verdict, when it came in June 1997, was something of a split decision – six of one and half a dozen of the other.

On the whole the case and the media exposure were devastating for McDonald's, for the judge ruled that the Corporation 'exploits children' with its 'misleading' advertising, is 'culpably responsible' for cruelty to animals, 'antipathetic' to unionisation and pays its workers low wages.[5]

Unfortunately, Helen and Dave failed to prove all their points, and so the judge ruled that they *had* libelled McDonald's and should pay £60,000 damages. The two refused and McDonald's didn't pursue it – more out of embarrassment, I imagine, than benevolence.

Later the defendants learned that McDonald's had hired spies to infiltrate London Greenpeace and agents to break into their offices and steal documents, and in September 1998 the pair sued Scotland Yard for disclosing confidential information to investigators hired by McDonald's, and received £10,000 in compensation and an apology.

Still angered by the judicial decision, the pair weren't about to give up, and in March 1999 they went to the Court of Appeal. The fight had taken its toll on both Helen and Dave, and the preparation for the appeal was gruelling – but a request for further time was denied by the court, despite medical evidence of their exhaustion.

Nevertheless they won. The Lord Justices made further rulings that it was fair comment to say that McDonald's employees worldwide 'do badly in terms of pay and conditions', and true that 'if one eats enough McDonald's food, one's diet may well become high in fat etc., with the very real risk of heart disease'.[6] The court went on to state that this last finding 'must have a serious effect on their [McDonald's] trading reputation since it goes to the very business in which they are engaged'.

Dave and Helen were spurred on by the backing of the vocal Anti-McDonald's Campaign, massive press coverage and a feature-length documentary, which was broadcast around the world, but predictably could not get a public screening in the UK, so had to be shown in private before an invited audience at the Riverside Studios in Hammersmith, London. The two took their case to the European Court of Human Rights (ECHR) to defend the public's right to criticise multinationals, claiming that UK libel laws were oppressive and unfair and that they had been denied a fair trial.

On 15 February 2005 the pair's twenty-year battle (and fifteen-year court battle) with the company concluded when the ECHR ruled that the original case had breached Article 6 (the right to a fair trial) and Article 10 (the right to freedom of expression) of the European Convention on Human Rights, and ordered that the UK Government pay the McLibel Two £57,000 in compensation. After this momentous victory, Helen and Dave made the following statement:

> The McLibel campaign has already proved that determined and widespread grass roots protests and defiance can undermine those who try to silence their critics, and also render oppressive laws unworkable. The continually growing opposition to McDonald's and all it stands for is a vindication of all the efforts of those around the world who have been exposing and challenging the corporation's business practices.[7]

The McLibel Two encouraged us all to question the nature and scope of all corporate activities, be they legal, illegal, morally defensible or morally dubious, and they prompted us to examine and reassess the regulatory systems currently in place that govern the actions of corporations – or, rather, the lack of them. I salute them.

Many others have followed in their footsteps, dedicated and honourable. In 2001 a group of demonstrators, including the environmentalist George Monbiot, were arrested for criminal damage during a protest at a genetically modified crop trial in Wales, and on 13 August 2007 over 2,000 environmental campaigners set up a camp on a field near Heathrow to protest at the damage caused by the airport and its seventy million passengers a year. The police drafted in 1,800 officers and Heathrow's owner, British Airways Authority (BAA), desperate to minimise any bad publicity, won a court ruling to ban the protesters. The problem is that with the new Terminal Five and projected expansion of a third runway, things at Heathrow can only get worse, so along with many others I have signed up to help purchase small plots of land in the path of the proposed runway.

In 2008 'climate camps' proliferated, one of which, Climate Rush founded by Tamsin Omond, organised an effective protest against the third runway on the roof of the Houses of Parliament. At the same time a jury at Maidstone Crown Court acquitted the Kingsnorth Six, Greenpeace activists who had been charged with causing £30,000 of criminal damage to a chimney at the coal-fired power station in Kent: they scaled the 200-foot stack and occupied it while they painted the name GORDON down the outside. Their defence of lawful excuse was unequivocally rooted in the immediate need to protect the property of another: the environment, people and wildlife. The 20,000 tonnes of carbon dioxide emitted daily from the power station is equivalent to the combined emissions of the thirty least-polluting countries in the world. Similar acquittals have been secured by those protesting against the Trident nuclear submarine and the development of the Hawk fighter jet by BAE Systems.

This movement is international, and communities worldwide are attempting to reclaim their heritage. A prime example is Nigeria, where oil companies like Shell have decimated the land with fires and oil spills, which turn into a hard brown crust several feet thick. The Carbon Disclosure Project (CDP), which monitors emissions by major British companies listed in the FTSE index, revealed in October 2008 that the total amount of carbon produced by Shell extracting and then burning oil and gas had reached 743 million tonnes in 2007, an amount that was higher than the total for Britain as a whole (587 million). Livelihoods in the Niger have been ruined by such activity, and opposition has been suppressed by the use of brutal military force. I joined the campaign in London to support Ken Saro-Wiwa, who was leading a number of local community groups in protest: he was arrested and executed by the Nigerian authorities. They never learn. You may kill the man, but you never kill the cause, and resistance has re-emerged with the Movement for the Emancipation of the Niger Delta. Then along comes Gordon Brown in July 2008, offering our troops to train Nigerian 'security forces' to restore order. Or should that read 'to restore oil profits'? The Saro-Wiwa family have since launched a legal action in a New York Federal Court against Shell alleging complicity in human rights abuses in the early 1990s in Nigeria.[8]

In 1996 the *Sea Empress* was grounded on rocks off the South Wales coast near Milford Haven, and about 72,000 tonnes of Forties light crude oil were released into the sea, devastating over sixty miles of coastline. The images of birds smothered and struggling against the sticky black oil were horrific. There had been many such disasters before this, notably the *Torrey Canyon* in 1967 and the *Exxon Valdez* in 1989, and I helped advise an environmental group over the *Sea Empress* spill. Without their vigilance, issues relating to such tankers would themselves have been submerged: their size; their construction and the need for a double hull; the provision of sea-going tugs; and the installation of land-based radar to reduce the risk of pilot error.

Another active and successful campaigning organisation is Viva!,[9] a vegetarian and animal-welfare charity of which I have been patron since its inception. Its founder, Juliet Gellately, is a ferocious campaigner who gave important evidence in the McLibel trial, and among her many awards are the *Daily Mirror*'s Pride of Britain, Linda McCartney Award for Animal Welfare. Her partner Tony Wardle is not only a great activist, but an exceptional researcher and writer too: he and Yvette produced films together for many years. In 2007 Tony researched and wrote *Diet of Disaster*, for Viva! Campaigns, cataloguing the environmental destruction engendered by meat and fish production – it is a devastating indictment of man's disregard for nature and the consequences for our planet.

I believe that powerful action can end animal suffering, protect the environment and bring fairness to the world's poor. Today, millions of children in the developing world die from hunger – and die alongside fields of high-quality food destined for the West's farmed animals. Animal feed is increasingly taking precedence over food for people.[10] The startling truth is that meat causes starvation. Worse, agriculture is the biggest user of fresh water (demanding up to 90 per cent of supplies in many poor countries), so a scarce resource is getting even scarcer.

It's now a common theme from major institutions such as the World Health Organisation that 'The human appetite for animal flesh is a driving force behind virtually every major category of environmental damage – deforestation, erosion, fresh water scarcity, air and water pollution and climate change.'[11] In September 2008 this opinion was supported by the United Nations chief climate expert Rajendra Pachauri, and by the Food Climate Research Network based at the University of Surrey. The animal-welfare group Compassion in World Farming has calculated that if the average UK household halved its meat consumption, that would cut emissions more than if car use were halved. In fact, aircraft produce around 3 per cent of greenhouse gases, and 13.55 per cent comes from all forms of transport, but livestock produces 18 per cent. Methane is lethal to our planet; it is a gas twenty-one times more damaging than CO_2. Both are hugely significant in meat production. Animal agriculture is responsible for over 100 million tonnes of methane a year: 85 per cent from digestion and 15 per cent from slurry lagoons.

The global-warming situation is far worse than anyone appreciated, and scientists at the Emergency Climate Conference in Copenhagen in March 2009, in preparation for a climate-change summit in December, described many of the developments as irreversible. The combination of warming ocean waters and melting ice sheets, especially land-based, is causing sea levels to rise twice as fast as predicted by the UN in 2007. Levels will rise by a metre or more by 2100, swamping coastal cities and obliterating the living space of 600 million people.[12] At the same time the Amazonian rainforest is converting from a beneficial carbon 'sink' that absorbs CO_2 into a detrimental carbon emitter, due to the prediction that one-third of its trees will be killed by even modest temperature increases over the next century.[13]

Meanwhile our insatiable drive for meat and fish escalates the deterioration even further. Every year, one billion animals face the barbarity of slaughter in Britain, while a further 4.5 billion fish and 2.6 billion shellfish are killed for the UK market. At sea, over-fishing has brought all the world's oceans to the point of collapse.[14]

Responsibility for the world in which we live, for the environment on which we place daily demands, rests with each one of us. International treaties and accords are important for setting agendas and frameworks, but at the end of the day we personally have to make choices that collectively reduce exploitation and the erosion of resources. We are the consumers. It is time to change the nature of that consumption to ensure that our planet has any chance of survival for us, let alone future generations. We can't do everything at once, but since watching *The Animals Film* I've tried to do my bit. If I stray, I turn to the Bible for inspiration – spiritual salsify and scorzonera with humble crumble.*

* The book I rely on most as the cook in our household is *Leith's Vegeterian Bible* by Polly Tyrer, Bloomsbury, London 2002.

20

JURIES IN JEOPARDY

The Fertiliser and Ricin Conspiracy Trials

The King, his crown placed squarely upon his full-bottomed wig, sat alongside the stern-faced Queen. They were to preside over an important trial. The jury was already in place busily assembling slates and pencils. The prisoner, Jack, 'the knave', stood in chains before them. As soon as the charge was put (the theft of special culinary delicacies), the King called for a verdict. Not yet, not yet. No evidence had been heard. The first witness had trouble with dates, the second refused to give evidence and the third knew nothing. The King, exasperated, repeated his demand for a verdict. The Queen lost patience. 'No, no. Sentence first, verdict afterwards.' 'Stuff and nonsense,' said the third witness loudly. Her name was Alice, and the King had already tried to remove her by spontaneously inventing rule 42 – anyone over a mile high had to leave court immediately. The Queen trumped this by ordering Alice's summary execution. 'Off with her head!' 'Who cares for you?' said Alice (who had grown to her full size by this time). 'You're nothing but a pack of cards.'*

How much easier it would have been to dispense with the trial – not be troubled by a lack of evidence, a jury of subservient small animals – and carry out the punishment without further ado. Quicker, cheaper and effective. Best of all, no footling lawyers.

For Alice, who awoke at just the right moment, it was but a

---

* An adaptation of *Alice in Wonderland*, with apologies to Lewis Carroll.

curious dream. For me, however, the incessant battle to preserve the centrepiece of our system of criminal justice – the hard-won right to trial by your peers – against the ever-present preying mantra of political expediency has been an enduring reality throughout my working life.

It was the Danes who evolved the twelve-man jury system, which seems then to have been borrowed by the English, who exported it to the rest of the world and now claim to have invented it. One possible precursor to the English jury trial was the *Lafif* in classical Islamic law and jurisprudence, which was developed between the eighth and eleventh centuries in the medieval Islamic world. The *Lafif* was a body of twelve members drawn from the neighbourhood and sworn to tell the truth, who were bound to give a unanimous verdict about matters that they had personally seen or heard. Quite where the number twelve came from is elusive. Trevor Grove muses that it might be from the twelve apostles and the twelve tribes of Israel.[1] Maybe it's got something to do with twelve months of the year, or the twelve days of Christmas, or the twelve times table, or maybe it's just an early disaffection with decimalisation.

Back in England in 1215, in the reign of King John, Article 39 of Magna Carta declared: 'No freeman shall be taken, imprisoned . . . or in any other way destroyed . . . except by the lawful judgment of his peers, or by the law of the land. To no one will we sell, to none will we deny or delay, right or justice.'

This document was really for the benefit of the landed and property-owning classes, but it has nevertheless provided a very useful fountain from which justice has flowed since, and it did put an end to trial by ordeal: fire, water and battle.

Significant landmarks in jury development came later when juries began to stand up to the judges and the courts: for example, against the notorious Star Chamber under the tutelage of kings, which was abolished in 1641, while the radical reformer and Leveller John Lilburne risked his life from 1637 (when he was only twenty-three years old) until his death twenty years later in defence of rights for freemen, including the independence of juries, which was incorporated into his *Agreement of the People* (1649): 'No judgment touching life, liberty or property but by jury trial.' Standing trial for his life four times, Lilburne spent most of his adult years in prison and died in banishment.

Gradually, over time, rights to sit on a jury were extended to women (in 1919) and to all on the electoral register except those involved in the law – such as police or barristers – but recently that disqualification has been dropped, and all except the mentally disordered or those whose previous convictions resulting in imprisonment can now be called to sit. So we have a truly democratic method of adjudicating at trial, but one that unfortunately many have sought to interfere with, weaken or remove altogether.

In September 1978 I was involved in a trial known as the ABC case. Why ABC? These were the initials of three individuals: Crispin Aubrey, who then worked on *Time Out*, the London listings magazine (and now an organic farmer in the West Country); my client John Berry, then a social worker who had been a corporal in Signals Intelligence in Cyprus (and now a probation officer); and Duncan Campbell, now scientific investigator and celebrated journalist, but then merely a scientific prodigy. They were charged under the Official Secrets Act because Duncan had published an article revealing for the first time the existence and purpose of GCHQ, the Government Communications Headquarters in Cheltenham, and as a consequence all hell broke loose. This was a very serious matter because they stood to get sentences of up to thirty years,[2] and the trial also exposed the practice of secret jury vetting by the prosecution.

In those days the names and addresses of the jury panel were available to all parties, and the prosecution had the power of 'stand by', which meant that without showing cause they could ask potential jurors to stand down and not serve. At the same time the defence had a limited power of peremptory challenge on jurors, again without cause. However, before the ABC trial the prosecution was clandestinely receiving intelligence from the security services with regard to potential jurors. We on the defence side were of course left completely in the dark.

In 1979 a group of young people, one of whom was the writer Ronan Bennett, was charged with a conspiracy to rob, allegedly for political purposes. The group was dubbed 'Persons Unknown' because the charge of conspiracy customarily includes the phrase 'with persons unknown' in the indictment, allowing the prosecution to keep their options open. I was instructed by James Saunders for one of four defendants in the jury trial, including Ronan – all of whom were acquitted. The judge ruled that the defence could itself make 'reasonable and necessary inquiries' about potential jurors with the benefit of legal aid. I thought this was a victory at the time, but I've changed my mind, and now I don't think that either side should be privy to any information about the jury panel. One of the reasons is that one juror who had been rejected by the Crown had been excluded on a spurious basis. He had written a pamphlet which had the words 'state' and 'individual' in the title. When the juror subsequently complained, it turned out he was a tax consultant and the leaflet contained advice about tax avoidance and nothing about political subversion.

What happens now is that if the trial involves highly charged or emotive events in which members of the public may have been caught up – such as bombings or disasters – or concerns particular organisations like the police or army, then the judge can be requested by either side to ask the jury panel if any of them (or their close friends or relatives) have been involved in any way, or are aware of any impediment to their returning an impartial verdict, with a view to excluding them. Under these circumstances jurors are remarkably honest and come forward if they feel they shouldn't be sworn in for that particular trial.

For some, the jury presents a real threat. The customary carping runs along the lines that jury trials take up too much time and money; an alternative tack is to suggest that juries don't understand complicated issues, or that they can be beguiled by fast-talking advocates. Then there is the old school of thought, which can barely contemplate the possibility of working-class, unemployed or black people appearing in a randomly chosen jury. Above all else is the terrible realisation, by those who regard themselves as having a monopoly on the truth, that juries might just take a different view and acquit. Such decisions are speedily characterised as 'perverse'.

In case you're thinking that this is some adventure in Wonderland, let me assure you that it's not. These are sentiments which have littered the legal landscape over the last forty years, and are expressed by all shades of established opinion, Tory and New Labour alike.

Principles stoutly supported and espoused in opposition are ditched with unseemly haste once the mantle of power is donned.

At the beginning of the 1970s, Lord Diplock undertook a review of the criminal-justice system in Northern Ireland at the height of 'The Troubles'. For me, rights matter most when the threat is greatest. Not for Diplock. He recommended the abolition of jury trial for a whole raft of offences, and in the process criticised lawyers and their unyielding adherence to what he regarded as 'technical' rules excluding unreliable confessions.[3] The fear I had then was that governments were using Northern Ireland as a testing ground for oppressive measures, to be imported to the mainland should they become necessary. I was part of a mission on behalf of the Haldane Society with Helena Kennedy, Nick Blake and Richard Harvey, examining the operation of this emergency legislation, and I remember standing with Gerry Adams in a doorway encircled by bullet holes from an assassination attempt the day before. Richard got over-excited and camera-happy outside Springfield Barracks just before we were due to have tea with the Lord Chief Justice, and he and his camera were temporarily detained at Her Majesty's Pleasure. Whatever else could be said about the lack of juries in Northern Ireland, having forthright talks over cucumber sandwiches with the Lord Chief Justice would never have been countenanced in England.

Although the number of trials heard at the Diplock courts dropped dramatically over the intervening years (to forty-nine in 2005), incredibly the courts remained legal until the Justice and Security (Northern Ireland) Act 2007 came into force, an act that nonetheless allows the Northern Ireland Director of Public Prosecutions to keep his options open by retaining a provision to issue a certificate in a case where it is felt a non-jury trial is appropriate.

By 1982 Lord Denning had advocated the end of random selection of juries from the electoral register, in part motivated by the verdicts in a Bristol riot trial and his conclusion that black jurors would never convict 'one of their own'. It was observations of this kind in his book, *What's Next in the Law*,[4] that forced his early retirement. This was the same judge who felt that the attempts by the Birmingham Six to pursue a civil action against the police presented 'an appalling vista'.

In 1986 Lord Roskill proposed that complex fraud trials should be conducted by a judge and two lay assessors, constituting what might be termed a professional jury. And then in 1988 a trio of senior legal figures led by Lord Hailsham, a former Lord Chancellor, demanded fundamental changes to the jury system. Hailsham thought it commanded more public support than it deserved, and his view was that London juries acquitted more people than they should because of their make-up. He went on to say: 'I do believe that we used to get a better class of jury before the abolition of the property-owning qualification.'[5]

During the dying days of the last Conservative government, Home Secretary Michael Howard wanted to reduce jury trial still further, and intended to do this by removing a defendant's right to choose this mode in what were known as 'hybrid' offences, which could be tried 'either way' – meaning either with a jury or without. The idea emanated from a recommendation by the Royal Commission on Criminal Justice under Lord Runciman in 1993, and was not supported by Jack Straw and Labour while they were in opposition. However, once Labour had been elected in 1997, the proposal reared its head again and was assessed to affect about 18,500 people a year. This was fought tooth and nail for over a year, and the government even threatened to use the Parliament Act to get it through, if the House of Lords stood in the way – at which point my close friend and colleague Baroness Helena Kennedy passionately marshalled the forces of reason and sense.

Undeterred, the Labour government has pursued other proposals to curtail the right to jury trial in the Criminal Justice Act 2003.[6] It has resurrected the complex fraud argument by allowing the prosecution to apply to a judge for a trial to be conducted without a jury. It also included a provision in the 2008 Counter-Terrorism Bill to prevent juries being summoned in certain inquests where it was not deemed to be in the public interest. This was dropped after the government received a well-deserved drubbing in the House of Lords over its plans for detention without charge for up to forty-two days, but with its usual disregard for reasoned opposition the government has reinstated these provisions in the Coroners Bill 2009.

On top of all these attacks, there has been a slow and often undetected diminution of the number of offences capable of being tried by a jury. This is accomplished by passing anodynely titled statutes (far more by Labour than by any previous government) in which there are clauses tucked away that knock off a few more offences which can be tried by a jury in the Crown Court. By now the vast majority of criminal justice, over 90 per cent, is dispensed in the lower courts by magistrates and district judges without a jury. At the same time New Labour has managed to create a further 3,600 *new* criminal offences, most of which are not susceptible to jury trial.

Yet when it suits governments, the good sense of juries is invoked as one of the arguments for relaxing long-standing rules intended to ensure the integrity and reliability of evidence. Once termed the 'golden thread of British justice' by judges and practitioners alike, the right to silence has been replaced by the 'adverse inference': if on arrest, on interview or in court a suspect refuses to speak, the jury is entitled to draw an unfavourable inference of guilt. Previous convictions and bad character are now more readily admissible, and in addition a wide range of hearsay evidence is allowed.

Despite all of this, my love affair with jury trial has remained untarnished throughout the years that I've had the good fortune to be able to address them. What I have found, and what I believe is unquestionable by anyone who has served upon a jury, is that jurors set about their task with exemplary responsibility and a conscientious attention to detail that knows no bounds. Ask anyone by whom they would prefer to be tried when it comes to something serious or a reputation is at stake, and almost without exception they will choose twelve fellow citizens.[7]

Many, many years ago when the Chelmsford Crown Court – or Quarter Sessions as it was known – was held in the Shire building in Chelmsford High Street, I had a short two-day burglary case which was relegated to a small courtroom at the top of the building, where the jury was housed on some fairly perfunctory benches next to the ones meant for the public. At the end of the trial the court clerk asked the jury to stand while the jury bailiff swore the usual oath to keep them in some private and safe place, before leading them to their room to consider their verdict. An hour later a note came from the jury with a question – a perceptive enquiry, and not one that anyone had thought to ask during the trial. The questioner at Chelmsford wanted to know whether the jury had to be sure that the defendant had stolen *all* the property listed on the indictment.

In those days, each time a jury returned to court the clerk would read out their names to check all were present and correct. This time they certainly were – plus one, making thirteen. None of us – especially the judge – could quite believe how we'd managed to get through a trial without noticing there were thirteen jurors, but in fact there hadn't been. On the second day of the trial a member of the public with nothing better to do on a rainy morning had sat himself down on the benches next to the jury box. When the clerk had asked the jury to stand before retiring, he stood up with them, and when they were then asked to follow the jury bailiff to the jury room, he followed as well. Once in the room, none of the jurors thought there was anything exceptional in this and merely took it as part of normal procedure – like an independent assessor joining them at the end of the case. And it was number 13 who had thought of the pertinent question. Unfortunately, we had to start all over again with another jury in another courtroom.

(This was by no means the first time in my experience that a question from the jury has had important consequences for a case, and I recall one trial where my cross-examination of a police officer concerned the accuracy of times that he claimed to remember with consummate recall to within a few seconds. As he was about to leave the witness box, a juror jumped up and asked if he could put one question, and this was permitted. The juror asked the police officer: could he recollect the exact time he entered the witness box? No chance.)

There is a serious point behind all this. One of the ways of easing the burden on jurors in long trials lasting several weeks, or even months, could be to have a number of standby or reserve members who are there from the beginning, hear all the evidence and can step in if one of the twelve falls ill. This would prevent the need to discharge the jury if the numbers fall too low for even a majority verdict: for example, below ten. In some parts of the USA such a system has been adopted and the reserves are called 'alternates'.

On a clear day with a fair wind behind them, I like to think that the majority of trial judges in front of whom I've appeared would accept that twelve minds are better than one, and that the twelve are less likely to be influenced by sanguine thoughts engendered by the case-hardened experience of a professional. The most obvious benefit, however, is that jurors are not agents of the state: they are not beholden to anyone or anything other than their own consciences, and their deliberations are beyond the reach of state interference. In criminal trials they return a simple verdict of either 'guilty' or 'not guilty'. They do not have to give reasons, although it has become abundantly clear in inquests that, if required to do so, they are more than capable of formulating detailed answers or of completing a comprehensive questionnaire.

Rather than restricting the role of juries, I think the time has come for an expansion of their work and recognition of the amazing contribution they make to our system. If you think about it, it's one of the few ways in which a citizen can perform a public duty and reach a decision that has both meaning and political significance. Public access and public participation are vital for any system of justice to attract confidence and trust, and it's mildly ironic that while the Labour government is eroding this at home, it is more than willing to extol its virtues on diplomatic trips abroad. Soon after his election in 1997 Tony Blair paid a visit to China, during which he exemplified the fairness of British justice with a mock jury trial, performed by British barristers in front of a Chinese jury and officials. It was a fitting demonstration of People's Justice – one of the most effective democratic processes our society permits.

If we are to accord this status to our citizens, they are due a far higher degree of respect and gratitude. On the practical front, while a number of improvements have been made over the last few years, it has been a painfully slow business, and has often been brought about by jurors themselves complaining about the conditions under which they labour. For example, in one trial they refused to continue until their remuneration was increased, and in another they wouldn't return to court until their food was more edible.

Imagine receiving a summons to serve on a jury for the first time. This has probably either happened to you or at least you know someone to whom it has. How much do you know about the process? Virtually nothing. You worry about what is involved: how long a case will last; whether you can get out of it because of your job, your health or a pre-booked holiday.

When you arrive at the court building, it's all a bit forbidding. You often hang about for hours, sometimes days, in facilities that can be fairly rudimentary in the older establishments. The court staff are usually very kind and understanding, but nevertheless it can be an irritating and frustrating experience.

If you do finally make it into court, you will then have the opportunity, if you wish, to explain to the judge why you need to be excused because of work, family or medical commitments. The judge will scrutinise each explanation carefully and will not accede to a request unless it is absolutely vital, because jury service is such an important public duty. The court clerk then opens a small box that contains cards with the names of jurors on the panel; a card is then selected at random and the name called out, until there are twelve.

Once you are selected to serve on a jury, the case is opened and the first witnesses called before you know where you are. The jury box where you sit is invariably cramped. In front of you is a tiny strip of wood about twelve inches deep, which masquerades as a kind of desk, and somehow you have to balance your notebook, pencil, numerous files (if the case has more than one exhibit), a glass and carafe of water on this narrow ledge.

This situation stems from the days when it was hoped that juries would only be seen and not heard; when they were almost considered to be tame voyeurs, like the creatures in Alice's jury, eating from the judicial hand that fed them. 'Don't write notes and don't ask questions' were the admonitions directed at juries by trial judges when I first began at the Bar.

Thankfully we've moved beyond that frame of mind, but the set-up itself has not. It could all be very different, especially given recent technological advances. There is no longer a need for anyone to keep a running note of the evidence; no need to depend on the judicial pen or counsel's fallible recollection. All evidence can now be recorded and transcribed via a system known as Livenote. As a participant speaks, his or her words are reproduced on computer screens allocated to the jurors, the judge, the lawyers, the defendant and the witness. This means that during the examination of a witness anyone can scroll back and check what has already been said by the witness, as well as by those who have gone before. It is a verbatim account, which can be made available on a daily basis either on disk or in hard copy, and the advantages are manifold – for barristers when examining witnesses and addressing the jury in speeches, for the judge when compiling his summing-up, and most significantly for the jury, who can take a complete record with them when they retire. No more wasteful arguments about who said what when. It is super-efficient and in the long run saves time, money and space.

Besides live testimony, all documentary material – and exhibits in particular – can also be reproduced on a separate screen and made available on disk. The screen itself can be split in a number of different ways to enable comparisons to be made with other documents, and passages of importance can be enlarged and highlighted. Where it has been necessary to reconstruct a document or, more significantly, the scene of an event, this can be done to great effect. In the Bloody Sunday Inquiry witnesses could be visually taken back to the streets and houses as they were in 1972. In the Diana/Dodi inquest witnesses could be transported to the Alma Tunnel and its approach road. Specific points or areas of interest can be identified and called up as 'hot spots'; it is then possible to swivel the graphic within a 360-degree arc in order to establish what lines of sight are available.

In an increasing number of investigations, film of one sort or another becomes relevant. Either a CCTV camera has captured an occurrence, or a passer-by has done so with a camera or mobile phone, or the police themselves have carried out covert surveillance by means of hidden cameras so small that they are undetectable. Provided the provenance, continuity and integrity of these films can be assured, far better images and compilations can be produced onscreen than ever before, and everything can be referenced and indexed at the touch of a button.

To date resources of this kind have been reserved for exceptional or high-profile cases such as the two mentioned above, the Stockwell inquest (see Chapter 21) and a couple of criminal trials in which I've been involved. It should be rolled out to all Crown Courts.

A further benefit of these innovations is Livenote's availability to the press and public at large, via the Internet. Public scrutiny is a very important safeguard, and for many people it is impossible to get to a court to watch the proceedings. Even if they could, the gallery in most courts is remarkably small. The real thing is nothing like the dramatised versions portrayed on television and, as with the House of Commons, it's time the cameras (under controlled conditions) were allowed in to record day-to-day trial developments in a routine and regular way.

Having all these resources makes no sense unless the jurors are encouraged to interact with the matters upon which they have to pass judgment. There should be no inhibitions about asking questions or raising queries, and in this way they will feel, and will be, involved. While it is not possible to have a dialogue with the jurors, whose deliberations are sacrosanct, their participation in court does provide an insight into the extent to which the various aspects of the trial are intelligible. The jury in the Stockwell inquest surpassed any I had known before, both by the number and the quality of their queries.

Addressing a jury is an odd sensation for a barrister. It is one-way traffic. No feedback. No conversation. Imagine sitting down in the same room with someone for months on end, talking to them about all manner of subjects, and getting no verbal response. Generally, for a defence lawyer, it's not until the end of the trial that you can speak directly to the jury by means of a final speech. (Sometimes an opening speech is allowable, if you are calling defence evidence of fact beyond the defendant's own.) You have to make assessments continually about how you think the jury are receiving you, and about what kind of people they are. How they look, how they dress, what books or newspapers they carry are less important than the body language that they unconsciously transmit. Even so, you can be terribly wrong. The juror who nods approvingly as you speak may just want you to go quicker; the one who shakes his head in apparent disagreement may have got wax in his ears; the diligent scribe may be assiduously listing all the points you've missed . . . and if one is asleep, you know you've had it.

There was one occasion when I spotted real consternation on the faces of the jury as I paced up and down in counsels' row close by. I move about a lot in order to liven up my presentation, and have the habit of removing my shoes (it relieves those varicose veins which trouble me) to reveal red socks, which have occasionally been mentioned in dispatches. My instructing solicitor at the time was an elderly and erudite managing clerk employed by a firm of solicitors in Hackney, who in his spare time was researching and writing a book about the joys of garlic and thought my general

health and welfare would benefit, were I to have a daily dose.
Noticing my socks, he suggested that I put a garlic tablet in each,
so that while I walked up and down the tablet would be crushed
and absorbed upwards. Those who consume garlic don't seem
to be aware of the effect on others, and I certainly wasn't, until
a court usher thought I should be alerted to the pungent cloud
drifting across the floor.

There are better methods of attracting the attention of jurors, and
I've always worked on the basis that they appreciate being engaged
in a way that allows them to be evidential detectives. Mostly the
evidence in cases tends to be circumstantial; rarely is there direct
evidence of a criminal act. The prosecution puts forward its
contention so that certain inferences can be drawn, and the defence
presents an alternative view.

Somewhere along the line there is a detail, an angle, a perspective,
an event that unlocks an avenue of thought – the missing pieces in a
jigsaw puzzle. It may have been overlooked or underplayed, but it
casts everything in a new light. In one of my favourite films, *Twelve
Angry Men*, starring Henry Fonda and E. G. Marshall (who also
featured in *The Defenders*), that is precisely what happens. At the
start the majority of the jury think it's all over bar the shouting and
that the defendant is guilty, but slowly doubts creep in when just
one juror encourages them to examine the evidence in more detail.
I often scour the newspapers when a jury is due to be sent out to
consider their verdict, to see if by chance the film is being shown on
one of the channels. I am assuming the power of art can help change
the course of reality . . .

My client Nabeel Hussein was a teenage student in his first year at
Brunel University. Against his better judgement and while caught
up in the early flush of student life, he was prevailed upon by others
to rent a lock-up in his name, using his bank account, thinking it was
for the short-term storage of builders' materials for his 'friends'. In
fact, unbeknown to him, the lock-up was used by others to store
a large quantity of fertiliser capable of being employed to make
explosives. This case became known as the Fertiliser Conspiracy.
In autumn 2006 Nabeel found himself charged with an extremely
serious conspiracy and standing trial at the Old Bailey – and,

because of the centrality of the lock-up, he was rated as the third most important defendant out of seven. If convicted, any sentence was likely to involve prison for more than twenty years.

To make my final speech a little more interesting and graphic I used an allegory to introduce the detail or event that lent a fresh perspective, one derived from the artwork of Banksy. There were several examples of his imaginative graffiti near the Old Bailey, which the jury could see for themselves, but I chose to use one of his installations which had just been on show in Los Angeles. Banksy had requisitioned an old warehouse, constructed a typical American living room and placed a real elephant in the middle of it, painted in the same colour and pattern as the wallpaper! Reactions by the American public ranged from a failure to notice the elephant at all, through an unwillingness to acknowledge its presence, to admiration for such a novel accessory. I think Banksy himself was trying to make a point about the war in Iraq.

I adopted the concept of 'the elephant in the room' for my speech to the jury because I wanted to emphasise a piece of evidence staring everyone in the face, which clearly indicated Nabeel's innocence, but which might have been overlooked. Unsurprisingly in a trial lasting over six months, amid the scores of witnesses and the hundreds of documents it's easy for relevant points to become submerged, and one of these was an event that had occurred shortly before Nabeel was approached about renting the lock-up. One of the co-defendants had suddenly pulled out of renting an entirely different lock-up not far from the one Nabeel was subsequently prevailed upon to hire. I asked the jury to closely re-examine the documents (regarding dates, times, purchase of the fertiliser, and so on), which revealed the enormous pressure on the group now encumbered with a huge quantity of fertiliser, to find an innocent dupe to front the whole operation.

The jury had a massive task because each of the seven defendants had a different case, and they considered their verdict for the longest time I've ever encountered, and possibly for the longest period ever recorded – nigh on seven weeks. The judge, Mr Justice Astill, recognised the jurors' diligence, and before sending them home let them know how much they were appreciated, in a laudatory homily delivered in public.

Nabeel was one of only two defendants acquitted at that trial, the other being defended by Helena Kennedy. I've no idea whether this result had anything to do with what either of us said in our final speeches, and from one trial to another you have to make an informed guess. You hone stories, anecdotes, analogies, strategies. You experiment with family and friends until they glaze over. The mirror in the bathroom is a little too close for comfort. If you make someone smile while you're talking, at least you know they're listening.

There are a couple of other stories that have helped liven up final speeches.

The first concerns two neighbours. Kitty has a retriever and Rodney a rabbit. Rod is going off for the weekend and asks Kitty to keep an eye on his house while he is away. Next morning, while reading her Saturday newspaper, Kitty casually looks over the fence to see her retriever shaking Rod's rabbit frenziedly by the neck. Rushing around to his garden in a panic, she rescues the rabbit from the jaws of her dog, but it is too late: the rabbit is well and truly deceased, passed on, gone to meet its maker. Only one thing for it – she takes the rabbit back home, washes it under the shower, dries it off with her hairdryer, fluffs up its fur and finally returns it to its hutch, propping it up against the wire. On Sunday night Kitty hears Rod parking his car, banging doors as he goes through his house into the garden. For a while there is an ominous silence. Kitty anxiously awaits. Soon there is a knock at her door and there stands Rod, distressed, shaking, with both fists clenched. 'Where have you been this weekend?'

'Er, nowhere,' comes the faltering reply.

'Did you bother to look over the fence?'

'I did, I did.'

'Did you see anything unusual or out of the ordinary?'

'Nothing, nothing at all.'

'Do you believe in the Second Coming?'

By this time the clenched fists are moving upwards. Kitty thinks the game is up and she is about to join the rabbit. Instead she is clasped in a warm embrace while Rod recounts, in an amazed and excitable tone, that only last week his rabbit had died, he'd buried it in the garden – only to find it moments ago resurrected, spruce and clean in its hutch!

The moral for those cases involving circumstantial evidence? You have to be careful before jumping to conclusions about what you think you see.

The second tale concerns two well-known characters. Sherlock Holmes and his assistant Dr Watson are on a camping trip in the Lake District, where they find it difficult to sleep through a somewhat chilly night. As they lie there, admiring the nocturnal sky, Holmes asks Watson what he makes of it. Watson, believing he should be seeking some eternal hidden truth, replies, 'From a meteorological point of view, it looks like a fine day ahead; astrologically Saturn is rising; horologically it's about 4 a.m.; and theologically it is a manifestation of our Lord's Grand Design.' Holmes pauses momentarily, as if absorbing such philosophical observations. Then he sits up, stares fixedly into the distance and says, 'No, my dear Watson, it's elementary. Someone has nicked our tent.'

The achievement in Nabeel's case was due not only to the jury, but also to my supportive legal team, Faisal Osman and Imran Khan. It's not just a matter of preparing all the schedules and statements, but also of providing the client with reassurance and care, hour after hour. In that way we probably spend more time on a case out of court than in it – a factor not always appreciated either by the public or by the politicians.

The acquittal of Nabeel after such a long trial and jury retirement was an occasion of unparalleled relief and joy, as a young, intelligent and highly artistic young man had been spared from an abyss. When you see a client every day for six months, living through some moments of extreme anxiety and others of supreme tedium, you become part of their lives. He was the same age as my youngest son Freddy and typical of everyone's teenage son. His mother was patient and generous and bore her anguish with great fortitude. She also bore me the occasional sensational hot curry.

Nabeel wrote to me afterwards:

How are you? I have moved into university and settled in just fine. I miss you, Mike, and often think about the trial and our conversations. I cannot believe this time last year I was giving evidence and now I am back at University, a student and free. It is a fantastic feeling. I will stay in touch as always and if there is anything I can ever do, please ask. Luv Nabeel.

What happens to the jurors after the case is over? They are expected to melt away back to their everyday lives, to carry on as if they had merely completed some obligatory errand, but in many instances the experience will have been onerous, soul-searching and traumatic. They may well have listened to heart-rending descriptions by witnesses, seen images of death and destruction, and heard about shameless exploitation and abuse. Crime and disaster cannot be neatly packaged.

Since 1989 in the USA projects have been undertaken to provide jurors, where necessary, with counselling in the form of therapy similar to the treatment given when people are suffering from post-traumatic stress disorder. There is a distinction to be made between those who experience the violence or disaster first-hand and those who do so second-hand, and we tend to concentrate our efforts more on the first category than on the second. It seems to me that this service should be made available by the NHS for jurors, should they want it, as a matter of course.

There was one trial, however, where I did discover afterwards what impact I'd had on the jury. At the time I hadn't a clue.

Mouloud Sihali was arrested in September 2002, the first of a series of arrests that led to a trial which became known as the Ricin Conspiracy. The arrests were used in the run-up to the war in Iraq to suggest that Britain was under threat from weapons of mass destruction, and represented the most cynical manipulation of the nation's fears.

On 5 January 2003 police found a few castor-oil beans – potentially the raw material for the poison ricin – in a flat in Wood Green, north London. They also claimed to have found the equipment needed to produce ricin, and recipes for ricin, cyanide and several other poisons.

The significant dates ticked by:

7 January 2003: Tony Blair publicly announced that 'The arrests which were made show this danger is present and real and with us now. Its potential is huge.' The case was cited as evidence for further terrorism laws.

8 January 2003: Britain's largest-circulation newspaper, the *Sun*, reported the discovery of a 'Factory of Death', and other newspapers warned on their front pages that 250,000 of us could have died, that a poison gang was on the loose, and talked about the killer poison with no antidote.[8] In fact, ricin is not a weapon of mass destruction: it is a substance that has only ever been used for one-on-one killings.

5 February 2003: US Secretary of State Colin Powell's speech to the UN endeavoured to build the case for the 2003 invasion of Iraq, as part of the alleged Abu Musab al-Zarqawi global terrorist network: 'The ricin that is bouncing around Europe now originated in Iraq – not in the part of Iraq that is under Saddam Hussein's control, but his security forces know all about it.'

20 March 2003: the USA, with the support of the UK, invaded Iraq.

30 March 2003: the head of US forces in Iraq announced: 'And it's from this site where people were trained and poisons were developed that migrated into Europe. We think that's probably where the ricin found in London came from.'

As late as February 2006, Gordon Brown described the so-called Ricin Conspiracy as a significant terrorism plot spanning twenty-six countries.[9]

It was in this context, representing Sihali at the trial, that on Wednesday 22 September 2004 I was confronted by an anonymous witness from the government research agency at Porton Down, who could only be referred to as 'H'. As it happened, the contents of the Wood Green flat had no direct connection with Sihali and therefore I was in half a mind whether or not to ask this witness any questions at all, so I had not prepared the cross-examination[10] as carefully as I normally would. I began by saying: 'I am sorry to detain you just a bit longer. I am only going to deal with a few loose ends arising out of what has been asked, if you would bear with me.'

This was a genuine attempt by me to reassure the witness that there wasn't much more to ask, and thereby gain his confidence, because at that point I had no idea how he might deal with fairly basic questions. Steaming in with strident assertions is usually counterproductive. I endeavour to be disarming – and, dare I say, even charming!

The first question I put was:

Question, MICHAEL MANSFIELD: Amongst the papers that you have in front of you, are there any notes about these events (that is, the events of 6 and 7 January);[11] conversations with the police prior to 20 March; the meeting on 20 March, and so on?

Answer, WITNESS 'H': No. No, there aren't. No.

Q: There are no notes?

A: No.

Q: Of any of the matters you've been telling this jury about, and his Lordship, made by you at any stage over these important days?

A: That's correct.

Q: Correct. Why not?

A: I think, at the time, we . . . we probably weren't in the habit of actually recording telephone calls and making, erm, copious notes.

Q: No, no. Not copious notes. Any notes at all? Were you not in the habit of making any notes about important decisions and stages, if you follow me? Was that not the habit at Porton Down?

A: Certainly not the habit in Porton Down, but I . . . I . . . I can't recall the notes. I cannot find the notes. Had I taken them, I cannot . . .

Q: We will take this slowly, please. Was it the habit at Porton Down generally, by people who worked at Porton Down, to make notes – some notes – about important decisions?

A: Yes. I believe that's true.

Q: You believe that to be true.

A: I have made notes. Erm, that's not unusual. But, unfortunately, erm, I can't find them.

Q: I will come to that.

A: Sure.

Q: So the answer to the question is generally you, particularly, would make notes about important decisions; yes?

A: Yes.

Q: Next stage: did you make notes with regard to this case about decisions taken either on the 6th or the 7th, or at any later date?

A: I cannot find the notes. I cannot remember.

Q: That is not an answer to the question. I will ask it again. Did you make notes about decisions taken on the 6th and the 7th or thereafter?

A: Yes, I would have made . . . I would have made notes.

Q: There is an obligation, is there not, to maintain records at Porton Down, generally?

A: Correct.

Q: That general policy applies to you, does it not?

A: It should do, yes. Yes.

Q: You are now, and were then, Operations Manager, were you not?

A: Correct, yes.

Q: One of the prime tasks you would have is to ensure the maintenance of a proper record of matters within Porton Down; correct?

A: Correct.

Q: Where would the files be kept in which records were made by you?

A: Probably in the office, but I'm not sure.

Q: You have accepted that you did make notes.

A: I should have done, yes, but . . .

Q: Are you wanting to change that and say that you did not?

A: I want to change to say that I didn't make notes, yes.

Q: Do you?

A: Yes.

Q: Anything else you want to change?

A: No, no.

Q: Do you find this amusing?

A: No. No.

Q: You didn't make any notes . . . [*continues*]

A: I said I'd made notes, but I cannot recall them actually being filed.

Q: Really? I'd like to know what your true position is . . . You see, you mentioned several times they're not available. How do you know they're not available, these notes that you would have made, or maybe you did not make . . . [*continues*]

[Lewis Carroll would have been proud of this!]

Q: We are just wanting the truth here. Are there notes that have disappeared?

A: There are no . . . I don't believe there are notes. I cannot . . . I cannot recall the . . . the notes.

Q: Nobody has asked you if you have any notes, at any stage before giving evidence? Is that right?

A: I can't . . . I can't recall, no.

Q: There is no point in keeping looking through those documents, as you do. There is nothing in there that is going to help you. I just want to ask you if there is any possibility of a cover-up going on here?

A: No. None whatsoever.

Q: You are quite sure?

A: Absolutely.

There should have been notes kept by the Operations Manager revealing what it was that the scientists had found, or actually had *not* found: ricin. And how much of the true position had been communicated onwards to the police and thence the politicians – or not.

In fact, all the testing on the samples from the Wood Green flat was done by 8 January 2003. The most that could ever have been said was that there was a very weak positive result for manufactured ricin, from a presumptive test carried out on a mortar and pestle. A presumptive test, as already described in relation to explosive traces (see Chapter 17), merely gives rise to the possibility of ricin among an infinite number of other substances, some of which have not even been identified. Dr 'A', who was the lead scientist, and a number of others with whom he worked, had arrived at the collective conclusion that the traces could not be attributed to ricin and that the result was to be regarded as negative, not positive. For the purposes of any investigator at the scene, it would still be necessary to take the utmost precaution for obvious health-and-safety reasons in case there were any poisonous traces. None of this had been revealed to the public before the trial, by which time of course British troops were well entrenched in Iraq.

I canvassed some of these points with witness 'H':

Q: There is a reason behind all of this, which you will appreciate, and I will put it to you so it is clear: unless you act responsibly and provide accurate information, other people will be misled themselves and mislead other people, an investigation could be skewed. All sorts of things can happen, can they not, if you do not provide the right information?

A: I wasn't aware of that at the time.

Q: Come along. Operations Manager not aware of that? Unless you provide the right accurate information—[*witness 'H' interrupts*]

A: I stand by my original comments that the overriding, erm, point of view from my point of view was the safety of the teams and people on the ground.

Q: No one takes issue with that for one moment. All you had to do – this is the key question, I suggest – all you had to do on the 7th, 8th or 9th was to communicate to somebody at SO13 [the anti-terrorist squad at New Scotland Yard]: 'Look here, the scientists think it's negative, that's their decision – no ricin detected, however for safety reasons we can't exclude it altogether.' You certainly should not go around telling the public that traces of ricin have been found … In other words, you tell the police the true position as you saw it. What is wrong with that?

A: Again, it . . . it didn't happen.

Q: Yes. What is wrong with it? Anything?

A: Well, I think we want to stress the fact that there was a . . . some doubt over the Elisa test [a scientific process relating to the detection of ricin].

Q: Did you tell them that on the 7th?

A: No.

Q: You see, what happened here, and this is what an officer at SO13 is claiming, is that they had no idea there was a problem with a positive result as communicated by you on the 6th until well into March, do you follow?

A: Correct.

Q: They had been misled, had they not?

A: I wouldn't say misled.

[The cross-examination continued in the same vein for many minutes . . .]

Q: Just concentrate, if you would not mind, on the mortar and pestle and traces of the manufactured ricin. You did not have a positive for ricin, did you?

A: It was reported as a positive.

Q: No. Sorry. 'Very weak positive for possible ricin amongst a number of substances.' That is actually the true situation, is it not? Very weak positive?

A: It was a weak positive. You're right, yes.

Q: 'For possible ricin, but it could be another substance.' You have no explanation, it would appear, for why you did not put that in the fax, so the police knew the true position.

A: I have no idea . . . idea why.

Q: You have no idea why you put that. Unless you wanted them to believe you had found manufactured ricin, did you?

A: No. I reported it as I . . . as I truthfully saw the situation.

Q: Did you?

A: Yes.

Q: One of the problems about all of this is that, in the end, there is a risk the public are going to be misled; the government are going to be misled. You do follow that, do you not?

A: Yes. [continues]

Q: Have you always worked in government service?

A: Correct.

Q: Linked to scientists and their investigations?

A: Scientific work, yes.

Q: So it would be fair to say, you would recognise perhaps even more than the scientists themselves, just how important it is, lest anyone is misled, for complete and accurate reporting of what is going on; do you agree?

A: Yes.

Q: But not only do you *not* report the full picture on the evening of the 6th, you never do until a week before 20 March. Do you agree?

A: Yes. [continues]

Q: You have no explanation for not even doing that, have you?

A: No. [continues]

Q: By the 8th, of course, you will have realised, and I'm not going through all the press cuttings – I think you obviously read the press. Do you?

A: Mm . . . hmm.

Q: You may not believe what they say of course, but in the press, on television, radio and all the rest of it, this story was top of the agenda, was it not?

A: I think it made the headlines, certainly.

Q: It certainly made the headlines. The way the story was often led into was: 'Traces of ricin found at an address in Wood Green.' That was the strapline, was it not?

A: Yes.

Q: You must have thought to yourself: 'Wait a minute, before this goes public, I thought, first it was confidential with the police and second, it's not right. I'm not going to let this go on.'

A: I certainly was surprised. Erm . . . yes, the first, confidential . . . I was surprised that it actually made the headlines.

Q: Not only that it made the headlines, but that it was wrong?

A: Wrong in regard to . . . ?

Q: They had not found it. It had not been confirmed. Possibly there was ricin, although Dr 'A' was saying it was a negative. Even on your version of all this, it just had not been excluded. It was not that they had found traces of manufactured ricin. It was just a possibility that could not be excluded. An entirely different spin was being put forward to the public, do you follow?

A: Yes.

Q: Right. Did you make the slightest effort to ring up SO13 or the press office at New Scotland Yard and say: 'What on earth is going on here?'

A: No. I didn't. [*continues in the same vein . . .*]

It is difficult to convey on paper the atmosphere in court during this cross-examination. I did not know, any more than anyone else, what the witness was going to say about the topics I covered, so you could hear a pin drop as anticipation mounted.

The trial hearings lasted almost a year, and the team of defence barristers was unusual for their range of different styles and talents: Michel Massih, QC, a flamboyant and passionate Palestinian; my junior Matthew Ryder, an assiduous lateral thinker; Marguerite Russell, forthright and assertive; Toby Hedworth, QC, calm, collected and effective; Danny Friedman, dynamo and technical wizard; the perceptive intellect of Ben Emmerson QC; combined with the exceptional diligence of a further three juniors. We all knew each other well and were able to work together easily, and when engaged in such a long trial this can make all the difference.

In April 2005 all the defendants save one were acquitted. Sihali was free, but still awaiting the outcome of an immigration application.

On 13 April 2005 Jon Silverman, legal-affairs analyst for the BBC, wrote:

This case . . . is notable for the way in which criminal investigations are shamelessly exploited for political purposes by governments in the UK and the United States, whether to justify the invasion of Iraq or the introduction of new legislation to restrict civil liberties. A key unexplained issue is why the Porton Down laboratory which analysed the material and equipment seized from a flat in Wood Green said that the residue of ricin had been found when it had not.[12]

The result of the trial was unacceptable to both prosecutorial and government authorities. So much so that I and many others at the Bar were concerned that the government would use this as an excuse to promote *non-jury* trials for terrorist-related cases. Sihali was rearrested four months later and returned to Belmarsh Prison in east London, where he had spent nearly two years awaiting his trial in the first place. The notice of reasons served upon him at the time of his re-arrest disclosed the same materials upon which he had been acquitted by the jury.

Uniquely, a number of jurors decided that they would voice their outrage publicly. What had been the point of them sweating over the niceties of evidence if the government was going to circumvent all that and achieve the same object without a trial?

In an interview in the *Observer*[13] one juror said that he was shocked when a number of the men they had freed after a seven-month trial were re-arrested: 'I was dumbfounded . . . During the trial there were clearly different degrees of evidence against different defendants. But in a couple of cases, the evidence was so flimsy you couldn't see where the arrest came from in the first place. To re-arrest them seemed totally unreasonable.' A female juror added that the trial revealed failures by the authorities: '[There was] poor intelligence, police having misinformation and not really understanding the background, the government willing something along because of the impending war and it gathered its own momentum . . . Now they are trying to justify why the arrests happened.'

One of the ricin jurors, speaking anonymously, told BBC's *Panorama*:[14] 'Before the trial I had a lot of faith in the authorities to be making the right decisions on my behalf . . . Having been through this trial I'm very sceptical now as to the real reasons why this new legislation is being pushed through.' A second added: 'I think they are probably a knee-jerk reaction to the recent terrorist incidents in London ... It's a classic example of the government's need to be seeming to do something to quell comment in the nation at large.' A third said that measures introduced in response to the 7 July bombings were 'draconian, ill-considered' and 'hastily put together'.

The jurors' public pronouncements were entirely justified and extraordinarily courageous. Of course jurors are not permitted to reveal the discussions they have in the jury room, but these jurors were not transgressing that rule: they were making a timely and powerful point about the rule of law. Why have a system for determining criminal liability which involves time, expense and the deliberation of jurors if, at the end of it all, a government can merely side-step the whole process or ignore the result by locking up the same innocent people without trial?

Physical torture is bad, but I think the worst kind of torture is psychological: where you imprison somebody and throw away the key, which is basically what the government was doing with foreign detainees in Belmarsh. No charge; no trial; no information about the real basis for the detention; representation by special counsel in secret hearings without the detainee. But it wasn't just Belmarsh – the government had turned its back on the rule of international law as well. (For example, the treatment of British resident Binyam Mohamed, a Guantanamo detainee, finally released in February 2009.)

What came as a complete surprise to me was that the ricin jurors did not stop at their expression of disgust, but wanted to help Sihali get out of Belmarsh and resolve his immigration problem. I managed to secure Sihali's release, but it was under the very strict and onerous conditions of a Control Order regime. This is equivalent to twenty-four-hour house arrest, where you can barely breathe without letting the authorities know what you are doing. Eventually there was a Special Immigration Appeals Commission hearing to decide whether the basis for his re-arrest – suspected terrorism – was justified, and fortunately they found that it was not. I was even more surprised when the jurors turned up to this hearing. This was unprecedented and a remarkable display of support by fellow citizens. It was then that I discovered that my Porton Down cross-examination had for them been a turning point during the trial, which changed their attitudes to government policy and pronouncements.

As for Sihali, finally cleared of the terrorism tag, in early 2009 he was still waiting to hear from the Home Office about his application for asylum. Still living in fear, he is convinced that deportation back to Algeria would mean inevitable torture.

The steadfastness and fortitude of these jurors form part of a long tradition of English juries who have held out against the state, and I believe this history should form part of the school curriculum.

The plight of two Quakers, William Penn and his son William Mead, is a case in point.[15] In 1670 they were charged with sedition and unlawful assembly for preaching in contravention of iniquitous laws aimed at suppressing Nonconformism. Penn encouraged the jury at the Old Bailey: 'You are Englishmen. Mind your privilege. Give not away your right!' Edward Bushell, the foreman, replied: 'Nor will we ever do it!', and the jury refused to convict the two despite the exhortations and threats of the judge. The threats were very real: the jurors were locked up for two nights, starved and, worst of all, denied tobacco, but they still held out, were fined by the judge for failing to convict and held in Newgate Prison until they paid up. Led by Bushell, four refused and remained in prison for seven months. There was an appeal[16] to the Lord Chief Justice Vaughan, who decided they should be released, proclaiming the right of juries to give their verdict by their conscience, irrespective of the judge's directions, and there is a plaque commemorating this jury's resilience on the ground floor of the Old Bailey. In appropriate trials I encouraged jurors I was addressing to go and look at it, and take strength from it. William Penn was later to become the founder of the state of Pennsylvania in the USA.

Since then there have been many other notable conscientious juries which have rejected draconian prosecutions, especially in some capital-punishment cases.

In a series of cases in the 1970s in which I was involved – brought under the Incitement to Disaffection Act, when peace activists were trying to persuade soldiers not to fight in Northern Ireland – juries refused to convict, while another high-profile case was that of

Clive Ponting in 1985: the civil servant was charged with breaking the 1911 Official Secrets Act after leaking two documents about the sinking of the Argentine ship, the *General Belgrano*, during the Falklands war. Ministers had misled the public into thinking the ship was threatening British lives, when in fact it was sailing away from the battle zone when it was attacked. Although the judge directed the jurors to convict, they ignored him and Ponting was acquitted.

In 1989 Michael Randle and Pat Pottle published a book[17] in which they confessed to their part in helping the double agent George Blake escape in 1966 from Wormwood Scrubs, where he was serving a forty-two-year sentence for espionage. Yet again, despite the judge's efforts, the jury disregarded his direction and acquitted.

There are a number of situations where the conscientious discretion and judgment of the jury will be essential to defend not only the interests of justice, but also the very vitality of our democracy: where the law itself is pernicious or oppressive; where its application by means of the process of prosecution and investigation is unfair and inhuman; where the role of the jury is subverted by overweening judicial authority.

E. P. Thompson, the celebrated historian, summed up the underlying principle of the jury system thus:

> The English common law rests upon a bargain between the law and the people. The jury box is where the people come into the court: the judge watches them and the jury watches back. A jury is the place where the bargain is struck. The jury attend in judgment, not only upon the accused but also upon the justice and humanity of the law.[18]

TAKING STOCK

Jean Charles de Menezes

He did not jump the ticket barrier; he was not wearing a bulky jacket; he did not fail to obey a command; he did not try to escape; he was not an illegal immigrant; his behaviour could not be attributed to cocaine; but, principally, he was not a terrorist. He was an innocent Brazilian electrician, trying to make his way in the world, late for work. He had a warm regard for the generosity of the British people, and above all there was abundant evidence that he had a genuine respect for the British police – until, that is, he was shot dead by two of them at point-blank range with seven hollow-tipped bullets, causing maximum internal head injuries.

His name was Jean Charles de Menezes. He was twenty-seven. This information was contained on identification documents in his pockets. They were available in a wallet that had been removed from his body within half an hour of the shooting and placed on a seat next to his body in the Underground train carriage.

It took over three years to dispel the myths surrounding this case which had been perpetrated in the media, some of them by the police themselves. On the day of the shooting Sir Ian Blair, the Metropolitan Police Commissioner, announced to the world in a press conference that an unnamed man had been shot during a terrorist-related investigation because he had failed to obey a challenge by police.

Jean Charles had been brought up just outside the small town of Gonzaga in a remote mountainous area of Brazil. He had always displayed an adventurous spirit, but unlike many of his contemporaries who migrated to the USA to seek new opportunities, he preferred a vibrant, eclectic environment in London. He persuaded his first cousin Vivian Menezes Figueiredo to join him, and they left Brazil together in spring 2005, arriving in London on 23 April. They went to stay with another cousin, Patricia da Silva Armani, who was living in a flat in a small block at the end of a cul-de-sac in Scotia Road in Tulse Hill, south London.

Jean Charles took casual work until he found what he wanted, a job with his friend Gesio, doing all the electrical work on a property in north London. Vivian spent the evening of Wednesday 20 July 2005 with Jean, when he expressed great hope and happiness for the future. Although she didn't realise it, it was the last time she was to see him.

On Thursday 21 July, between 12.36 and 13.11, there were four attempted suicide bombings in London. Three were at Underground stations (the Oval, Warren Street and Shepherds Bush) and the fourth was on a bus on Hackney Road. A fifth device was recovered the next day on common ground at Little Wormwood Scrubs. No one was injured, unlike the suicide bombings in the capital two weeks earlier on 7 July, which also took place at three Underground stations (Aldgate, King's Cross and Edgware Road) and on a bus in Tavistock Square: fifty-six people were killed and 977 injured.

No one should underestimate the traumatic effect these terrible events had on everyone, especially the travelling public in London: without question a sense of fear and trepidation filled both mind and body. Unlike the Blitz and the Provisional IRA campaigns in the past, there had been no warnings. Unsuspecting innocent citizens had been blown to pieces. No one was untouched by events. On the morning of 7 July I had travelled by public transport to Gatwick airport in order to catch a flight to Holland, where I was doing a case at The Hague. All my children (now adult) lived and worked in London and all used public transport to get around; Jonathan, Anna, Leo and Kieran would have been going to work in Oxford Circus, Canary Wharf, Holborn and Clerkenwell; Freddy was using the overground train to reach his school.

When I arrived at the house where I was staying in The Hague the television news had been on continuously for hours. In a sense, the further away you are from events like these, the worse it is. Telephone lines are blocked, mobile phones are not being answered, and it takes hours of anxious enquiry and waiting until the final picture emerges. During that time you can be sure of nothing; you can't assume anything. In Holland the time was one hour in advance of London, and the various commitments I had that day in a war-crimes trial had to be honoured. I have often been handed dramatic messages during cross-examination and speeches (births, deaths and marriages among them), but this was on quite a different scale, and I remember being totally distracted all day.

Thankfully, the family was safe, and like the rest of London showed customary resilience. Neither they nor the injured and their families were to be deterred from the monumental task of piecing their lives back together and continuing their daily business, even though it would never be quite the same again, and within hours people were braving the public-transport system.

Vivian, Patricia and Jean Charles were no different. Hesitant but determined, they carried on, with Jean Charles telling Vivian that 'We need to pray and hope for the best.'

On 22 July, the morning after the failed bombings, Vivian, who was working as a cleaner in Surbiton, left her block of flats before Jean Charles, walking down the stairs and out of the communal front door. The flat above hers in the same block – number 21 – was being used by two people, Abdi Omar and Hussain Osman. It was empty that day, but neither this nor the identity of the occupants was known to Vivian.

She crossed the end of the cul-de-sac, close to a parked black Nissan Primera (P579 UBB), which had been insured by Omar but was registered to another address in west London, 61A Portnall Road, near the Harrow Road. As she walked the short distance further along Scotia Road she was oblivious to an innocuous, unmarked van parked up by a lamp post on the opposite side. Vivian was being filmed. Inside the van was a surveillance officer who, for reasons of security, was only ever known by the pseudonyms Frank, Tango 10 or call-sign 50. He was not a policeman, but a soldier on attachment to an undercover Special Branch (SO12) team working under the code colour Red. The van was stationary and he had been on his own in this position since about 6.30 that morning: his brief was to keep a lookout for anyone coming out of number 21, especially anyone resembling either Omar (codenamed Regal Wave) or Osman (codenamed Nettle Tip). They were both linked to the same block as Vivian, and were considered by senior command officers to bear a strong likeness to CCTV images of the bombers at Warren Street and Shepherds Bush stations the day before.

It was immediately obvious to anyone on the ground – although not for some hours, it appears, to those back in the control room at New Scotland Yard – that Frank could not see the front door of flat number 21. All he could therefore do was assess whether someone coming from the main door of the nine-flat block matched the images he had of the two suspects. All the surveillance officers thought the one of Osman was particularly poor, while the command officers thought the opposite. It had been copied from a gym-membership card and showed Osman's head and shoulders only. The surveillance officers had had only a short time to familiarise themselves with the image; not all of them even took a copy with them. The reason? Underlying SO12 policy was a worry that highly trained and experienced officers might lose or drop the photograph and compromise the whole operation.

Five or six occupants left the block that morning between 7.45 and 8.30 and, like Vivian, all of them could easily be excluded because of their sex, age or colour.

At 9.33 a.m. Jean Charles emerged. It was a fine and dry summer's day with clear visibility. He was wearing a denim jacket, jeans and a dark T-shirt. He wasn't carrying anything. No bag. No rucksack. He walked calmly by the van on the opposite side. He was not filmed.

Frank, who by now had been on duty for over three hours, had been caught short and was relieving himself in a bottle. The camera was not running continuously in order to conserve both film and battery. He only had one hand free, but he couldn't use this to switch on the camera because he was having to use a handheld airwave radio to transmit messages. This in turn was because the main Cougar headset radio system had broken down and could only receive messages. If this were not so serious, you might imagine it had been lifted straight out of a scene from the *Keystone Cops*.

Initially Frank thought Jean Charles was a white European, recorded in amorphous police-speak as 'IC1 [Identity Code One], male'. On that basis he concluded that this man could be ignored like the others – until, however, Jean Charles passed close to the van. At this point Frank had second thoughts and uttered the fatal words: 'Worth somebody else having a look.'

By this time there were two squads of undercover officers in the area: the original Red team and now the Grey team, numbering approximately twenty in all. None of them had placed themselves in positions where they could obtain anything more than a fleeting glimpse during Jean Charles's six-minute walk to the nearest number 2 bus stop on Tulse Hill, and the majority did not see Jean Charles at all during this phase. There were, however, six surveillance officers, in cars and on foot, in the short stretch of Upper Tulse Hill and the corner of Tulse Hill where the bus stop was situated. They could not positively discount Jean Charles, nor could they positively identify him as a suspect. For the rest of his journey (only half an hour) that is how it remained. No surveillance officer reported to control that he *was*, or *was not*, the suspect Nettle Tip.

Four of the six officers were armed. In this they were not alone. Unbeknown to them and to Jean Charles, this same short stretch of road contained at least another six armed officers in unmarked cars, part of the specialist firearms unit CO19. Three hours late (not their fault), they had come as back-up for the surveillance teams should an armed intervention be required, and the first two cars had arrived minutes before Jean Charles walked past on the pavement opposite the Territorial Army Centre they were intending to use as a forward holding base.

This was a critical moment in the whole operation. The one thing missing was an order to stop Jean Charles boarding the public-transport system: pretty important if he had been a suicide bomber, given what had happened over the previous two weeks.

Jean Charles got on the number 2 bus bound for Brixton. Ivor (codename), a surveillance officer, did likewise. They both sat downstairs and the CCTV cameras on the bus recorded clips of Jean Charles behaving in a perfectly normal way. No bulky clothing; nothing untoward; still not carrying anything.

About five minutes later (9.45 a.m.) the bus had reached Brixton, where Jean Charles got off, intending to continue his journey northwards by Tube. Partly because of the previous day's events the station was closed, so he contacted his employer by mobile phone and reboarded the same number 2 bus. Ivor, who had followed him off the bus, sensibly decided not to draw attention by getting back on with Jean Charles.

The bus was now heading towards Stockwell Underground station, and Jean Charles hoped this one would not be closed. He sat upstairs on the top deck. Along the route another officer called Laurence (codename) took over 'the follow' on the bus. Nothing occurred until Jean Charles got up and started down the stairs because he saw that the Tube station was open. Laurence immediately transmitted this information.

While before this the police may not have realised exactly where Jean Charles would get off, they certainly knew now. In fact the day before some of the bombers had entered the Underground system at Stockwell. So once again, if he were a suicide bomber, it was imperative that he should be stopped before he entered the station, or at the very latest before he went down the escalators to the platforms. What was missing was an effective order to do so.

As Jean Charles left the bus near the National Westminster bank, some armed surveillance officers were already on the pavement before him. One of them was Ivor and he was alert to the fact that surveillance is sometimes best kept covert by staying ahead of the target. Anticipating, rightly, that Jean's destination was the Underground station, he went in first and positioned himself in the doorway of a chemist shop on the right-hand side as you enter. The time was now around 10 a.m., and the walk from the bus stop to the station takes no more than two or three minutes.

Yet again, the surveillance officers were unaware that their armed back-up had also either just arrived at the junction outside the station or were in a line of traffic just beyond the traffic lights on Stockwell Road, opposite the station entrance. The lead car in the line contained one of the officers (C2), who eventually shot Jean Charles on the train, and another contained a team leader codenamed Ralph. Unbeknown to him and to Ivor, there was yet another car with armed CO19 officers, one of whom was codenamed C12, who also shot Jean Charles. This car had taken an entirely different route from the main convoy and almost certainly was the first CO19 vehicle to reach the junction, having driven straight up Clapham Road. There were therefore a minimum of nine armed officers – three surveillance and six specialist firearms – available to effect an intervention. In contrast to what the surveillance officers claim they had reported, the firearms officers firmly believed by this point that they had heard over the radio Jean Charles being positively identified with phrases like 'It's him' or 'It's definitely him' or 'It's our man', and naturally they thought this meant he was a suicide bomber from the day before. If these words were spoken, it has never been established who said them.

Ivor watched Jean Charles at close quarters as he passed by on the station concourse to collect a *Metro* newspaper from the stand nearby, and assessed, rightly, that he himself was in a prime position to detain the subject. There was another armed surveillance officer a few feet away to help him, and Ivor offered by radio to do so. He waited and waited as precious seconds ticked away. What was missing, for the third time, was an effective order.

All Jean Charles's movements from the moment he left the bus, then walked along the pavement and through the station concourse to the escalators were monitored on a variety of CCTV cameras. His behaviour was perfectly normal.

No effective order was given until Jean Charles was already on the escalator descending deep into the station. It was too late. His fate (although not according to C12 and C2) was already sealed.

It was an armed officer who jumped over the ticket barrier and was mistaken for a terrorist. C12 and C2 rushed down the escalator, weapons loaded and ready to fire. They could no longer be contacted because none of their radios worked underground. They were in plain clothes, not readily identifiable as police officers, and moved swiftly along the platform, maintaining their covert approach by keeping their guns out of sight until they reached the open doors of the carriage.

Ivor was already on the train, oblivious to their impending arrival. He had assumed that he should continue to follow the target until such time as his identity could either be confirmed as a suspect or discounted. For example, if Jean Charles used a cash machine or a mobile phone with traceable numbers, this might help; but Ivor thought this could take some considerable time and in the end might not happen at all. Ivor had sat down in the same row of seats as Jean Charles, facing the platform, but a few places to his left.

Ivor recognised that the men in civilian clothing were from CO19 and assumed, this time wrongly, that they must know something he didn't – namely that the target was in fact a suicide bomber about to detonate a bomb. He got up and crossed the carriage in front of Jean Charles to the doors of the train, stuck his foot out to prevent them closing and the train from leaving, and pointed directly at Jean Charles, shouting, 'That's him!' – which merely reinforced what the firearms officers had in mind. None of them had actually seen Jean Charles at any stage during the pursuit.

Ivor turned to face Jean Charles who was a matter of only a few feet away from him and who, almost certainly in response to being pointed at, had got up from his seat. Ivor grabbed him in a bear hug, restraining both his arms and pinning him back in the seat. It took no more than five to ten seconds for the firearms officers to enter the carriage, lean over Ivor and discharge their weapons nine times.

Another firearms officer who approached the scene walking down the inside of the carriage mistook Ivor for the suspect. Ivor was dressed in similar denim clothing to Jean Charles, and had a similar olive complexion. In addition he had a rucksack, which he placed on the floor by the doors to the train. Ivor was dragged away and pinned to the carriage floor with a gun to his head. Once subdued, he was bundled off the train onto the platform and put up against the wall, until he was able to confirm his identity as an undercover police officer.

The accounts of what happened in the carriage, especially by C12 and C2, were seriously at odds with those of the civilian witnesses who were sitting nearby. Crucially, C12 claimed that as he entered the carriage he shouted 'Armed police!', raised his right arm to shoulder level and pointed his handgun straight at the face of Jean Charles. In spite of this, they both asserted that Jean Charles advanced threateningly towards them and, using the same terminology in their original statements, both officers thought Jean Charles's jacket was 'bulky' – a feature they are trained to consider might conceal a bomb. When, at the subsequent inquest, I confronted them with the CCTV photographic evidence and with the jacket itself, they had to concede that they were wrong.

No civilian witness saw the sequence that the officers described, and they were all adamant that there was no shout of 'Armed police!' Interestingly, no other firearms or surveillance officer saw such a sequence of events with C12's gun out in front at arm's length, although some claimed to have heard the words 'Armed police' from the direction of the platform. C2, who was following C12 onto the train, did not see or hear what C12 said or did at that point.

Allowances must be made for selective vision, perceptual distortion, intermittent recollection and the pressure of the occasion. The divergence, however, with the passengers is too great to be explained in this way.

There were between seventeen and nineteen passengers in the same carriage as Jean Charles, most of whom had got on the train a few stops before Stockwell. A number, like him, were running late and were wary about using the Tube. Some scrutinised who got on, what they looked like, what they were carrying and so forth – all very natural reactions at a time of tangible tension. It seemed that the train had been stuck in the station for an abnormally long time. The nervous and impatient disembarked to try a different route. Others remained and tried to preoccupy themselves with books and magazines. An unfortunate few had ringside seats. What happened next was unimaginable carnage, almost as bad as the bombs themselves. Only one person was killed, but numerous others, their families and friends have had their lives marked for ever, just like those affected by the atrocities of 7 July.

Sitting right opposite Jean Charles, with their backs to the platform, were a young couple, Ralph Livock and Rachel Wilson. Mr Livock remembered three men with pistols and another with a weapon that looked like a rifle, and at the inquest was asked questions[1] by Nicholas Hilliard, QC, on behalf of the coroner:

Question, NICHOLAS HILLIARD: Did you have any idea who they were?
Answer, RALPH LIVOCK: Absolutely not. They had no identifying ... well, on the television you see people with caps or jackets. There was nothing like that. They looked like ... one of my initial thoughts was it was all a game and they were a group of lads who were just having a laugh, in a very bad taste laugh, but just having a game on the Tube because they were just dressed in jeans and

T-shirts, but with firearms.

Q. Did you hear anything said about police?

A. No, certainly not. And I remember that specifically, because one of the conversations that Rachel and I had afterwards was that immediately afterwards we had no idea whether these were police, whether they were terrorists, whether they were somebody else, we just . . . we had no idea.

Ms Wilson was asked similar questions:[2]

Question, NICHOLAS HILLIARD: Then several men have come on to the train, do I have that right?

Answer, RACHEL WILSON: Yes.

Q. Can you say how many?

A. Several, three, four, five, that sort of number.

Q. How were they dressed?

A. Casually, not in any uniform.

Q. Did you have any idea who they were?

A. None whatsoever.

Q. Was anything said at any time during the incident to give you a clue as to who they were?

A. No, and I know this because, similar to Ralph's statement, first I thought they were messing around, then I thought they were terrorists and it was only when I left the carriage and the . . . somebody moved me gently out of the way that I figured they must have been good guys, and apart from that I just didn't know who they were.

Q. Specifically, did you hear anybody shout 'Armed police'?

A. If I had heard that, I would have thought they were police, so no.

On the same side of the carriage as Jean Charles, a few seats to his left, sat Anna Dunwoodie, and when Ivor first got on the train he sat down immediately to her left. She was asked questions[3] by Jonathan Hough on behalf of the coroner:

Answer, ANNA DUNWOODIE: It's a really odd thing to try to describe, because my memory is that right in the carriage where we were actually we were all very still, I think maybe because it was so unexpected, and me and the people around me, my memory is that we all sat quite still and were quiet. Further away, where I guess people had more of a chance to react, I could feel that there were people getting out of their seats further along the carriage and again, you know, a sense of panic from the passengers. But I also felt that there was a sense of panic from the men in the doorway and a sense that maybe they weren't quite sure what was going to happen next or what they were going to do next and I found that very frightening.

Question, JONATHAN HOUGH: You say this in your statement: 'I thought that the other men outside the carriage were the man's accomplices [the man who pointed] but that he was the main threat.'

A. I did think that at the time, yes.

Q. When you first saw these various men, what did you think they were about?

A. I thought . . . I mean maybe what was frightening was that I didn't know what they were about . . . [*continues*]

Q. As you very fairly say, your memory is one of snapshots?

A. My memory is one of snapshots, that's true. I would like to say, though, that the thing about whether or not I heard 'police', I am very, very clear on because I was . . . I absolutely had no idea who they were and I was looking for a clue as to who they might be, and if anybody had said 'police', I would have latched on to that, I think.

The coroner, Sir Michael Wright, often interceded and asked his own questions of witnesses. He asked Anna Dunwoodie:

Question, SIR MICHAEL WRIGHT: What was it you saw or sensed that made you think that they [the police] were in a state of panic? I know it's a difficult question, so do your best.

Answer, ANNA DUNWOODIE: I think that . . . partly I think it was because the man who I now know as the surveillance officer [Ivor] really seemed to me to be frightened.

Q. Yes?

A. Or hyped up, maybe, if that's a way to describe it. And when he was calling the other men in, they seemed . . . you know when people are full of adrenaline and they move quickly and their movements are a bit jerky, and things just felt like they were a bit out of control, that's what it felt like. I think in a small place like a carriage, you pick up on that kind of thing quickly.

Later on Anna Dunwoodie was asked:

Q. You also say that you could see the expression on the man's face who actually had the gun pointed at his neck, that's Mr de Menezes; can you remember anything about that expression now? A. I remember that his eyes were closed and I remember that he had . . . you know, it's a hard thing to try to explain, but his eyes were closed and he looked almost calm, which again I hesitate to say that, but . . . I guess he had a gun pressed, and there wasn't very much he could do about it.[4]

From the moment I first heard about these tragic events I was eager to help in whatever way I could, as it seemed to me there were major issues of principle and organisation to address at all levels of the police. I have spent my working life in contact with the police, both in and out of court, and I have attended their conferences, seminars and meetings at Hendon, Bramshill and New Scotland Yard. I've done so in the firm belief that it is always possible to contribute towards transparency, accountability and respect for human rights.

Throughout the rest of 2005 there were a number of campaign and support meetings organised on behalf of the de Menezes family. I had strong feelings about how they were being treated – the delay, the misinformation and the lies – so I went along to a couple of them to see if I could lend a legal perspective. In particular I wished to pass on my experiences with other families, as President of the National Civil Rights Movement (NCRM), since there is always a risk that the hard lessons of the past are half-forgotten or wasted. Families in distress need to know what their options are, and most importantly which bland assurances dished out by the authorities need to be ignored.

As always, being instructed to represent the family was largely a matter of chance. They had engaged a firm of solicitors, Birnbergs, with whom I had worked closely on many occasions. There were three wise women in the firm who had matchless expertise: Harriet Wistrich, Marcia Stewart and Gareth Peirce. I became involved in 2006 shortly after the Director of Public Prosecutions (DPP) had decided that no individual officer would be prosecuted for a criminal offence, but that instead the Office of the Commissioner of the Metropolitan Police would stand trial in a notional sense for an offence in contravention of Health and Safety legislation. Another barrister, Henrietta Hill, a super-efficient fast thinker, was already on board for the family and was to be my junior.

Our first job was to challenge that decision. Usually the clients are based in the UK and can easily be consulted, but in this instance Jean Charles's mother Maria, his father Matosinhos and his brother Giovani were all in Brazil, and contact had to be made through a Portuguese interpreter, Agnes Nunes, who was proficient, empathetic and patient. She remained with the case throughout all its stages and without her, agreements, decisions and understanding would have been unattainable. Fortunately there were other members of the family – cousins and a close friend in London – who stayed on in the UK despite immigration and employment complications: Vivian, Patricia, Alessandro Pereira and Erionaldo da Silva. They were unstinting in their efforts to keep the flame of hope alight, which was not easy through the years of waiting, disappointment and disenchantment with a system of justice which rarely provided any satisfaction. Their quest was given strength every step of the way by two ardent campaigners, Yasmin Khan and Asad Rehman, who had put the family in touch with Birnbergs in the first place.

Like most relatives and friends of victims at an inquest, they had not been present when the death occurred, and their beliefs about what must have happened are born out of their intimate relationship with and understanding of the dead person. The clear and collective message being conveyed by the de Menezes family had two principal themes. First, Jean Charles's mother was convinced that if he had been challenged by armed police in a controlled manner soon after he had left home and before he mounted the number 2 bus, or even when he had left the bus outside Stockwell Underground station, he would have cooperated fully and still been alive. Second, she felt that Jean Charles would never have advanced threateningly towards armed police and that he had been shot mercilessly by firearms officers.

Challenging a decision not to prosecute any officer for murder or manslaughter is done by way of judicial review. You have to be able to demonstrate to the reviewing judges in the Divisional or Administrative Court that the decision is unreasonable, in the sense that the Director (DPP) has omitted to take into account something he should, or that he has taken into account something he shouldn't. This is termed the Wednesbury* Unreasonableness Test. Persuading the judges that *they* might have taken a different decision if they had been Director is not enough.

Another difficulty is that you may not have all the necessary evidential material. In this instance it was in the possession of the Director himself for the purposes of the Health and Safety prosecution, and it was with the Independent Police Complaints Commission (IPCC)[5] for the purposes of their original investigation. None of it had been made public, and the IPCC report was only made available to the family on a very restricted basis, with crucial parts of it redacted – that is, blanked out, usually with a black felt-tipped pen, so that the words cannot be read – to begin with. We did not have the statements of any of the civilian witnesses from the train; we did not have the prepared statements made by CO19 officers in conjunction with each other;[6] plus we knew that the shooters had refused to answer any questions when interviewed by the IPCC. The standard of proof required for murder or manslaughter, whether in an inquest or a criminal trial, is the same. It is very high, 'beyond reasonable doubt': a jury must be sure. Our submissions were rejected, although the force of the argument was acknowledged to be relevant to the Health and Safety prosecution, which was set down for October 2007. Meanwhile nothing could be said by the family in public because of the *sub judice* rule and the risk of prejudice to that trial.

We made strenuous attempts to get the inquest opened and under way, even though there was a trial in prospect, because the trial was expressly going to deal with a separate (albeit connected) issue – whether the health and safety of the public at large had been put at risk by the decisions and actions cumulatively taken by the police officers involved. There was no legal requirement to show that this

---

* This is not some midweek crisis, but the name of a case in which this was decided.

in particular had caused the death of Jean Charles. In due course the jury in the Health and Safety trial were specifically directed to exclude this aspect as a matter for the inquest.

The delay for the family in Brazil was unbearable, and for those in the UK intolerable. We were also concerned that there was no guarantee at the end of the trial that the inquest would necessarily be resumed. There were rumours that some Interested Persons[7] might oppose such resumption, on the basis that most of the factual matters had already been canvassed. Our attempts on this score also failed. We all had to wait until the end of the trial in November 2007 in the guarded hope that we would not face further disappointment.

During 2006 the two most senior officers involved in the case, Commanders John McDowell and Cressida Dick, were both promoted to the rank of Deputy Assistant Commissioner (DAC). You might have thought that consideration for a move of this kind could have been deferred until the end of the inquest. The family was not just dismayed, but unutterably shocked.

The relatives attended the trial of the Office of the Commissioner at the Old Bailey – sitting alongside a dock with no one in it, a somewhat bizarre and unreal occurrence. Many key witnesses were not called (for example, the shooters and the passengers), because of course they were not directly relevant to what was being litigated during the trial. Nor did Sir Ian Blair, the Commissioner, give evidence. A combination of nineteen different failures by different police officers on 22 July 2005 was alleged by the prosecution. They could be aggregated in a way which was not legally possible when examining the individual acts and omissions of particular officers, for example in relation to an allegation of manslaughter.

The Office of the Commissioner was convicted. It was not possible to tell from the verdict which of the nineteen failures the jury found proved to their satisfaction. How the Office felt about this we shall never know. What we do know is that it was fined, and effectively the public footed the bill. The person who filled the office continued to do so. He did not seem too perturbed, and he did not finally step down until two weeks before the end of the inquest in December 2008. The trial judge, Mr Justice Henriques, observed during his sentencing remarks that the Office of the Commissioner had made no concessions with regard to any of the nineteen allegations. What the family noted with dismay was that part of the defence at the trial had involved an attack upon Jean Charles, as if it were his own behaviour that had resulted in his death. A more muted form of this was to resurface during the inquest.

It is not difficult to imagine the distress and anguish suffered by the family through these tortuous months. By the beginning of 2008 it was agreed that there should be an inquest, but the place and date had not been fixed.

Southwark Coroner's Court in Tennis Street, Bermondsey, is quaint and friendly, but incommodious. It was really not built to accommodate more than one of everything: one coroner, one clerk, one lawyer, one member of the public and one member of the press – hardly enough room for the numbers anticipated in this case. There is a historic but silly rule (which it is intended will be changed in the Coroners Bill 2009) whereby inquests have to be heard within the jurisdiction of the coroner dealing with the body. Nowadays this is quite unnecessary, and it is about time that fully resourced court premises are available in all the major conurbations, financed by central government. The coroner's office and Southwark Council had an uphill struggle to find somewhere big enough and affordable, given that the council would have to find the money from its own budget.

Quite exceptionally, the most unusual and delightful venue was provided at the Oval cricket ground – but the inquest could not commence until South Africa, Sri Lanka and India had finished their business with England, which involved another unavoidable delay until the end of September. The main hearing room was in the John Major Suite: I don't know whether he minded, but it was thought politically correct to remove his portrait in order to maintain an atmosphere of impartiality. The corridors leading to the room displayed a series of sepia photographs and lithographs depicting the history of the ground from village cricket to commercial bonanza, one of the most fascinating of which was an image taken during the Second World War, when everything had been cleared in order to convert the ground into a prisoner-of-war camp.

Each group of lawyers had its own conference room, which during the cricket season would have been an expensive box from which to view the game, and at one end of the room was a pair of sliding glass doors, which led onto the terrace overlooking the pitch. The room we were allocated was quite high and had a panoramic view across south London, and I enjoyed arriving early to witness the September sun pouring in through the windows. Down below they had begun the laborious task of digging up the pitch in order to lay new turf for next season, which reminded me of some protesters I had represented once who did just the same – only they didn't replace the turf: they were campaigning for the release of George Davis, imprisoned for a robbery in north London. Even more of a distraction was a lone fox that appeared from the Pavilion end and performed a mighty fine run up to the wicket.

Preparing for a case of this size takes a massive amount of time and effort. As I'm not exactly computer-literate with everything contained within the slimline confines of a laptop, I can often be seen with a wheelbarrow-type contraption lugging supermarket cardboard boxes filled with old-fashioned ring-backed files, the ones that have a habit of breaking open of their own accord and releasing hundreds of pages indiscriminately onto the floor. A perennial problem. A close colleague, Tanoo Mylvaganam, suffered the misfortune of high winds on the imposing York central railway station, which blew her papers, like confetti, across the platform onto the track. Normal service could not be resumed until every sheet had been retrieved. Headline writers next day had a field day – BARRISTER'S BRIEFS HOLD UP TRAINS!

For the de Menezes inquest, the paperwork encompassed all the stuff amassed by the IPCC during its six-month investigation, extra materials brought about by the Health and Safety prosecution, and further documentation generated for the inquest itself. In total, I would estimate, about 22½ wheelbarrows' worth.

Reading all this material was far from straightforward because two-thirds of the witnesses were anonymous, yet there was no consistency about this. Sometimes they were referred to by their rank, sometimes by their role, sometimes by a letter or a combination of letters, or by a combination of letters and numbers, and sometimes by an arbitrary first name not their own. To make life even easier, departments within New Scotland Yard were also known by a combination of letters and numbers. For operational purposes when they came together to act as a group or unit – I expect you're getting the hang of it – they were all allocated different colours: red and grey for surveillance, black, orange and green for firearms. (In one of my earliest cases, before the introduction of screens, the security services were so protective of their witnesses that they proposed putting paper bags over heads with holes cut out for eyes, nose and mouth.)

On top of all this, in the bundles and bundles and pages and pages of documents to scrutinise, you suddenly turn the page and find that whole sections have been redacted for security reasons. Often this has been done in a hurry and not very professionally. Hold it up to the light and every letter's in sight. They should have used that much-advertised washing powder . . .

Once I have mastered the fundamental material, I then have to work out a strategy commensurate with the central tenets of the family's beliefs, and this is the most interesting stage for me. If the family are right, then using that premise I go back to the drawing board as if I were the senior officer in charge that day. As a matter of common sense, what should have happened? And then, could it have been accomplished? Finally, what prevented a different result? These are interrelated questions, and the answer to one also answers another. I am mindful to avoid the benefit of hindsight, and not to impose superhuman powers and perception on everyday human affairs.

The drawing board for me starts with the scene of the crime. As in the Jill Dando case, I need to re-examine the minutiae of what has been left behind by the perpetrator. Not rocket science, I admit. There are obvious shortcomings when you try to do this at a distance, and nearly three years down the line, but in this case it revealed some important neglected material.

The suicide bombers on 7 July had left their signature at the scene. At least one rucksack used on that occasion contained identification documents relating to the bomber. The police, aware of this on 21 July, tasked detectives to search the various rucksacks accompanying the unexploded bombs, but before they could do so each had to be made safe by bomb-disposal experts. The one at Shepherds Bush was troublesome and took longer to clear than the rest. By 2.15 in the early hours of 22 July a gym card had been discovered bearing the name Hussain Osman. The membership related to the South Bank Club in Wandsworth Road, and this was checked out in the middle of the night. It was a joint membership in two names with two cards, one relating to Osman and the other to Abdi Omar. Osman had joined some two years before. There was one address for the two cards: 21 Scotia Road.

All this information reached Commander McDowell at New Scotland Yard, the officer in overall charge, around 4 a.m. on the Friday. By 4.55 a.m. he had recorded and set his strategy – for this address to be controlled and contained by surveillance, with specialist armed back-up as soon as practicable. It was an urgent and sensible priority. What was neglected was whether there was any more information, particularly pictorial, that could assist in the description of the two men. How else could an effective manhunt be carried out?

I've always found it difficult to believe that there was an 'intelligence vacuum' surrounding the bombings in July 2005, as was asserted by New Scotland Yard. Either there was a lack of joined-up thinking about information gathered by different intelligence agencies, or those agencies had not been doing their job. Some of the victims of the bombings have already called for a full public inquiry into this, but there are criminal trials and inquests still ongoing.*

One trial has already taken place. In 2007 six men were convicted of conspiracy to murder on 21 July 2005, and one of them was Hussain Osman. Another was called Omar, but was *not* the one linked to 21 Scotia Road who was *Abdi* Omar. It was accepted that Abdi had no involvement with the attempted bombings. It is worth noting nevertheless that senior officers thought he bore a good likeness to the CCTV images from Warren Street; had he happened to emerge from Scotia Road that morning, he too would have been at risk of being shot.

In relation to the trial of the attempted bombers in 2007 I had for a short time represented a co-defendant named Adel Yahya, and I recalled some surprise evidence served by the prosecution, which disclosed Yahya with a number of others on a camping trip in Cumbria. It was suggested by the prosecution that this was a jihadist training camp. What caught my attention, and continued to do so in 2008, was that the trip was in May 2004, a year before

* See footnote to p. 224

the attempted bombing. The camp had been monitored closely by Special Branch (SO12), and had been filmed over a number of days. There were a large number of still photographs, something in the region of 400. Now Special Branch does not go to the bother of such an expensive expedition (codenamed Ragstone) on a whim or a fancy. There must have been some intelligence behind it all, the detail of which is still not known. A collection of photographs that big, showing people and vehicles, ought to have opened a veritable Pandora's box of potential associations. Beyond an initial flurry of interest, we were led to believe that it remained dormant until 22 July 2005, presumably housed in a Special Branch archive at New Scotland Yard.

I couldn't remember if Osman had attended the camp, so in the run-up to the inquest I telephoned one of the lawyers who had represented him at the trial, Jim O'Keeffe. He was extremely helpful, and luckily had kept a number of the relevant documents in store. He dispatched them immediately. Osman had indeed been at the camp. He featured prominently in a large number of photographs, many of which had been exhibited at his trial by the Metropolitan Police. Hit number one.

Number two was even more dramatic. Along with the photographs sent down by Jim O'Keeffe were others taken in quite a different situation. These were also exhibited at his trial, but where had they come from? To my astonishment they had been discovered in the rucksack found at Shepherds Bush.

This was completely new information to those of us representing the de Menezes family. The detailed investigation by the IPCC had not uncovered it; preparations by the prosecution in the Health and Safety trial had not done so; nor had investigations carried out on behalf of the coroner. The police had assembled five teams of barristers for the inquest, to represent the Commissioner, the Command team, the shooters, the remainder of the firearms officers and all the surveillance officers. All manner of visual aids were provided by New Scotland Yard, most tellingly schedules relating to the bombings on the 7th, the attempted bombings on the 21st, the suicide bombers, their arrests and the outcome of their trials. Funny how no one at the Yard spotted the omission of any reference to these photographs for the purposes of the inquest.

An hour or so after the gym card had been found, the same detective who had continued to examine the contents of the rucksack found an envelope in a side pocket containing torn-up documents, and some of these were photographs. He diligently pieced them together, and discovered that they were wedding portraits of a man and a woman: he had no doubt that the man was Osman. He photographed the reconstruction in order to preserve the originals for other forensic examination and, having completed this, telephoned his superior, the detective in charge of this aspect, Superintendent MacBrayne, and informed him of the results of his handiwork.

Almost at the same time as this information was coming through, MacBrayne and another senior officer, Detective Chief Inspector Patrick Mellody, were having a long and intense meeting with Commander McDowell. Not a word was uttered about the additional rucksack photographs. MacBrayne had taken it upon himself – without ever seeing the original, reconstituted photographs or a photographic copy – to decide that they would be of no use to the manhunt. They did not bear a name or a date and he was concerned to preserve any fingerprints. At the inquest I reminded him that potential fingerprints would only apply to the original photographs, and anyway the gym-card photograph being relied upon was likely to be at least two years old. None of this explains why he didn't mention the photographs to anyone between 4.30 and 9.30 a.m., even though he had attended numerous meetings.

But these were not the only photographs neglected during these early meetings, despite the presence of DCI Mellody, an extremely experienced and senior member of Special Branch, the department responsible for Operation Ragstone. Pretty well everything else about the operation, except the photographs, was discussed. Commander McDowell agreed during my subsequent questioning that he would have expected there to be photographs on an operation of this kind.

In fact the 400-odd photographs from the camp depicted approximately fifteen Asian males in combat clothing. The black Nissan Primera (P579 UBB) parked near 21 Scotia Road was in Cumbria, as were a number of other vehicles, among them a blue VW Golf (L199 FPA) registered to Yeshiembet Girma at another address in Stockwell. This was the woman in the wedding photographs. By placing the photographs in the order in which they were taken, it was possible to discern who was most closely associated with the vehicle – the person who could be seen walking towards it, standing next to it and sitting in it. That man was Hussain Osman.

Oh, say the police, but we had not made that connection by 21 July. We go to the trouble of taking all these photographs, but we don't go to the trouble of following them up in that way. Too much an invasion of privacy, too disproportionate. In that case, it is difficult to imagine how they would describe the original excursion by Special Branch. And by the way, what about the information coming from the Stockwell mosque?

When Detective Superintendent MacBrayne came to give evidence at the inquest, I asked to see his original notes, made in two red hardbacked daybooks on the morning of 22 July in relation to the various meetings he had attended with Commander McDowell. They had not been examined before. I spotted some important words written alongside information about Yeshiembet Girma: 'wife of Osman'. These entries were preparatory to a meeting at 7 a.m. If they knew this then, it would not have taken long for the intelligence unit, situated right next door to the control room at Scotland Yard, to detect that the man standing next to the car registered in her name in the Ragstone photographs compared favourably with the images from the rucksack. This in turn would have provided the surveillance officers with a much better range of material, particularly as it showed Osman full stature, giving a rough estimate of his build and height.

Among the pre-inquest materials was a DVD of a television documentary[8] presented by the well-known investigative journalist Peter Taylor (who had done similar work in relation to Bloody Sunday). I saw the programme when it was first transmitted and remembered it mainly for footage taken in Israel, illustrating different methods of dealing with suicide bombers, and Henrietta and I both thought we should watch it again. This time, of course, we paid far greater attention to detail. Near the beginning was an observation (almost an aside), in which Peter Taylor mentioned that Osman had been known for his connection with a mosque in south London. Further research by Harriet, my solicitor, showed that this topic had also been mentioned on Channel 4 News. It appears that over the two years preceding July 2005 Osman had been attending a mosque in Stockwell, and had made his presence felt in unwanted ways. He was known there under his own and another name. This had been reported by one of those running the mosque to the Borough Commander in Brixton, and this person had also contacted a unit within Special Branch at New Scotland Yard entitled Muslim Liaison. The police claimed that they only knew about the alternative name, and not about the name of Osman. Exactly what information the police have in their files about this has not been revealed.

There was yet another line of enquiry that could have borne fruit before the fatal shooting, and which could have helped to exclude Jean Charles. Osman had a driving licence bearing his photograph, but this was not obtained from the DVLA in Swansea until midday on 22 July. The initial explanation for this was that it could only be accessed during office hours and it would take some time. I think we are all aware that the slightest traffic transgression is tracked down promptly these days. Data is centralised and computerised, and I found it difficult to accept that the emergency services – properly authorised – could not get to it within an hour or so at the most. A little later in the inquest, after some checking had been done, it was conceded that in July 2005 there was a hotline for police out of office hours, which would have produced the necessary goods within an hour and a half.

So far, by my reckoning, we've reached double figures in relation to photographic materials of Osman available before 9.33 a.m. on 22 July. Without any of this, small wonder that surveillance was hindered. In the control room at New Scotland Yard the poor identification process was compounded by confusion and bad communication, as Jean Charles went from being a 'possible' suspect to 'definitely not' the suspect, back to a 'possibility' and then a 'certainty'. This variation occurred over a period of roughly seventeen minutes.

Identification is notoriously difficult and fraught with subjective judgement. You can fail to recognise someone you know, or go up to someone you don't know thinking it is someone you do. Judges in criminal trials are obliged to issue a caution to juries where identification is an issue, especially fleeting-glance cases, with detailed directions about the risks of misidentification. Lawyers call this the 'Turnbull'* direction.

With all these qualifications in mind, what was required that morning was someone in command to think through how it was going to be possible to implement Commander McDowell's strategy set at 4.55 a.m. It couldn't be formulated in a vacuum, or left to float somewhere in the ether, and an obvious candidate to do so was McDowell himself.[9] I reminded him of his obligations as Gold Commander, as outlined in the Association of Chief Police Officers' Manual, to oversee and review implementation.

First, the overriding concern and urgency for London was to ensure, so far as was humanly possible, that no potential suicide bomber would be allowed onto any form of public transport.

Second, Scotia Road was linked to two suspects and the Nissan parked outside. It could be a bomb factory, a safe house, a store or even a decoy. While of course a suspect might not return to what the police call a 'footprint' address, knowing he'd left his details in the rucksack, this cannot be safely assumed, and anyway there might be others associated with him still there. All things considered, it was the best lead at the time, whatever else might come on stream later.

Combining these two points, therefore, what had to be calculated was how much time and space were needed to stop any potential bomber from 21 Scotia Road before they reached the bus.

To make these calculations you need to have the base data: the geographical layout, the streets, the premises, the points of ingress and egress, and the nearest public transport. These strategic parameters determine what has to be done tactically to achieve the desired objective, yet this was not something readily appreciated by some of the police witnesses I questioned at the inquest.

Nearly all the relevant data could have been ascertained within a matter of minutes. If someone had referenced a detailed map, of the type commonly used by the police, the answers were there, but no one did. It would have shown that number 21 is not a discrete property with a visible front door – something which took the control room some two hours to appreciate; it would also have revealed that Scotia Road is a cul-de-sac with only one exit for both

---

* Not an expression used by toreadors, just the name of another case.

cars and pedestrians, and that once through this 'pinch point' you can only turn left or right, and that the closest bus stops are right there, on opposite sides of the road. Walking that distance could be estimated at two to three minutes, with another three to four minutes to the next nearest bus stop – the one used by Jean Charles.

No one in the control room seems to have troubled themselves with these calculations: far too busy with manuals, meetings and matters of greater moment. It's always someone else's responsibility to tiddle about with the nuts and bolts.

Someone who did concern himself with these nuts and bolts was Derek (codename), the Red surveillance team leader on the ground at Scotia Road, who was repeatedly alerting the control room to these points and wanted the nearest bus stop suspended or the route diverted to allow more time. Cressida Dick, the Designated Senior Officer (DSO)[10] appointed specifically for this part of the operation in case a critical shot was required, did not know where any of the bus stops were, let alone how long it would take someone to reach one.

Unless everybody, from top to bottom, realises the minimum window of opportunity for an intervention before public transport is reached, there is a risk that they will fail to tailor the role they are performing to the exigencies of the moment. It's unlikely you will achieve a positive identification within three to six minutes, and the best you're going to be able to do is make an obvious elimination. Trojan 84, one of the most impressive inquest witnesses, as well as an experienced and perceptive firearms tactical advisor, used the phrase: 'The stakes are high'.[11] Therefore, to pre-empt the possibility of a suicide bomber getting on a bus, all those not expressly eliminated (Jean Charles and one other) would need to be intercepted. Trojan 84, unlike Cressida Dick, took the view that this could have been done with the firearms resources that had arrived in the stretch of Upper Tulse Hill along which Jean Charles had walked – and Trojan 84, unlike Cressida Dick, was actually on the ground that day.

These are factors no one in command sat down and discussed, or communicated through briefings to others. We were constantly reminded by the senior officers about the pressures of the day, the fast-moving dynamic nature of the exercise and the uniqueness of confronting a failed suicide bomber. This is fair. But it is precisely these elements that police officers are trained to handle. Pressure, stress and split-second decision-making are the order of the day. And it's not as though there was any shortage of brainpower corralled around Cressida Dick. Besides the Gold Commander, McDowell, there were a minimum of eleven senior officers on hand: Dick herself had brought in a particular colleague to advise and challenge her decisions; there was a senior investigating officer (control-room Silver Commander) and his deputy; a senior firearms tactical advisor; two senior Special Branch officers; four control-room managers and coordinators; and two inspectors preparing to act as location Silver commanders.

For certain operations the police have devised a pyramid of responsibility designated by the terms Gold, Silver and Bronze. Usually there will be one Gold Commander at the top, but there may be a number of Silvers and Bronzes below. Part of the problem in this instance was that the control-room Silver wasn't in the building when the strategy was set and the location Silver, who takes charge of the scene on the ground, did not arrive at Scotia Road before Jean Charles departed (nearly five hours after the strategy decision). The main reason for this protracted delay was that the firearms team (black), deputed to go to Scotia Road, did not come on duty until 7 a.m. They then had to be kitted up, briefed at Leman Street police station in the City of London, and travel to the Nightingale Lane rendezvous point near Clapham Common in south London for a second more detailed briefing before dispersing to the target location in Scotia Road, Tulse Hill. The scale of this lacuna crystallised at the inquest for the first time, when it emerged that there was, all along, an overnight standby CO19 team (orange) kitted up, sitting in the canteen in New Scotland Yard together with a tactical firearms advisor, by 5.30 a.m. ready to go. There was also an inspector available to accompany them as Location Silver. None of this appears to have been known by Commander McDowell who was on duty throughout this period or by DSO Cressida Dick, who had come on duty at 7 a.m. but who had been present in New Scotland Yard at least an hour before that.

There was another problem for Cressida Dick. She missed the window of opportunity altogether. She was unaware of Jean Charles's departure from the block of flats until he was already on the number 2 bus nearing Brixton. Quite how she managed this is a little perplexing. At least two witnesses, Pat (codename) the surveillance monitor and someone else sitting behind in the control room, said that Dick and her coterie of officers *were* alerted to this. Maybe she was not expecting a bomber to emerge that day and was not prepared for the possibility of one. Maybe she was distracted by the late arrival of her loggist, whom she had to instruct about the day's events. Senior officers involved in crucial decision-making rely upon someone else to keep a diary of events and decisions for them, because clearly they don't have time to do it themselves. Cressida Dick had asked for one to be appointed two hours before he actually arrived at about 9.40 a.m. As the loggist had missed all the briefings, he had to be put in the picture and brought up to date.

What followed was bizarre. As we know, the levels of identification fluctuated from one extreme to the other, but at the point when it appeared that Jean Charles was discounted as a suspect, another team of officers was brought into play. An arrest car containing three unarmed anti-terrorist squad officers from SO13 was deputed to intercept the bus, detain the suspect and question him for intelligence purposes. It did not use the route of the bus and the following surveillance officers, but cut across south London to Stockwell before the bus reached the station. As far as they were concerned, he was not a potential terrorist and they were not near 21 Scotia Road, which meant they could clear the way ahead of them, trumpeting their impending arrival by the familiar 'blues and twos' – blue light and siren, for the uninitiated. It was probably the first police car to arrive at this important junction where everything was to unfold minutes later, and as it turned into Stockwell Road, the bus was coming towards them from the opposite direction. The car continued flashing and blaring, past the bus, did a U-turn and came up behind the target. If there had been a suicide bomber on the top deck of the bus, he would have had a wonderful bird's-eye view and plenty of advance warning. The arrest squad, having got themselves into position, were then told that Jean Charles *was* the suspect after all and that they should hold off (because they were not an armed unit).

Meanwhile back at the ranch, teams of specialist CO19 firearms officers had taken up the trail. Five out of six cars followed the route of the bus, but the sixth followed the route of the arrest car. In the traffic conditions which pertain in the London rush hour it would have been far quicker to have sent the two motorcycles that were on standby at Nightingale Lane near Clapham Common. You may think dear old Frank in the back of the van had a problem, but so did the motorcyclists. Their radios didn't work either, and trying to use a mobile with all that headgear and gauntlet gloves in the awful traffic noise was a trifle tricky. So they couldn't be deployed.

It wasn't that much better for those who went in the cars. This time it was the main radio system Cougar, which was supposed to provide the channel of communication between the pursuit cars and the control room, that was playing up: for some cars it wasn't working at all, for others it was intermittent, and for yet others it was indistinct.

Besides this, the line of contact between the teams and the control room was convoluted. There were several different options: an individual car could radio a message, in the hope that other cars on the same channel would hear it; if surveillance, the message might have to go via the team leader James onwards to the monitor Pat at New Scotland Yard; alternatively, Pat might just have heard it over the airwaves anyway; on the other hand he might not, or he might have misheard it. That could explain how a message from James to the effect that 'It's possibly him' could have been construed by Pat as 'They believe it's him' and overheard by firearms as 'It's him'.

When dealing with firearms, messages to and from the control room would probably have had to go through a number of hands: the firearms team leader on the ground to the firearms tactical advisor (Trojan 84) or the Silver Commander, who would then use a mobile phone to contact the tactical firearms advisor in the control room (Trojan 80), who would then have to tell Cressida Dick. At any one of these stages one might not be able to get through on the phone because the other was otherwise engaged, and this is what happened to the two tactical advisors. None of this is very propitious for split-second, fine-tuned decision-making, and effective orders in these circumstances are well nigh impossible.

I did suggest to Cressida Dick that she should have been listening herself to significant radio traffic from the surveillance team, which could have been broadcast in the control room over the speakers without the need for an intermediary. These broadcasts should have been (and now are) recorded for everyone's benefit, each speaker being identified via their call-sign, so that exactly what has been said and by whom is readily available. If there is another operation being handled at the same time (which there was at 61a Portnall Road), then another DSO on another channel could be monitoring developments on the ground with a headset.

If you are not on the spot, you need up-to-the-minute (indeed, up-to-the-second) precise information about the movements and positions of all the individual key players and the target. In this day and age such a requirement is plainly achievable through state-of-the-art technology. At the inquest I relied on ancient analogies derived from the war. Given my age, I'm sure there were those who were asking themselves: which war is he on about? Well, the Second World War – not that I was up and about too much at the time. What was available even then were wall charts plotting the positions of ships, planes and military units; this could be done with little flags, pins, small models and in some cases lights. Nowadays, with all the electronic tracking devices and the ability to visualise the vehicles transmitted by these devices, it must be possible to contrive an instantaneous overview.

Even without this, all that Cressida Dick needed to do at that time was procure a large-scale map of the area and project it onto the control-room wall. (This had been done in the past.) It could then have been someone's sole responsibility to ensure, through direct communication with the units on the ground, that everybody's progress was monitored as it happened; and this information could have been transferred onto the map for the benefit of everyone in the control room.

As it was, the majority of the information was being received sporadically and in a piecemeal fashion. Mainly it was coming through the mobile phone being used by Trojan 80, the firearms tactical advisor in the control room; via a mobile phone being used by the Silver Commander with the unit on the ground; and through a phone being used by Cressida Dick. The result of this method was that confusing messages were being received and no one knew precisely where any of the cars were. As we have seen, outside Stockwell Tube station, at the junction opposite the entrance, there were three or four armed surveillance officers on foot, two or three cars with specialist armed officers and the SO13 car: quite sufficient to carry out a controlled armed intervention. Ralph (codename), the firearms team leader, described in evidence how he thought this could have been done by encircling Jean Charles in the middle of the road as he crossed to the station. It would have been done from positions of cover, but the actual tactics could not be revealed for reasons of confidentiality.

What actually happened in the control room is that when Cressida Dick first ordered CO19 to do the stop, she was told by Trojan 80 that they were not in a position to do so. She then considered the desirability of using SO12 officers who are not so highly trained, one of whom, Ivor, had volunteered to 'lift him'. She cancelled CO19 and decided to order SO12. She was then told that CO19 were in a position to carry out the stop. She countermanded SO12 and reordered CO19, but it does not appear that either of the commands to SO12 was received. In any event, by the time she issued a final order to stop – not an order authorising a critical shot – Jean Charles was already down the escalators. This much was clear from her decision log, as well as from other witness evidence. At the inquest, however, she stated that she would not have used CO19 if she had known that Jean Charles was going down the escalator.

The real regret here is that if Ivor had done 'the lift', Jean Charles would still be alive. I asked Ivor at the inquest if he would be kind enough to demonstrate how he would have done it – something that had not been requested before and breaking one of the basic rules of advocacy: never ask a question to which you do not know the answer. His technique was graphic, simple and effective. To preserve the element of surprise he and another officer, Ken (codename), would have approached Jean Charles from behind as he negotiated the ticket barrier, with his Oyster card in his right hand and the *Metro* newspaper in his left: in that moment of preoccupation, Ivor and Ken would have grabbed an arm each and physically restrained him. Both officers had guns and handcuffs. It would be unwise to force a suspect to the ground in these circumstances in case there was a bomb hidden in his clothing, but as was obvious to these officers, Jean Charles did not have a rucksack, did not have any telltale wires protruding from his jacket sleeves or any initiation device, pad or switch in his hands. Had anyone had the presence of mind, the barriers could have been temporarily closed and locked as soon as Jean Charles left the bus, so that no one could have gone down the escalators.

I wanted to find out whether such a straightforward technique had been practised within CO19. After 9/11 somebody must have anticipated the prospect of a suicide bomb attack in London, which might be delivered in a number of ways, most obviously by a person on foot. This was likely to be in a crowded urban situation: a shopping precinct, a high street, a railway station, an airport, an Underground train or a bus. It would not be possible in these scenarios to carry out a controlled armed challenge without provoking the very event you are trying to prevent. If you are sure the person has a bomb, does that justify undercover officers shooting the person dead on the spot without warning? On the other hand, if you are not sure – and this is the more likely scenario – how do you deal with somebody who might be a suicide bomber? These are questions that have not received public scrutiny, but which in a democracy require public debate and approval. We all need to be clear what it is we expect our police force to do in our name. The use of lethal force must be contained within agreed parameters of principle, and there must be unambiguous rules of engagement. Ironically, a letter written by Sir Ian Blair, following a meeting with the Prime Minister Tony Blair and dated the very day of the attempted suicide bombings, was canvassing these points. The Commissioner was going so far as to suggest that the time had come for a policy empowering police to kill suicide bombers on sight.

These were all questions largely beyond the remit of the coroner's court, but Ivor's technique was not. The coroner has the power at the end of an inquest to make recommendations which may be necessary in order to reduce a repetition of risks resulting in death (Rule 43). Within fifty-six days the Commissioner and the Metropolitan Police Authority are required to provide a written explanation of what they have done or propose to do; and if nothing, why not?

So had CO19 been practising similar methods for an urban setting? This was an operationally sensitive topic, and not much could be extracted from the officers I questioned. In the end there was a concession that it certainly hadn't been practised before July 2005.

Yet since 9/11 2001 the British police have been planning and preparing for suicide attacks. There have been working parties, research, visits to Israel, Pakistan and Sri Lanka, mock exercises in street conditions on computers and on tabletops. What this had thrown up by July 2005 was a policy codenamed 'Kratos', which contemplated the delivery of a 'critical shot' (meaning a fatal one). There is huge reticence in police circles about using the word 'kill', probably because it sounds too brutal, so the concept is dressed up in language like 'neutralising', 'nullifying', or 'negating the threat'. It is argued that doing anything less, such as shooting at other parts of the body or using a stun or laser gun, may not eradicate the threat.

The term Kratos has been amplified and overtaken by other codewords, and I am not at liberty to disclose what is currently involved. At the time, however, Kratos covered two different situations. The first contemplated a spontaneous call from a member of the public or a police officer, reporting a suspected suicide bomber. Since there might be hundreds of such calls, each one would have to be assessed, usually by an on-call DSO, who would decide whether action should be taken and what resources were available for such action: for example, an ARV (Armed Response Vehicle, on standby in London, with an average response time of twelve minutes) or a specialist unit. If reliable intelligence became available that the person was about to detonate a bomb, the DSO could authorise a critical shot. If there was no intelligence and no obvious signs of a bomb (a belt, vest or wires), then the individual firearms officer would have to make his own assessment. But does this involve a warning or not? The normal Association of Chief Police Officers (ACPO) firearms manual permits an officer to exercise his or her own discretion and not issue a warning if this would endanger life. This goes without saying, because to do so would alert the target; and anyway in ordinary firearm, non-suicide situations such as a hostage-taking or a kidnap, the threat is more obvious. The Kratos policy on the other hand *did* suggest a warning, which yet another tactical firearms officer, codenamed Andrew, said takes the form of: 'Armed police; stand still; show us your hands.' How else would you assess whether the person was a suicide bomber?

It was precisely these considerations that lay behind the evidential conflict at the inquest. The officers claimed they had made an assessment by shouting 'Armed police!' and by observing the bulky jacket, Jean Charles's reaction, etc., whereas I suggested that they had made a covert approach without shouting anything, because they had predetermined that he was a suicide bomber and had no time for a proper assessment within the five to ten seconds from their first seeing Jean Charles to shooting him.

According to the passengers, and to the verdict of the jury, no challenge was made to Jean Charles. It seems to me that it should be obligatory to issue a warning or challenge where the person may not be a suicide bomber, and where there is no intelligence and no visible evidence to suggest that he is.

The second situation covered by Kratos was known by another codeword – 'Clydesdale' – which had no application to Stockwell: where the police have specific intelligence that a suicide bombing is going to take place, they can mount an operation in advance with clear authorisation for a critical shot. Clydesdale would therefore apply to major public events like Trooping the Colour, a state visit, a political party conference or the Olympics – in other words, something pre-planned.

As the inquest entered its closing weeks in November 2008, after a wait of nearly three and a half years and almost eight weeks of intense evidence, the family felt that their concerns had been aired and that police witnesses had been held to account in the witness box. But the most important stage, the deliberations of the jury and their verdict, were yet to come. The family was expectant and hopeful that at last it would experience justice being done, and being seen to be done.

After lengthy submissions, the coroner ruled that he was withdrawing two verdict options from the jury: unlawful killing (murder) against C12 and C2, and unlawful killing (manslaughter) against Commanders McDowell and Dick and Trojan 80. This left lawful-killing and open verdicts only.

The considerations for each version of unlawful killing are different. In relation to murder, there has to be sufficient evidence to prove this allegation to the criminal standard so that a jury can be *sure*. Where self-defence or defence of others is pleaded, a jury has therefore to be satisfied so that they are sure the officers did *not* have an honest, albeit mistaken belief that they were defending themselves and others against an imminent threat of death. The coroner's judgment was that no properly directed, reasonable jury could find that the officers either did not have or may not have had such a belief. If a jury were so to find, then it could be characterised as 'perverse'. On behalf of the family, I did not agree. I contended that there was a perfectly satisfactory evidential basis (the passengers' evidence, for example) capable of giving rise to a safe inference by the jury of unlawful killing.

This poses, and has posed in the past, a serious conundrum in cases where police officers kill, because their justification is nearly always self-defence. Does this mean that they can hardly ever be prosecuted for murder, let alone face a similar allegation in an inquest? There are judges in the Divisional Court who believe that the verdict of unlawful killing (murder) should never be left at an inquest in police cases, because it would be tantamount to a criminal conviction for murder without the protections afforded by a criminal trial. They also argue that such a verdict risks breaking the rule in inquests that prohibits specific findings of criminal or civil liability. I think this is quite unacceptable, because the use of lethal force should be subject to the processes of legal scrutiny and adjudication, if for no other reason than for public confidence and accountability. An inquest may be the only legal vehicle for doing this.

Perversely, the opposite of inculpation – namely exoneration – *is* permissible. What tends to happen in inquests is that the converse verdict of *lawful* killing is left. This is mainly because the standard of proof for this finding is far lower: that of the civil standard, on the balance of probabilities (more likely than not). So all a police officer has to do is show that it is more likely than not he was defending himself or others. My argument here is they can't have it both ways. Either there is no verdict of unlawful *or* lawful killing made available to juries; or they should *both* be available with the same standard of proof. I favour the latter, on the civil standard, and any unlawful-killing verdict would not be tantamount to a criminal conviction, whatever the tabloids might like to think. This is because, under inquest rules, no individual can be named or found criminally liable in any verdict. It would then be for the DPP to decide whether a criminal prosecution, on the criminal standard, should follow.

It is a common practice, where lawful killing is left for the jury, for an alternative 'open' verdict to be left. This is to provide for a situation in which the jury is agreed that there is insufficient evidence to cross the threshold of proof required for the short-form verdict – here, more likely than not, lawful killing. It is not intended to cover a situation in which the jury merely cannot agree on a specific verdict like lawful killing. Therefore where a jury returns an open verdict and rejects lawful killing, there may be those among their number who – while believing that the evidence is insufficient to prove it was probably lawful – may nevertheless consider it was unlawful. But the opportunity to argue this position has been withdrawn. It is of interest that this jury, after they had retired, did ask a question about these options.

The manslaughter allegation is more complicated. There are a number of different elements that have to be proved to the criminal standard against each individual quite separately. Legally speaking, you cannot combine a number of different acts and omissions committed by different individuals (aggregation) and put them in the pot against one individual. So against any one person – in this case a senior police officer – it has to be shown: first, that there was a duty of care owed by that officer to Jean Charles; second, that there was a breach of that duty by some act or omission by the officer; third, that the particular breach contributed to the cause of death; and finally, that that breach could be characterised by a jury as a grossly criminal act or omission. The coroner was not satisfied that these four elements had been made out, save in part as against one of the individuals. I argued otherwise.

The verdicts discussed above are known as 'short-form' simply because they are attempts to summarise a particular cause of death. As such they plainly do not cover the whole chain of events that preceded it. In order to meet this need and comply with the requirements of the European Convention on Human Rights, juries in inquests are now permitted a narrative verdict. There is no stipulated form for this, and within the various rules about liability and so on they can use whatever words they like. This is a new development, and unfortunately judges (high and low) are worried about trusting juries to get it right. Better, they say, to set limited questions to which the answers are equally limited: 'Yes', 'No' or 'Don't know'.

This is an extremely important fresh dimension. Whereas it may not be possible to demonstrate failures to meet the criteria within manslaughter, it will often be possible to identify a whole range of acts or omissions which contributed more than minimally to the death. Advocates in inquests cannot make speeches or submissions to the jury, but they can (when requested) assist the coroner on matters of law, and this is done in the absence of the jury. At the de Menezes inquest there was intensive argument on what narrative questions should be left, with little agreement between us and the five police teams, leaving the coroner's team bravely trying with consummate grace and good humour to balance the scales between us. Besides the individual areas that we thought should be addressed, we wanted the jury to have the liberty to add overall observations of their own, because we did not believe that the lawyers had the monopoly on this. In particular I felt it important that the jury should be able to qualify any contributory cause that they found in terms of its level of gravity: how much of a cause was it? I was unable to persuade the coroner of this.

When the coroner announced his rulings, it was a bitter pill for the family to swallow. Despite all the delays, lies, misleading statements, legal setbacks and disappointments, they had always maintained hope and above all their dignity.

As the coroner began his summing-up on the penultimate day of the inquest, we decided to see even at this late stage whether it was possible to get the Divisional Court to intervene. I focused only on one part of the rulings, the section about what the jury can do in relation to a narrative verdict. Launching a judicial review is quite a palaver, because you have to find a judge who is available to hear it at short notice, assemble all the necessary forms and notices, and put together bundles of documents from the inquest and files of legal authorities. Given that the judge will not be familiar with what has been going on at the inquest, you have to be in a position to summarise what has happened so that the relevance of the complaint you are making can be seen in context. A lot of midnight oil was burned by Marcia and Henrietta to get it completed, and by me in thinking – or was it sinking?

In comes the Wednesbury Unreasonableness Test once more.

We did not get leave, and this was the last straw for the family. It was an extremely tense and emotional stage, exacerbated by the fact that half the family were back in Brazil. When you are driven to distraction there is often no alternative. And so at the eleventh hour, on the last morning, just before the remaining couple of hours of the coroner's summing-up, the family decided they no longer wished to participate and no longer wished to be represented in the hearings. After all the time and effort that had been expended, a great deal of soul-searching was undertaken by decent and responsible people to reach a decision of this kind.

It was only the third time in the whole of my career that I have ever stood up in front of a court to announce my withdrawal. For me, it goes against the grain and, where there is a choice, I always prefer to stay in there and fight every inch of the way. But then it's not about me. I had, and have, complete respect for this family, which has survived against all the odds. Equally I had, and have, complete respect for a decision when there was really no other option left.

Suddenly I found myself packing up all those boxes, clearing the room overlooking the cricket pitch and leaving the Oval without a result. I was thrust into a vacuum, powerless to do anything about whatever might happen in court thereafter. I never lost faith in the capacity of the jury to restore the family's confidence in the system. This was partly due to the nature of the numerous questions they had asked throughout, passed to the coroner on small pieces of paper, which by this stage filled a container the size of a shoebox.

No sooner had the jury retired than they started asking more questions. They wanted to know what they should do about unlawful killing, and whether there were other things they could say, beyond the questions set by the coroner as part of the narrative. Too right. I could hardly believe it. These were precisely the points we had been making a few days before, to both the coroner and the Divisional Court, although of course the jury didn't know this.

Waiting for a verdict when you're not involved is even worse than when you are. I was not there to see the jury when they started and finished their deliberations each day; I was not there to see what they looked like, how lively or tired they were or what body language they displayed. Then there are the rumours that usually percolate the corridors. If they want lunch, does it mean they're going into the afternoon? If they want to come in early or stay late, does this mean they're close to a conclusion? It's probably all nonsense and way off the mark, but you cannot avoid engaging in this kind of speculation. Only I couldn't.

It was worth the wait. I was at home working at my desk, listening to BBC Radio 4. The one o'clock news came on as usual and there it was, the first item: I'd never heard a verdict in that way before. It started with the open verdict, and I knew exactly what that meant. The jury was not able to find that C12 and C2 had probably acted in self-defence. Amazing! But there was more to come. The jury unanimously rejected two of the mainstays of C12's assertion of self-defence: that he had warned Jean Charles by shouting 'armed police' and that Jean Charles had nevertheless advanced threateningly towards him. I don't usually jump up and down – unbecoming in a wig and gown and inappropriate in a courtroom – so it was the first time I'd been able to let off steam over a verdict. I jumped!

All those film scenes are complete fantasy. I'm thinking in particular of the one of the freeing of the Guildford Four in *In the Name of the Father*, with Emma Thompson as Gareth Peirce leaping over the court benches like some crazed gazelle. Totally impossible, improbable and out of character . . . Great drama, though.

Besides the open verdict, these were the other resounding and significant findings of the de Menezes inquest:

CORONER, SIR MICHAEL WRIGHT: The short-form verdict is either lawful killing or open verdict. What is your verdict?

FOREMAN OF THE JURY: Open verdict.

SIR MICHAEL WRIGHT: Thank you. Question 1: did Officer Charlie 12 shout the words 'Armed police' at Mr de Menezes before firing? Yes, no or cannot decide?

FOREMAN OF THE JURY: No.

SIR MICHAEL WRIGHT: I should have asked you in relation to the verdict: is that a unanimous verdict or by a majority?

FOREMAN OF THE JURY: It's a majority.

SIR MICHAEL WRIGHT: How many agreed and how many disagreed?

FOREMAN OF THE JURY: Eight agreed, two disagreed.

SIR MICHAEL WRIGHT: In answer to question number 1, the one you have just given, is that unanimous or by majority?

FOREMAN OF THE JURY: That is unanimous.

SIR MICHAEL WRIGHT: The second question is: did Mr de Menezes stand up from his seat before he was grabbed in a bear hug by Ivor? Yes, no or cannot decide?

FOREMAN OF THE JURY: Yes, and that's unanimous.

SIR MICHAEL WRIGHT: Thank you. Did Mr de Menezes move towards officer C12 before he was grabbed in a bear hug by officer Ivor?

FOREMAN OF THE JURY: No, and that's unanimous.

SIR MICHAEL WRIGHT: Thank you. Turning to the factors for consideration, do you consider that any of the following factors caused or contributed to the death of Mr de Menezes: (a) The suicide attacks and attempted attacks of July 2005 and the pressure placed upon the Metropolitan Police in responding to the threat?

FOREMAN OF THE JURY: Cannot decide, sir.

SIR MICHAEL WRIGHT: Again, is that inability to decide by a majority or unanimous?

FOREMAN OF THE JURY: That's a majority of eight to two.

SIR MICHAEL WRIGHT: Thank you. (b) A failure to obtain and provide better photographic images of the suspect Hussain Osman for the surveillance team?

FOREMAN OF THE JURY: Yes, that's unanimous.

SIR MICHAEL WRIGHT: (c) A failure by the police to ensure that Mr de Menezes was stopped before he reached public transport?

FOREMAN OF THE JURY: Yes, unanimous, sir.

SIR MICHAEL WRIGHT: Thank you. (d) The general difficulty in providing identification of the man under surveillance, Mr de Menezes, in the time available and in the circumstances after he had left the block at Scotia Road?

FOREMAN OF THE JURY: No, and that's unanimous.

SIR MICHAEL WRIGHT: (e) The innocent behaviour of Mr de Menezes, which increased the suspicions of some officers?

FOREMAN OF THE JURY: No, that's a majority of eight to two, sir.

SIR MICHAEL WRIGHT: Thank you. (f) The fact that the views of the surveillance officers regarding identification were not accurately communicated to the command team and the firearms officers?

FOREMAN OF THE JURY: Yes, unanimous.

SIR MICHAEL WRIGHT: (g) The fact that the position of the cars containing the firearms officers was not accurately known to the command team as the firearms officers were approaching Stockwell station?

FOREMAN OF THE JURY: Yes, unanimous.

SIR MICHAEL WRIGHT: (h) Any significant shortcomings in the communications system as it was operating on the day between the various police teams on the ground and with New Scotland Yard?

FOREMAN OF THE JURY: Yes, unanimous again, sir.

SIR MICHAEL WRIGHT: (i) A failure to conclude at the time that surveillance officers should still be used to carry out the stop of Mr de Menezes at Stockwell station, even after it was reported that specialist firearms officers could perform the stop?

FOREMAN OF THE JURY: Yes, unanimous.

SIR MICHAEL WRIGHT: That concludes your verdict. I am very much obliged to you, Mr Foreman, thank you.

FOREMAN OF THE JURY: Thank you.[12]

A number of the factors unanimously decided upon by the jury as contributing to the death of Jean Charles de Menezes had been strongly argued for on behalf of the family: the availability of better photographs (b); the window of opportunity (c and d), i.e. that Jean Charles could have been stopped before he got onto public transport and that the difficulties of identification in that period were not a hindrance, because the police only needed to stop those people who were clearly *not* women, children, the elderly and obviously white men; the inaccurate communication of identity (f); the whereabouts of the CO19 cars (g); the shortcomings in the communication systems (h); and finally the failure to use Ivor to detain him (i).

The jury's verdict and findings as a whole should be a sign of hope for the future. They should promote and provoke a serious reappraisal by the police of what went wrong and how to remedy it. What the family found depressing – as did those of us representing them – was any real recognition from start to finish that anything had gone wrong. At no stage were the main players prepared to make any major concessions. Where was the humility that Sir Ian Blair had urged upon his officers before the inquest began?

What it needed on day one or two, straight after the killing, was a heartfelt apology, an assumption of responsibility, recognition of failure and a willingness to identify the faults and put them right. We are all human; we all make mistakes, big and small; we are all sympathetic to the enormous dangers faced by police officers. But they must stand up and be counted when it goes wrong, just as much as when it goes right.

The current approach of institutional reticence and denial which permeates the culture of the police (just as it did during the Stephen Lawrence inquiry) has to be admitted and transformed. There is no point in our recommending change, or trusting that changes have been made, if the police really don't accept that there's a need for it.

Once again the process has been tortuous and painful. A family has had to push the police authority right up to the wire before there is even a glimmer of hope. The Lawrence family had to wade through a trial, internal enquiries, an inquest and a public inquiry before an eleventh-hour concession by the Met; here, the de Menezes family had to wade through an IPCC inquiry, a trial and an inquest until belated concessions, contended for by the family throughout that inquest, were finally made by the Metropolitan Police Service (MPS) in response to the coroner's report in February 2009.

These were essentially:

a A system for strategy implementation
b Provision of command continuity
c DSO role clarification (this term has now been abandoned)
d Effective systems of communication (now provided by *Airwave*)
e Standardisation of terms used
f Surveillance-officer radio identity
g Provision of onscreen maps depicting locations and premises
h Provision of tracker technology
i Improved and standardised techniques and terms for identification
j Improved acquisition and deployment of photographic material
k Joint briefings of operational personnel.

Such progress is to be welcomed and the benefits are awaited.

What has not been satisfactorily addressed or publicly debated are the rules of engagement with regard especially to the delivery of a critical shot. A convoluted and somewhat laboured concept has been invoked – the Conflict Management Model. Strip away the police-speak, and all it amounts to, as ever, is the good sense and discretion of the individual firearms officer. This is not even straightforward for the majority of mainstream firearms situations where challenges are normally issued. For example, within the recent past a chair leg in a plastic bag has been mistaken for a shotgun, a cigarette lighter for an automatic hand gun, and during 2008 and 2009, to May, a further six fatal shootings by police have been reported and are being investigated by the IPCC. It is quite unreasonable to depend on discretion for the extreme situations presented by possible suicide bombers, where the most likely scenario is one in which there is little or no reliable intelligence, only suspicion, and there are no obvious physical indicators, only ambiguity.

In these circumstances there have to be practised procedures for the surprise detention of the suspect in crowded urban environments that do not involve the use of arms and a critical shot; failing this, there have to be clear and obligatory protocols, which must include words to the effect: 'Armed police, stop, stay still, hands up'.

In the absence of these, there will undoubtedly be more innocent citizens shot dead. This cannot be permitted.

LAW, NOT WAR

Yes, We Can!

On the corner stood a mysterious, flat concrete bunker, with a small iron gate that appeared to be rusted into place. Hidden by a wall seven feet high, it could barely be seen from the street, and over ten years I never saw anyone enter, let alone come out. If I opened my sash window in the building next door and leaned out, looking to my right, I could see the roof of the building. It was bigger than I had originally thought, with odd little bits of greenery, fern and buddleia, taking root in the cracks. It's all gone now, replaced by a commercial job several storeys high.

My window was in number 14 Tooks Court. When I first set up chambers, there was a rumour current that the bunker next door contained a secret entrance to an underground tunnel, and a local workman told me that he thought it was connected to Downing Street, so that the Prime Minister could do a runner if under attack from irritating protesters or the occasional more serious bazooka – though quite why he would want to pop up next to me I'm not sure.

Maybe the workman was not so far off the mark. In January 2009 an unusual property came onto the market: six interlinked stretches of tunnel about one and a half miles long, capable of housing 8,000 people. It comes complete with canteen, restaurant, recreation room, cinema, bar, telephone exchange, generators and an artesian well. At least that's what they had at one time.[1] This unique bargain basement runs a hundred feet below High Holborn, Chancery Lane, and Furnival Street adjacent to Tooks Court. It was originally built by London Transport as a bomb shelter during the Blitz, but towards the end of the war the tunnels and their contents became classified information subject to the Official Secrets Act. MI6 took them over under the cryptic title of the Inter-Services Research Bureau, followed by the Public Record Office and its classified archives. Latterly British Telecom used them to operate a huge exchange, which had been earmarked during the Cuban missile crisis in 1962 for a post-nuclear communications centre, and for a hotline between the Kremlin and the White House. The tunnels remained classified information, referred to only as the Kingsway or 2147 tunnels, right up to 2005.

These are elaborate provisions to deal with the horrors of war, and it would be comforting to imagine that the tunnels' obsolescence and impending sale marks a magic milestone towards a new world order. By the beginning of the third millennium you might have thought it would not have been beyond the wit of man or woman to have devised an effective method of conflict resolution without descending into the mire of massacre, death and destruction. I mean, if they can put a man on the moon ... 'Why not put all of them there?' says a sizeable chunk of womanhood: mildly uncharitable, but it might be a solution.

Meanwhile what to do? It's certainly not for want of trying by those who care; the trouble is that there are quite a few who don't. Some believe it will sort itself, but I don't think so. We have just witnessed the catastrophic results of three decades of unregulated, untrammelled economic free enterprise in the marketplace, and inevitably it's the weak, the impoverished, the vulnerable and the disempowered who are hit the hardest. The same applies to power-crazed individuals and states that employ terror to further their aims. Some continue to put their trust in politicians: need I say more? Some throw up their hands in the face of seemingly impossible odds and retreat. Some simply decide to put up with the situation as it is.

I am a firm believer in change. It is an intrinsic part of the natural order to which we are all subject, and it is the one thing that cannot be stopped. Therefore either we control change or we are controlled by it. The bigger the force, the bigger the need for collective effort. No one person can do it alone, but that's not the same as saying that an individual contribution, however small, is meaningless or ineffectual. Each endeavour is a cause that has an effect. It may not be immediately discernible; it may take more than a lifetime. It is the absence of endeavour which permits the ascendancy of doctrines suffused with the 'might is right' attitude and 'gunboat diplomacy'. In words frequently attributed to Edmund Burke, the Irish-born eighteenth-century Whig politician, 'It is necessary only for the good man to do nothing for evil to triumph.'

The endeavour I have in mind is something to which we can all contribute, but as a lawyer it is something towards which I feel a special obligation. I've tried to keep a measured focus on maintaining a flame lit by others far more inspirational and creative than me. We are custodians of a movement that should be treasured rather than trashed: peaceful coexistence within a recognised and respected international rule of law. Up jump the Hobbesian cynics, the moaners and groaners, the new-age realists. 'Utopian claptrap!' they chant in unison. 'It hasn't worked, it doesn't work, and it never will.' Without realising it, they have in fact touched the void, the vacuum. It's time for a little taste of Utopia, a little vision of value in an era of mad materialism.

The movement and its concepts are a temporal pinprick compared with the history of the universe or even humankind, and patience and perseverance are required in abundance before the full fruits of its growth can be gathered.

Amazing sacrifices have been made. Blood, sweat and tears have been shed over at least three centuries by progressive thinkers from all parts of the world. To let this go would be an unbearable betrayal.

An early protagonist was the eighteenth-century English political philosopher Tom Paine (1737–1809). He has never been adequately recognised and certainly wasn't flavour of the month at the time in England, so he fled abroad and became an influential figure in two revolutions, the American and the French: quite good going for one lifetime. Both revolutions spawned seminal written constitutions and documents delineating basic human rights: *The Declaration of the Rights of Man and of the Citizen* approved by the National Assembly of France in 1789, and the *United States Bill of Rights* in 1791. Paine has been credited with the first use of the term 'United States' when writing his incisive pamphlet entitled *The Crisis*[2] in support of the American War of Independence. He is probably best remembered for *Rights of Man*, part one of which was published in 1791 and was dedicated to George Washington.

What tends to get overlooked is that his thesis about the necessity for a union of states also has resonance for a union of nations. This has been summarised succinctly by John Keane, who like me is a Professor at the University of Westminster:

> Paine argued that the best antidote to war is the formation of an international confederation of nationally independent and peacefully interacting civil societies that keeps an eye on the international system of nation-states, taming their bellicose urges. He was certain that democratic republican states, guided by civil societies held together by reciprocal interests and mutual affection, would make for a new global order freed from the curse of war.[3]

I have been a long-time admirer of Paine's courage, his enterprise and his evocative prose, and it was a privilege to deliver the biennial Tom Paine Lecture at the University of East Anglia in 2003, and to address the Tom Paine and Headstrong Societies in Lewes, Sussex, on more than one occasion.

The notions which Paine articulated became the bedrock for a line of innovative, bold initiatives that punctuated the history of the twentieth century, and it is no accident that they, and Paine's constructs, were underpinned by statements of principle about the rights of the individual. If you're trying to outlaw war and promote peace, it helps to know why. What is it you are striving to protect by the advent of peace? So, unsurprisingly, the right to life is top of the bill.

There are many landmarks in the twentieth century, but the ones worth selecting are: the League of Nations (1919); the Kellogg-Briand Pact (1927–8, where an American Republican combined with a French socialist to outlaw war); the United Nations Charter (1945); the Universal Declaration of Human Rights and the European Convention on Human Rights (1948), a spectrum of covenants covering several political, economic, social and cultural rights; the Geneva Conventions (1957);[4] and the Second Treaty of Rome in 1998.[5]

No one is labouring under any illusion about these initiatives. They are fragile. Not all nations have signed up, and the ones that have occasionally withdraw when it suits them, or else employ the veto; others don't pay their dues, and many cannot afford to do so. For those who break the rules, what are the sanctions? Who provides the enforcers, the international police? On top of this is the over-arching concern that the whole edifice is too embedded in the ethos of Western industrialised states and the European Enlightenment.

These reservations cannot be ignored, but there is no reason to surrender. The concepts of respect, arbitration and reconciliation attract universal understanding, even if the methods of fulfilment differ.

One method that has steadily gathered momentum and approval is a judicial structure of courts which transcend national boundaries and provide universal jurisdiction and accountability. The International Court of Justice in The Hague, referred to as the ICJ or the World Court, has been in place for a number of years, settling disputes of principle between member states. Most recently, for the first time, an International Criminal Court (ICC)[6] has been established at The Hague. This is a permanent body intended to replace the ad hoc tribunals that have been dealing with specific theatres of war – Nuremberg and Tokyo after the Second World War; the International Criminal Tribunal for the former Yugoslavia (ICTY)[7] after the genocide in the Balkans; others in Africa dealing with genocide in Rwanda and Sierra Leone; and another in Cambodia trying five senior Khmer Rouge leaders accused of genocide thirty-five years ago, which opened in April 2009. The ICC took years of negotiation and diplomacy to forge, and while the vast majority of the world nations signed up, a few did not. Among those that did not were the USA and Iraq, probably because they thought they might be among the first in the dock.

Member states are given first bite at the cherry to bring suspects to book. This may be too much to ask. The infrastructure may not be in place; the culprits may be viewed as local heroes; all the witnesses may be too intimidated to come forward. Occasionally on a local level there is a reticence to participate lest it be thought that the whole process might reopen rather than heal old wounds. If a suspect cannot be tried locally, then the International Criminal Court may take over. In March 2009 the court for the first time issued an arrest warrant against a serving president – President Bashir of Sudan, for seven counts of war crimes in relation to Darfur.

The UK incorporated the ICC into domestic legislation in 2001,[8] just as it incorporated the European Convention in 2000, and everyone in my chambers was singularly proud when one of our number, Adrian Fulford, became the first British judge there. The court is concerned with offences that could not be more fundamental – genocide, crimes against humanity and war crimes – and the sort of behaviour that might be involved is not difficult to envisage: murder, abduction, kidnapping, torture, rape and disappearances. There are, however, two areas upon which consensus has not so far been reached: the crime of aggression and the definition of terrorism. Once again this may be because some of the major nation states are more than a little sensitive about their own track records.

Against this background my own focused contributions pale into insignificance, but I sincerely hope they have helped towards establishing some of the indispensable bricks in the wall of peace and justice (you certainly can't have one without the other); and they do show what is possible even on the smallest scale. No one should imagine they can't make a difference.

In the early 1980s I joined forces with a number of other lawyers who wanted to supplement the exemplary work carried out by Amnesty International, which has consistently exposed the plight of political prisoners worldwide. As lawyers, we wanted to assist in practical ways.

A trio of us thrashed out both the name and the design logo: InteRights. Nothing world-shattering, but you'd be amazed how much longer it takes to sort out the colour of the wallpaper as opposed to the nature of the room it's in. InteRights is now a well-established and highly respected international centre for the legal protection of human rights, facilitating essential legal challenges in different corners of the world. Not long after its inception I parted company with it, when I felt that its emphasis on referral and academic research was too great, but this has since changed. What I had in mind was an agency more akin to Médicins Sans Frontières or Avocats Sans Frontières, which are now very active in a variety of war zones.

During the 1990s there were three very different groups to which I lent wholehearted support, each of them employing different techniques and legal avenues to promote the twin objectives of peace and human rights.

The first was a consortium of non-governmental organisations (NGOs) that came together in a worldwide campaign known as the World Court Project,[9] one of whose main purposes was to petition the ICJ in The Hague for a declaratory judgment in 1996 about the illegality of nuclear weapons. There are of course several aspects to this: the possession of such weapons, the threat of their use and finally their actual use, and in a sense the ICJ is a creature of the United Nations and is normally approached either by states themselves or by agencies of the United Nations, such as the General Assembly. The court's opinion, although only advisory, is one of the highest authority. The issue was given careful and lengthy deliberation by fifteen judges after full hearings involving all the interested states and UN agencies. On this occasion forty-three states (a record number, including the USA, UK and France) filed written submissions, and twenty-two (including the NATO nuclear states) made oral statements.

The ruling was historic in that it considered the threat or use of nuclear weapons to be generally illegal, and states have an obligation to conclude negotiations on their elimination.[10]

The element of elimination is crucial. The Nuclear Non-Proliferation Treaty (NPT) signed by the major nuclear powers in 1968 reflected a significant bargain struck at that time. In exchange for allowing the five major nations (including the UK) to retain their nuclear capability, it was understood that they would only be deployed for collective protection, particularly of the weaker non-nuclear powers. At the same time there was supposed to be a staged reduction in this capability, to the point of elimination. Nearly forty years later that has not been achieved, which is all the more poignant when you consider the fuss that has been made by some of the five major powers about North Korea and Iran.

Mordechai Vanunu paid a very heavy price as a whistleblower on nuclear capabilities. In 1986 he provided the *Sunday Times* with information and photographs about Israel's clandestine nuclear facilities below the Negev Desert at Dimona. Israel has never come clean about their existence, nor has it allowed international inspection, and its nuclear programme is almost certainly in breach of the 1968 NPT. If you combine this with Israel's breaches of international law and UN resolutions, the result comes close to the very rationale that the international coalition used for the invasion of Iraq.

Vanunu was entrapped in London by a Mossad agent and lured to Rome, where he was drugged and kidnapped for his onward journey to Israel. Once there, he was put on trial in secret, shackled in every way (including tape across his mouth) and sentenced to eighteen years' imprisonment, most of which he served in conditions of severe physical confinement, including eleven years in total isolation.

He was finally released in 2004. Beside his own internal courage and strength, one of the ways in which hope has been kept alive for him has been the combined efforts of organisations[11] and individuals everywhere. I was but one of many who relentlessly demonstrated and petitioned for his release, and then for the lifting of ongoing extraordinary restrictions on his freedom of movement. Vanunu is still virtually under house arrest in East Jerusalem. He is awaiting the result of a ruling about a further three-month prison sentence imposed for 'talking to foreigners' – who happened to be from the media.

The UK has also set an appalling example in relation to nuclear proliferation, which has continued right up to the minute, with revelations that the government plans to spend £3 billion on new warheads for the Trident submarine nuclear system.[12] Most Trident warheads are 100 kilotonnes – about eight times larger than the bomb used on Hiroshima – and most of the submarines carry at least six of these. Such enormous destructive power, combined with the ability to cause untold human suffering and damage to future generations from radiation effects, makes these weapons incapable of complying with humanitarian law, because in effect they are disproportionate and indiscriminate.

Fortunately there are groups of citizens similar to Mordechai Vanunu and those involved in the World Court Project, stretching from New Zealand right across to Canada, who are prepared to keep a close watch on this form of the arms trade. On 1 July 2008 a cross-party group representing sixty-nine members of the European

Parliament from nineteen European Union member states launched a
Declaration in support of the Nuclear Weapons Convention to mark
the fortieth anniversary of the NPT. The appeal calls for multilateral
negotiations to prevent proliferation and achieve non-discriminatory
nuclear disarmament.[13] President Obama lent his weight to these
efforts in a speech in Prague on 6 April 2009. He made clear that he
would 'aggressively' push for the Senate to ratify the Comprehensive
Test Ban Treaty and that he will 'strengthen' the NPT. 'The basic
bargain is sound,' he said. 'Countries with nuclear weapons will
move towards disarmament, countries without nuclear weapons
will not acquire them and all countries can access peaceful nuclear
energy. If we are serious about stopping the spread of these weapons,
then we should put an end to the dedicated production of weapons-
grade materials that create them. That's the first step.'[14]

The second group with which I became involved from its
inception is the Kurdish Human Rights Project (KHRP).[15] The
Kurds are a dispossessed nation, bearing many similarities to the
Armenians and the Palestinians. Many of the Kurds live in the
Zagros Mountains which border Iraq, Iran, Syria, Turkey and the
former Soviet Union. The diaspora involves millions of people in
each of those areas. The Kurds have been bombed and exterminated,
their villages and livelihoods razed to the ground. In 1992 a project
was inaugurated on a non-partisan basis dedicated to the human
rights of all people in the Kurdish region. At the beginning it was
difficult to raise awareness and garner support, as the plight of these
people was not high on anyone's agenda, but persistence has paid
off. I was happy to become a patron and speak whenever needed,
and under the leadership of Lord Avebury, Kerim Yildiz and Mark
Muller, QC, this has become one of the most successful campaigns
of its kind. The KHRP has brought thousands of cases before the
European Court of Human Rights concerned with extra-judicial
killings, disappearances and destruction of property, and each case
has resulted in real benefits on the ground.

You don't have to be a lawyer to take action. Tom Carrigan found
himself in a spot of bother a few years ago and was represented by
two members of my chambers. Once the dust had settled after his
brush with the law, he became a professional photographer and
visited Halabja in Kurdistan, Iraq. Saddam Hussein had attempted

to wipe out the Kurdish population there in the 1980s; he had not succeeded and they were attempting to rebuild what had been destroyed. Tom made a film about the reconstruction and produced many strong images, which were exhibited in Tooks Chambers in 2008. But it didn't stop there. He is returning to Halabja with money he has raised, to help build a much-needed children's playground.

The final example also shows what can be done by both lawyers and non-lawyers working together. Some say that what happens on the other side of the world has little or nothing to do with us: it's their problem, let them get on with it. However, if we are right to believe that there is a universality about certain intrinsic values and rights, then it matters not where the invasion or the denial takes place. That value is indivisible, and any attack upon it is also an attack upon each one of us. In the words of Martin Luther King, 'Injustice anywhere is a threat to justice everywhere.' A collective response is the only true defence.

Anne Wright realised this is much as anyone, and once her family had grown up, she left the comfort and security of her north London home in order to perform extremely dangerous work in Colombia. For over ten years lawyers there representing disempowered communities and workers have suffered all kinds of harassment and even death, and have banded together in a collective (Lawyers' Collective José Alvear Restrepo, CAJAR).[16] Their lives are watched day and night, and the repression is endless; physical attacks happen regularly and without any warning. Twenty to thirty lawyers and human-rights defenders are killed or attacked every year in Colombia alone, simply for going about their job.

Anne joined Peace Brigades International (PBI), established in 1981,[17] to provide what they call 'protective accompaniment': you become a shadow for a threatened lawyer as they go about their work. In that way the risk of assault or death is reduced and you provide an extra pair of eyes to watch the watchers. Needless to say, it cannot guarantee that the anonymous assassins will be deterred, but PBI is effective in dissuading violence towards persecuted activists by creating what they term a 'space for peace'.

I had met Anne over thirty years ago when I had played rather stolid football alongside her husband and the wizardry of his South

American colleagues. When I heard from her about the precarious predicament of the lawyers she accompanied, I felt some form of extra support had to be marshalled in the UK, so I met the President of the lawyers' collective in London and suggested that individual lawyers under threat could be sponsored by lawyers in England, with a hotline that could be used in times of emergency. This might also be a means of mobilising international political opinion. The Bar Council Human Rights Committee has taken the lead in coordinating action and support for lawyers in Colombia.

In December 2002 I was asked to address a packed meeting organised by the Kurdish HRP at St Paul's Cathedral, and an audience of over 2,000 came along, mainly to hear the softly spoken but intellectually incisive Noam Chomsky. He was a hard act to follow, and the only way I felt I could retain audience interest after a riveting and detailed exposition of the build-up to the Iraq war was to give an intimate description of the harrowing conditions of a prison cell in Guantanamo Bay, which at that stage was not familiar to many people. I suggested that instead of the spurious dossier about Iraq's supposed weapons of mass destruction (WMD), a dossier of Blair/Bush illegalities should be sent to the International Criminal Court. In the first instance it's the job of the British Government to investigate and prosecute any potential crime covered by the three offences within the ICC jurisdiction, which is why they have been incorporated into domestic UK legislation. Over the subsequent months I did not notice or anticipate any interest or appetite for this by the British authorities, especially as the Attorney General would have to give permission for such a prosecution and he was the very person who had endorsed the war as lawful in the first place.

In March 2004 at a press conference at the House of Commons I launched a petition, organised by Legal Action Against the War (LAAW) and signed by other lawyers and politicians, requesting the newly formed ICC in The Hague to investigate the possibility that the UK government had committed war crimes in Iraq. I concentrated on this offence because there were obvious violations by coalition forces in the use of cluster bombs and depleted uranium which have an indiscriminate effect upon people and the environment. It was more difficult than you might imagine finding prominent lawyers prepared to put their reputations on the line, but

I have a stalwart friend and comrade in Ian Macdonald, QC, who kindly stood alongside me.

'Why do you want to put Mr Blair in the dock?' 'How are you going to do it?' 'What sentence will he get?' 'Is there any chance of success?' These were just a few of the many questions posed by the media, but of course our object is to highlight not only 'war crimes' but the illegality of the war itself. It is not an attack on personalities, more an issue of principle. At the end of the day it may not be Tony Blair's sole responsibility, but there is a need to ensure much greater transparency and accountability in such areas. Presently the prerogative powers enable certain executive decisions, such as signing treaties and declaring war, to be taken without the need for parliamentary consent and without effective remedy in the courts which regard such decisions as matters of high political policy which are 'non-justiciable'. This remarkable anomaly has to end.

On the one hand, when it suits a government – particularly when faced with political opposition that takes to the streets – 'the rule of law' is espoused in the event of public disorder. On the other hand, the crucial decision about such grave matters as going to war, which involves the loss of life as well as huge economic resources, is often taken with scant regard to the same principle.

This is why, as a lawyer, I felt that it was necessary, with others, to take a stand through the courts, because history has demonstrated that silence is the handmaiden of oppression. Perhaps the most important aspect of all of this for me, with all my children and grandchildren, is the example being set for future generations. The example or message is clear: 'might is right'. How can we expect those growing up and watching this spectacle to abide by the law in their domestic lives when such flagrant disregard has occurred on the international stage, played out on our television screens day after day? First invasion, then torture and rendition. In the wake of the return of British resident Binyam Mohamed, a dossier has been provided to the Metropolitan Police for an investigation into allegations of maltreatment against him and twenty-eight other British citizens held in Guantanamo Bay and elsewhere in which MI5 and MI6 are said to have been complicit.[18]

A more testing dilemma arose when George Galloway was on the phone from the Middle East, and the maverick MP came straight to the point: was I prepared to represent Saddam Hussein, who had just been discovered in his underground hideout, in his trial for war crimes?

Saddam was an oppressor of the worst kind, and I had represented his victims; but there was a substantial risk that he would not get a fair trial. I took time to think this one through – about twenty-four hours – but in the end I turned it down because I did not feel that I could conscientiously represent him especially given the plight of my client in the Iraqi hijack case (see Chapter 13). Nor was I comfortable returning other cases to which I was already committed. Unquestionably there were breaches of the fair-trial principles in the way that Saddam, although in an Iraqi court, was effectively tried by the Americans, not by an international court, and I don't believe he should have been executed, because in principle I am opposed to the death penalty (see Chapter 16). I never regretted my decision. Fortunately I have not often had to face dilemmas similar to the invitation to defend Saddam Hussein, because I have been publicly active in a number of political campaigns and there is an element of self-selection in the way cases come my way. People who are sympathetic to the issues I feel strongly about want me, and those who aren't don't.

The charter upon which the United Nations is founded was carefully crafted, and provides a clear scheme for peace within a staged framework. At one and the same time it attempts to minimise the risk of war, while appreciating the need for self-defence. Plainly if a real and immediate threat is posed by another state, there may be circumstances in which it is necessary for the threatened state to take unilateral action. The preconditions involve absolute necessity because there is no other alternative, and the response itself must be proportionate, discriminate and specific. It should only continue in such an emergency until such time as the United Nations itself can take over. This explains all the deceit and Dodgy Dossier nonsense about WMD and the myth of the forty-five-minute threat.

What should happen is that the United Nations keeps control of an escalating series of events where tension is running high and there is a risk of war. The charter suggests all manner of alternative means for achieving a peaceful solution. These necessarily involve diplomacy, but beyond that there may be the imposition first of economic sanctions and then of military ones. Ultimately it may be incumbent on the United Nations to intervene with a peacekeeping force. These various stages require the authority of the UN through its General Assembly and Security Council, and the authority is usually couched in terms of a resolution. That is why Tony Blair assured us that we would not go to war without a second resolution. One in which the UN finally determined that Iraq *did* possess WMD, *had* broken previous resolutions and resolved that military intervention by coalition forces with UN support *could* take place. That resolution was never passed.

The USA and the UK had predetermined for at least six months, by their deployment of troops on the ground, that invasion was a foregone conclusion. (Oliver Stone's film *W* has a wonderfully underplayed scene with George and Tony in a woodland setting, discussing the inevitability of the situation.)

On 17 November 2008 Lord Bingham, once Lord Chief Justice and senior Law Lord, gave a resounding endorsement to the view that the war lacked legitimacy. Addressing the British Institute of International and Comparative Law, he said, 'If I am right that the invasion of Iraq by the US, the UK, and some other states was unauthorised by the Security Council, there was a serious violation of international law and the rule of law.'[19]

Both the Preamble to the UN Charter and Article One deserve to be written on the walls of all our schools and colleges as an agenda for the future, but as far as I can ascertain, they barely get a mention. I make no excuse for setting them out at the end of the chapter.

I have been fortunate to experience the workings of international justice first-hand at the International Criminal Tribunal for the Former Yugoslavia (ICTY) in The Hague, and in 2003–4 I was again away from home for a case that lasted a year and a half – this time flying back and forth between London and Holland, leaving Yvette all week with Freddy, by now a wonderful, socially aware, opinionated teenager. It was tough, but necessary.

There was a team of lawyers from the UK, some from my chambers, and one from the USA, and we were extensively assisted by Dutch lawyers, interns from the United States, Albanian interpreters and researchers from Kosovo. This was the first time I had appeared in a trial at The Hague. The set-up was quite different and it took some time to acclimatise, but fortunately two of my English co-counsel were extremely experienced and had edited the two leading textbooks in the field. The whole process was challenging and exciting. Both the substantive law and procedure are still in their infancy and developing fast; the most interesting part for me was its eclectic nature, deriving its precepts from many different jurisdictions, although the English Common Law has had a singular influence.

Several trials were taking place at the same time, with the court hearing one case in the morning and another in the afternoon. For example, our court, with a different panel of three judges, was being used to try Slobodan Milosevic, who was accused of crimes against the Albanians among others, whereas the person I was representing was an Albanian in Kosovo accused of offences against the Serbs.

Lawyers from all over the world came together to take on these cases – from Canada, the USA, France, the UK, Italy, the Balkans, Australia and Africa. The mix was incredible, and because we were all crushed into a tiny communal robing room there was some pretty interesting intellectual frisson, though the *raison d'être* for everyone was the same: securing a fair trial for the defendants appearing there. It was a crucible of exchange in which ideas being forged in one trial might feed into another, and everything was televised, so you had up-to-the-minute commentary on developments.

My client was Fatmir Limaj, born on 4 February 1971 in the village of Banja, Mališevo municipality, Kosovo. During the 1998–9 Kosovo war, Fatmir earned something of a hero's reputation as a commander in the Kosovo Liberation Army (KLA), and led many civilians up into the mountains to escape the oppression of Milosevic's forces, where they were given shelter and sustenance. After the war he was one of the founders of what is now Kosovo's second-largest political party, the Democratic Party of Kosovo (PDK): he became deputy leader and a successful, much-admired politician.

Suddenly in 2003 the ICTY charged Fatmir, Isak Musliu and Haradin Bala with war crimes against Serbs and Albanians suspected of cooperating with Serbs during the Kosovo war.

The indictment against Fatmir read:

On the basis of individual criminal responsibility [Article 7(1) of the statute of the tribunal] and on the basis of superior criminal responsibility [Article 7(3)] he is charged with: five counts of crimes against humanity [Article 5] – imprisonment; torture; inhuman act; murder – and five counts of violations of the laws or customs of war [Article 3] – cruel treatment; torture; murder.

The trial commenced on Monday 15 November 2004 in Trial Chamber No. 1, in front of a triumvirate of international judges consisting of Judges Parker (presiding), Thelin and Van den Wyngaert.

Lawyers are entitled to dress in the robes of their home country, but I much preferred the ones customarily used in The Hague. For a start, there was no need for a wig, or a detachable stiff collar, both of which I find decidedly irritating. Instead I wore a floor-length black gown with full sleeves and a row of buttons down the front. Quite fetching really, and reminiscent of a Nonconformist priest. But its real advantage was the complete coverage it provided. Some lawyers wore a suit underneath, some just a T-shirt and jeans – and others rather less than that.

The allegations against Fatmir and his co-defendants were complex. In early 1998, after years of increasing tension and violence, armed conflict commenced between Serb forces and the Kosovo Liberation Army (KLA) in Kosovo, a development consistent with the KLA's general approach of active, armed resistance to Serb rule and occupation. It was alleged that until at least August 1998 the KLA targeted (by means of intimidation, imprisonment, violence and murder) both Serb and Albanian civilians who were perceived to be either refusing to cooperate with or resisting the KLA by non-military means.

Fatmir Limaj and Isak Musliu were said to have exercised both *de jure* and *de facto* command and control over KLA members operating a prison camp in the village of Lapusnik. Fatmir was accused of maintaining and enforcing the inhuman conditions in the camp, which included inadequate food and medical care, and of participating in or aiding and abetting the torture and beatings of the detainees, resulting in some deaths.

According to the indictment, shortly before 26 July 1998 Serb forces regained the area around the prison camp, and as a result the KLA abandoned it. Haradin Bala and another guard were said to have marched about twenty-one detainees from the camp into the Berisha Mountains. On the way they apparently met up with Fatmir, who gave orders, and shortly afterwards they were divided into two groups: the prisoners in one group were released, while those in the other were shot.

These were obviously very serious charges, and Fatmir knew he faced many, many years in prison if convicted. He was a tall, striking and imposing individual whose charisma was almost tangible. Here was a man who was deeply convinced about the moral purpose of the struggle in which he had participated, and during which he had attempted to maintain high standards of discipline and conduct among those he led.

In England the legal profession is divided between barristers and solicitors, with solicitors bearing the burden of investigation in preparation, and barristers that of presentation. In countries where this is not the case, a firm of lawyers carries out the whole exercise. Generally speaking, defence lawyers appearing in international cases in The Hague do not have this system of support. I was therefore faced for the first time in my career with the job of doing everything from start to finish. I've always wanted the opportunity to do so, because I felt it would give me a better idea about the quality of the material and evidence available to back up my case: a hands-on approach quickly reveals the pitfalls to be avoided.

Karim Khan, my co-counsel, had been to Kosovo before and was extremely familiar with the hurdles facing us there, as well as the complexities in The Hague. It was going to be necessary to visit all the relevant locations, discover pertinent witnesses willing to come forward, and have them interviewed without fear or favour – no mean task in a war-torn country where suspicion and bitterness run rife.

For my first visit Yvette came along too – as she often has on trips – both to support me and out of an abiding interest in things political. We were to meet Fatmir's family (though he himself was in custody in The Hague) and try to set up a defence group of people to undertake the tasks I had identified. I don't think I was fully prepared for what lay in store, and without Karim's generous and even-tempered demeanour we might not have got very far.

Kosovo is a small, mountainous country with, as we were soon to discover, a very attractive, welcoming and intelligent population. Their whole country – villages, towns, roads, communications, farms, trees, livelihoods and lives – had been decimated during the war. At the time I visited, the United Nations had the task of policing the country and overseeing a programme of regeneration while final-status talks continued with the Serb authorities.

Met at the airport by a driver and a bodyguard (who turned out to be Fatmir's brother), we drove through much new, solid, rather ugly, perfunctory architecture into the capital, Priština, and one of the first features I noticed was the presence of abundant American and British flags: I soon learned that there was a real sense of gratitude felt by the huge population of Albanian Kosovars for the support they have been given. This was no Iraq. We arrived at the Victory hotel, which was clean and comfortable, and were made very welcome, but we were rather shaken to be awoken the following morning by the sound of gunfire. A lot of political progress had been made since the war, but there was the occasional eruption of suppressed tension. It was an isolated incident, but it did make me think what it must be like to represent people in countries really on the front line, such as Palestine. I honestly don't know if I'd have the courage, and those lawyers who do are only to be admired.

On the way to meet Fatmir's family, the route took us through the very mountains into which he had escorted thousands of civilians from beleaguered villages, and I shall never forget those images that flooded our television screens of so many huddled figures trailing up steep slopes away from their homes: women with their babies, young children, the old, sick and feeble. The young men had either joined the KLA to fight or had been driven out of Kosovo into Albanian border refugee camps, or were the unlucky ones who had been captured and summarily massacred in large numbers.

Our jeep stopped to show us the life-saving, improvised shelters and bread ovens made in the caves and crevices in the rocks high in the mountains – the resourcefulness of people under such dire circumstances was staggering. It was Fatmir's dedication to his community which was largely responsible for their eventual salvation and, as it turned out, his own as well.

We were taken around Fatmir's area of command – which, our guide pointed out, did not cover the area of the prison camp, whatever the prosecution maintained had happened there – and saw the deserted regional headquarters of the KLA, which had been housed in a remote farmhouse. Across the road at the top of this desolate mountain was a small graveyard, with a series of graves in two semicircles, and it was distressing to read the simple inscriptions: one nineteen-year-old youth lay alongside another of eighteen, then two aged twenty and so on, one after the other surrounded by tattered flags of the KLA fluttering in the bitter wind. There was an eerie silence as Yvette and I stood together, both realising that any one of these young men could have been our son Freddy, had he been born in Kosovo. So many adolescent lives had been sacrificed for an independent homeland.

We went to the so-called prison camp, which consisted of two large outbuildings and a ramshackle series of farmhouses ranged around a courtyard. The advantage of site visits like this is that they bring home a reality which can never be replicated in the courtroom. It was a grey day with a mist hanging over the hillside and buildings, and it seemed such an inconsequential place to have witnessed the inhumanity alleged by the prosecution. The only people left were an elderly couple, and the old man said he knew nothing of such awful events in his home.

The authorities were determined that they were going to be seen to be even-handed in the treatment and trials of both Serbs (in the form of Milosevic) and Albanian Kosovans, and it wasn't going to be easy to clear Fatmir's name.

Kosovo is a predominantly Muslim country, which was evident as soon as we arrived at Fatmir's home. We took off our shoes and were very warmly welcomed by a reception committee of at least fifteen men of varying ages seated on a long padded bench that ranged along one wall of the quite sizeable room, while the women, some very elderly, were seated on the floor at their feet; none of them appeared to speak any English and we certainly didn't know any Albanian. We were formally introduced to Fatmir's parents, and Fatmir's father beckoned me to sit alongside him. Yvette hesitated – oh, help me, Allah, was she going to start an international incident?

Very sweetly, she gestured to Fatmir's mother and patted the space next to her on the bench by my side. The mother graciously rose from the floor and accepted the offer, and thus a thousand-year-old cultural custom was shattered. I then variously 'signed' or had translated my intention to defend Fatmir to the best of my ability. On my left, I noticed Yvette was communicating sympathy through her eyes to Fatmir's anxious mother: 'Michael will set him free,' she seemed to be saying. No pressure, then!

We were invited to take a meal with certain of the gathering, and this time we sat on a large rug on the floor with Fatmir's brothers and some cousins – and were embarrassed to be served by Fatmir's wife and sisters-in-law, who remained in the background in the adjoining kitchen. The elders on the bench watched carefully as we digested the delicious food while Yvette tried to engage the women in conversation – and suddenly Mirjeta Namani, one of the sisters-in-law, started speaking to us in near-perfect English about the case. She was highly articulate and explained that she was studying law, which was just the break we needed. I was looking for someone to lead the Kosovo legal team and this young woman seemed to be the perfect answer.

We spent another day meeting Fatmir's campaign group; having long discussions with representatives of all the political factions then vying for power; and enjoying dinner with extremely charming friends and colleagues of Fatmir. But then I really ran into trouble, it appeared there was a reticence about Mirjeta, a woman, leading our research team.

Well, I can be stubborn when necessary. She was ideally suited to the job, keen and efficient, and there was no male equivalent – but even if there had been, on principle I was not minded to acquiesce. This impasse lasted a number of weeks. Every time I thought Mirjeta had started work, there would be a deadly quiet; no sign of the important witness statements we needed for the trial. I knew she was eager to do this investigative work, but there'd be nothing – only silence. When I persisted, the silence turned into excuses suggesting that she wasn't available. It was pretty infuriating, but there was no way I was giving in over this one.

Eventually I went back to Kosovo to sort it out and draw up protocols for the collection of evidence in a systematic and judicious manner by non-lawyer volunteers. There was a very steely blue-eyed, handsome party leader who I thought could help. He was one of those people who would make a brilliant poker player: he gave nothing away, and was completely inscrutable and economical with words. I sat opposite him in a café and told him how it was. 'You want me' (and they really did want this arrogant Englishman Michael Mansfield, whose reputation had preceded him), 'and I have to have Mirjeta to head the investigative unit.' I resisted blurting out, as if it were *The Last Gunfight at the OK Corral*, 'Either that, or I leave now', as these guys had probably wielded a weapon or two during the war. Still, I stuck to my guns – and heigh ho, Mirjeta did my research; meticulous and invaluable it was too. (By the way, Mr Steely Blue Eyes, Hashim Thaçi, was elected the first Prime Minister of an independent Kosovo in February 2008.)

By now we had built a good team (which I codenamed PROMICK – because the UN force was called UNMIC) and a coherent case. Fatmir was adamant that he had nothing to do with human-rights atrocities, but rather was defending Albanian communities against the Milosovic regime, and he did this by setting up small, local defence units for the villages and by taking them to safety in the mountains when things got really bad. A large measure of the evidence against him was either tenuous or tainted by sectarian prejudice.

During the many months the trial lasted I had plenty of opportunities to sample the delights of The Hague. Most places, including the seafront and the centre of town, were within walking or cycling distance, which helped burn off the seductive patisserie. I had the small red collapsible bike, with a sturdy luggage rack on the back which was useful for passengers: standing room only. The art galleries – one of which contained Vermeer's *Girl with a Pearl Earring* and his beautiful dramatic stormy skylines over Delft – were wonderful, but the high spot was the International Jazz Festival. Freddy, Yvette and I enjoyed the last one before it moved to Rotterdam, in a venue right opposite the court building, and the place was packed to bursting, with music flooding out of every nook and cranny from stunning artists, young and old. Joss Stone and Jamie Cullum in particular gave barnstorming performances.

On Tuesday 30 August 2005 I delivered my final submissions to the tribunal.

I don't ever read a final speech: I use trigger notes and extemporise, so normally I don't have a record of exactly what I have said. This is the only time I have a transcript, because in The Hague it's normal procedure (unlike the UK) to record everything, including speeches, not just the evidence.

I started by quoting the words of Noel Malcolm in his introduction to *Kosovo: A Short History*:[20]

> The Yugoslav crisis began in Kosovo, and it will end in Kosovo. One can hear this saying almost anywhere in the former Yugoslavia; it's one of the few things on which all parties to the conflicts of the 1990s seem to agree.

I went on to describe the ICTY's fourfold mission. The fourth purpose is very significant: to 'contribute to the restoration of peace by promoting reconciliation in the former Yugoslavia'.

After that, it was important in the speech to establish the role of the KLA as a defence force against a superior oppressor, and to suggest to the judges what they might do in Fatmir's situation:

> If you were abroad watching your homeland being destroyed, almost in a war of attrition, conducted by a heavily armed Serbian force, it is unsurprising that you might want to come back and help. As we say, this is not some act of opportunism by Fatmir Limaj, or any of the others who came back. Think of it for one moment. If you'd left Kosovo and you were in Switzerland (as was Fatmir) or Italy or Sweden, wherever, how much easier would it be for you to say, 'I'm not going back there. Let the others do the fighting.' So the mere fact of a return, I would submit to you, is a significant one, risking lives. And a lot of people died; of that there is no doubt. And Fatmir's description to you ... you'll remember was a graphic one ... People are coming back in small groups, crossing the border. Yes, arms are coming over the border because they have but few themselves, as I've mentioned, the odd hunting rifle here and there. There's no point coming back and saying to villagers, 'Well, just use your pitchforks' when they come in. You only have to think across to Africa at the moment and what has happened in Darfur and elsewhere. Are people supposed to say,

'No, no, no, it's all right, you can do what you want, you can
come through, you can destroy all of us; all of our existence can be
destroyed, and we'll just leave.' Or are they to do what anybody, I
think, would submit is a natural and legitimate aim, and that is to
protect what little is left? And that is effectively what Fatmir did.

Above all, I wanted to demonstrate that Fatmir was a respected and
responsible leader who would not contemplate using any kind of
irresponsible, let alone inhuman treatment. There was a stream of
witnesses – diplomatic, political and expert – who were familiar
with Fatmir's efforts during the war and after, in the process of
reconstruction. They spoke volumes about his determination and,
above all, about his pluralist, multicultural approach. None of this
could easily be reconciled with a man who would undoubtedly have
had to countenance torture if the prosecution were right. In these
circumstances I chose in particular a witness who had gone with
Fatmir to the mountains with the thousands of people who were
seeking refuge there. His name was Fadil Bajraktari.
'He was the mountain teacher,' I told the tribunal:

You may remember during an emotionally charged day, in which
he recalled what had happened in that autumn period to the
children, particularly the children, and the way in which shelter
was provided by Fatmir Limaj; food provided by Fatmir Limaj
and schooling provided by Fatmir Limaj. You saw the photographs
of the makeshift tents and the conditions under which this was
done. Medical supplies provided by Fatmir Limaj and, most of all
perhaps, something which he has contrived to do throughout, and
again it is in stark contrast to the allegations in the indictment, is
to provide hope and inspiration. And he did it in a particular way
for this individual.

I quoted his evidence:

When we went to the mountains I was feeling worse and worse
and the medical team came from the Red Cross from Geneva
and they told me they wanted to take me abroad to be cured;
but Fatmir's idea to have a school to teach the children made

me refuse. I told those doctors that I won't come. I decided to stay with the children. I proposed to them [the Red Cross] to take two young mothers who are about to give birth instead. I couldn't leave those children there, even if I would feel well again and my kidneys would become better. I didn't want that life. I wanted to be close to the children because my life was with them. Believe me, the miracle happened. I didn't go to the doctor again. I didn't need that surgery any more. The kidney stones, I passed them out myself. I didn't need the surgery any more. That's what happened to me. Today I'm fit as a fiddle. I don't suffer any more. But it was Fatmir who taught me how to become a teacher; a teacher of those children: 'The Teacher of the Mountain', as they called me.

Haunting testimony of one individual, but of course hope and inspiration often springs not only eternal, but from the individual.

Many witnesses had spoken about the vision that Fatmir had for Kosovo, so I ended my address to the judges:

It's a vision which of course some in politics, and Martin Luther King, would call a dream. Interestingly in a book published recently, entitled *The Palace of Dreams*, the first International Booker prize-winner this year, Ishmael Kadare, the Albanian writer, described a regime against which he'd set his own face (and one no doubt against which Fatmir Limaj would have set his face) – a totalitarian regime rather than a democratic one. In the book he describes the need for a Master of Dreams; in other words, those who have a facility to have visions that will govern the destiny of states. If I may end what I have to say to you with Fatmir Limaj's own words about this vision: 'I very much believe that if we don't take the initiative of creating, building trust among us, nothing will succeed, no matter what UNMIC does. I regret to say, in Kosovo we should have brave people, people who are willing to assume responsibilities upon their own shoulders, and not to do things only for the sake of the international community . . . We should do things because this is in the interest and for the benefit of the people . . .'

In November 2005, Fatmir was acquitted by the ICTY, one of the very few defendants at The Hague who have ever been acquitted on all counts. It was a moment of great elation for the people of Kosovo, and it was also a moment for reflection and for reconciliation.

The day we won, Fatmir insisted that Karim and I return immediately with him to Kosovo to share in the victory: optimistically, a flight had been booked in case of this eventuality, and we departed in the late afternoon from Amsterdam via Vienna to Priština, where the welcome was enormous and overwhelming. The road between the airport and the main stadium in Priština was lined with people singing, shouting, laughing, crying and waving the national flag. It was an honour to witness tens of thousands of Kosovans in a tumultuous thanksgiving, which brought the country to a standstill.

We went straight into the stadium, but because of the huge crowds – and lest I got lost attempting to follow Fatmir's swift passage towards the waiting audience of around 100,000 – I was lifted off my feet by two bodyguards, and ended up close by Fatmir's side. His speech was spellbinding. As I don't speak Albanian I didn't understand a word of it, but then I didn't need to, because the chanting and cheering at every word made clear what was meant. It was nothing short of pure exhilaration, and occasionally I would detect the shout 'Mansfieldi! Mansfieldi!'

The motorcade continued from Priština, travelling through the night and covering the length and breadth of the land, visiting families and communities that had given Fatmir support during the war and the trial. No unmade, unmarked road was too far, no tiny hamlet too small, no family too few in number. At each point the greeting was the same – from an elderly, gravel-lined face that sprang to life, with tears of joy and an ever-spreading smile. The most poignant part was the nocturnal homage paid at the many war cemeteries of young men in their prime who had paid with their lives fighting for freedom and justice. They did not live to see the triumph, but it was palpable that night. Even autonomy for Kosovo lay within reach.

The next morning at Fatmir's family home there were more ceremonies and celebrations, though I was a little worse for wear, having had no sleep and no change of clothing, as the whole visit had been totally unexpected. A marquee had been erected, with a table and chairs at one end, and the male elders of the family, including Fatmir, sat there for several hours receiving the good wishes and blessings of people from all over Kosovo. On some occasions Karim and I would be invited to sit with them while the exchanges were translated for us. The bonds of friendship were firm and unfailing.

Once the numbers dwindled it was time for a dance, something I always find hard to resist, even if I've never done it before and I've no idea what is expected. We formed a circle of thirty or forty people, and people could join in or drop out as they pleased. There was an infectious drumbeat that got us all going and I relied heavily upon my memories of *Zorba the Greek*, which – had they known – would probably not have gone down too well. What I hadn't really noticed, owing to the euphoria that had anaesthetised all our senses, was that the ground beneath our feet had acquired a farmyard quality from the overnight rain and the heavy stamping. I had come straight from court in clothes that were not best suited for such hopping around and retained a certain country air all the way back on the plane.

The celebrations were momentarily dampened when we were put on notice that the prosecution, not satisfied with the result, were going to try and get Fatmir's acquittal overturned on appeal, but that seemed to me a pretty hapless exercise, because it would be no more than a rerun of the trial, suggesting that the tribunal had not applied the proper standard of proof. It failed on all counts. In September 2007 came the announcement: 'The Appeals Chamber finds that the Trial Chamber reasonably found that Fatmir Limaj does not incur criminal responsibility for any of the offences charged in the indictment.' Today Fatmir is still a free man and is once again active in politics: he ran for Mayor of Priština in the elections held on 17 November 2007 and won, and at the time of writing is a minister in the government of the Republic of Kosovo.

All in all, it was a great job done by everyone – and it's good to be able to say that now and again.

As a result of the experience at The Hague I feel invigorated and renewed. The ICTY court has shown the possibilities of both prosecution and defence. The ICC has now established an innovative unit to assist and support victims and their families, who have so often been neglected by the judicial process: I hope to be involved with this work one day. It is important that the principles that are being applied receive the necessary moral and financial support from the international community. No longer is it so easy for tyrants, oppressors and murderers to evade justice. They may hide, but they can't run any more, for fear of arrest.

It took a Spanish magistrate to finger General Pinochet, who – staggeringly – had been allowed into the UK by the Labour administration to visit Margaret Thatcher. Eventually, under the pretext of ill health, he was returned to Chile to face trial.

And in September 2005 Doron Almog, an Israeli general, arrived at Heathrow airport on an El Al flight.[21] Between 2000 and mid-2003 he had been head of Israel's Southern Command, responsible for operations in Gaza, which included the demolition of an estimated 1,100 Palestinian homes. Once again the British Government failed to make any plans for his detention. Daniel Machover is an Israeli citizen and a solicitor with the London firm Hickman Rose, who represents clients from the Palestinian Centre for Human Rights and individuals whose homes were bulldozed and whose families were bombed in Gaza. He persuaded the police that General Almog should be arrested if he set foot on British soil, the intention being to initiate a private prosecution under UK statutes incorporating the Geneva Convention. (The necessary legal paperwork and preparations had been assembled with the assistance of Steve Kamlish, QC, and Paul Troop from my chambers.) Someone tipped off the general and he refused to get off the plane, and the British police, fearing an armed confrontation, backed down, when all they needed to have done was prevent the plane from taking off. General Almog may have escaped on that occasion, but increasingly those who commit crimes against humanity in future may have to think twice before they do so, and certainly before they travel abroad.

The Charter of the United Nations[22] reads:

CHAPTER I: PURPOSES AND PRINCIPLES
Article 1

The Purposes of the United Nations are:

1 To maintain international peace and security, and to that end: to take effective collective measures for the prevention and removal of threats to the peace, and for the suppression of acts of aggression or other breaches of the peace, and to bring about by

peaceful means, and in conformity with the principles of justice and international law, adjustment or settlement of international disputes or situations which might lead to a breach of the peace;

2 To develop friendly relations among nations based on respect for the principle of equal rights and self-determination of peoples, and to take other appropriate measures to strengthen universal peace;

3 To achieve international co-operation in solving international problems of an economic, social, cultural, or humanitarian character, and in promoting and encouraging respect for human rights and for fundamental freedoms for all without distinction as to race, sex, language, or religion; and

4 To be a centre for harmonising the actions of nations in the attainment of these common ends.

The long arm of international law stretches across national frontiers. It's not foolproof and it's not always fair, but without it the world would be a far poorer place.

I am ever optimistic.

Acknowledgements

My sincere thanks and appreciation to those who have helped me in producing a memoir of my legal career . . .

Anthony & Robina Masters – Anthony's untimely death jolted me into creating this as a commemoration of his joie de vivre.

Bill Swainson, Senior Editor, Bloomsbury – patience personified, thoughtful and perceptive – what more can one hope for in an editor?

Sean Magee, who helped shape and frame the book with sensitivity and professionalism.

David Hooper for the scrutiny of his legal eagle-eye.

Anna Simpson, Editor, always good humoured, efficient and positive.

Mandy Greenfield, Catherine Best and Vicki Robinson for meticulous copyediting, proofreading and indexing respectively.

The team at Bloomsbury including Colin Midson, Ruth Logan, Nick Humphrey, Penny Edwards and Polly Napper.

Nigel Warner, for writing our very first outline so long ago I can now hardly recall . . .

Camilla Cameron for her unstinting support as my PA for ten years and for garnering valuable research; and Natasha Coburn who has recently stepped into her capable shoes with enthusiasm and competence.

The clerks at Tooks, who are a collective team of wizards at endless information retrieval.

My family, for allowing me to trespass on their privacy where it touches on my legal life – especially my great children: Jonathan, Anna, Louise, Leo, Kieran and Freddy, and my gorgeous grandchildren: Larissa, Elyse, Charlotte, Myles and baby Luca.

And my darling wife Yvette, for her electronic, intellectual, inspirational skills.

Notes

Criminal cases may involve at least two stages – trial and appeal. Records relating to these stages are many and various. The primary record of trial is made by a shorthand writer or stenographer; it can then (but not always) be converted into a transcript. Copies may be held by the court, the firm of shorthand writers or the firm of solicitors involved. These will only exist because someone has requested one for some purpose. The transcript will have a case number reference which includes the year of the trial, the number given to the case by the court which appears on the indictment and sometimes initials, maybe referring to a defendant. For example: 2000/111111/MM.

If, however, a transcript hasn't been produced it may still be possible to procure one if you have some idea of the name, place and date of the trial. But this will have to come from the firm of shorthand writers at the time, which will require payment for the transcription.

Nowadays there is an increasing use of 'Livenote', an instantaneous transcription service that usually ends up on the Internet. Presently there are very few criminal trials recorded in this way. A transcript from this source could come from, for example, www.sellers.co.uk. In the case of high-profile public inquiries or inquests full transcripts are easily available on the Web. Enter the case name and 'transcripts' into a search engine and it should come up.

If a case has gone to appeal the process of transcript recovery is much the same. Once again there will be a case number, usually incorporating the year in which the application for leave was lodged, the number allocated to the application individually for each applicant, plus letters referring to who knows what. In forty-two years, I've never bothered to ask! For example 2000/1111/M1.

Besides transcripts, cases are reported. This is mainly done for the purpose of highlighting points and decisions on matters of law. These reports do not provide a verbatim account of what has transpired at trial or on appeal but what they do provide is the rationale for rulings and judgments. Not all decisions are reported. Some may appear in short form, summarised in newspapers such as *The Times* and the *Independent* and specialist journals such as the *Criminal Law Review* (CLR). Full reports are available in law libraries under different titles, such as *All England Law Reports* (AER), *Weekly Law Reports* (WLR) and *Criminal Appeal Reports* (CAR). These reports are often published many months and sometimes years after the judgments themselves. They are arranged by date, volume number, followed by the initials of the report series, and page number within the volume. For example [2000] 1 CAR 55.

Most of these law reports are available on the Web if you are a member of a legal network; they can be very expensive. For example, try Westlaw and Casetrack.

Chapter 1: 'Michael, You See What You Want to See!'

1 The Doppler Effect: when a source of light (or sound) is moving towards or away from an observer (radial velocity) the photons (or sound waves) show a shift in wavelength from what would be observed for a stationary source. The sense of the shift is towards longer wavelengths for receding objects and shorter wavelengths for objects coming towards us.

Chapter 3: Drugs, Rock and Law

1 Michael Mansfield, 'Private Drug Use – No Crime?', *Drugs & Society*, Macmillan Journals, London, July 1973, vol. 2, no. 10, pp. 10–11.

Chapter 4: Prints and Impressions

1 Gordon Carr, *The Angry Brigade, the Cause and the Case: Britain's First Urban Guerillas*, Victor Gollancz, London, 1975.
2 Marshall McLuhan's *The Gutenberg Galaxy: The Making of Typographic Man* (University of Toronto Press, Canada, 1962) is a pioneering study in the fields of oral culture, print culture, cultural studies and media ecology.
3 Lord Justices Swinton Thomas, Garland and Longmore, Judgment no. 9704481S2, 17 December 1998; *The Times*, 18 December 1998, p. 15.
4 James Randerson, 'Study questions reliability of fingerprint evidence', *Guardian*, Friday 23 March 2007.

Chapter 5: Parents at Risk

1 Lady Bracknell interviewing Jack/Ernest about his background in *The Importance of Being Earnest* by Oscar Wilde, Penguin Classic, London, 1995.
2 The Confidential Enquiry into Maternal and Child Health (CEMACH) was established in April 2003. It replaces CESDA (the Confidential Enquiry into Stillbirths and Deaths in Infancy) and CEMD (the Confidential Enquiry into

Maternal Deaths); this gives it a truly perinatal focus, but its remit is now wider and includes all childhood death.

3 Trial transcript, 5 March 2002, pp. 941–3, my cross-examination.
4 The long QT syndrome (LQTS) causes an abnormality of the heart's electrical system. The mechanical function of the heart is entirely normal. The electrical problem is due to defects in the heart-muscle cell structures known as ion channels. These electrical defects predispose affected persons to a very fast heart rhythm (arrhythmia) called 'Torsade de Pointes' (TdP), which leads to a sudden loss of consciousness (syncope) and may cause sudden cardiac death.
5 Lord Justice Judge's judgment [2004] EWCA Crim. 1; 2 CAR7; 1 WLR 2607; 1 AER 725, given on 19 January 2004 in Angela Cannings appeal; conviction quashed on 10 December 2005.
6 From BBC News on the Cannings appeal, 10 December 2003; see also Angela Cannings, with Megan Lloyd Davies, *Against the Odds, A Mother's Fight to Prove Her Innocence*, Time Warner Books, London, 2006.
7 Stephen Howard, 'Abuse case couple lose fight to get children back', *Independent*, 12 February 2009
8 Lord Justice Gage and Justices Gross and McFarlane, Case no. 200403277, 21 July 2005, 2006 1 CAR 55.
9 Tooks Court became Tooks Chambers when we moved location from Tooks Court itself to Clerkenwell in 2004.
10 Kevin Callan, *Kevin Callan's Story*, Little, Brown, London, 1997, p. 14.
11 Philip Wrightson, Dorothy Gronwall and Peter Waddell, *Head Injury: The Facts*, Oxford University Press, New York, 1998.
12 From my Foreword to Kevin Callan, *Kevin Callan's Story*, Little, Brown, London, 1997, p. ix.
13 Jane Merrick, 'Cuts to Forensic Watchdog', *Independent*, 22 March 2009
14 *Frye v. United States*, 293 F. 1013 (D.C. Cir. 1923).
15 The Daubert Test arose out of the United States Supreme Court case *Daubert v. Merrell Dow Pharmaceuticals*, 509 US 579 (1993).
16 Sourced from Esther Rantzen, *Esther: The Autobiography*, BBC Books, London, 2001, ch. 13, pp. 293–4.

Chapter 6: 1984

1 *Financial Times*, 4 March 1985.
2 Bernard Jackson and Tony Wardle, *The Battle for Orgreave*, Vanson Wardle Productions, Brighton, 1986, ch. 3, p. 37.
3 Ibid., ch. 6, p. 76.
4 Hansard HC Deb 20 June 1991 vol. 193 cc463–81; see also: http://hansard. millbanksystems.com/commons/1991/jun/20/business-of-the-house
5 See: www.thepeoplescharter.com.
6 See: http://news.bbc.co.uk/onthisday/hi/dates/stories/february/15/newsid_3455000/3455083.stm.
7 See: www.activistslegalproject.org.uk.

Chapter 7: The Slenderest Thread

1 'Bailey' is defined as a courtyard of a castle formed by spaces between the defences which surround the keep.
2 Cited in both Brian Cathcart, *Jill Dando, Her Life and Death*, Penguin, London, 2001, ch. 15, pp. 279–80, and S. C. Lomax, *The Case of Barry George*, Kempton Marks, Hertford, 2004, ch. 6, p. 128.
3 The Parabellum pistol was developed by Georg Luger in Germany, c. 1898. The Parabellum name comes from the ancient Latin saying, 'Si vis Pacem,

Para bellum,' (If you want Peace, prepare for War). See www.world.guns.ru/handguns/hg67-e.htm if you must.

4 Cited in Lomax, *The Case of Barry George*, ch. 2, p. 31.

5 Justin Davenport, 'Yard to investigate Serbian's bar boast that he killed Dando', *Evening Standard*, Monday 23 February 2009.

Chapter 8: The Need to Know

1 Sections 8(i) and 8(iii) respectively of the Coroner's Act 1988.

2 See: www.inquest.org.uk.

3 Size and tonnage specifications from the *Marchioness Inquiry Report*, vol. 2, annex D, p. 1; speed specification from the *Marchioness Inquiry Report*, vol. 1, para. 10.19, p. 1: both The Stationery Office, February 2001.

4 'Marchioness hands lost for years', BBC News Online, 8 December 2000. See: http://news.bbc.co.uk/i/hi/uk/1061472.stm.

5 The *Marchioness Inquiry Report*, vol. 1, para. 15.56, p. 153, Right Honourable Justice Clarke and panel.

6 Ibid., para. 16.32, p. 174.

7 Ibid., para. 21.2, p. 251.

8 Oral evidence taken before the Home Affairs and Work and Pensions Committees, Thursday 10 November 2005.

9 *The Stephen Lawrence Inquiry/Macpherson Report*, The Stationery Office, February 1999, ch. 13, para. 25.

10 From material provided to the Stephen Lawrence/Macpherson Inquiry, which began on Tuesday 24 March 1998.

11 *The Stephen Lawrence Inquiry/Macpherson Report*, ch. 19, para. 8.

12 Ibid., ch. 8, para. 7.

13 This reference is at 7.31 in the transcript of the hearings of the Stephen Lawrence/Macpherson Inquiry; a version of part of the protracted surveillance appears in the appendices to *The Stephen Lawrence Inquiry/Macpherson Report*.

14 *Archbold: Criminal Pleading, Evidence and Practice*, Thomson Sweet & Maxwell, London, 2007, paras 13-1 to 13-104, p. 1431 onwards.

15 Doreen Lawrence, *And Still I Rise*, Faber and Faber, London, 2006, pp.185–6.

16 *The Stephen Lawrence Inquiry/Macpherson Report*, ch. 8, paras 8.2 and 8.3 respectively.

17 Ibid., para. 8.3.

18 Jamie Doward, 'New report says racism still rife in police force', *Observer*, Sunday 15 February 2009, p. 5.

Chapter 9: The Trouble with Ireland

1 Patrick Bishop and Eamonn Mallie, *The Provisional IRA*, Heinemann, London, 1987, p. 9; and Marianne Elliott, *Wolfe Tone*, Yale University Press, London, 1989, pp. 392–5.

2 A paralegal who assists a solicitor's firm by attending court, interviewing witnesses and visiting clients in prison.

3 Suzanne Breen, 'Old Bailey bomber ashamed of Sinn Fein', *The Village*, 7 December 2004; see: www.irishfreedomcommittee.net/news/december_2004.

4 Don Mullan and John Scally, *Eyewitness Bloody Sunday: The Truth*, Merlin, Dublin, 2002, p.xli.

5 *The Bloody Sunday Inquiry/Saville Report*, Day 260/46/3 to Day 260/53/22.

Chapter 10: That Little Tent of Blue

1 Material presented in court – an article written by Wadi Williams while an inmate at Hull Prison; see: http://libcom.org/history/1989-the-risley-prisoners-uprising.
2 Ibid.
3 Michael Mansfield and Maggie Raynor, *Whale Boy*, Mantra Publishing, London, 1991.
4 Material from Nicki Jameson and Eric Allison, *Strangeways 1990: A Serious Disturbance*, Larkin Publications, London, 1995 quoted in the *Guardian*.
5 Prisons Security Act, 1992, *Archbold*, 2009, p 2689, paras. 28-217 to 28-218.
6 Anne Owers, Chief Inspector of Prisons, 'Prison System at a Crossroads, Warns Chief Inspector', Press release re Annual Report 2006–2007, 30 January 2008, see www.inspectorates.homeoffice.gov.uk/hmiprisons.

Chapter 11: The Magic Bullet?

1 Prof. Brian Caddy (Strathclyde University), Review commissioned by the Forensic Science Regulator, November 2007.
2 Transcript of Omagh judgment, Neutral Citation No. (2007) NICC 49 Ref. WEI 7021, esp. paras 62–4, pp. 20–23.
3 Sean O'Neill, 'Defence lawyers ready to seize on DNA doubts', *The Times*, 24 January 2008.
4 Caddy Report, November 2007; *A Review of the Science of Low Template DNA Analysis*, April 2008; see: police.homeoffice.gov.uk/publications/operational-policing.
5 Paul Foot, *Who Killed Hanratty?*, Jonathan Cape, London, 1971; and Paul Foot, *Hanratty, the Final Verdict*, Macmillan, London, 1997.
6 Rod Chaytor, 'I'd rather have died in jail than admit a murder I didn't do', *Daily Mirror*, Saturday 5 July 2003.
7 Ibid.
8 Sandra Laville, 'Twenty-seven years on', *Guardian*, 12 March 2009.
9 *R v. Deen*, *The Times*, 10 January 1994, CA; and *Archbold*, 2009, paras 14–58, p. 1585.
10 Iain Haddow, 'Debating ethics of DNA database', BBC News Online, Wednesday 9 January 2008; see: http://news.bbc.co.uk/1/hi/uk/7177152.stm.
11 Ibid.
12 Peter Walker, 'European court rules DNA database breaches human rights', *Guardian*, 4 December 2008.

Chapter 12: Cops and Robbers

1 Transcript of the judgment of the Court of Appeal, Lord Justice Roch and Justices Hidden and Mitchell, Wednesday 30 July 1997, Ref. 96/5131/S1, p. 47.
2 Ibid., p. 57.
3 Ibid., p. 89.
4 Ibid., p. 137.
5 Gisli Gudjonsson, *The Psychology of Interrogation, Confessions and Testimony*, John Wiley & Sons, Chichester, West Sussex, 1992.
6 Appeal of Engin Raghip, Judgment Ref. 90/5920/51, 91/4944/51, 91/4945/51, Court of Appeal Criminal Division 5 December 1991.
7 Ibid, pp. 4–6.
8 Ibid, pp. 18–19.
9 Michael Mansfield and Tony Wardle, *Presumed Guilty*, Heinemann, London, 1993, ch. 8, p. 96.
10 Clive Walker and Keir Starmer, *Miscarriages of Justice*, Blackstone Press, London, 1999, p. 39.

Chapter 13: The Switch

1 Letter in Lord Acton's *Life of Mandell Creighton*, cited in *Oxford Dictionary of Quotations*, Oxford University Press, Oxford, 2nd edition 1953, p. 1.
2 From material at the trial of the alleged Iraqi hijackers, Old Bailey, 1997, in front of Mr Justice Wright.
3 Court of Appeal judgment, Thursday 17 December 1998, Ref. 9707758/51.
4 From material in the Court of Appeal, 1998, in front of Lord Justice Rose.
5 A precis of the Terrorism Act 2000, Section 1, and the Terrorism Act 2006, Section 34.
6 Fabio Bourbon, *Egypt Yesterday and Today, Lithographs by David Roberts, RA*, American University in Cairo Press, 1996, pp. 173–5.
7 Mahatma Gandhi explains his philosophy, way of life and the concept of non-violence (*ahimsa*) in his autobiography *The Story of My Experiments with Truth*, Navajivan Trust, 1927.
8 From an email from her husband Omar, in evidence at the trial of Tahira Tabassum at the Old Bailey, April 2004.

Chapter 14: Lifting the Lid

1 Convicted of the (sexual) murder of a young girl in 1976, Stefan Kiszko spent sixteen years in prison until he was released in 1992. He died of a heart attack the following year at his mother's home, aged forty-four; his mother, who had waged a long campaign to prove her son's innocence, died six months later. A detective and a forensic scientist were charged with perverting the course of justice, but the case was halted at committal because of 'the lapse of time'. See Stewart Tendler, 'Two are Accused of Perverting Justice', *The Times*, 12 May 1994.
2 Michael Mansfield and Tony Wardle, *Presumed Guilty*, Heinemann, London, 1993, p. 55.
3 Judith Teresa Ward, 1993, 96 CAR 1, p. 56.
4 Ibid., p. 51.
5 Dominic Kennedy, 'Uncovered: Police notes cast doubt over Eddie Gilfoyle murder', *The Times*, 20 February 2009; 'New evidence prompts police review of murder case', *The Times*, 21 February 2009.
6 The Criminal Cases Review Commission (CCRC) is the independent public body set up in 1995 to investigate possible miscarriages of justice in England, Wales and Northern Ireland. (Previously this had been left to the Home Secretary.) The Comission assesses whether convictions or sentences should be referred to a court of appeal. See: www.ccrc.gov.uk.

Chapter 15: Shared Experience

1 Charles Dickens, *Bleak House*, Penguin English Library, London, 1984, p.178.
2 Ibid, p.182.
3 Lord Scarman's *The Scarman Report* (25 November 1981, The Stationery Office), which resulted from an official inquiry into rioting in the Brixton neighbourhood of London, concluded (amongst other recommendations) that the police had become too remote from their communities and that local citizens should have more input into police policy-making.
4 Tandana – the Glow-worm website (archiving the Bradford Twelve case). See: www.tandana.org.

Chapter 16: The Execution

1 Jane Officer (ed.), *If I Should Die*, New Clarion Press, Cheltenham, 1999.
2 Cited in Marie Mulvey Roberts, *Out of the Night*, New Clarion Press, Cheltenham, 1994, p. 245.
3 *Death Sentences and Executions in 2007*, Amnesty International, issued April 2008
4 Robert Verkalk, 'China Spearheads Surge in State Sponsored Execution', *Independent*, 24 March 2009.
5 Amicus derives its meaning from the legal term *amicus curiae*, which is used to describe lawyers who intervene in cases to provide advice and information on issues that are being litigated.
6 See: www.amicus-alj.org.
7 The African Prisons Project's founder, Alexander McLean, won the Beacon Fellowship Award 2007; see: www.africanprisons.com.
8 The Murder (Abolition of Death Penalty) Act 1965, Section 1, *Archbold*, 2009, p. 707, para 5-236.
9 Transcript of Case no. 9706415/S2, p. 10.
10 See their judgment at Neutral Citation No: (2003) EWCA, Crim. 3556, para. 90.
11 Although her sister Muriel Jakubait, in her book *My Sister's Secret Life* (Constable & Robinson, London, 2005) argues that Ruth was the victim of a secret-service conspiracy run by Dr Stephen Ward, who was later linked to the Profumo/Keeler scandal.
12 Ministry of Justice, *Murder, Manslaughter and Infanticide: Proposals for Reform of the Law*, Consultation Paper, July 2008; see: www.justice.gov.uk/publications/cp1908.
13 Jakubait, *My Sister's Secret Life*, ch. 15, pp. 235–6.
14 Peter and Shirley Adams, *Knockback* (Duckworth, London, 1982) contains their letters.

Chapter 17: No ExSkuse

1 The full chronology of events was as follows:
   • Trial, 15 August 1975 before Mr Justice Bridge.
   • Appeal, March 1976 before Lord Chief Justice Widgery.
   • Application for a civil action against the police and Home Office for injuries in custody, 17 January 1980, before Lord Denning, Master of the Rolls.
   • Appeal to House of Lords, November 1981, upheld Denning's judgment.
   • Second appeal, referred back by Home Secretary, Douglas Hurd, 20 January 1987.
   • Second appeal, 2 November 1987, before Lord Lane, Lord Chief Justice in Court Number 12, Old Bailey, denied 28 January 1988.
   • Third appeal before Lord Justice Lloyd, 4 March 1991.
   • Release date, 4 p.m. 14 March 1991
2 Ludovic Kennedy, *Ten Rillington Place*, first published by Victor Gollancz, London, 1961.
3 Chris Mullin, *Error of Judgement*, Poolbeg, Dublin, 1987.
4 Lord Denning's judgment, 17 January 1980, on the Birmingham Six's action against the police, cited in Mullin, *Error of Judgement*, p. 243.
5 Arthur Koestler, *The Roots of Coincidence*, Vintage, London, 1973.
6 Mullin, *Error of Judgement*, pp. 311, 325–8.
7 Ibid.
8 Ibid.
9 Terry Kirby, 'Decision to Halt Birmingham Six case "exceptional"', *Independent*, 16 October 1993.

10 Seamus Boyd, 'Birmingham Six Reflect on their Lost Years', BBC News NI, 14 May 2002.

Chapter 18: Big Brother

1 John Ezard, 'Did love turn Orwell into a government stooge?', *Guardian*, 21 June 2003.
2 Timothy Garton Ash, 'Under the blanket', *Guardian*, 10 July 2003.
3 David Leigh and Paul Lashmar, 'Revealed: how MI5 vets BBC staff', *Observer*, 18 August 1985.
4 There is a sinister pro-Nazi website – PzG.biz – where you can buy a recording of the song. The memorabilia on offer are advertised as 'helping you create the ultimate Adolf Hitler, Third Reich Nazi military collection'. Nice.
5 Leigh and Lashmar, 'Revealed: how MI5 vets BBC staff'.
6 Ibid.
7 Hugo Young and Cathy Massiter, *MI5's Official Secrets*, 20/20 Vision for C4, 1988. Sean O'Neill and others, 'No Secrets, No Risk', *The Times*, 17 April 2009.
8 Sean O'Neill et al., 'No Secrets, No Risk', *The Times*, 17 April 2009.
9 Annie Machon, *Spies, Lies and Whistleblowers*, The Book Guild, Lewes, Sussex, 2005, ch. 2, p. 44, confirms that there was an MI5 file in existence.
10 See: www.the-hutton-inquiry.org.uk.
11 Republic, the Campaign for an Elected Head of State and a British Republic: www.republic.org.uk.
12 *Middleton v. HM Coroner for West Somerset*, 2004 2 AC 182.
13 *R v. Greater Manchester Coroner*, case Tal (1985) QB 67.
14 From the official Diana/Dodi inquest transcript, available at: www.scottbaker-inquests.gov.uk/hearing_transcripts/031007am.htm, p.81: 17–23.
15 Operation Paget Inquiry report: overview, p. 4; see: www.direct.gov.uk/en/Nl1/Newsroom/DG_065122.
16 www.scottbaker-inquests.gov.uk/hearing_transcripts/031007am.htm, 07.04.2008, pp.6–7.
17 Ibid., 24.10.2007, p. 47.23 to p. 48.2.
18 Ibid., 24.10.2007, p. 73.17 to p. 75.16.
19 Ibid., 24.10.2007, p. 10.3–6 and p. 23.9 to p. 23.12.
20 Ibid., 24.10.2007, p. 25.16 to p. 25.18.
21 Ibid., 12.03.2008, p. 82.2.
22 Ibid., 11.10.2007, p. 6.2–12 and p. 12.24 to p. 13.25.
23 Ibid., Inquest. Doc. 0006335.
24 Ibid., 15.01.2008, p. 109.17–19.
25 Ibid., Inquest. Doc. 0010117.
26 Ibid., 18.02.2008, p. 2.19–22.
27 Princess Diana/Martin Bashir, *Panorama*, 20 November 1995; transcript at: www.bbc.co.uk/politics97/diana/panorama.html.
28 www.scottbaker-inquests.gov.uk/hearing_transcripts/031007am.htm, 10.01.2008, p. 52.12–23.
29 Andrew Pierce, 'Diana's Letters to PMs will remain Secret', *Daily Telegraph*, Thursday 19 February 2009, p. 2.
30 www.scottbaker-inquests.gov.uk/hearing_transcripts/031007am.htm, p.81: 17–23 Inquest. Doc. 0058847, p. 2.
31 Ibid., 4.03.2008, p. 64.4–8.
32 Ibid., Inquest. Doc. 0060705, p. 6.
33 Ibid., Inquest. Doc. 0061066.
34 Ibid., 14.01.2008, p. 86.7–11.
35 The Regulation of Investigatory Powers Act 2000; see www.opsi.gov.uk/acts/

acts2000/ukpga_20000023_en; *Archbold*, 2009, pp. 2476–92, paras 25–368 to 25–380.

Chapter 19: Milk, Muck and Methane

1 *The Animals Film*, directed by Miriam Aloux and Victor Schonfeld, Channel 4, 1981, released on DVD in September 2008.
2 Duncan Campbell, *That Was Business, This Is Personal*, Secker & Warburg, London, 1990.
3 'Over the past 15 years, McDonald's has threatened legal action against more than 90 organisations in the UK, including the BBC, Channel 4, the *Guardian*, the *Sun*, the Scottish TUC, the *New Leaf Shop*, student newspapers and a children's theatre group. Even Prince Philip received a stiff letter. All of them backed down and many formally apologised in court'; taken from Franny Armstrong, 'Why won't British TV show a film about McLibel?', *Guardian*, 19 June 1998.
4 See: www.mcspotlight.org.
5 Ibid.; see also link to Mr Justice Bell's judgment on 19 June 1997.
6 Appeal judgment, Wednesday 31 March, Court 1, Royal Courts of Justice, pp. 247 and 264 – this publication can be found at www.mcspotlight.org.
7 See: www.mcspotlight.org.
8 Nick Mathaison, 'Shell in Court over alleged role in Nigeria executions', *Observer*, 5 April 2009; see also the Center for Constitutional Rights at www.ccrjustice.org; see also *Wiwa v. Royal Dutch Petroleum and Earthrights International* at www.earthrights.org/legal/shell.
9 Viva! was founded in 1994 by Juliet Gellately, who is the organisation's director; she also founded Viva!'s sister group, a registered charity called the Vegetarian & Vegan Foundation, in 2002; see: www.viva.org.uk.
10 Tony Wardle, *Diet of Disaster*, Viva Campaigns, Bristol, 2007, p. 18. An area of land the size of five football pitches will grow enough meat to feed two people or enough soya to feed sixty-one.
11 Ibid, p. 23, taken from WorldWatch Institute, Washington.
12 Michael McCarthy, 'Sea levels rising twice as fast as predicted', *The Independent*, Wednesday 11 March 2009, p. 1.
13 David Adam, 'Too late to save Amazon...', *Guardian*, Thursday 12 March 2009, pp. 14–15.
14 Tony Wardle, *Diet of Disaster*, p. 37. Back in 2003 the International Council for the Exploration of the Seas warned that 82 per cent of all fish stocks were not within safe biological limits – that is, they were on the road to extinction.

Chapter 20: Juries in Jeopardy

1 Trevor Grove, *The Juryman's Tale*, Bloomsbury, London, 1998. One of the rare but excellent overviews of the jury system, from someone who served on one.
2 After a long and tortuous process, the 'spying' charges against Berry were dropped, and the two journalists Albury and Campbell received conditional discharges for other minor offences.
3 Richard Harvey's pamphlet *Diplock and the Assault on Civil Liberties*, published by the Haldane Society of Socialist Lawyers (London, 1980), is an invaluable analysis of the Diplock period.
4 Lord Denning, *What's Next in the Law*, LexisNexis Butterworths, USA, 1982.
5 Richard Ford and David Sapsted, 'Hailsham Backing for Jury Reforms', *The Times*, Wednesday 2 November 1988.
6 Criminal Justice Act 2003, Section 43 in *Archbold*, 2009, pp. 493–4, paras 4-267a to 267c.

7 Research undertaken for the Royal Commission on Criminal Justice under Lord Runciman, CM2263 HMSO London, 1993.

8 'Seventh Man Arrested in London Ricin Case' *Associated Press*, 8 January 2003; 'More Plotters With Ricin May Be on the Loose, London Police Say', *Associated Press*, 8 January 2003; 'The sober truth about Ricin', *Argus*, 9 January 2003.

9 Gordon Brown, 'Full text of Gordon Brown's speech to the Royal United Services Institute in London', BBC, 13 February 2006; see: http://news.bbc.co.uk/1/hi/uk_politics/4708816.stm.

10 The cross-examination is taken from a transcript in my possession. It took two to three hours and, were it to be printed in full, it would occupy sixty pages, so I have edited the material slightly – hopefully without distorting the meaning of the questions or the answers; [*continues*] denotes a break in continuity.

11 These were the dates when scientists were called in to examine whether in fact there was any ricin in the flat.

12 Jon Silverman, 'Comment: Questions Unanswered', BBC, 13 April 2005; see: http://news.bbc.co.uk/1/hi/uk/4442479.stm.

13 Martin Bright, Home Affairs Editor, 'Ricin Jurors attack new terror laws', *Observer*, 9 October 2005.

14 Panorama, *Blair vs Blair*, BBC, 9 October 2005.

15 *Howell's State Trials*, vol. 6, p. 951 (6 How. 951); 230. 'The Trial of William Penn and William Mead, at the Old Bailey, for a Tumultuous Assembly: 22 Charles II. A.D. 1670. [Written by themselves.]'; see: www.constitution.org/trials/penn/penn-mead.htm.

16 Bushell's appeal, 1670, Law Reports Vaughan, p. 135.

17 Michael Randle and Pat Pottle, *The Blake Escape – How We Freed George Blake and Why*, Harrap, London, 1989.

18 E. P. Thompson, 'Sold Like A Sheep for a Pound', Review of George Rudé, *Protest and Punishment*, New Society, 14 December 1978.

Chapter 21: Taking Stock

1 The transcripts for the Stockwell inquest are available online at: www.stockwellinquest.org.uk/hearing_transcripts; the list of witnesses for each date is listed in a main index; the indexes for the day's proceedings come at the *end* of the day's transcript. The Ralph Livock cross-examination was on 30 October 2008, pp. 14-15.

2 Ibid., 30 October 2008, p. 55.

3 Ibid., 3 November 2008, p. 13; [*continues*] denotes a break in continuity.

4 Ibid., 3 November 2008, p. 17, lines 16-25.

5 The Independent Police Complaints Commission (IPCC) is an organisation that has overall responsibility for the system for complaints against the police. See: www.ipcc.gov.uk. Statistics of fatal shootings are reported each year at www.ipcc.gov.uk/death_report.

6 A practice now frowned upon by the Divisional Court. Mark Saunders was shot by police on 8 May 2008 and in September 2008 his sister, Charlotte Saunders, judicially reviewed the unfairness of police officers colluding over their notes and statements.

7 IP is a term specific to inquests; in other tribunals they are called 'parties'.

8 *Stockwell – Countdown to Killing*, Panorama, BBC1, 8 March 2006.

9 Stockwell inquest, transcript of my cross-examination of Commander McDowell on 25 September 2008, pp. 35-142.

10 Ibid., transcript of my cross-examination of DSO Cressida Dick on 7 October 2008, pp. 9-200.

11 Ibid., transcript of my cross-examination of Trojan 84 on 16 October 2008, pp. 1-54.

12 Ibid., transcript of jury verdict on 12 December 2008, p. 10, line 5 to p. 13, line 8.

Chapter 22: Law, Not War

1 The first journalists allowed down to inspect the tunnels were Andy McSmith (see 'A taste of how the other half lived in the blitz', *Independent*, 18 October 2008) and Maev Kennedy (see '100 ft down, the capital's cold war warren gives up its final secrets', *Guardian*, 18 October 2008).

2 Thomas Paine, *The Crisis*, Penguin 60s, Pamphlet no. xiii (1783), London, 1995, p. 79.

3 John Keane, *Tom Paine, A Political Life*, Bloomsbury, London, 1995, pp. 303–4.

4 *Archbold*, 2007, paras. 19-367 to 19-369, p. 1913; see also *Archbold International Criminal Courts*, 3rd edition, Rodney Dixon and Karim A. A. Khan, Sweet & Maxwell, London 2009.

5 The first Treaty of Rome in 1957 led to the Common Market/European Union.

6 See the ICC website at: www.icc-cpi.int.

7 See the ICTY website at: www.icty.org.

8 *Archbold*, 2007, para. 19-351, p. 1906 to para. 19-366, p. 1913; see also *Archbold International Criminal Courts*, 3rd edition, Rodney Dixon and Karim A. A. Kham, Sweet of Maxwell, London 2009.

9 The World Court Project is part of Abolition 2000, a global network to eliminate nuclear weapons; see: www.abolition2000europe.org.

10 IALANA (International Association of Lawyers Against Nuclear Arms) in conjunction with the IPB (International Peace Bureau) and the IPPNW (International Physicians for the Prevention of Nuclear War) led World Court Project, a worldwide campaign that resulted in a historic opinion from the ICJ (International Court of Justice) in July 1966. For the opinion see: www.ialana.net/worldcourtproject.

11 For Mordechai Vanunu, see: www.vanunu.org; for Amnesty International, see: www.amnesty.org.uk; for the Medical Foundation for the Care of Victims of Torture, see: www.torturecare.org.uk.

12 Mathew Taylor, 'Britain plans to spend £3bn on new nuclear warheads', *Guardian*, 25 July 2008.

13 For details, see: www.abolition2000europe.org.

14 Katherine Ling, 'Obama's Nuclear Non-proliferation Plan', *New York Times*, 6 April 2009.

15 See the KHRP website at: www.khrp.org.

16 Information via the Latin America Bureau at: www.lab.org.uk.

17 Peace Brigades International (PBI) is a non-governmental organisation working to promote non-violence and to protect human rights. It currently has projects in Colombia, Mexico, Guatemala, Nepal and Indonesia. See: www.peacebrigades.org.

18 Mark Townsend, 'Police Probe 29 UK Torture Cases', *Observer*, 5 April 2009.

19 Richard Norton-Taylor, 'Top judge: US and UK acted as "vigilantes" in Iraq invasion', *Guardian*, 18 November 2008. Edited from thousands of hours of testimony by Richard Norton-Taylor, *Justifying War* was one of Nicolas Kent's exemplary series of tribunal plays (including the Stephen Lawrence inquiry) at the Tricycle Theatre, London. I was superbly played by Jeremy Clyde in both.

20 Noel Malcolm, *Kosovo: A Short History*, Pan Books, London, 2002, p. xliii.

21 Andy McSmith, 'Keeping the peace?', *Independent*, 20 February 2008, pp. 10–11.

22 See: www.un.org/aboutun/charter5.

Further Reading

I have drawn on a wide range of sources in the writing of this book. Here is a select list, organised by chapter and broken down under the headings 'General', and the name and date of an individual case. Where a case appears as a subheading, in capitals, this denotes one in which I have appeared or played a part, and the stage (eg trial or appeal) at which this occurred. The list also contains film or television documentaries which I feel are relevant, most of which can be accessed online, via the relevant TV channel or the British Film Institute at www.bfi.org.uk. All Web links are live at the time of going to press.

Most laws and statutes can be found at the UK Statute Law Database, part of the Office of Public Sector Information, in the National Archive at: www.statutelaw.gov.uk or in law libraries, most of which are linked to universities.

There is also a practitioner's reference book which is published every year and contains the principal statutes and case precedents. Known as Archbold, its full title is *Criminal Pleading, Evidence and Practice*, published by Thomson Sweet & Maxwell. Each source shows the page number (p.ooo) and the paragraph number is hyphenated (para oo-ooo).

Chapter 3: Drugs, Rock and Law

GENERAL

The Defenders, CBS, 1961–64.

Devlin, Lord Patrick, *The Enforcement of Morals*, Oxford University Press, Oxford, 1965.

Glatt, Pittman et al., *The Drug Scene in Great Britain*, Edward Arnold, London, 1967.

Hart, Professor H. L. A., *Law, Liberty and Morality*, Oxford University Press, Oxford, 1969.

Mansfield, Michael, 'Private Drug Use – No Crime?', *Drugs & Society*, Macmillan Journals, London, July 1973, vol. 2, no. 10, pp. 10–11.

Masters, Anthony, *The Seahorse*, Atheneum, New York, 1966.

Mill, John Stuart, *On Liberty*, Hackett, Indianapolis, 1978.

SEARLE & OTHERS APPEAL, 1971

R v. Searle, (1971) Crim. LR 592.CA; see also *Archbold: Criminal Pleading, Evidence and Practice*, Thomson Sweet & Maxwell, London, 2009, p. 2602, paras 26–69.

'OPERATION JULIE' TRIAL, 1978

Lee, Dick and Pratt, Colin, *Operation Julie*, W. H. Allen, London, 1978.

AMEER AND LUCAS TRIAL, 1977

Ameer & Lucas v. R., (1977) CLR 104, before H. H. J. Gillis.

THE CAMBRIDGE TWO (WYNER & BROCK) APPEAL, 2000

Masters, Alex, *Stuart, A Life Backwards*, Harper Perennial, London, 2006.

www.cambridgetwo.com/history/his.htm.

Appeal, December 2000, before Lord Justice Rose, Mr Justice Longmore and Mr Justice Ouseley, judgment ref. (2001)1 WLR 1159; (2001) 2 CAR 3; (2001) 2 CAR 48; (2001) CLR 320. See also *The Times*, 28 December 2008.

Chapter 4: Prints and Impressions

GENERAL

Joad, Professor C. E. M. (contributor), *The Brains Trust*, BBC Radio and TV, 1941–61.

Lindsay, A. D., *The Modern Democratic State*, Oxford University Press, Oxford, 1947.

Kieckhoefer, Hartmut, Ingleby, Michael and Lucas, Gary, 'Monitoring the physical formation of earprints: Optical and pressure mapping evidence', as part of the FearID research consortium, School of Computing and Engineering, University of Huddersfield, 30 May 2006; see: linkinghub.elsevier.com/retrieve/pii/S0263224106000662.

Wallander, BBC1, 7 December 2008.

THE ANGRY BRIGADE TRIAL, 1972

Burns, Alan, *The Angry Brigade: A Documentary Novel*, Quartet Books, London, 1973.

Carr, Gordon, *The Angry Brigade, the Cause and the Case*, Victor Gollancz, London, 1975.

Christie, Stuart, *My Granny Made Me an Anarchist*, Christie File, Part I 1946–64, ChristieBooks, Hastings, 2002; see: ChristieBooks.com.

McLuhan, Marshall, *The Gutenberg Galaxy: The Making of Typographic Man*, University of Toronto Press, Canada, 1962.

GILBERT 'DANNY' MCNAMEE APPEAL, 1998

Randerson, James, (re Dr Itiel Dror) 'Study questions reliability of fingerprint evidence', *Guardian*, Friday 23 March 2007.

Woffinden, Bob, 'The "Hyde Park bomber" has become a landmark for British justice', *Guardian*, 17 December 1998; see: www.innocent.org.uk/cases/dannymcnamee/index.html.

Court of Appeal, 17 December 1998, before Lord Justices Swinton Thomas, Garland and Longmore, transcript of judgment no. 9704481S2.

MARK KEMPSTER APPEAL, 2001

Kieckhoefer, Hartmut, Ingleby, Michael and Lucas, Gary, 'Monitoring the physical formation of earprints: Optical and pressure mapping evidence', as part of the FearID research consortium, School of Computing and Engineering, University of Huddersfield, 30 May 2006; see: linkinghub.elsevier.com/retrieve/pii/ S0263224106000662.

Trial in March 2001, Southampton Crown Court; see: www.ccrc.gov.uk/ NewsArchive/news_461.htm - 17k - 29 October 2007

First appeal (2003) EWCA 3555; second appeal (2008) [2008] EWCA Crim. 975; 2 CAR 19.

Chapter 5: Parents at Risk

GENERAL

Daubert v. Merrell Dow Pharmaceuticals, 509 US 579 (1993).

Frye v. United States, 293 F. 1013 (DC Cir. 1923).

ANGELA CANNINGS TRIAL, 2002; APPEAL, 2003

Cannings, Angela, with Lloyd Davies, Megan, *Against the Odds, A Mother's Fight to Prove Her Innocence*, Time Warner Books, London, 2006.

Confidential Enquiry into Stillbirths and Deaths in Infancy (CESDI), 7th Annual Report 2000; see also those for the following years at www.cemach.org.uk.

Sweeney, John, *Angela's Hope*, BBC TV, December 2003.

Taylor, Matthew, 'Cot death expert to face investigation', *Guardian*, 11 December 2003.

Appeal judgment, 19 January 2004, before Lord Justice Judge; conviction quashed on 10 December 2003[2004] EWCA Crim1; 2 CAR 7; 1 WLR 2607; 1 AER 725.

SHAKEN BABY APPEALS, 2005

Lorraine Harris and others

Court of Appeal hearing 21 July 2005 before Lord Justices Gage, Gross and McFarlane, case number 200403277, (2006) 1 CAR 55.

See: http://news.bbc.co.uk for 21 July 2005.

See Crown Prosecution Service website, at www.cps.gov.uk/newes/pressreleases/ archive/2005.

ANGELA AND IAN GAY APPEAL, 2006

Sweeney, John, 'Child killers and legal lunacy', *Sunday Times*, 4 March 2007.

www.telegraph.co.uk/news/uknews/1513666/Did-boy's-body-produce-salt-that-killed-him.htm.

KEVIN CALLAN APPEAL, 1994–5

Callan, Kevin, *Kevin Callan's Story*, Little, Brown, London, 1997.

Wrightson, Philip, Gronwall, Dorothy and Waddell, Peter, *Head Injury: The Facts*, Oxford University Press, New York, 1998.

CHILDREN AT RISK

Rantzen, Esther, *Esther: The Autobiography*, BBC Books, London 2001.

The Victoria Climbie report was published on 28 January 2003, see; www.victoria-climbie-inquiry.org.uk.

Lord Laming's report on the 'Baby P' case is available via http://news.bbc.co.uk/1/hi/england/7938826.stm.

Chapter 6: 1984

ESTABLISHING TOOKS CHAMBERS

Williams, Kyffin, *Across the Straits*, Duckworth, London, 1973.

www.tooks.co.uk.

MINERS' STRIKE, ORGREAVE TRIAL, 1984

Atkins, Chris (Director), *Taking Liberties*, Revolver, May 2007, available at www.revolvergroup.com.

Benn, Tony, MP, Question in the House re compensation for miners and the BBC media coverage, Hansard HC Deb 20 June 1991 vol. 193 cc463–81; see also: http://hansard.millbanksystems.com/commons/1991/jun/20/business-of-the-house.

Challinor, Raymond, *A Radical Lawyer in Victorian England, W. P. Roberts*, I. B. Tauris, London, 1990. Roberts courageously represented the mining communities in their struggle for trade union rights.

Connelly, Steve (Director) and Vanson, Yvette (Producer), *Taking Liberties*, BBC Community Programme Unit, 1984.

Jackson, Bernard and Wardle, Tony, *The Battle for Orgreave*, Vanson Wardle Productions, Brighton, 1986.

Jones, Mark, *Killed on the Picket Line: The Story of David Gareth Jones by his Father*, New Park Publications, London, 1985.

Macgregor, Ian, *The Enemies Within*, William Collins, London, 1986.

Milne, Seumas, *The Enemy Within*, Verso, London, 1994.

Thatcher, Margaret, *The Downing Street Years*, HarperCollins, London, 1993.

'Statistics on Police Operations', *Financial Times*, 4 March 1985.

Vanson, Yvette (Director/Producer), *The Battle for Orgreave*, Vanson Wardle Productions, Channel 4, 1986. Available at www.journeyman.tv or www.bfi.org.uk

www.h2g2.com is contributed to by people from all over the world. Launched in April 1999, the BBC took over the running of the site in February 2001 as part of a drive to develop innovative online services. www.bbc.co.uk/dna/h2g2/brunel/A9361334 at 12 February 2006 is a personal description of events at Orgreave.

WAPPING DISPUTE, 1986.

http://news.bbc.co.uk/onthisday/hi/dates/stories/february/15/newsid_3455000/3455083.stm.

www.uhc-collective.org.uk/webpages/toolbox/legal/advice_4_legal_observers2.htm.

Legal observers information, see: www.activistslegalproject.org.uk. www.thepeoplescharter.com.

Chapter 7: The Slenderest Thread

GENERAL

Legal Action Group, see: www.lag.org.uk.

BARRY GEORGE TRIAL 2001, FIRST APPEAL, 2002

Court of Appeal Law Reports (2002) EWCA Crim. 1923; (2003) CLR 282; *The Times*, 30 August 2002.

Cathcart, Brian, *Jill Dando, Her Life and Death*, Penguin, London, 2001.

Davenport, Justin, 'Yard to investigate Serbian's bar boast that he killed Dando', *Evening Standard*, Monday 23 February 2009.

Lomax, S.C., *The Case of Barry George*, Kempton Marks, Hertford, 2004.

Chapter 8: The Need to Know

GENERAL

Matthews, Paul (ed.), *Jervis on Coroners*, Sweet & Maxwell, London, 12th edition, 2006. See sections 8(i) and 8(iii) of the Coroner's Act 1988.

INQUEST is a charity that provides a free advice service to bereaved people on contentious deaths and their investigation, with a particular focus on deaths in custody. See: www.inquest.org.uk.

Thomas, Leslie, Straw, Adam and Friedmann, Danny, *Inquests: A Practitioner's Guide*, Legal Action Group, London, 2008.

THE MARCHIONESS PRIVATE PROSECUTION, 1992; INQUEST, 1994; PUBLIC INQUIRY, 2000–1

Clarke, Lord Justice, *Marchioness Inquiry Report*, vols 1 & 2, The Stationery Office, February 2001; for some of the findings of the inquiry, see vol. 1, pp. 153, 174, 251.

Corporate Manslaughter and Homicide Act 2007, *Archbold*, 2009, p. 1933, para 19-117.

For chronology of events, see: www.geocities.com/jndenio/ChronTable.htm

www.methodist-central-hall.org.uk/history.

STEPHEN LAWRENCE INQUEST, 1993; RESUMED, 1997; PRIVATE PROSECUTION, 1995; PUBLIC INQUIRY, 1998–9

The Stephen Lawrence Inquiry/Macpherson Report, The Stationery Office, 1999; see appendices and at 7.31 in the transcript of the hearings for a version of part of the protracted surveillance of the suspects; ch. 8, p. 43, para. 8.2 for Neville Lawrence; para. 8.3 for Michael Mansfield's closing remarks and conclusions. For Michael Mansfield's verbatim opening remarks on Day 2, 24 March 1998, see also Doreen Lawrence, *And Still I Rise*, pp. 185–6.

Front-page article, 'MURDERERS', *Daily Mail*, 14 February 1997.

Greengrass, Paul (Director), *The Murder of Stephen Lawrence*, Vanson Productions co-production with Granada, 2000. Available at granadamedia.com.

Lawrence, Doreen, *And Still I Rise: Seeking Justice for Stephen*, Faber & Faber, London, 2006.

Lee Wright, Peter (Producer), and Vanson, Yvette (Executive Producer), *The Stephen Lawrence Story*, Vanson Productions, Channel 4 TV, 1996; *Hoping for a Miracle*, Channel 4, Vanson Productions, 1999. Available at www.channel4.com or www.bfi.org.uk.

Mayberry, David, *Black Deaths in Police Custody*, Hansib Publications, London, 2008.

RICKY REEL INQUEST, 1999

Judd, Terri, 'Family claim "victory" after inquest returns open verdict on Reel death', *Independent*, 9 November 1999.

For the National Civil Rights Movement, see: www.ncrm.org.uk.

JAMES MILLER INQUEST, 2006

Dowell, Ben, '"Breakthrough" in Gaza death case', *Guardian*, 7 August 2007.

Times Online and Agencies, 'Film-maker murdered by Israeli soldier, inquest finds', Times Online, 6 April 2006; see: www.timesonline.co.uk/tol/news/world/middle_east/article702674.ece.

TOM HURNDALL INQUEST, 2006

Hurndall, Jocelyn, *Defy the Stars: The Life and Tragic Death of Tom Hurndall*, Bloomsbury, London, 2007.

Joffe, Rowan (Director) and Block, Simon (Writer), *The Shooting of Tom Hurndall*, Channel 4, 2008.

DUBLIN/MONAGHAN BOMBINGS, 1974; INQUEST, 2004

Mullan, Don, *The Dublin & Monaghan Bombings*, Wolfhound Press, Dublin, 2000.

O'Neill, Edward with Whyte, Barry J., *Two Little Boys*, Currach Press, Blackrock, 2004.

www.dublinmonaghanbombings.org.

OMAGH INQUEST, 2000

http://news.bbc.co.uk/onthisday/hi/dates/stories/august/15/newsid_2496000/2496009.stm.

www.guardian.co.uk/uk/2002/jul/26/northernireland.

Mansfield, Michael, 'Truth Must Not be the Final Victim', *Guardian*, 14 December 2001.

Chapter 9: The Trouble with Ireland

GENERAL

Adams, Gerry, *Hope and History: Making Peace in Ireland*, Brandon, London, 2003.

Bishop, Patrick and Mallie, Eamonn, *The Provisional IRA*, Heinemann, London, 1987.

Bowyer Bell, J., *The Secret Army, The IRA, 1916–1979*, Academy Press, Dublin, 1979.

Campbell, Beatrix, *Agreement! The State Conflict and Change in Northern Ireland*, Lawrence and Wishart, London, 2008.

Elliott, Marianne, *Wolfe Tone: Prophet of Irish Independence*, Yale University Press, London, 1989.

Geraghty, Tony, *The Irish War: The Military History of a Domestic Conflict*, HarperCollins, London, 2000.

Lapsey, Sarah (ed.), *Children in Crossfire, I Have a Dream*, YES! Publications, Derry, 2005.

O'Mahony, Sean, *Frongoch, University of Revolution*, FDR Teoranta, Killiney, 1987.

Reed, David, *Ireland: The Key to the British Revolution*, Larkin Publications, London, 1984.

Taylor, Peter, *Brits: The War Against the IRA*, Bloomsbury, London, 2001.

THE PRICE SISTERS' TRIAL, 1973

Breen, Suzanne, 'Old Bailey bomber ashamed of Sinn Fein', *The Village*, 7 December 2004.

For information on the Trial of 14 November 1973, see: http://news.bbc.co.uk/onthisday/hi/dates/stories/november/14/newsid_4724000/4724181.stm.

For a description of force-feeding, see: www.irishfreedomcommittee.net/news/december2004.

'Ulster's Price Sisters: Breaking the Long Fast', *Time*, 17 June 1974.

www.time.com/time/magazine/article/0,9171,879325,00.html.

THE BRIGHTON BOMBERS/THE SEASIDE CONSPIRACIES TRIAL, 1984

For Martina Anderson interview, see: www.tallgirlshorts.net/marymary/martina.html.

http://news.bbc.co.uk/onthisday/hi/dates/stories/june/25/newsid_2519000/2519673.stm.

Parry, Gareth, 'Patrick Magee convicted of IRA terrorist attack', *Guardian*, 10 June 1986.

Roisín de Rossa interviews Ella O'Dwyer, see: http://republican-news.org/archive/1998/December17/17ella.html.

BLOODY SUNDAY SECOND PUBLIC INQUIRY, 1999–2004

Bloody Sunday and the Report of the Widgery Tribunal, The Irish Government's Assessment of the New Material, June 1997.

Daly, Edward, *Mister, Are You a Priest?*, Four Courts Press, Dublin, 2000.

Kent, Nicolas (Director), *Bloody Sunday – Scenes From the Saville Inquiry*, Tricycle Theatre, London, 2005; edited from thousands of hours of testimony by Richard Norton-Taylor, this was one of an exemplary series of tribunal plays in which I was superbly played by Jeremy Clyde.

McCann, Eamonn (with Maureen Shiels, Bridie Hannigan), *Bloody Sunday in Derry, What Really Happened?*, Brandon, Derry, 2000.

McCann, Eamonn (ed.), *The Bloody Sunday Inquiry: The Families Speak Out*, Pluto Press, London, 2006.

Mullan, Don (and Scally, John), *Eyewitness Bloody Sunday, the Truth*, Merlin, Dublin, 2002.

O'Dochartaigh, Niall, *From Civil Rights to Armalites: Derry and the Birth of the Irish Troubles*, Cork University Press, Cork, 1997.

Pringle, Peter and Jacobson, Philip, *Those Are Real Bullets, Aren't They?*, Fourth Estate, London, 2000.

Sierz, Aleks, 'Bloody Sunday – Scenes from the Saville Inquiry', *The Stage*, Wednesday 20 April 2005.

The Widgery Tribunal Report at: Hansard HC Deb 19 April 1972 vol. 835 cc519-28; see also: http://hansard.millbanksystems.com/commons/1972/apr/19/northern-ireland-widgery-tribunal-report.

www.bloody-sunday-inquiry.org/transcripts/Archive.

Chapter 10: That Little Tent of Blue

GENERAL

Owers, Anne, Chief Inspector of Prisons, 'Prison System at a Crossroads, Warns RNS Chief Inspector', press release of 30 January 2008 re Annual Report 2006–7; see: www.inspectorates.homeoffice.gov.uk/hmiprisons.

Stern, Vivien, *Bricks of Shame*, Penguin, London, 1987.

PARKHURST SIEGE, 1983

Beam, Roger, 'Mirror man helps to end jail siege', *Daily Mirror*, 6 January 1983.

RISLEY RIOTS/WADI WILLIAMS TRIAL, 1990

Mansfield, Michael and Raynor, Maggie, *Whale Boy*, Mantra, London, 1991.

Tumim, Stephen, Chief Inspector of Prisons, Annual Report, 1988.

Williams, Wadi, article written while an inmate at Hull prison; see: http://libcom.org/history/1989-the-risley-prisoners-uprising.

STRANGEWAYS/PAUL TAYLOR TRIAL, 1992

Allison, Eric, 'Breaking Point', *Guardian*, 20 February 2006.

Jameson, Nicki and Allison, Eric, *Strangeways 1990: A Serious Disturbance*, Larkin Publications, London, 1995.

'Rioting Inmates Take over Strangeways', see: http://news.bbc.co.uk/onthisday/hi/dates/stories/april/1/newsid_4215000/4215173.stm; for Prisons Security Act, 1992, in *Archbold*, 2009, S1, p. 2689, para. 28-217.

Chapter 11: The Magic Bullet?

GENERAL

An Audience With ... Michael Mansfield, QC. Recordings and transcripts are available at www.celebrityproductions.info/displayer_list_productions.php.

Laville, Sandra, 'Twenty-seven years on', *Guardian*, 12 March 2009.

O'Neill, Sean, 'Defence lawyers ready to seize on DNA doubts', *The Times*, Thursday 24 January 2008.

Trial of Sean Hoey before Mr Justice Weir, 20 December 2007; transcript judgment at Neutral Citation No. (2007) NICC 49 Ref: WEI 7021.

DNA

Caddy, Prof. Brian (Strathclyde University), Review commissioned by the Forensic

Science Regulator, November 2007; Report: *A Review of the Science of Low Template DNA Analysis*, April 2008; see: police.homeoffice.gov.uk/publications/operational-policing.

Levy, Harlan, *And the Blood Cried Out*, HarperCollins, London, 1996.

JAMES HANRATTY APPEAL, 2002

Court of Appeal Law Reports (2002) EWCA Crim. 1141; (2002) 2 C.A.R. 30; (2002) CLR 350; (2003) 3 AER 534; *The Times*, 16 May 2002.

Foot, Paul, *Who Killed Hanratty?*, Jonathan Cape, London, 1971.

Woffinden, Bob, *Hanratty, The Final Verdict*, Macmillan, London, 1997.

MICHAEL SHIRLEY APPEAL, 2003

Court of Appeal transcript of judgment before Lord Justice Laws, Mr Justice Gage and Mr Justice Mitting, No. 2001/02302/X1; (2003) EWCA Crim. 1976.

Chaytor, Rod, 'I'd Rather Have Died in Jail than Admit a Murder I Didn't Do', *Daily Mirror*, 5 July 2003.

DEEN APPEAL, 1994

Court of Appeal judgment before Lord Chief Justice Taylor, *R v. Deen*, *The Times*, 10 January 1994; see also *Archbold*, 2009, p. 1585, para. 14-58.

DNA DATABANK

For ruling on databanks, see: www.echr.coe.int for European Court of Human Rights case reports.

Haddow, Iain, 'Debating ethics of DNA database', BBC News Online, 9 January 2008; see: http://news.bbc.co.uk/1/hi/uk/7177152.stm.

Travis, Alan, '17 Judges, One Ruling', *Guardian*, 5 December 2008.

Walker, Peter, 'European Court Rules CAN Database Breaches Human Rights', *Guardian*, 4 December 2008.

Chapter 12: Cops and Robbers

GENERAL

Gillard, Michael and Flynn, Laurie, *Untouchables: Dirty Cops, Bent Justice and Racism in Scotland Yard*, Cutting Edge Press, Edinburgh, 2004.

McLagan, Graeme, *Bent Coppers*, Orion, London, 2003.

Paddick, Brian, *Line of Fire*, Simon & Schuster, London, 2008.

Walker, Clive and Starmer, Keir, *Miscarriages of Justice: A Review of Justice in Error*, Blackstone Press, London, 1999.

BRIDGEWATER FOUR (PAT MOLLOY) APPEAL, 1997

Foot, Paul, *Murder at the Farm: Who Killed Carl Bridgewater?*, Review, London, 1997.

Graves, David, 'Bridgewater Four Convictions Quashed', *Daily Telegraph*, 31 July 1997.

Shaw, Don (Writer) and Drury, David (Director), *Bad Company*, BBC2, 1993.

For the Criminal Justice and Public Order Act 1994 (Sections 34 to 39), see *Archbold*, 2009, main section 34, p. 1743, para 15-414, and section 35, p. 508, para 4-305; see also: http://www.legislation.hmso.gov.uk/acts/acts1994/Ukpga_19940033_en_4. htm#mdiv34.

Transcript of Court of Appeal judgment before Lord Justice Roch, Mr Justice Hidden and Mr Justice Mitchell, sub. nom. Michael Hickey, 30 July 1997, no. 1996/5131/S1; Law Report (legal professional privilege) Molloy, (1997) 2 C.A.R. 283.

BROADWATER FARM RIOTS (MARK LAMBIE) TRIAL, 1987; ENGIN RAGHIP APPEALS, 1988, 1991

Gudjonsson, Gisli, *The Psychology of Interrogations, Confessions and Testimony*, John Wiley and Sons Ltd, Chichester, West Sussex, 1992.

Kennedy, Ludovic, *Ten Rillington Place*, Pan Books, London, 1963.

Rose, David, 'They created Winston Silcott, the beast of Broadwater Farm. And they won't let this creation lie down and die', *Observer*, 18 January 2004.

Summers, Chris, 'Malign and corrosive gangsters', BBC News Online, 17 May 2002.

Court of Appeal transcript of judgment in Engin Raghip and others, 5 December 1991 1990/5920/S1 pp. 4–6, 18–19, 34–36; sub. nom. Silcott (1992) 1 WLR 291; *The Times*, 9 December 1991.

CARDIFF THREE (STEPHEN MILLER) APPEAL, 1992

Bennetto, Jason, 'Police officers among 22 held over quashed murder convictions', *Independent*, 25 April 2005.

Mansfield, Michael and Wardle, Tony, *Presumed Guilty*, Heinemann, London, 1993.

Sekar, Satish, *Fitted In*, The Fitted In Project, Notting Hill, London, 1997.

Vanson, Yvette (Producer/Director), *Presumed Guilty*, presented by Michael Mansfield, Vanson Wardle Productions for *Inside Story*, BBC2, 1991.

Appeal report, sub.nom. Paris (1993) 97 CAR 99; (1994) CLR 361; *The Times*, 24 December 1992; *Independent*, 17 December 1992.

For prostitute trial perjury charges, see: http://innocent.org.uk/cases/cardiff3_1/ index.html.

CARDIFF NEWSAGENT (MICHAEL O'BRIEN) APPEAL, 1999

O'Brien, Michael with Lewis, Greg, *The Death of Justice*, Y Lolfa Cyf, Talybont, Wales, 2008.

Sub. nom. Darren Hall, (2000) CLR 676; *The Times*, 16 February 2000; *Independent*, 27 March 2000.

Chapter 13: The Switch

GENERAL

Deery, Phillip, *Malaya, 1948: Britain's 'Asian Cold War'?*, International Center for Advanced Studies, New York University; 'The Cold War as Global Conflict', Working Paper 3, April 2002.

IRAQI HIJACK TRIAL, 1997; APPEAL, 1998

'Iraqi Hijackers Jailed "to deter others"', BBC News Online, 5 November 1997; 'Iraqis Found Guilty of Hijack', BBC News Online, 1 November 1997.

Terrorism Act 2000, Section 1, and Terrorism Act 2006, Section 34 in *Archbold*, 2009, pp. 2322–23, para 25-56.

Trial of alleged Iraqi hijackers, Old Bailey, 1997 before Mr Justice Wright, Court of Appeal transcript of judgment before the Vice President, Lord Justice Rose, Mr Justice Rougier and Mr Justice Johnson, sub. nom. Mustafa Shakir Abdul-Hussain, 17 December 1998, no. 1997/07785/S1; Law report (1999) CLR 570.

BOTMEH AND ALAMI TRIAL, 1996; APPEAL, 1998

Appeal report (2001) EWCA Crim. 2226; (2002) 1 WLR 531; (2002) 1 CAR 28; (2002) CLR 209; *The Times*, 8 November 2001.

Brittain, Victoria, 'A vision from Rugby Prison', *New Statesman*, 1 December 2003.

'Embassy Bomb Appeal Rejected', BBC News Online, 1 November 2001.

Foot, Paul, 'MI5 & human error', *Guardian*, 31 October 2000.

Gandhi, Mahatma, *The Story of My Experiments with Truth*, Navajivan Trust, India, 1927.

Machon, Annie, *Spies, Lies and Whistleblowers – MI5, MI6 & The Shayler Affair*, The Book Guild, Lewes, Sussex, 2005.

Shayler, David, 'MI5 bugged Mandelson', *Mail on Sunday*, 24 August 1997.

TAHIRA TABASSUM TRIAL, 2004

Clough, Sue and Boffey, Chris, 'Bomber's widow cleared of failing to inform police', *Daily Telegraph*, 9 July 2004.

Dodd, Vikram, 'It's not about the truth. Someone had to pay', *Guardian*, 9 July 2004.

SAAJID BADAT TRIAL, 2007

Dodd, Vikram, 'Former grammar school boy gets 13 years for shoe bomb plot', *Guardian*, 23 April 2005.

Honigsbaum, Mark and Dodd, Vikram, 'From Gloucester to Afghanistan: the making of a shoe bomber', *Guardian*, 5 March 2005.

Chapter 14: Lifting the Lid

GENERAL/NON-DISCLOSURE

Bennathan, Joel, 'Defendants are severely disadvantaged by current legislation on evidence', *The Times*, 25 July 2000.

Dyer, Clare, 'Legal "safeguard" risks injustice', *Guardian*, 3 March 2000.

Emmerson, Ben, 'Prosecution in the dock', *Observer*, 14 November 1999.

Langdon-Down, Grania, 'The whole truth and nothing but? Non-disclosure of evidence has led to some 200 wrongful convictions', *Independent*, 7 December 1999.

Mansfield, Michael and Wardle, Tony, *Presumed Guilty*, Heinemann, London, 1993.

Woffinden, Bob, 'No, you can't see. It might help your client', *Guardian*, 4 May 1999.

www.innocent.org.uk/misc/disclosure.html.

JUDITH WARD APPEAL, 1992

Ward, Judith, *Ambushed*, Vermilion, London, 1993.

Court of Appeal Law Reports before Lord Justice Glidewell, (1993) 96 CAR 1; (1993) CLR 312; (1993) 1 WLR. 619; (1993) 2 AER. 577.

European Convention on Human Rights, Article 6 (fair trial) as incorporated in the Human Rights Act (HRA) 1998 S6, *Archbold*, 2009, p. 1802, para 16-57.

Judith Ward v. The Queen UK (1992) (the M62 Bombings); appeal judgment prepared by Dr Robert N. Moles; see: netk.net.au/UK/Ward.asp.

M25 (MICHAEL DAVIS) TRIAL, 1990; DAVIS & ROWE APPEAL, 1993

Court of Appeal Law Reports (1992 & 1993) 97 CAR 110; *The Times*, 24 April 2000.

www.guardian.co.uk/uk/2000/jul/22/race.world.

www.homepage-link.to/JUSTICE/Rowe/index.htm.

EDDIE GILFOYLE APPEALS 1995, 2000

Kennedy, Dominic, 'Uncovered: Police notes cast doubt on Gilfoyle Murder', *The Times*, 20 February 2009; 'New evidence prompts police review of murder case', *The Times*, 21 February 2009.

Court of Appeal Law Reports (1996) 1 CAR 302.

Chapter 15: Shared Experience

DEPTFORD FIRE INQUEST, 1981

Howe, Darcus, *From Bobby to Babylon*, Race Today Publications, London, 1988.

Le Rose, John, 'The New Cross Massacre Story', *Black Parents Movement & Race Today*, London, 1984.

Scarman, Lord, *The Scarman Report*, The Stationery Office, 25 November 1981.

For the first inquest, see: www.guardian.co.uk/uk/1981/may/14/race.world.

For the second inquest, see: www.guardian.co.uk/uk/2004/feb/02/race.ukcrime.

THE BRADFORD TWELVE AND NEWHAM SEVEN TRIALS, 1981

Malik, Kenan, 'Born in Bradford', *Prospect* magazine, October 2005.

Powell, Enoch, MP, 'Rivers of Blood' speech, 20 April 1968; see: http://news.bbc.co.uk/onthisday/hi/dates/stories/april/20/newsid_2489000/2489357.stm.

Tandana, the Glow-worm website (archiving the Bradford Twelve case), see: www.tandana.org.

FRANK CRITCHLOW (MANGROVE) TRIAL, 1993

Howe, Darcus, 'If I pleaded guilty, said the lawyer, I'd get five years', *New Statesman*, 4 December 1998.

Mills, Heather, 'Restaurant that became a Symbol for Radicalism', *Independent*, 13 October 1992.

For transcript of Colville, all the sinners saints, see: www.rbkc.gov.uk/events/intransit/podcast_tran_colville.asp.

Chapter 16: The Execution

GENERAL

Arriens, Jan (ed.), *Welcome to Hell*, Ian Faulkner Publishing, Cambridge, 1991; see also: www.lifelines-uk.org/LLnews.asp.

Death Sentences and Executions in 2007, issued in April 2008, and *Death Sentences and Executions in 2008*, issued in April 2009, both Amnesty International, see www. amnesty.org.uk.

Levine, Stephen (ed.), *Death Row: An Affirmation of Life*, Glide Publications, San Francisco, 1972.

Officer, Jane (ed.), *If I Should Die*, New Clarendon Press, Oxford, 1999.

Robbins, Tim (Director), *Dead Man Walking*, Working Title, 1995; see www. workingtitlefilms.com.

Sakharov, Andre, cited in Mulvey Roberts, Mary with Zephaniah, Benjamin, *Out of the Night*, New Clarendon Press, Cheltenham, 1994.

Stafford-Smith, Clive, *Bad Men*, Weidenfeld & Nicolson, London, 2007.

Thomas, Merrilyn, *Life on Death Row*, Piatkus, London, 1989.

For African Prisons Project, see: www.africanprisons.com.

For Amicus (President, Michael Mansfield, QC) and the assisting of prisoners on death row, see: www.amicus-alj.org.

The Murder (Abolition of Death Penalty) Act 1965, Section 1 *Archbold*, 2009, p. 707, para. 5-236.

MAHMOUD MATTAN APPEAL, 1998

Court of Appeal transcript of judgment before Lord Justice Rose, case no. 1997/06415/S2, 10.

RUTH ELLIS APPEAL, 2003

Jakubait, Muriel and Weller, Monica, *Ruth Ellis, My Sister's Secret Life*, Constable & Robinson, London, 2005.

Court of Appeal judgment before Lord Justice Kay, (2003) EWCA Crim. 3556, para. 90.

The Homicide Act 1957, Sections 1, 2 & 3 in *Archbold*, 2009, p. 1916 paras 19-20, 19-66 and p.1912, para. 19-52.

SARAH THORNTON APPEAL, 1995

Ministry of Justice, *Murder, Manslaughter and Infanticide: Proposals for Reform of the Law*, Consultation Paper, July 2008, see: www.justice.gsi.gov.uk/publications/cp1908.

Nadel, Jennifer, *Sara Thornton*, Victor Gollancz, London, 1993

Court of Appeal Law Reports (1966) 2 CAR 108; (1996) 1 WLR 1174; (1996) 2 AER 1023; (1996) CLR 597; *The Times*, 14 December 1995 and 6 June 1996; *Independent*, 19 December 1995.

For Southall Black Sisters, see: www.southallblacksisters.org.uk

PETER ADAMS

Adams, Peter and Shirley, *Knockback*, Duckworth, London, 1982.

Chapter 17: No ExSkuse

GENERAL

Bennett, Ronan, *Double Jeopardy: The Retrial of the Guildford Four*, Penguin, London, 1993.

Conlon, Gerry, *Proved Innocent*, Hamish Hamilton, London, 1990.

Hill, Paul with Bennett, Ronan, *Stolen Years*, Transworld, London, 1990.

Kennedy, Ludovic, *Ten Rillington Place*, Victor Gollancz, London, 1961.

Kennedy, Ludovic, *Truth to Tell* (Collected Writings), Bantam Press, London, 1991.

Kennedy, Ludovic, *Thirty-Six Murders*, Profile Books, London, 2002.

Koestler, Arthur, *The Roots of Coincidence*, Vintage, London, 1973.

Sheridan, Jim (Director), *In the Name of the Father*, Hell's Kitchen Films, 1993.

Walker, Clive and Starmer, Keir (eds), *Miscarriages of Justice*, Blackstone Press, London, 1999.

Woffinden, Bob, *Miscarriages of Justice*, Coronet, London, 1986.

BIRMINGHAM SIX SECOND APPEAL, 1987; THIRD APPEAL, 1991

Callaghan, Hugh and Mulready, Sally, *Cruel Fate*, Poolbeg Press, Co. Dublin, 1993

Faul, Fr Denis and Murray, Fr Raymond, *The Birmingham Framework*, Pamphlet published in Armagh, no date.

Gilligan, Oscar (ed.), *The Birmingham Six: An Appalling Vista*, Litereire Publishers, Dublin, 1990.

Hill, Paddy Joe and Hunt, Gerald, *Forever Lost, Forever Gone*, Bloomsbury, London, 1996.

Jessel, David, *Rough Justice*, BBC, exposed miscarriages of justice between 1980 and 2007.

Jessel, David, *Trial and Error*, Channel 4, featured 15 cases between 1993 and 1999; see also Jane Robins, 'Channel 4 to axe "outdated" criminal justice show', *Independent*, Friday 16 July 1999.

McKee, Grant and Franey, Ros, *Time Bomb*, Bloomsbury, London, 1988.

Mullin, Chris, *Error of Judgement*, Poolbeg, Dublin, 1987.

Mullin, Chris and Tremayne, Charles, a series of documentaries, including 'The Birmingham Six: Their Own Story' and 'Who Bombed Birmingham', for *World in Action*, Granada Television, 1985.

Vanson, Yvette (Director), Bennison, Ishia (Producer), *The Birmingham Wives*, for Everyman, BBC 2, Vanson Wardle Productions, 1989, available at the British Film Institute archive at: www.bfi.org.uk.

For the application for a civil action against the police and Home Office for injuries in custody, 17 January 1980, before Lord Denning, Master of the Rolls, see judgment cited in Chris Mullin, *Error of Judgement*, Poolbeg, Dublin, 1987, p. 243.

For the second appeal on 2 November 1987 before Lord Lane, Lord Chief Justice in Court Number 12, Old Bailey, denied 28 January 1988, see Court of Appeal Law Reports sub. Nom. Callaghan, (1988) 86 CAR 181; (1988) 1 WLR 1; (1988) 1 AER 287; (1988) CLR 107.

For the third appeal before Lord Justice Lloyd, 4 March 1991, see Court of Appeal Law Reports sub. nom. McIlkenny, (1992) 93 CAR 287; (1992) 2 AER 417.

Chapter 18: Big Brother

GENERAL

Ezard, John, 'Did love turn Orwell into a government stooge?', *Guardian*, 21 June 2003.

Foot, Paul, *Who Framed Colin Wallace?*, Macmillan, London, 1989.

Garton Ash, Timothy, 'Under the blanket: Orwell sends us a posthumous warning about trying to manipulate the BBC in a time of war', *Guardian*, 10 July 2003.

Hain, Peter, *Political Trials in Britain*, Allen Lane, London, 1984.

Hollingsworth, Mark and Fielding, Nick, *Defending the Realm: MI5 and the Shayler Affair*, André Deutsch, London, 2000.

Kennedy, Helena, *Just Law: The Changing Face of Justice*, Chatto & Windus, London, 2004.

Leigh, David, *The Frontiers of Secrecy*, Junction Books, London, 1980.

Leigh, David and Lashmar, Paul, 'Revealed: how MI5 vets BBC staff', *Observer*, 18 August 1985.

Machon, Annie, *Spies, Lies and Whistleblowers*, The Book Guild, Lewes, Sussex, 2005.

Orwell, George, *Nineteen eighty-four*, Harcourt Brace, London, 1949.

Wright, Peter with Paul Greengrass, *Spycatcher*, William Heinemann, London, 1987.

Young, Hugo and Massiter, Cathy, *MI5's Official Secrets*, 20/20 Vision for C4, 1985.

For Republic, the Campaign for an Elected Head of State and a British Republic, see: www.republic.org.uk.

For RIPA, the Regulation of Investigatory Powers Act, see: www.opsi.gov.uk/acts/acts2000/ukpga_20000023_em or *Archbold*, 2009, p. 2416–92, paras 25-368 to 25-380. This statute permits the government interception of specified communications.

For the official website of the Public Inquiry by Lord Hutton, see: www.the-hutton-inquiry.org.uk.

For *The Newsline*, the daily paper of the Workers' Revolutionary Party, from May 1976 to the present, see: www.wrp.org.uk.

DODI AND PRINCESS DIANA INQUESTS, 2007–8

Brown, Tina, *The Diana Chronicles*, Century, London, 2007.

Burrell, Paul, *A Royal Duty*, Penguin, London, 2003.

For official inquest transcripts, see: www.scottbaker-inquests.gov.uk/hearing transcripts.

Administrative Court Judicial Review before Lord Justice Smith, Mr Justice Collins and Mr Justice Silber in March 2007, sub. nom. Henri Paul (2007) EWHC 408 (Admin); (2008) Q.B. 172; (2007) 3 W.L.R. 503; (2007) 2 A.E.R. 509; (2007) 95 B.M.L.R. 137; (2007) Inquest L.R. 17; (2007) 157 N.L.J. 366.

Middleton v. HM Coroner for West Somerset 2004, 2 AC 182.

R v. Greater Manchester Coroner, case Tal (1985) QB 67.

For the transcript of Martin Bashir's *Panorama* interview with Princess Diana, see: www.bbc.co.uk/politics97/diana/panorama.html.

For the Operation Paget Inquiry report, see: www.direct.gov.uk/en/Nl1/Newsroom/DG_065122.

Chapter 19: Milk, Muck and Methane

GENERAL

Aloux, Miriam and Schonfeld, Victor (Directors), *The Animals Film*, Channel 4, 1981

Campbell, Duncan, *That Was Business, This Is Personal*, Secker & Warburg, London, 1990.

Lane, Carla, *Instead of Diamonds*, Michael Joseph, London, 1995.

For Climate Rush, founded by Tamsin Omond, Climate Suffragettes, see: www.climaterush.co.uk.

THE MCLIBEL TWO

'McLibel pair get police payout', BBC News Online, 15 February 2005.

Armstrong, Franny, 'Why won't British TV show a film about McLibel?', *Guardian*, 19 June 1998.

Morris, Dave, and Steel, Helen, 'McWorld on Trial', *The Raven*, issue 43, Freedom Press, 2002; see: www.anarres.org.au.

Schlosser, Eric, *Fast Food Nation: The Dark Side of the All-American Meal*, Houghton Mifflin Harcourt, New York, 2001.

Vidal, John, *McLibel, Burger Culture on Trial*, Macmillan, London, 1997.

For judgment day verdict, 19 June 1997; for 'Victory for McLibel Two Against UK Goverment', 15 February 2005; and for story of agents' infiltrations, see: www.mcspotlight.org.

SEA EMPRESS

Marine Accident Investigation Bureau (MAIB) Report, The Stationery Office, London 1997.

VIVA!

Adam, David, 'Too late to save Amazon...', *Guardian*, 12 March 2009.

McCarthy, Michael, 'Sea levels rising twice as fast as predicted', *Independent*, 11 March 2009.

Wardle, Tony, *Diet of Disaster*, Viva Campaigns, Bristol, 2007.

www.viva.org.uk.

Chapter 20: Juries in Jeopardy

GENERAL

Article 39 of the Magna Carta, 1215, in the reign of King John, see: www.fordham.edu/halsall/source/mcarta.html.

Criminal Justice Act 2003, Section 43 in *Archbold*, 2009, pp. 493–4, para. 4-267 A-C.

Denning, Lord, *What's Next in the Law*, LexisNexis Butterworths, USA, 1982.

Devlin, Patrick, *Easing the Passage: The Trial of Dr John Bodkin Adams*, Bodley Head, London, 1985.

Ford, Richard and Sapsted, David, 'Lord Hailsham on juries', *The Times*, 2 November 1988.

Grove, Trevor, *The Juryman's Tale*, Bloomsbury, London, 1998.

Harvey, Richard, *Diplock and the Assault on Civil Liberties*, Haldane Society of Socialist Lawyers, London, 1980.

Hostettler, John, *The Criminal Jury Old and New*, Waterside Press, 2004.

Kafka, Franz, *The Trial*, Vintage, London, 1999.

Lief, M., Caldwell, H. M. and Bycel, B., *Ladies and Gentlemen of the Jury: Greatest Closing Arguments in Modern Law*, Touchstone, New York, 1998.

Lumet, Sidney (Director), Fonda, Henry (Co-producer), *12 Angry Men*, 1957.

Penn, William and Mead, William, *Howell's State Trials*, vol. 6, p. 951 (6 HOW 951).

Royal Commission of Criminal Justice under Lord Runciman, 1993, see: www.criminal-courts-review.org.uk/ccr-01.htm.

www.livenote.com.

PERSONS UNKNOWN TRIAL, 1979

www.saunders.co.uk. My instructing solicitor.

Flintoff, John-Paul, 'The angry young man grows up', *Independent*, 31 July 1998.

King-Hamilton, QC, Alan, *Nothing But the Truth*, Weidenfeld & Nicolson, London, 1982.

THE FERTILISER CONSPIRACY (NABEEL HUSSEIN) TRIAL, 2006–7

Philippe Naughton, 'Five given life for fertiliser bomb terror plot; Link to 7/7 bombers can be revealed for the first time', Times Online, 30 April 2007.

http://news.bbc.co.uk/1/hi/uk/6610131.stm.

RICIN (MOULOUD SIHALI) TRIAL, 2004–5; SIAC HEARING, 2006

Blair vs. Blair, *Panorama*, BBC1, 9 October 2005; for full transcript, see: www.bbc.co.uk/panorama.

Bright, Martin, 'Ricin jurors attack new terror laws', *Observer*, 9 October 2005.

Brown, Gordon, 'Speech to the Royal United Services Institute in London', 13 February 2006; for full text, see: http://news.bbc.co.uk/1/hi/uk_politics/4708816.stm.

Campbell, Duncan, 'The ricin ring that never was', *Guardian*, 14 April 2005.

Sihali, Mouloud, statement at www.campacc.org.uk/Library/Sihali_270606.doc.

'More Plotters With Ricin May Be on the Loose, London Police Say', *Associated Press*, 8 January 2003.

'Seventh Man Arrested in London Ricin Case', *Associated Press*, 8 January 2003.

'The sober truth about Ricin', *Argus*, 9 January 2003.

http://news.bbc.co.uk/go/pr/fr/-/1/hi/uk/4433459.stm.

http://news.bbc.co.uk/1/hi/uk/4433459.stm.

www.mi5.gov.uk/output/page602.

Chapter 21: Taking Stock

JEAN CHARLES DE MENEZES INQUEST, 2008

Rudd, Jonathan (Director), *Stockwell*, ITV1, 2009, based on the Health and Safety Trial, 2007.

Mark Saunders was shot by police on 8 May 2008. His Sister, Charlotte Saunders, Judicially reviewed the unfairness of police officers colluding over their notes and statements in September 2008, see: www.independent.co.uk/news/uk/crime/the-killing-of-mark-saunders-929877.html, and www.telegraph.co.uk/news/1934958/Chelsea-shooting-Barrister's-family-'stunned'-at-gun-rampage.html.

www.stockwellinquest.org.uk/hearing_transcripts – the list of witnesses for each date is listed in a main index; the indexes for the day's proceedings come at the *end* of the day's transcript.

Chapter 22: Law, Not War

GENERAL

Farebrother, George and Kollerstrom, Nicholas (eds), *The Case Against War (in Iraq)*, Legal Inquiry Steering Group, Hailsham, 2003.

Kennedy, Maev, '100 ft down, the capital's cold war warren gives up its final secrets', *Guardian*, 18 October 2008.

McSmith, Andy, 'A taste of how the other half lived in the blitz', *Independent*, 18 October 2008.

THOMAS PAINE

Ayer, A. J., *Thomas Paine*, Secker & Warburg, London, 1988.

Foner, Eric, *Tom Paine and Revolutionary America*, Oxford University Press, Oxford, 1976.

Grayling, A. C., *Towards the Light: The Story of the Struggles for Liberty & Rights that made the Modern West*, Bloomsbury, London, 2007.

Keane, John, *Tom Paine, A Political Life*, Bloomsbury, London, 1995.

Nelson, Craig, *Thomas Paine, His Life, His Time and the Birth of Modern Nations*, Profile, London, 2007.

Paine, Thomas, *The Crisis*, Penguin 60s, Pamphlet no. xiii, (1783), London, 1995.

Paine, Thomas, *Common Sense*, Penguin, London, 2004.

INTERNATIONAL LAW AND WAR CRIMES

Bowring, Bill, *The Degradation of the International Legal Order?*, Routledge-Cavendish, Abingdon, 2008.

Foley, Conor, *The Thin Blue Line: How Humanitarianism Went to War*, Verso, London, 2008.

Jorgensen, Nina, *Responsibility of States for International Crimes*, Oxford University Press, Oxford, 2000.

McSmith, Andy, 'Keeping the Peace?', *Independent*, 20 February 2008.

Norton-Taylor, Richard, 'Top judge: US and UK acted as "vigilantes" in Iraq invasion', *Guardian*, 18 November 2008.

Robertson, Geoffrey, QC, *Crimes against Humanity: The Struggle for Global Justice*, Penguin, London, 2000.

Rose, Michael, *Washington's War: From Independence to Iraq*, Weidenfeld & Nicolson, London, 2007.

Sands, Philippe, *Lawless World, Making and Breaking Global Rules*, Penguin, London, 2006.

Stone, Oliver (Director), *W*, Lionsgate Entertainment 2008.

Wood, Nicholas, and Pellens, Anabella, *War Crime or Just War? The Iraq War 2003–2005, The Case Against Blair,* South Hill Press, London, 2005.

Zyberi, Gentian, *The Humanitarian Face of the International Court of Justice*, Intersentia, Utrecht, 2008.

For the International Criminal Tribunal for the former Yugoslavia, see: www.un.org/icty or www.icty.org.

Geneva Conventions (1957), *Archbold*, 2009, p. paras 1913, 19-367 to 19-369. For International Criminal Court incorporated into UK legislation in 2001, see: www.icc-cpi.int; see also *Archbold*, 2009, p. 1906, para. 19-351 to p. 1913, para. 19-366; *Archbold International Criminal Courts*, 3rd edition, Dixon, Rodney and Khan, A. A. Karim, Sweet & Maxwell, London 2009.

WORLD COURT PROJECT, 1996

Mothersson, Keith, *From Hiroshima to The Hague*, International Peace Bureau, Geneva, 1992.

Taylor, Mathew, 'Britain plans to spend £3bn on new nuclear warheads', *Guardian*, 25 July 2008.

For the World Court opinion, see: http://disarm.igc.org/oldwebpages/worldct.html.

The World Court Project is part of Abolition 2000, a global network to eliminate nuclear weapons, see: www.abolition2000europe.org .

MORDECHAI VANUNU

For the latest by Vanunu himself, see: altahrir.blogspot.com/2006/01/vanunus-trial-what-happened.html.

www.amnesty.org.uk.

www.torturecare.org.uk.

www.vanunu.org.

INTERNATIONAL HUMAN RIGHTS

For the Kurdish Human Rights Project, see: www.khrp.org; www.torturecare.org.uk.

For the Latin American Bureau, see: www.lab.org.uk.

For Peace Brigades International, see: www.peacebrigades.org.

FATMIR LIMAJ/ICTY IN THE HAGUE, TRIAL AND APPEAL, 2004–7

Di Giovanni, Janine, *The Quick and the Dead: Under Siege in Sarajevo*, Phoenix House, London, 1994.

Doucette, Serge R. and Thaci, Hamdi, *Kosovar Moral Democracy or Kosovo Greater Serbia*, Europrinty, Priština, 2004.

Judah, Tim, *Kosovo, War and Revenge*, Yale University Press, New Haven and London, 2002.

Malcolm, Noel, *Kosovo: A Short History*, Pan Macmillan, London, 2002.

Rupnik, Jacques, *Balkans Diary*, Kosovar Action for Civil Initiative, Priština, 2004.

Stephen, Chris, *Judgement Day: The Trial of Slobodan Milosevic*, Atlantic Books, London, 2004.

Under Orders: War Crimes in Kosovo, Human Rights Watch, London, 2001.

For the United Nations Charter, see: www.un.org/aboutun/charter 1389.

Transcript Reference and case no. at Trial IT-03-66-T; for Appeal, see IT-03-66-A, p. A1058 – A1670, or see: www.un.org/icty/transe66/050830Ed.htm.

Index

A NOTE ON THE AUTHOR

Michael Mansfield QC was born in 1941 and educated at Highgate School and Keele University. Called to the Bar in 1967, he established Tooks Chambers in 1984 and became Queen's Counsel in 1989. He has represented defendants and their families in criminal trials, appeals, inquests and inquiries in some of the most controversial legal cases the country has seen, particularly where issues of civil liberty have arisen; he is President and Patron of numerous organisations including the Haldane, Amicus and Viva!, Professor and Honorary Fellow of many universities as well as being a regular contributor to public debates on human rights issues. His books include *Presumed Guilty* (with Tony Wardle), *The Home Lawyer* (edited by Yvette Vanson) and, for children, *Whale Boy* (illustrated by Maggie Raynor). He lives in London with his wife, former documentary film-maker Yvette Vanson, and their son Freddy.